OF COURAGE
AND DETERMINATION

OF COURAGE AND DETERMINATION

The First Special Service Force, "The Devil's Brigade," 1942–44

COLONEL BERND HORN
MICHEL WYCZYNSKI

DUNDURN
TORONTO

Copyright © Bernd Horn and Michel Wyczynski, 2013

All rights reserved. No part of this publication may be reproduced, stored in a retrieval system, or transmitted in any form or by any means, electronic, mechanical, photocopying, recording, or otherwise (except for brief passages for purposes of review) without the prior permission of Dundurn Press. Permission to photocopy should be requested from Access Copyright.

Editor: Nigel Heseltine
Design: Jennifer Scott
Printer: Webcom

Library and Archives Canada Cataloguing in Publication

Horn, Bernd, 1959-
Of courage and determination : the First Special Service Force, "the Devil's Brigade", 1942-44 / by Bernd Horn and Michel Wyczynski ; foreword by Charlie Mann.

Includes bibliographical references and index.
Issued also in electronic format.
ISBN 978-1-4597-0964-5

1. First Special Service Force--History. 2. World War, 1939-1945--Regimental histories--Canada. 3. World War, 1939-1945--Regimental histories--United States. 4. Combined operations (Military science). I. Wyczynski, Michel, 1953- II. Title. III. Title: First Special Service Force, "the Devil's Brigade", 1942-44. IV. Title: Devil's Brigade, 1942-44.

D768.153H67 2013   940.54'1271   C2013-900820-9

1 2 3 4 5   17 16 15 14 13

  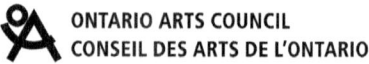

We acknowledge the support of the **Canada Council for the Arts** and the **Ontario Arts Council** for our publishing program. We also acknowledge the financial support of the **Government of Canada** through the **Canada Book Fund** and **Livres Canada Books**, and the **Government of Ontario** through the **Ontario Book Publishing Tax Credit** and the **Ontario Media Development Corporation**.

Care has been taken to trace the ownership of copyright material used in this book. The author and the publisher welcome any information enabling them to rectify any references or credits in subsequent editions.

J. Kirk Howard, President

Visit us at
Dundurn.com
Definingcanada.ca
@dundurnpress
Facebook.com/dundurnpress

Dundurn	Gazelle Book Services Limited	Dundurn
3 Church Street, Suite 500	White Cross Mills	2250 Military Road
Toronto, Ontario, Canada	High Town, Lancaster, England	Tonawanda, NY
M5E 1M2	LA1 4XS	U.S.A. 14150

TABLE OF CONTENTS

Foreword		7
Introduction		9
1	A Few Desperate Men: The Rise of Commandos and the Raiding Concept	13
2	"Mastery of the Snows": The Plough Project	29
3	A Growing Web: The Canadian Connection	41
4	"Hazardous Duty": Recruiting and Selecting the Force	51
5	The Other War: The Bureaucratic Battle to Sustain the Canadian Component of the FSSF	67
6	Forging the Forcemen: Two Distinct Identities — One Common Legacy	85
7	No Room for Weakness: Training for the Plough Project	103
8	Without Hesitation: Creating a Potent Striking Force	121
9	Kiska: The Battle That Never Was	143
10	Where Eagles Dare: The Battle for Mount La Difensa	165
11	Death in the Mountains: Mount Majo	187
12	Anzio and the Race to Rome	207
13	To the Bitter End: Operation Dragoon and the Fight Through Southern France	239
14	Disbandment	263
15	Epilogue	277

Annex A	Consent to Serve Declaration Form	295
Annex B	The FSSF and Operation Jupiter: A Historical Clarification	299

Notes 305
Glossary 389
Acknowledgements 395
About the Authors 397
Index 399

FOREWORD

Since the end of the Second World War much has been written about the First Special Service Force (FSSF), also popularly known as the "Devil's Brigade." As a Canadian veteran of the FSSF, the numerous articles, books, documentaries, and movies that have been produced on the Force never cease to interest me. One aspect I have always noticed is that most accounts are dominated by the American perspective. In that light, this volume, *Of Courage and Determination — The First Special Service Force, 1942–1944*, is refreshing. While capturing the spirit and achievements of the "Black Devils" as a whole, the authors have also managed to tell our story from a distinctly Canadian vantage point.

Comprehensive and detailed, this account encapsulates every aspect of the FSSF experience: its theoretical genesis; the Herculean task of selecting and recruiting tough, young, and capable Canadian volunteers to serve on the Force; and the bureaucratic and political struggles required to ensure its survival. Moreover, the authors have managed to capture with accuracy and historical detail, the drama and significance of our combat operations from the dry run at Kiska in the Aleutians to our legendary exploits in Italy and France.

This book is a testament, as the title suggests, to the courage and tenacity of the Forcemen, both American and Canadian, who undertook a unique experiment, that is to say the complete integration of soldiers from two nations under the banner of a single North American formation. Simply put, we served shoulder to shoulder through thick and thin. It never mattered whether you were a Canadian or an American — we were all brothers in arms — members of the Force. That is what connected us together and allowed us to persevere through some of the greatest tests one can withstand in war. In that vein, the esprit de corps and cohesion — forged through hardship and shared experience and tempered in the furnace of savage combat — leaps from the pages of this book. Without question, this volume is an exemplary account of the dynamic history of what is widely considered one of the Second World War's premier fighting formations.

Ultimately, this book will become one of the key sources for the history of the First Special Service Force. For Canadians, it will undoubtedly become the definitive work on the Canadian component of the Force. As such, the authors deserve our thanks for once again making the effort to not only document, but also capture the spirit and drama of the efforts and sacrifices of Canadian veterans who demonstrated the courage and fortitude — those who dared — to serve in Canada's neophyte airborne and commando units. Their efforts to ensure that this part of our military history is not lost is greatly appreciated.

Charlie Mann
Director Emeritus
Canadian Military Liaison Officer
1st Special Service Force Association

INTRODUCTION

The onset of the Second World War proved to be the catalyst for many innovations. It was the stage for new concepts, tactics, organizations, technology, and weapons. One of these innovations was the explosion of special operations forces (SOF), defined in its most basic form as organizations consisting of individuals who were specially selected, specially trained, and given special missions. The war spawned such legendary organizations such as the British commandos, the Special Air Service (SAS), the Long Range Desert Group (LRDG), the U.S. Rangers, and the Canadian/U.S. First Special Service Force.

In the desperate early days of the war when the AXIS war machine seemed virtually unstoppable, the British Combined Operations Command Headquarters worked hard at initiatives that could strike the Germans and tie down their military resources and interfere with their war industry. The FSSF was born from this intent. The concept was daring and innovative. And, the FSSF was to be a hard-hitting force driven by courage and determination. Crucially, it was to live up to these expectations.

The original idea was hatched in the spring of 1942 by a British scientist, Geoffrey Pyke, who wanted to develop an over-snow vehicle that would provide mobility and allow a specially trained force to run a hit-and-run guerrilla war in Norway, tying down German forces and attacking key hydroelectric plants, particularly those manufacturing heavy water for the German atomic weapon program. Some thought was also put to using the force to destroy the Ploesti oil fields in Romania or to destroy hydroelectric facilities in Italy. Overall, the planners reasoned that attacks on any of these targets with a hard-hitting raiding force would not only damage Germany's vital war industry, but would also tie up German forces that would now be required to protect facilities and chase down an elusive guerilla force.

The Americans accepted the project and Prime Minister Winston Churchill and Lord Mountbatten very quickly convinced the Canadians to participate as well. The decision for Canada was easy. The Ogdensburg Agreement, signed in 1940, had already led Canada down the path of defence co-operation for the security of North America. This newest idea was just another mechanism to further Canadian/U.S. ties. The politics made sense, but the effect went deeper — much deeper.

As a result, a Canadian/U.S. brigade-sized formation was created with Canadians and Americans serving side by side, wearing the same American uniform, in a military command that was completely integrated. At inception, the Canadians contributed 697 all ranks to the formation, representing approximately a quarter of the total number of troops.

The FSSF, under the command of Colonel Robert T. Frederick, became a unique and inspiring formation. When the call went out for volunteers, the organizers looked for young, strong, robust men who had experience living off the land, preferably with work experience in the North as miners or lumberjacks. Preference was given to resilient, independent, self-reliant individuals who could undertake hard physical conditions and endure harsh environments and not only survive, but thrive. Although selection criteria and practices varied, in the end the real selection criteria became whether or not an individual could survive the training.

This became the acid test for Frederick and the Force: it wasn't what an individual said they could do. it was what they could actually do. The indoctrination began with parachute training, but not the three week course. Volunteers were given 48 hours of instruction and then thrown out of an airplane. If they passed that, they went on to the rest of the training. Gruelling marches in the mountains, demolitions training, small arms training on all Allied and enemy weapons, ski training, unarmed combat with some of the most proficient instructors in the world, all contributed to transforming volunteers into an elite fighting force.

Important in all of this was the fact that Frederick, and he was supported by the governments and military commanders of both great nations, did not want a mixed force. It was a unified, combined force that had Canadians and Americans mixed throughout the formation. There was no distinction. They wore the same uniform, used the same weapons. Canadians served under American officers and non-commissioned officers (NCOs), and Americans served under Canadian officers and NCOs. Quite simply, it was impossible to tell the difference between the soldiers of either nation.

In addition, from the start, Frederick allowed no rivalry or competition based on Canadian versus American. They were one team. Not surprisingly, very quickly, it no longer mattered. They were brothers-in-arms and nobody saw themselves as Canadian or American — just as Forcemen.

INTRODUCTION

Although the original mission was scrubbed in October 1942 for a number of political, operational, and logistical reasons, both countries saw the value in this highly trained force, as well as the political implications, undertones, and message it sent. It was a North American formation representing the best of both nations, united against a common enemy and fighting for a just and noble cause. As such, the FSSF was kept alive and deployed for operations.

Its first mission, fittingly, was in defence of North America. In the summer of 1943, the FSSF was sent to seize the island of Kiska in the Aleutian island chain. The Japanese, unbeknownst to the Allies, had already withdrawn from the cold, desolate island, so the formation saw no real fighting. But it proved to be a good test of its members.

The FSSF was then sent to Italy, where it cut its teeth in combat and carved its name into military history legend. Its first task was to seize the towering Mount La Difensa, a seemingly impregnable German defensive stronghold on the top of a 945-metre mountain that was holding up Lieutenant-General Mark Clark's 5th Army, which was trying to punch its way through to Rome. The 5th Army had tried unsuccessfully for weeks, and at great human cost, to eject the Germans from the mountain redoubt. However, they repeatedly failed.

The task was then given to the FSSF. On the night of 2/3 December 1943, the Forcemen scaled the rear of the mountain, which included a 70-degree, 305-metre veritable cliff using ropes and sheer courage and tenacity. By using an approach that the enemy had discounted as impassable, the FSSF surprised the German defenders and after two hours of vicious hand-to-hand combat seized the peak and began to push the Germans from the mountain itself.

The next days were spent consolidating defensive positions and pushing the Germans from the adjacent peaks and valleys. Rain, snow, and perpetual freezing winds made life miserable on the mountain tops. Enemy shelling and sniping added to the misery. As did the lack of food, water, and adequate clothing. Everything had to be carried up the mountain and wounded had to be carried down the steep, muddy, and slippery trails. One stretcher took six men and each trip up or down took anywhere from eight to eleven hours.

The rest of December and most of January was spent in these conditions fighting from one mountain top to the next to clear the enemy from their defensive positions to allow 5th Army to breakout into the Liri Valley and move on to Rome. In the desperate conditions and against a formidable foe, the FSSF achieved what others could not and in so doing earned legendary status. But it came with a cost. By the end of January it had suffered 80 percent casualties. But its feats were unrivalled.

After a short rest the Force was thrown into the fire once again. The stalled and imperilled beachhead at Anzio required immediate assistance. The FSSF was thrown into the front line on 2 February 1944 and remained in position for 99 days without relief. The Force's aggressive patrolling struck fear into the Germans opposite them and earned them the title of "Black Devils." When the breakout came in late May, the Force once again set the example and eventually became the first Allied troops to enter the Eternal City — Rome — on 4 June 1944.

With the Allied push into Europe, the FSSF spearheaded the invasion of Southern France on 15 August 1944 by capturing key island fortresses that could interfere with Allied landings during Operation Dragoon. The Force then proceeded to advance along the French and Italian Riviera clearing the enemy from their mountain positions. With the war quickly winding down, the FSSF assembled on 5 December 1944, in Menton, France, for its next assignment. However, that was not to pass. The great experiment now came to an end — the Force was disbanded.

The disbandment came as a shock and surprise to the members of the FSSF. The North American experiment had proven to be a success. The Force, despite administrative difficulties, was, from the perspective of most of the soldiers, the embodiment of warrior spirit, kindred spirit, a demonstration of how close Americans and Canadians truly are. Frankly, as noted by *Time* magazine, "the Force had lived up to its promise of becoming one of the Army's elite — a tough, secret, widely trained outfit that had fought its way through some of the hottest spots of World War II."[1] In the end, the FSSF demonstrated that no task was too great and no mission too daunting, as the Force was made of courage and determination.

1

A FEW DESPERATE MEN:
The Rise of Commandos and the Raiding Concept

> There comes from the sea, a hand of steel that plucks the German sentries from their posts.[1]
> — Prime Minister Winston Churchill, October 1942.

As dramatic and inspiring as the prime minister's words were, they were not delivered from a position of strength. Rather, they were born from weakness. The era of peace following First World War was a low point for Allied military development. Debt-ridden governments faced with a war-weary public and an international depression were loathe to expend time or effort, much less money, on their armed forces. After all, large inventories of equipment and weaponry remained after the bloody global conflict ended in 1918. Moreover, a vindictive and very restrictive armistice ensured that their recent enemy would never rise again to challenge their military power. The conservative and anti-intellectual military hierarchy was no more insightful or innovative. Doctrinal development stagnated. Simply put, the Allies settled into a trench-induced myopia, dabbling in mechanization but never fully embracing, much less understanding, its significance. This failure would bring them to the brink of disaster.

And so, as the Allied soldiers cowered under cover, trying to escape the reach of German attacking aircraft, their military commanders and political masters were aghast at how quickly their defensive plans were being crushed. Although given a preview almost 10 months prior, in the fall of 1939 when German forces sliced through Poland, the onslaught on Norway in April 1940, and the Low Countries and France the following month, appeared to catch the Allies completely off guard.

Undeniably, the Allies were entirely unprepared for this new form of warfare. The German Blitzkrieg unleashed on the West showcased new doctrine and tactics that they developed in the interwar years. In the simplest terms, the Blitzkrieg centered on rapid manoeuvre and firepower executed by combined arms forces that penetrated deep into the enemy's lines to achieve psychological dislocation rather than just mere physical destruction. Speed and flexibility of the attack were paramount. Exposed flanks were of secondary importance. The object was to destroy the opponent's command and control. To achieve this the Germans placed an emphasis on mechanized forces, specifically tanks, as well as close air support and airborne forces.

In the end, the speed and multi-dimensional battlefield simply overwhelmed and paralyzed the Allied forces deployed to defeat the enemy offensive. The German success was due to mobility which was achieved by a combination of concentration, firepower, surprise, and combined arms co-operation. The destruction of the West took 46 days, but it was decided in only 10.[2] As such, on the night of 2 June 1940, the last of the British soldiers were evacuated from the beaches of Dunkirk, France. However, the desperate withdrawal resulted in the loss of virtually all their heavy equipment, weapons, and vehicles.[3] Britain, now braced for what seemed to be the inevitable conclusion to the German master plan — the invasion of England.

Devoid of any major equipment or weapons, and encumbered by a doctrine and war making methodology that was now clearly defunct, England was on the precipice of disaster. Simultaneously, it had to re-equip, rebuild, and retrain its armed forces. And this, in addition to preparing the island for defence. It seemed that Britain had no other choice but to surrender the initiative and dig-in and wait for the inescapable onslaught.

However, this was not the case. Even though British equipment was still smouldering on the beaches of Dunkirk, the combative Churchill declared in the House of Commons on 4 June 1940, that "we shall not be content with a defensive war."[4] He was well aware that to win a war meant ultimately offensive action. Moreover, only through offensive action could an army provide the needed confidence and battle experience to its soldiers and leaders. Furthermore, only offensive action could sustain public and military morale. And finally, offensive action represented a shift in initiative. By striking at the enemy, inherently an opponent is forced to take defensive measures which represents a diversion of scarce resources.

That afternoon, Churchill penned a note to his chief of staff of the War Cabinet Secretariat, General Hastings Ismay. "We are greatly concerned ... with the dangers of the German landing in England ...," he wrote, "why should it be thought impossible for us to do anything of the same kind to them?" He then added, "We should immediately set to work to organize self-contained, thoroughly-equipped raiding units."[5] After all pondered Churchill, "how wonderful it would be if the Germans could be made to wonder where they were going to be struck next, instead of forcing us to try to wall in the island and roof it over!"[6] Vice-Admiral Lord Louis Mountbatten put it in simpler terms. "We cannot win this war," he asserted, "by bombing and blockade alone."[7]

On 6 June, Churchill sent yet another missive to Ismay. "Enterprises must be prepared," he directed, "with specially trained troops of the hunter class who can develop a reign of terror down these coasts, first of all on the butcher and bolt policy; but later on, or perhaps as soon as we are organized, we should surprise Calais or Boulogne, kill and capture the Hun garrison and hold the place until all the preparations to reduce it by siege or heavy storm have been made, and then away." He then curtly directed the "Joint Chiefs of the Staff to propose me measures for a vigorous, enterprising, and ceaseless offensive against the whole German-occupied coastline." The prime minister added the requirement for deep inland raids that left "a trail of German corpses behind."[8]

Churchill's ruminations and subsequent missive were passed to the chief of the imperial general staff (CIGS), General Sir John Dill. The CIGS wasted no time. He passed the problem to one of his general staff officers, Lieutenant-Colonel Dudley W. Clarke with direction to find means by which the offensive spirit of the Army could be fostered until it was in a position to resume the offensive. Clarke began work immediately. "The mind of the entire nation — and above all of the Army," recalled Clarke, "had been turned violently to Defence to the exclusion of all else." But Clarke, like Churchill and a few others, realized that "even the lightest threats, if only they could be produced, must compel the Germans to turn in the midst of their feverish invasion preparations to organize defence and divert troops to guard this enormous front line [occupied Europe]."[9]

To Clarke the solution was simple — guerrilla operations. He recalled his childhood in the Transvaal and the stories of how the outnumbered Boer commandos had tied down thousands of troops and denied victory to a superior army for years. These stories were reinforced by his study of military history, as well as his own experience in Palestine in 1936 during the Arab Rebellion, where a motley selection of armed Arab bands tied down an entire British Army corps and their auxiliaries. Therefore, he proposed that the concept of guerrilla warfare was the best model the British could adopt under the present conditions.

As such, Lieutenant-Colonel Clarke proposed that "commandos," the term taken directly from the Boer War experience, be established to first, create a threat to divert German resources, and second, restore the offensive spirit to the British Army.[10] Dill passed the idea to Churchill who leapt on it immediately. After all, it appealed to his character. Winston Churchill, himself an accomplished adventurer, journalist, and soldier, held a heroic and romantic image of war. Moreover, he maintained "an almost abstract attachment to the offensive."[11] He believed that audacity and willpower constituted the only sound approach to the conduct of war.[12] He later revealed his mind set to President Franklin D. Roosevelt. "[The] essence of defence," he asserted, "is to attack the enemy upon us — leap at his throat and keep the grip until the life is out of him."[13]

His zeal for the offensive was overpowering and caused great consternation for his generals. General Archibald Wavell stated that Churchill "always accused commanders of organizing 'all tail and no teeth.'"[14] Similarly, General Sir Alan Brooke recalled that the prime minister was "like a child that has set its mind on some forbidden toy." He elaborated that "It is no good explaining that it will cut his fingers or burn him. The more you explain, the more fixed he becomes in his idea."[15]

And so it was. Despite resistance from many senior military commanders who felt that valuable resources were being frittered away for no valuable return at a time when the nation faced invasion, Churchill pressed on. In a remarkable display of military efficiency, by 8 June 1940, General Dill received approval for the creation of the commandos and that same afternoon, Section MO9 of the War Office was established. Four days later, Churchill appointed Lieutenant-General Sir Alan Bourne, the adjutant general of the Royal Marines as "Commander of Raiding Operations on Coasts in Enemy Occupation and Advisor to the Chiefs of Staff on Combined Operations."[16]

Clarke's concept was coming to life. He could now establish his "picked bands of guerilla fighters who would harry the long enemy coastline in order to make him [Germans] dissipate his superior resources."[17] In all, 12 commando units consisting of 500 men broken up into a headquarters and 10 troops each, were proposed. Incredibly, Lieutenant-Colonel Clarke was also directed to mount a cross-channel raid "at the earliest possible moment."[18]

The next hurdle was actually raising the force. It was considered axiomatic from the beginning that no existing Army units could be made available for raiding operations, nor could any personnel be diverted from the necessity of Home Defence. The corollary condition was one of stringent economy. So acute was the shortage of equipment and weaponry that commandos were "armed, equipped, organised and administered for one task and one task only — tip-and-run raids of not more than 48 hours from bases in England against the Continent of Europe."[19] The problem was so severe that a commando unit drew its full complement of weapons, such as submachine guns, from a central pool only when it was about to set out on a raid.[20]

For manpower, Clark was somewhat more fortunate. The cadre of Nos. 1 and 2 Commandos were harvested from the 10 independent companies that were raised earlier in the year to harass the advancing Germans in Norway. The 10 independent companies, each consisting of approximately 20 officers and 270 men, were raised largely from second-line Territorial Army divisions in April 1940. These units were designed exclusively for raiding and as such were self-contained in a ship which was to be their floating base. They had no garrison and were billeted in private homes in coastal towns. However, the chaos created with the German assault on Norway forestalled any real preparation. There was practically no training for the militia soldiers or leaders of the independent companies before they were deployed to that beleaguered country.

Although eager and keen, they had little skill or equipment and no transport. Under the overall command of Lieutenant-Colonel Colin Gubbins, they were ordered "not to offer any prolonged resistance but should endeavour to maintain themselves on the flanks of the German forces and continue harrying tactics against their lines of communications." However, the German advance was too rapid and the five independent companies that actually made it to Norway in time, were withdrawn by early June. In the end, they conducted no raids and very little action that could be called guerrilla warfare. In fact, overall, there was very little contact with the enemy.[21]

A FEW DESPERATE MEN

A group from No. 4 Commando walk by a collapsed Goatley boat upon returning to New Haven U.K. after the Dieppe Raid, 19 August 1942.

Nonetheless, their disbandment provided an immediate pool of manpower. However, the inexperience of the territorial troops was seen as incompatible with the intended concept and as a result, under pressure from Churchill, recruiting for the remaining commandos was done by asking for volunteers for "special service of a hazardous nature" from the regular army.[22] Prospective candidates were required to be fully trained men. Commanding officers were picked from the volunteers and then they were given a free hand to choose their own officers, who in turn were dispatched to various units to select their own men.

The theoretical construct for selection was sound. The nature of commando operations dictated that volunteers were to be the best possible material. As such, initially, officers and men were hand-picked from volunteers. "Great care," revealed one report, "was taken in the selection of officers and men and from the outset they were specially picked units."[23] Recruiters wanted intelligent, young, exceptionally fit individuals who demonstrated courage, endurance, initiative, and resourcefulness, as well as self-reliance and aggressiveness. Marksmanship and the ability to swim were also essential skills required. The selecting officers also tried to pick candidates who were mechanically inclined, able to drive motor vehicles and immune to air or sea sickness.[24]

"I looked for intelligence and keenness," recalled Brigadier John Durnford-Slater, the first commanding officer (CO) of No. 3 Commando. "What I was seeking and what I obtained," he explained, "were men of character beyond normal." He added, "I intended that every soldier in the Commandos should be a potential leader; that he must be mentally and physically tough and must radiate cheerfulness, enthusiasm and confidence."[25]

Lord Lovat and Captain Boucher-Myers of No. 4 Commando following Operation Jubilee, the Dieppe Raid.

Significantly, they did not select a full complement of NCOs. They preferred to promote from within once their own men proved themselves.

The men drawn to the commando idea very quickly coalesced the concept that was expected. Raiding was their primary role. In essence, they were to be trained to be "hard hitting assault troops" who were capable of working in co-operation with the Navy and Air Force. As such they were expected to capture strong points, destroy enemy services, neutralize coastal batteries, and wipe out any designated enemy force by surprise as detailed by higher headquarters.[26] They were also told that they would have to become accustomed to longer hours, more work, and less rest than the other members of the armed forces.

Predictably, the commando idea attracted a like-minded group of aggressive, action-orientated individuals who quickly shaped the essence of the commando idea. "There was a sense of urgency, a striving to achieve an ideal, an individual determination to drive the physical body to the limit of endurance to support a moral resolve," explained one veteran officer. "The individual determination," he added, "was shared by every member of the force, and such heights of collective idealism are not often reached in the mundane business of soldiering."[27] Together they forged a "commando spirit" that comprised of determination; enthusiasm and cheerfulness, particularly under adverse conditions; individual initiative and self-reliance; and finally, comradeship.[28]

Once selected, the next requirement was to get them organized and trained. Much like the former independent companies, the commandos were not put in barracks, but rather each man was given a subsistence allowance and was required to find his own accommodation and food. Commanding officers touted this practice to be of great value because it increased a man's self-reliance, made him available for training at any time of the day or night, and eliminated the loss of manpower due to the perennial demands of administrative duties and tasks inherently associated with any garrison setting.[29] The commandos troops appreciated this aspect as well. "It is the greatest job in the Army that one could possibly get, and it is a job that, if properly carried out, can be of enormous value," asserted Major Geoffrey Appleyard. He added, "no red tape, no paper work ... just pure operations, the success of which depends principally on oneself and the men one has oneself picked to do the job with you ... it's revolutionary."[30] Many agreed. That is why the "RTU" (return to unit) became the CO's most powerful punishment.[31]

Initially, training was the responsibility of the individual commando unit COs. However, in December 1940, the castle grounds at Achnacarry, Scotland, became a holding unit of the special training centre until December of the following year when it officially became the Commando Depot. Its purpose was to achieve a level of uniformity and concentration in the early stages of a commando recruit's training. Once a commando recruit completed his basic course at the depot, he was dispatched to the Commando Holding Unit where he underwent further advanced collective and combined arms training prior to being posted to an active commando unit.[32] The standards were unrelenting. Individuals who failed to meet the requisite training requirements were immediately returned to their original units.

Nonetheless, whether at the depot, holding unit, or at the unit, commando training was exceptionally gruelling. Long marches (up to 64 kilometres in a 24-hour period), strenuous assault courses, cliff climbing, and a myriad of exercises that focused on arduous and exhausting activities were routinely undertaken. Blank ammunition was unheard of. The requirement for realism, as well as mental and physical challenge, necessitated the use of only live ammunition and bombs. As its foundation, the training was intended to make soldiers tough and willing to endure and strive for mission completion regardless of the hardship or obstacles they faced.

At its core, the training was designed to achieve a number of goals. First, it was devised to foster the offensive spirit — an ever present eagerness to "have a go" at the enemy. Second, it nurtured the belief that darkness and the night was an aid rather than a deterrent in "closing with and attacking the enemy." Equally important, it made the soldier self-reliant and gave him the ability to act, whenever necessary, on his own initiative to accomplish the mission. As well, the training brought him to a level of physical fitness akin to that of a trained athlete.

Infantrymen of the 3rd Canadian Infantry Division undergoing gruelling commando training — scaling near vertical cliffs, Seaford, England, 21 July 1942.

The training program also had a very tangible practical side. It taught specific skills that were crucial to raiding. The soldiers became familiar with the sea and with ships and small craft, and learned how to "live off the land" and scale cliffs and mountainous terrain. Additionally, commando soldiers were taught infiltration tactics, demolition and sabotage techniques, parachuting, and the "art of bluff and low cunning."[33]

At the end of the program, the commando units could:

- conduct assault landings before first light to seize and destroy coastal defence batteries or installations;
- land in the dark in rough weather and on rocky coasts in areas where defences were deemed to be weaker;

- land under cliffs to conduct scaling operations to strike where the enemy least expected attacks;
- penetrate behind the enemy lines either by infiltration in small parties or by landing on the coast from surface craft, submarines, or flying boats to conduct night assaults against headquarters, tank harbours, communications facilities or lines of communication, and/or ambush enemy forces moving forward to the battle area;
- infiltrate airfield perimeters to destroy aircraft;
- conduct raids to obtain identification and other information;
- create tension, disruption, and anxiety;
- combine units to create large-scale diversionary raids designed to induce the enemy to commit his reserves.[34]

Although the commandos began to attract the requisite amount and type of manpower, and even though they had a high-level sponsor, predictably, they quickly met resistance. "As ever," lamented Brigadier Anthony Farrar-Hockley, "a new concept, a new organization tends to be resisted, even at a peak of crisis in a nation's affairs."[35] Resistance emanated from both the War Office and particularly from operational commanders. Not surprisingly, many felt that the diversion of resources during the critical period of likely

Canadian assault landing exercise, 1 October 1942.

invasion was not sound. And even once this threat passed, many still felt that the investment in commandos and raiding was not worth the return. "Descending on the enemy, killing a few guards, blowing up the odd pillbox, and taking a handful of prisoners," critiqued Major-General Julian Thompson in later years, "was not a cost-effective use of ships, craft and highly trained soldiers."[36]

Furthermore, directors and commanding officers were upset by the prospect of losing some of their best men to calls for volunteers for the special duty. "The resistances of the War Office were obstinate," reflected Churchill, "and increased as the professional ladder was descended." He explained that "the idea that large bands of favoured 'irregulars,' with their unconventional attire and easy-and-free bearing, should throw an implied slur on the efficiency and courage of the Regular battalions was odious to men who had given all their lives to the organisation and discipline of permanent units." He added, "The colonels of many of our finest regiments were aggrieved."[37] One official report acknowledged that "Home Forces have consistently used their predominating influence at the War Office to thwart the efforts of those well disposed to us."[38]

In addition, dispersions, often due to the behaviour of the commando soldiers themselves, soon tarnished their reputation. Although everyone cheered their offensive strikes against the enemy, their less than textbook discipline soon took its toll. "There had grown up in the Commandos a tradition," conceded David Stirling, the founder of the SAS and a former commando officer, "that to be a tough regiment it was necessary to act tough all the time in the barracks and on leave, and they were liable to be badly dressed, ill disciplined and noisy in the streets...."[39] He was not alone in his observations. "Discipline at the Commando is very unsatisfactory," complained one medical officer, "I have had reports to the effect both from officers and men; a service policeman told me that they were the worst of men he had ever come across.... Lack of discipline is followed by lack of morale and crime.... we are in a position of knowing that out of every five men we train one is a potential coward or criminal." He added, "The men are all volunteers and are free to go from the unit when they choose; many of them have a mistaken idea of the danger attached to the job, encouraged by highly coloured press reports; their self esteem is excessive and they think that they have a right to behave as free agents and disregard discipline."[40]

Whether deserved or not, a negative perception emerged that was soon reflected in how others treated the commandos. For instance, "high officials" referred to them as the "unmentionables."[41] The media often described them as toughs, gangsters, and cutthroats. And not surprisingly, the effort by the commandos to obtain royal ascent and have HRH Princess Margaret Rose appointed as their colonel-in-chief was refused on the grounds that it might tend to "perpetuate the commandos."[42]

Fortunately for the commandos, despite the opposition, they survived as an entity and the raiding concept was pushed forward. Much of this was due to Churchill's active interest and aggressive mentorship. On 18 June 1940, Churchill prompted Ismay, the CIGS, for a report. To Churchill commandos represented offensive power and were just as effective in Home Defence as they were for raiding. As such, he demanded to know what had been done "about storm troops." He visualized a force of "at least twenty thousand Storm Troops or 'Leopards'" poised "to spring at the throat of any small landings or descents."[43] Weeks later, he wrote Anthony Eden, the secretary of state for war to stress the requirement for his unconventional but extremely offensive forces. "If we are to have any campaign in 1941," he stressed, "it must be amphibious in its character and there certainly will be many opportunities of minor operations all of which will depend on surprise landings of lightly equipped mobile forces accustomed to work like packs of hounds instead of being moved about in the ponderous manner which is appropriate to the regular formations." Churchill emphasized that "we must develop the storm troop or commando idea."[44] Frustrated with the seemingly endless resistance from within the military, he suggested to Eden that an example should be made of "one or two" of the reluctant officers.[45]

The initial raids did little to help the fledgling commandos win support from their detractors. The first raid was conducted less than three weeks after Churchill authorized the creation of commandos, on the night of 23/24 June 1940, by 120 commando troops who were landed at various points on the French coast south of Boulogne. Their mission was to determine the nature of the German defences and capture prisoners. The raid, bemoaned Lieutenant-Colonel Clarke who accompanied the expedition, "was a muddle from start to finish."[46] In all, very little was accomplished. The next raid was launched several weeks later, on the night of 14/15 July. It too was unimpressive. "The raid was a very amateurish affair," confided Lieutenant-Colonel Durnford-Slater, the designated raiding commander, "from which we were very fortunate to return." He explained that "everything was faulty from the higher direction in London down to the landing craft and our own training."[47] The intent was to conduct a small raid on the Channel island of Guernsey to seize some prisoners and gather as much information as possible, as well as inflict the maximum number of casualties on the Germans. However, the execution failed to meet the aim. Neither of the two groups participating achieved any real success. "The raid was," conceded Durnford-Slater, "a ridiculous, almost a comic failure." He explained that "We captured no prisoners. We had done no serious damage. We had caused no casualties to the enemy ... we had cut through three telegraph cables." He added, "A youth in his teens could have done the same."[48]

He was right. The poor results provided further ammunition for their critics. They also earned the censure of those who supported the commandos and raids. Churchill angrily directed that there be no more "silly fiascos like those perpetrated at Boulogne and Guernsey." He asserted that "The idea of working all these coasts up against us by pinprick raids is one to be strictly avoided."[49]

Nonetheless, the commandos and the raiding policy were allowed to evolve. But, Churchill wanted the commando idea and the raiding concept to be conducted properly. Overall, the commandos came under the control of the Combined Operations Command (COC) which was responsible for raiding operations to harass the enemy and cause him

OF COURAGE AND DETERMINATION

Commandos evacuate a wounded comrade.

to disperse his forces. In essence, COC was the mounting authority for all raids from Northern Norway to the western limit of German-occupied France.[50] Two days after the second fiasco, on 17 July 1940, Churchill appointed Admiral of the Fleet Sir Roger Keyes, the hero of Gallipoli and Zeebrugge, as the director of combined operations command. "The truth of the matter," confided Keyes to a friend, "is these irregular troops are very unpopular in certain quarters in the War Office. But, as you know, the Prime Minister is determined that five thousand shall be specially trained and available for raiding operations under my direction."[51] The change in command was also meant to mark the transition in policy from small to larger-scale raids even though, for lack of enough ships and trained men, they could not be undertaken immediately.[52]

Despite the best efforts of the 68-year-old Keyes, he could not gain the co-operation of others, namely the chiefs of staff of the different services. The growing strain and enmity between Keyes and others, not surprisingly, resulted in his eventual removal. Keyes was replaced by Lord Louis Mountbatten in October 1941, who was given the title "Chief Advisor of Combined Operations" and the rank of acting commodore. Approximately, six months later in April 1942, Churchill, desperate for offensive action, appointed Mountbatten the chief of combined operations and promoted him to the rank of vice-admiral, as well as the equivalent honorary rank of lieutenant-general in the Army and air marshal in the Air Force. Churchill also made him a de facto member of the Chiefs of Staff Committee. As such, Mountbatten was the only individual other than the King to have rank in all three services.[53]

Churchill now pressed the young, energetic, and well-connected Mountbatten to make real progress. "My task, he [Churchill] told me," revealed Mountbatten, "was to continue the Commando raids in order to keep up the offensive spirit, gain essential experience, and to harass the enemy."[54] He added, "above all, I was to prepare in every possible way for the great counter-invasion of Europe." The prime minister summed up his expectations succinctly. "I want you [Mountbatten]," he directed, "to turn the south coast of England from a bastion of defence into a springboard of attack!"[55]

In the end, despite the rocky start, with time came more experience and skill, and with that, success. Undeniably, commando raids commenced slowly. Only three were conducted in 1940, 10 in 1941, and 21 in 1942.[56]

For many, despite the slow start and relative short history, commando raids were proving themselves successful and achieving their aim. They raised public morale, forged a record for perseverance and toughness, and brought tactical, and at times, arguably, strategic success. For instance, the raid on the Italian Tragino Aqueduct on 10 February 1941, conducted by seven officers and 31 NCOs and men was intended to cut the pipeline that took water from the Sele River to the arid province of Apulia and the strategically important ports of Brindisi, Taranto, and Bari. Although the raid caused only minimal physical damage, it had far-reaching implications. The Italians became so unnerved by the operation that they diverted valuable manpower and resources in its aftermath for the protection of every vital point in the country.[57]

Another raid, in March 1941, against the Lofoten Islands (located off the Norwegian coast), specifically the ports of Stamsund, Henningsvaer, Svolvaer, and Brettesnes, aimed to destroy oil installations, factories key to the war effort and enemy shipping, as well as to capture prisoners.[58] "The raid," gloated Lieutenant-Colonel Durnford-Slater, "could hardly have been more successful." He added, "we destroyed eighteen factories; had sunk twenty thousand tons of shipping in harbour; had sent nearly a million gallons of oil and petrol up in smoke ... taken 216 Germans and sixty quislings [Norwegian collaborators] ... seized maps, code systems, valuable documents ... and we carried off three hundred loyal Norwegians who volunteered to continue their country's fight from Britain."[59] But, the greatest coup was the capture of spare wheels for the German cipher machine that was given the codename "Enigma." This was of vital importance for the decrypting of German code traffic which provided the Allies with one of their greatest wartime advantages. All this was achieved without losing a single man.[60]

Later in the year, in December, a raid was mounted in Norway, this time against Sör Vaagso, with a diversionary attack once again in the Lofoten Islands. The primary goal this time was to prevent German forces from being moved to the Eastern Front. The tactical aim was to destroy the garrison, demolish the local fish-oil factories, sink shipping, seize Quislings, and bring home volunteers for the Free Norwegian Forces. As such, the commandos were successful. They wrecked German installations, destroyed 15,000 tons of German shipping, small industry, warehouses, stores, and a small dockyard. In addition, they captured 98 prisoners and four Quislings.[61] Of greater importance, was the impact the raid had on the German psychology. A week following the raid, Hitler decreed that "Norway is the zone of destiny in this war" and he demanded unconditional obedience to his directives concerning its defence.[62]

But Norway was not the only area of continuing success. On 27/28 February 1942, another raid with strategic implications was conducted against a known German radar installation in Bruneval, France that housed the state-of-the-art *Würzburg* radar system that vectored German fighter aircraft onto individual British bombers. The intent of the raid was to capture radar components for the experts at the Telecommunications Research Establishment. The assault was extremely productive. First, the captured equipment had far-reaching effects on British radar development and electronic countermeasures, specifically the development of chaff. Moreover, it buoyed public morale at time when Britain had just lost two battleships, as well as the city of Singapore in the Far East.[63]

Yet another example of a successful raid with strategic implications was the attack on the French port of St. Nazaire, on the night of 27/28 March 1942. Its purpose was to destroy the only dry dock on the Atlantic coast large enough to service the German battleship *Tirpitz*, which the Allies feared could slip into the Atlantic as a surface raider and play havoc with the vital Allied convoys from North America. In a remarkably bold attack, an old destroyer, the HMS *Campbeltown*, laden with five tons of explosives bluffed its way past the enemy defences and rammed the dry dock. A party of 268 commandos then landed and proceeded to destroy essential machinery and infrastructure of the dock. The destroyer itself exploded the next morning when its timed charges detonated.[64]

This sampling of raids conducted in the first two years of the commandos' existence is not all-encompassing. However, it does provide insight into the nature of their successes. Moreover, Hitler's extreme reaction to the commando raids was a tangible, albeit dark, indicator of their success. His "Commando Order" of 18 October 1942, that directed that "all men operating against German troops in so-called Commando raids in Europe or in Africa are to be annihilated to the last man ..." provides further testimony to the effectiveness of the commandos and the raiding policy. Enemy intelligence summaries bluntly acknowledged that "men selected for this sort of Commando [mission] by the enemy are well trained and equipped for their task."[65] So incensed was the German dictator by their constant attacks that he ordered them killed "whether they be soldiers in uniform ... whether fighting or seeking to escape ... even if these individuals on discovery make obvious their intention of giving themselves up as prisoners." He insisted that "no pardon is on any account to be given."[66]

Undeniably, the creation of commandos and the raiding policy that they made possible was born from a position of incredible weakness. Devoid of equipment, adequate weaponry, and a modern doctrine for warfighting, Britain needed a means to bolster morale, maintain an offensive spirit, develop battle experience, and spread out German military resources. Highly trained and motivated commandos executing an aggressive raiding policy were seen as the solution. And, in the process, the ground was prepared, in spite of opposition from many senior military commanders, for the birth of modern special operations forces.

The commando experience made the idea of specially organized and specially trained units of intrepid individuals who revelled in challenging and highly dangerous small-unit actions that called forth innovation, individualism, and initiative more widely accepted, or at least tolerated, in an institution known for its conservatism and traditionalism. However, this conditional acceptance existed largely only at the beginning of the war when the years were filled with disaster and loss, with defeat looming on the horizon. In this chaotic storm of despair, special units helped cover up weakness and met specific needs that conventional forces were seen as too unwieldy or poorly trained to accomplish. As such, commandos, Long Range Desert Group, the Special Air Service, the Special Operations Executive, and many others emerged to maintain the war effort until larger conventional forces could crush the German war machine. It was in this period of weakness and crisis, that another requirement necessitated the creation of yet one more special unit to raid the northern reaches of the Nazi empire to destroy its war-making potential and components critical to its atomic weapons program. Although the idea originated in England, the unit that would become the First Special Service Force was a distinctly North American affair.

2

"MASTERY OF THE SNOWS":
The Plough Project

We must obtain mastery of the snow as we have of the sea ... This would enable us to move over snow at speeds greater than that of the enemy and to go where he cannot follow.[1]
— British Scientist, Sir Geoffrey Nathaniel Pyke.

The rise and near reliance on special operations forces (SOF) to strike back at the Germans at the beginning of the war was as much a result of Britain's weakness after its expulsion from Europe in the early summer of 1940, as it was due to the aggressive hands-on approach to the conduct of the war by the British prime minister. As such, Winston Churchill and his carefully groomed confederate, Lord Louis Mountbatten, the newly appointed chief of combined operations and fourth member of the Chiefs of Staff Committee responsible for the strategic conduct of the war, continued to support aggressive schemes, regardless of their seemingly unorthodox nature. What conservative, tradition-bound, and imagination-stunted military staff viewed as outlandish, unmilitary, and preposterous, Churchill and a small circle of like-minded innovators often considered as daring, fresh, and full of promise.[2] In the end, their collective support, senior positions, and tenacious manner of imposing their will, more often than not ensured that their initiatives were pursued.

It was precisely this formula that would have significant consequences for North America. In September 1941, an eccentric, widely despised, but according to Mountbatten, brilliant British scientist, named Geoffrey Nathaniel Pyke developed a theory that he believed was quite revolutionary and instrumental to the Allied war effort.[3] In short, Pyke visualized snow as the "fourth element — a sea which flows over most of Europe each year and which usually tends to act as a brake on military operations."[4] With the development of a new special snow vehicle, Pyke postulated that a small British raiding force could overcome this "fourth element" and attack and tie down a vast number of German troops.[5] Moreover, according to Pyke, the Allied force could cripple key German war industries.

This "new" vehicle was key to the concept of "mastery" of the snow. Pyke insisted that the possession of new cross-country snow machines would allow access to large tracts of Norway and the Carpathians, and allow Allied soldiers to move over snow at greater speeds than the enemy and into areas they could not follow, particularly up steep gradients and into wooded terrain. In the simplest form, Pyke was calling for the mechanization of the ski. The War Office, however, was not interested. In its view, this was just another wild idea that required additional manpower, research, and production capacity. Furthermore, the overworked general staff saw in it as just another version of commando operations, which had not proven overly successful to date in their estimation.[6] As well, they were still struggling with the transition to mechanization of the Army — anything else, particularly such a questionable requirement as snow operations, could wait — indefinitely.

Nevertheless, almost eight months later in March 1942, fortunes changed for Pyke and his radical concept. His proposal reached the ear of the chief of combined operations and he was, not surprisingly, very interested. Pyke jumped at the opportunity. He caught Mountbatten's attention immediately by asserting that his plan addressed the perennial strategic problem of how to compel the enemy to draw off the largest amount of resources from the primary theatre of war at relatively small cost to friendly forces on a scale and at a time of their choosing. In light of the continued weakened state of the Allies at this point in the war, it was a very pertinent issue. Pyke then hammered home his point. He insisted that a force of perhaps a thousand British soldiers could tie down a force of a half million Germans.[7]

Pyke's focal point was Norway. He explained that most of that Scandinavian country was under snow for more than six months of the year and that in the south 18 hours of each winter day was cloaked in darkness. Furthermore, he explained that although the Germans seized and occupied the country they did so only by virtue of occupying major towns and cities and fortifying coastal areas. Pyke asserted that in essence, the Germans were occupying the population, which required a relatively small commitment of resources. However, if they were forced to occupy the country, they would be forced to tie up an unduly large military force. Pyke now connected the dots. He argued that the interior of Norway, which was Europe's most sparsely populated country, provided a commando force a large tract of territory for manoeuvre. "If there were to be landed by parachute men with machines able to travel fast and far not through but on the snow," explained an excited Pyke, "able to carry arms for attacking and explosives to destroy bridges, tunnels, railway tracks, hydro-electric stations … equipped to maintain themselves in any part of the country, however high and desolate to launch frequent attacks on vital objects" then the Germans would be compelled to sink larger forces into defence of that country.[8]

The importance of his plan became readily apparent. Pyke insisted that the development of his snow machine and the corollary raiding force would eliminate Norway as an economic asset to Germany by the destruction of the hydroelectric stations. He further explained that 49 percent of the hydroelectric power generated in Norway was concentrated in only 14 stations, thus, a raiding force could focus on a small number of targets yet achieve a high payoff. Simply put these power stations were key to serving particular industries that were critical to the German war effort. For example, Norwegian molybdenum was an important steel-hardening alloy and it represented 70 percent of the German supply, 95 percent of which came from deposits from the Knaben mine in the south of Norway. In addition, Finnish nickel refined in Norway represented 70 percent of the German intake, while Norwegian aluminum and copper represented 8 percent.[9] In all, the impact of Pyke's recommended operation on Norwegian hydroelectric capacity would be substantial. The targeted sites would incapacitate 970,000 kilowatt hours of production out of Norway's total of approximately two million kilowatt hours.[10]

Pyke also posited that the raiding force would provide another useful strategic results. For instance, he argued the inserted force would lead the way for an eventual reoccupation of Norway, as well as a link with the Russians. Moreover, he insisted that it would be a means of destroying German bases in northern Norway that threatened the Allied supply line to Russia. Finally, Pyke pointed out that its existence alone would necessitate a large German military presence in an anti-guerrilla/sabotage role.[11]

Pyke's vision, however, also spilled over to other snow-covered territories. He argued that the vehicle and raiding force(s) could be utilized in "destroying a large proportion of the oil refining capacity and a considerable proportion of the oil producing capacity of Rumania."[12] In all, Rumania was supplying approximately three million tons of oil annually to the Axis powers. The oil came from approximately 5,000 oils wells clustered in various fields within a 50-mile radius of Ploesti.[13]

In addition, Pyke asserted that his concept could be used for the destruction of "as much as seventy per cent of the Italian hydro-electric power."[14] The Italian option, however, was problematic. This capacity was concentrated in only 12 power stations, but, they extended along the northern Po River watershed from the French border to across Italy. But more important, the actual impact of a temporary stoppage on the German war effort would be minimal. Italy contributed no critical materials or products that could not have been provided by German capacity.[15]

The Plough Project's boldness, aggressive offensive nature, and undeniable economy of effort appealed to Mountbatten, as it did to Churchill once he had been briefed. "Never," penned a jubilant prime minister, "will so few immobilize so many."[16] Moreover, the plan provided another important potential benefit — a means of striking at Germany's atomic weapons program.

The spectre of Hitler gaining access to an atom weapon quickly began to weigh on Allied leaders and scientists. Churchill himself conceded that the idea of Germany attaining the atomic bomb "lay heavy on my mind."[17] After all, Otto Hahn, a German physicist successfully discovered atomic fission in December 1938.[18] And, with Hitler's

OF COURAGE AND DETERMINATION

Member of the Lovat Scouts participating in a winter tactical exercise in Jasper Park, Alberta.

stunning success in overrunning Europe in the spring of 1940, the German physicists were provided with an amazing windfall. Suddenly, they had access to heavy water (deuterium oxide)[19] from the Norsk-Hydro plant in Vemork (Rjukan), Norway; thousands of tons of uranium ore from the Union Minière in Belgium; the use of the only cyclotron,[20] albeit not completely finished, in existence in Paris; and access to the doyen of nuclear physicists, Niels Bohr, in Occupied Denmark.[21] Therefore, when British Intelligence, in the summer of 1941, discovered that the Norsk-Hydro plant was in the process of increasing its heavy water production 10-fold, it became clear that the Germans were actively involved in atomic weapon research.[22] Planners quickly realized that the heavy water could be the weak link in the German program. Not surprisingly, the Norsk-Hydro facility, which was located in inhospitable terrain, nestled between

Above: *Lord Louis Mountbatten.*

Right: *Prime Minister Winston Churchill was a fervent supporter of the Plough Project.*

two mountains, became a priority target.²³ As such, the Plough Project promised the possibility of being another extremely effective tool for eliminating what was viewed as a potential catastrophe in the making. It made it just that much more alluring to Churchill and Mountbatten.

In the end, as appealing as the "Plough" concept was, on so many different levels, it was beyond the British capacity at that time. They had neither the manpower, nor the industrial production capacity to undertake it. However, by March 1942, their Americans allies, who had just entered the war a few months prior, provided a possible avenue to exploit. What is more, for Churchill, the project provided a potential respite. It could act as a diversion to get the impatient Americans to drop their naive and ill-advised idea of invading Europe in

1942. As such, in the early spring of that year, the concept was pitched to U.S. Army Chief of Staff General George C. Marshall and Harry Hopkins, President Roosevelt's representative, when the two Americans came to England to discuss Allied strategy, namely the opening of a western front against the Germans. During the numerous discussions, the issue of diversionary attacks arose. Without hesitation, Lord Mountbatten proceeded to outline Pyke's concept.

The chief of combined operations explained to the Americans that his headquarters had been studying an operation (code named "Plough" — derived from a suitable cover name for the vehicle, i.e., snowplough), which he described as an ideal diversion and a possible mission for his commandos. He conceded, however, that after consulting with war production agencies, it became apparent that Britain, for practical and technical reasons, could not produce the special vehicle in a timely manner. British engineers estimated it would take approximately four years. Churchill wanted the vehicle operational in nine months. As hoped, the idea caught Marshall's imagination and he agreed to a fuller meeting on the subject at a later date.[24]

The follow-on meeting occurred on 9 April 1942, at Chequers, Prime Minister Churchill's country home. Geoffrey Pyke himself was there to explain his bold plan. At the end of the meeting, General Marshall decided, after deliberations with his staff, that the project, including the design and production of about 1,000 special snow machines, was not a difficult task for American ingenuity and industry.[25] "It was agreed," wrote Churchill for the minutes, "that the United States authorities would undertake to develop and manufacture the necessary armoured fighting snow vehicles."[26] And so, the Plough Project became a reality.

However, the reception in the United States was not overly promising. Although General Marshall provided a letter of introduction, American military officers were as skeptical as their British counterparts in the War Office when they were first told of the idea. The incredibly short time line of nine months to design, produce, and field the machines only made the overall scheme seem so much more silly. Adding to the problem was Pyke's abrasive, contentious, and rude manner. Initial meetings in Washington, D.C., with American officers could not have gone more badly. They questioned the actual military feasibility of the plan and developed a strong dislike for Pyke to the point that they completely cut him out of follow-on discussions.

Adding to the growing skepticism and apathy of the American staff officers tasked with the project was a negative estimate on the entire Plough operation. Lieutenant-Colonel Robert T. Frederick, an artillery officer assigned to the Operations Division of the General Staff, was saddled with the chore of completing an assessment of the military viability of the British plan.[27] By early May, his analysis was complete and his appraisal was scathing. First, he highlighted the lack of aircraft capable, or available, to lift the snow machines. The few possible aircraft capable of lifting such weight were simply not viable. For example, the British Lancaster bomber was just in mass production and heavily committed to the

General George C. Marshall, Chief of Staff, U.S. Army

bombing campaign and the American C-54 transport plane was still in the prototype phase. Gliders were also discounted because their use would necessitate half the raiding force being made up of glider pilots. A seaborne insertion, reasoned Frederick, would negate surprise. In addition, he argued that the effort would interfere greatly with preparations and manufacturing of equipment for the invasion of Europe.

Furthermore, Frederick pointed out that there was no sound evacuation plan, therefore, he believed it was a suicide mission that sacrificed men needlessly. He insisted, true to his conventional roots and traditional military mindset, that there was no proof that a small band of men, scattered throughout Europe could engage and occupy a large number of enemy troops. He asserted that sabotage by native Norwegians or a bombing program could achieve the same results. In the end, he concluded that Plough was a great theoretical concept but a rather contemptible military plan.[28]

Predictably, Pyke now largely marginalized, came to the conclusion that his idea was coming to naught. Fortuitously for Pyke, in June 1942, Lord Mountbatten arrived in Washington, D.C., to discuss the invasion of Europe with Roosevelt and his chiefs of staff. While in America, he used the opportunity to discuss the Plough Project with Pyke. He was quickly inundated with complaints. Other than his own personal ostracism, by both the American officers and his own British military superior, Pyke also revealed flaws in the research program. To date, only one prototype vehicle was being examined and it was too large to fit into an aircraft. It seemed there was little interest in developing other models. As a result, Mountbatten made some internal personnel changes and sought a meeting with General Marshall's assistant chief of staff, Major-General Dwight "Ike" Eisenhower to discuss progress made to date. As such, Mountbatten and Pyke shared their concerns that the project was not receiving the attention it merited. To underscore the British commitment to the scheme, Mountbatten subsequently personally delivered a message from Churchill to President Roosevelt confirming the prime minister's strong interest in Operation Plough.[29]

OF COURAGE AND DETERMINATION

Not surprisingly, the American intransigence was swiftly nipped in the bud. Eisenhower quickly followed up on his promise to invigorate the American participation in the Plough Project. The negative report particularly piqued his ire. Eisenhower raged at his staff and demanded to know how they could so off-handedly criticize a plan that was approved and so strongly supported by Churchill and Mountbatten. Political reality now over-rode sound military judgment. Regardless of Frederick's estimate or his staff's assessment, Eisenhower announced point blank that Operation Plough would proceed. As far as he was concerned, he had no choice. He had already told the British that the Americans were proceeding with the project at full speed.[30]

Eisenhower met personally with Frederick and informed him that he would not sign the report. Moreover, he directed Frederick to call Army Ground Force Headquarters (AFG HQ) to assign an officer to assume command of the project. Initially, Lieutenant-Colonel H.R. Johnson was designated as commander. His tour of command barely lasted days. Johnson and Pyke, upon their first meeting immediately had a falling out. Johnson made it clear that he had neither the time, nor the inclination to solicit or even consider counsel from a civilian scientist, particularly one as irregular and unorthodox as Pyke. Pyke immediately complained to Mountbatten who promptly met with Johnson and Frederick. During the meeting, Johnson indicated his willingness to support the project if it was a serious initiative. However, he made it clear he was not anxious to become involved in a theoretical exercise. Mountbatten said little and after a short time dismissed the portentous officer. By that evening, Lieutenant-Colonel Johnson had been replaced.[31]

As an ironic twist, the very officer who so capably criticized the Plough Project earlier on, was now appointed as its new commander. On 16 June 1942, the coastal artillery officer, Lieutenant-Colonel Frederick, was removed from his staff position and directed by General Marshall to "supervise and be responsible for all development of material and planning for accomplishment of the Plough Project, and for the procurement and organization of such forces as are necessary for the project."[32] This mandate included Marshall's direction to "all

General Dwight D. Eisenhower overcame initial staff resistance in pushing forward the Plough Project in the U.S.

agencies of the War Department" to "cooperate with and assist" Frederick with his mission. Moreover, Frederick was designated to command the force once it was organized.[33]

The Plough Project broke down into two very distinct and separate problems. The first was the development of the special snow vehicle. The second was organizing and training the special raiding force that would man the vehicles. The initial priority was placed on developing the special snow vehicle. This would prove to be quite a challenge.

The target date for the completion of the Plough vehicle, that is the design, testing, and full production, was only nine months. Churchill wanted his snow machines ready for operational deployment by the end of December 1942. This Herculean task fell to Brigadier-General Raymond G. Moses, the American Army General Staff G-4, who was overall in charge of the snow machine program. Brigadier-General Moses very quickly co-ordinated with both the Office of Scientific Research and Development (OSRD) and the War Production Board. As a starting point, they utilized the tentative specifications developed by the British. In short, the snow machine was required to be capable of:

a. Movement over hard and soft snow.
b. Limited movement over non-snow terrain, if possible.
c. Carrying two tons, in final version, with possible development of smaller machines for non-cargo-carrying missions such as reconnaissance.
d. Transportation by any of four means — glider, parachute, Alan Muntz wings,[34] and seaborne craft.

It was also required to meet the following characteristics:

a. Speed on level ground — 20 miles per hour.
b. Slope capacity — 20 per cent (1 in 5) essential.
c. Radius — 250 miles.
d. Small armor desirable up to proof against small-arms fire.
e. Small silhouette.
f. Maneuverable, to turn in its own length.
g. Silent, free-running, capable of free downhill run.
h. Braking — able to stop on slope.
i. Variable pitch screw, if Archimedian screw development employed.[35]

In late April 1942, Geoffrey Pyke and a young British Commando officer, Major E.A.M Wedderburn, who was also a winter warfare expert, as well as Brigadier Nigel Duncan, the British Combined Operations liaison officer in Washington, D.C., visited Brigadier-General Moses to discuss British expectations. Amazingly, they tabled the requirement for 600 vehicles by the end of October, only six months away! Despite severe misgivings, after consulting with the OSRD technicians, the Americans agreed.

To meet the new timeline, Brigadier-General Moses assured the OSRD team that they would receive the fullest cooperation from the State and War Departments; top priority from the selected manufacturer; assistance to assemble every type of snow machine in existence for testing; and access to any and all specialists required. The actual task of building the "Plough" vehicle was in the hands of Palmer C. Putnam from the OSRD. He quickly determined that the snow machine in question needed to be wide-tracked with a lightweight, watertight hull powered by an automobile engine.[36] His next step was to travel to Mount Rainier near Fort Lewis, Washington to test existing vehicles. These included the Army's Eliasson toboggan (a toboggan powered by a motorcycle engine with a canvas belt studded with oak slats which bit into the snow for propulsion), Russian propeller-driven sleds, a civilian Archimedean screw-driven vehicle, and even a standard issue jeep. These tests quickly determined that something innovative and new was required.

As a result, Putnam refined his design requirements and passed the new design instructions and specifications to a design team in New York by telephone. He demanded that blueprints be developed and sent to Washington the next day. As ordered, the blueprints arrived and both military representatives and civilian scientists met with Brigadier-General Moses to discuss the suggested solution. And thus, the "Weasel," or more formally the Cargo Carrier, Light, T-15, was born.[37]

As if by providence, design and manufacturer were soon to collide. Concomitant with the testing and design work, the automotive firm Studebaker uncovered a large stock of Champion motor parts in its various plants and depots, sufficient to build 2,000 Champion motors. From the sketchy details available, the auto manufacturer felt that these engines would be adequate to power the Weasel. A quick meeting between Putnam, Major Wedderburn, and the vice-president of Studebaker, Ray E. Cole, resulted in the design coming to life. Studebaker immediately adopted a 24-hour production cycle to meet OSRD's priority demand that four pilot models at $100,000 each be produced as quickly as possible. The technical problem of producing extremely wide, light-gauge rubberized steel tracks was given to research engineers of the tire manufactures of both Firestone and Goodrich.[38] Despite the advancements made, the clock was still relentlessly ticking.

Development of the Weasel moved forward rapidly. Prototype vehicles were ready for evaluation in early July 1942, but the problem became finding a suitable testing ground. Failure to find an adequate snow testing range, meant the four prototype Weasel vehicles were put through their paces on the Michigan-Indiana sand dunes. Moses and the OSRD were satisfied enough that they directed Studebaker to commence with the production of 600 vehicles.[39] In the end, Studebaker produced 1,000 Weasels.

The vehicle met with much criticism. In short, it failed to meet the requirements set out: It was difficult to transport by air, there being only a limited number of aircraft capable of carrying it; its top end speed was only 24 kilometres per hour; it could only

The T-15 Weasel over-snow vehicle, code-named "Plough."

climb a grade of 15 percent; and its range was a dismal 120-128 kilometres. Nevertheless, it was still recognized as the most practical all-around snow machine available.[40] As such, vehicles were made available for training the Plough force.

And so, by mid-August, Project Plough appeared on the rails. The vehicle problem was solved. The target was refined to Norway, with little objection being forwarded by Allied headquarters in regards to the decision to drop Rumania and Italy as Plough Force objectives. Moreover, planning now focused on how to extract the raiders once their mission was done. Three possible plans — landing craft extracting groups assembled on the coast; flying boats picking up members from isolated fiords; and individual groups travelling in Weasels moving east to cross into Sweden, leaving a trail of demolished bridges and other infrastructure in their wake — came under detailed scrutiny.

But for Frederick, a more immediate problem required resolution, namely, that of organizing the actual Plough Force. This became Frederick's first issue of business upon taking on the role as commander of the Plough Project. He now learned that Canadians and Norwegians would also make up part of the force. As such, he was quickly whisked away from Washington, D.C., to accompany Mountbatten and Pyke on a staff visit to Canada to discuss the possibility of Canadian participation in Operation Plough. Very quickly, the Canadian connection was about to turn a British idea into a unique North American undertaking.

3

A GROWING WEB:
The Canadian Connection

The cream of Canada's hard-fighting army youth is training in the United States today for "aerial commando" raiding which one day soon will make the German and the Jap think cyclones have struck where they thought they were safe and secure.[1]

— Reporter Don Mason, August 1942.

Although neighbours and allies in the current global crusade, ironically the Plough Project's Canadian connection was not the genesis of American or Canadian co-operation. Rather it was the idea of Winston Churchill.[2] Initially, he visualized a force composed of American, British, Canadian, and Norwegian troops. However, demands on their limited resource base and the fact the war was expanding as momentum shifted to the Allied cause meant the British had to pull out. The Norwegians also abandoned the project early on, fearing that their participation might trigger German reprisals against civilians in occupied Norway. And so, the Plough Project very quickly became a North American endeavour.

Canada's involvement, however, did not begin with the visit of Lord Mountbatten, Colonel Frederick, and Geoffrey Pyke to Ottawa on 11 June 1942. In fact, there was a Canadian tie from the beginning of the Plough Project discussions. In April 1942, the British requested assistance from Lieutenant-General A.G.L. McNaughton, the Canadian Overseas Army commander and former president of the Canadian National Research Council (NRC), who was widely known for his interest in scientific research and "things technical." Not surprisingly, the British quickly received the full co-operation of McNaughton, who directed his staff to ensure that "all available particulars of existing snowmobiles and other similar snow-crossing transport equipment" be made available to the British authorities.[3] McNaughton's call for co-operation also extended to the NRC, who were asked for the same material, as well as all their work on the snow performance of aircraft skis.[4] In addition,

OF COURAGE AND DETERMINATION

The Plough Project called for American and Canadian soldiers who were at home in the harsh winter/arctic environment.

McNaughton arranged to loan an officer trained in winter warfare and a technical officer familiar with winter transport equipment to the British mission.[5]

These informal ties soon became a much larger web. As mentioned earlier, on 11 June 1942, the British-American delegation led by Mountbatten met with Lieutenant-General Kenneth Stuart, the chief of the general staff, and Major-General John Murchie the vice-chief of the general staff (VCGS). At this time the chief of combined operations outlined the Plough Project and asked that the Canadians co-operate to the fullest, including the provision of combat forces. Stuart quickly agreed to the proposal. At

Lieutenant-General Andrew "Andy" G.L. McNaughton, Canadian overseas commander.

42

A GROWING WEB

this point in the war, Canadians, particularly the combatants who had joined to fight and were now sitting idle in England without seeing action for over two years, were eager to join the active war effort.[6] This bold and offensive scheme seemed perfect to galvanize both military personnel and the public. Moreover, it increased the level of co-operation between the Americans and Canadians.[7]

Having secured Canadian participation in principle, Mountbatten departed and left Frederick and Pyke to work out the necessary details. Frederick clearly spelled out that Canadian combat troops would be required to serve on the force, although he had no idea how many at this stage. The Canadians took an instant liking to Frederick. Conversely, like their American counterparts earlier, they developed a negative impression of Pyke. As a result, Pyke was stymied in his attempts to have control of the Plough Project taken over by Canadians. His incessant demands fell on deaf ears. Murchie informed John Ralston, the minister of national defence (MND), that "it appeared that he [Pyke] had got off on the wrong foot in Washington and now wanted to move the control of the project to Canada."[8] But the Canadians would have none of it. They were not prepared to take on a new project, especially at the risk of offending their relatively new American allies. The Canadians made it a point of principle and a condition of their participation that the Americans bear primary responsibility for the Plough Project and they demanded that any discussion on priority or plans be addressed to them. In fact, the CGS insisted, "the first step to be taken in this project from our point of view is to establish clearly the channels of responsibility

The Honourable John Ralston, MND, meeting with General Eisenhower at SHAEF headquarters, Paris, France.

through which it will be handled."[9] To ensure there was no mistake as to the origin of this requirement, it was further articulated that "any representations which he [Pyke] may wish to make with respect to the alteration of our plans are to be made in the first instance to the U.S. War Department and not directly to the Canadian authorities."[10]

Follow-on discussions and planning continued between the Department of National Defence (DND) and the U.S. War Department. On 20 June 1942, Lieutenant-Colonel W.A.B. Anderson, the Canadian representative of the General Staff in Washington, D.C., conducting the joint planning, informed his superiors in Ottawa that General J.T. McNarney, the U.S. deputy chief of staff of the Army requested that Canada provide 500 all ranks, including an officer to act as second-in-command for the Force, as well as the commanding officer of the Canadian contingent.[11] This represented half of the 1,000 man force that the Americans envisioned.[12]

It was now time to pony up. And, as always, commitment of Canadian troops required the blessing of the risk averse Canadian prime minister, William Lyon Mackenzie King. The MND, a former battalion commander and colonel in the First World War, met with the prime minister on 26 June 1942. As a result of this meeting, King formally authorized the Canadian participation and the next day Ralston forwarded the necessary approval to the CGS.[13]

The prime minister's ready acquiescence to the joint venture was not overly surprising. After all, on 18 August 1940, in the aftermath of the Fall of France and in the shadow of the imminent invasion of England, King entered into a series of discussions between himself and President Roosevelt relating to the mutual problems of defence. This resulted in the Ogdensburg Agreement, which was nothing short of a continental defence pact. Among other things it established the Permanent Joint Board of Defence (PJBD), which was charged with co-ordinating the joint defence planning between the two countries. "The common approach of the governments of Canada and the United States," extolled King, "to the problems of North American defence was formally recognized in the Ogdensburg agreement."[14] In accordance with the pact, the PJBD, which had four to five members, mainly military, from each country, became responsible for the "broad consideration of the defence of the north half of the Western Hemisphere."[15] Prime Minister King himself explained to Parliament that due to the global scope of the conflict, "recommendations were made from time to time by the joint board [PJBD] for the development ... of projects of vital importance to the two nations for common defence and for the effective prosecution of the war."[16] As such, the idea of an integrated unit was not outside his threshold of acceptance, particularly in light of the ongoing Canadian/American co-operation.[17]

With the Canadian commitment formally authorized, all that remained was to determine the actual size of the contribution required. By 7 July 1942, the Americans had finalized the establishment for the Plough Force. In total, the combat echelon numbered 1,167 all ranks and the support component to the force added up to an additional 521

A GROWING WEB

Canadian Prime Minister William Lyon Mackenzie King (centre) meeting with U.S. President Franklin D. Roosevelt (left) and British Prime Minister Winston Churchill, in Quebec, during the Quadrant Conference, 18 August 1943.

personnel.[18] This in turn triggered the MND to approve, on 14 July 1942, the dispatch to the U.S. of the necessary Canadian contingent that now numbered 47 officers and 650 other ranks.[19] Two days later, a special meeting was held at NDHQ to determine how the Canadian commitment could be achieved. This would be no easy feat. Incredibly, the Canadians were to be in the U.S. for training by 1 August — approximately two weeks later. Obviously, shortcuts would be required. As such, the planners decided that to avoid undue publicity for this secret force and to gather the necessary number of troops required in such a short period, they would recruit the necessary personnel at the same time as they were attracting volunteers for the 1st Canadian Parachute Battalion. This would also provide a measure of security since it would cover and disguise the true nature of the force. Therefore, logically, it was decided to name the Canadian component of the Plough Project the 2nd Canadian Parachute Battalion (2 Cdn Para Bn).[20]

However, the creation of 2nd Canadian Parachute Battalion was not the only Canadian tie to the Plough Project at this juncture. Concomitant with the military efforts were the scientific. The NRC provided what support they could in the way of research data and expertise. In addition, Canadian technology and testing sites were also tapped. The Americans quickly requested samples of the Bombardier snowmobiles in existence at the time. As a result, on 10 July 1942, the MND contacted C.D. Howe, the minister of the Department of Munitions and Supply, who's own ministry was working on a snowmobile prototype and asked for the release of one of the Bombardier vehicles it currently possessed. Of the three held by the Department of Munitions and Supply (i.e., a standard six-passenger, a standard 12-passenger, and a special model), Ralston demanded only the use of the 12-passenger snowmobile "for most urgent test purposes."[21]

The Department of Mines and Resources was also recruited to assist with the Plough Project. The Americans very quickly realized the potential of Western Canadian test sites and targeted Jasper National Park, specifically the Athabasca Glacier as a potential location. However, the myriad of crevasses on the glacier made the site unworkable. However, Jasper's Columbia Glacier and the Saskatchewan Glacier in Banff National Park did provide the necessary conditions. As such, the Department of Mines and Resources was asked to clear temporary paths into the sites so that the requisite testing could be carried out.[22]

By mid to late August the testing had been completed. The Bombardier snow machine with its forward skis and plywood cabin for personnel installed on its rear tracks was put through its paces. However, in the end, the Weasel still won out and remained the

Bombardier staff assembling military snowmobiles in Valcourt, Quebec.

A GROWING WEB

designated vehicle for the Plough Project. In all, although snow conditions were limited (i.e., only "spring snow"), the tests still provided an opportunity to compare alternate snowmobiles, as well as derive important data that resulted in follow-on research and testing for improving the Weasel design. For example, the proper depth of grousers, ice build-up in the sprockets, the design of bogie wheels, and the structural make-up of the track were all issues that were addressed and improved as a result of the Canadian tests.[23]

Meanwhile, as the scientists and Studebaker Corporation engineers raced to design and build the requisite over-snow vehicle, Colonel Frederick wrestled with the establishment of the human component of the Plough force. One of his first challenges was to find a name for this embryonic unit. Once again, the necessity of covering the true identity of the Force ruled out using any variation of the names "commando," "rangers," "airborne," or "parachute infantry" because they would invariably attract undue attention and they were already taken and referred to distinct forces.[24]

One popular idea was to name the combat unit the "Braves." Frederick explained, "Because the history of both the United States and Canada is so rich in Indian lore, we believe that a term derived from the Indians would be fitting in describing the Force of both nations."[25] The connection with Natives also prompted Frederick and his subordinate commanders to consider in combination with the formation moniker using the name of eight Indian tribes to identify the FSSF's subunits.[26] Additionally, the FSSF adopted the motto. "None but the brave can be free."[27]

In the end, Colonel Frederick kept the motto but arbitrarily selected the title First Special Service Force for his force — a name that sounded innocuous enough to hide its real intent. Moreover, to further conceal the special nature of the FSSF combat role, the designation of subordinate organizations (i.e., regiments, battalions, companies, platoons, and sections) followed the standard infantry nomenclature to avoid any unwarranted attention. In the end, his choice of name was actually quite insightful, as later in the war the Special Services Branch was established as an entertainment organization to assist with raising the morale of the troops overseas.[28] As such, the FSSF at least on paper seemed innocuous enough.

Despite having made a formal decision on the name, the "Braves" motif, in particular its Native connotation, stuck with the Forcemen, albeit not the formation itself. This was most likely a result of the shoulder patch insignia that was allocated to the FSSF shortly after its approval — a spearhead with a red background on which the letters U.S.A. are spelled out in white thread horizontally across the top of the spearhead and CANADA spelled out vertically, also in white thread, along the axis, as well as collar dogs comprised of two crossed arrows.[29] In fact, later at Anzio in 1944, the unit newspaper was called *The Braves Bulletin*.[30]

The naming of the Force, however, was of far less importance than its actual organization. This became another key concern for Frederick. Although it had to be light in nature — it also had to be self-sufficient, particularly in the form of raw combat power. As such, the FSSF was broken into two separate echelons — combat and support. Canadians served only in the combat echelon but they were not segregated. The FSSF was completely integrated, with American and Canadian personnel serving together under a unified command structure. This meant that personnel were required to obey the orders of their respective superiors regardless of nationality.

The combat echelon, consisting of 1,167 men of which 567 were Canadians, was organized into three regiments, each of two battalions.[31] The regiments comprised approximately 600 men and were commanded by a full colonel. The battalions in turn numbered 300 and were led by a lieutenant-colonel. Battalions were divided into three companies of approximately 100 men in the charge of a captain. The hierarchy broken down further within the companies to three platoons each consisting of two sections of 12 to 16 men. At each level down to the platoon, a headquarters element ensured the efficient functioning of the respective organization and co-ordination with the greater whole.[32]

The FSSF shoulder insignia.

The section was the basic fighting block for the Force — each being similar in strength and armament. Each section was led by a staff-sergeant and in theory included three demolition experts, a medic, two mechanics, a navigator, a radioman, two grenadiers, and a light machine gunner.[33] Originally, four weasels were also assigned to each section, however, in practice this was never realized.

The support echelon or service battalion for lack of a better term, as already noted, had no Canadian participation. It was also unique of sorts. It was responsible for the complete administration, supply, and maintenance of the entire Force. In essence, the support echelon, or service battalion of approximately 546 all ranks was created to relieve the combat echelon from the distraction of any non-combat or general duty (GD) tasks that are normally the bane of existence of all combat units in a garrison setting. Due to the tight timelines to get the Plough Force ready any distraction from training was simply detrimental to mission success. As such, the FSSF Service Battalion provided the necessary manpower so that the combat echelon could focus its efforts and train undisturbed.

An important note worth mentioning is the fact that overall, even though the Canadians would only represent approximately a third of the combat echelon of the

Force throughout its history, they occupied about one-half of the leadership positions. This was a function of the generally older age and greater amount of experience of the Canadian officers. In the end, most of the battalion commanders and senior sergeants were Canadians, while most of the junior officers were Americans.[34]

Ironically, despite the initial attempts to disguise the true nature of the force, political expediency, a need to fuel public morale, and a desire to prove that the Allies were now creating the offensive tools necessary to strike back at the Nazis fed a media frenzy. Although not surprising since the Allies had for so long been on the defensive and on the receiving end of the war, it did render the efforts at secrecy superfluous. And so, just as the Force was assembling in Montana in early August to commence training for its sensitive mission, a myriad of official announcements and newspaper articles exploded into the public domain.

The American and Canadian governments agreed to announce the creation of the force at the same time, on 6 August 1942, although the FSSF was actually activated on 9 July 1942.[35] The Canadian press release, made by the MND, revealed "the formation of a joint Canadian-United States force to undergo special training for offensive warfare including parachute training, marine landings, mountain fighting and desert warfare." The announcement also mentioned that the unit, called the First Special Service Force, would demand "rigid physical requirements and other qualification similar to those of parachute troops." It also stressed that Canadians and Americans would serve together in the unit, "which will have a distinctive uniform."[36]

The American media release was no less revealing. The U.S. under-secretary for war, Robert P. Patterson, announced the creation of "a new American-Canadian force of super-specialists in offensive warfare." He outlined that the new unit was "a unique combat unit composed of specially qualified men skilled in all offensive operations, including marine landings and mountain and desert warfare." He also divulged that the "super-commando force," designated the FSSF, would be answerable directly to the U.S. deputy chief of staff of the Army, Lieutenant-General J.T. McNarney.[37]

The announcement also managed to pique the ire of the Canadian political and military leadership. Patterson's release also boasted that the "Canadian contingent will be the first to serve as a part of a United States Army unit" and that "Canadians and Americans will wear the same uniform," which in practice became the American combat uniform. For the Canadian leadership, who for so long fought to maintain their distinct identity within the British political and military framework, that seemingly simple statement created a degree of angst.[38] Nonetheless, the Canadians pressed on.

In the end, the initial attempts at keeping the nature of the Force secret were somewhat derisory. The media frenzy that was unleashed with the press announcements clearly laid out the FSSF's special status and role. Newspapers across the country and throughout the United States reported on the new unit of "super-specialists in offensive warfare" and the new "elite" Canadian-American "super-commando unit." They highlighted the FSSF's composition of "picked men" and its ability "to go anywhere, at any time." The FSSF was described as a "fast, furious hard-hitting force." In addition to listing the unit's offensive capabilities, the media reports went on to speculate that the FSSF would be a "continental American edition of the Commandos of the British Army."[39] One article went so far as to describe, "bailing out at the 1,500 foot level and making the descent in less than a minute, swift ski runs down mountain slopes and scaling wall-like cliffs are but a few of the thrills in the life of a ski-paratrooper."[40] Little was left to the reader's imagination.

And so, Churchill's "rumination of a North American Force" now came to pass. The unique and fully integrated FSSF did not stealthily creep into history but rather exploded onto the scene through a well-orchestrated media campaign. However, as is so often the case, the public quickly forgot and the unit returned to obscurity — for the time being. Nevertheless, regardless of the American emphasis on the U.S. component and control of the Force, it was undeniable, that Canadian participation in the First Special Service Force was pervasive. Beginning with the provision of expertise to a budding British raiding scheme, it evolved into Canada's full participation in an endeavour that proved as challenging as it was unique.

The concept of complete integration, with Canadian and American personnel serving under a unified command was a bold experiment. However, this risk acceptance, not surprisingly, had a pragmatic and political basis. First, it was understood that the integration of personnel would more effectively facilitate administrating, equipping, and training the Force, which from the start was acknowledged by both parties to be an American responsibility. Moreover, the Canadian political and military leadership was always adamant that the planning, development, and conduct of the project also be the exclusive purview of the U.S. War Department.[41] Simply put, the Canadian leadership was not interested in the tactical or strategic value of the Plough Project. Rather, the commitment to provide 50 percent of the combat echelon personnel seemed like a harmless enough request — one that entailed only 700 personnel at a time when manpower was not an issue, but getting Canadians into combat was.

As such, the invitation appeared fortuitous. It was a means of highlighting the nation's commitment and preparation for the offensive; a means of giving Canadian soldiers, who were chomping at the bit to get at the German enemy, an opportunity for action; and a method to deepen the political ties between Canada and the U.S.

Even so, the nation's leaders still demanded the right to authorize the employment of the Canadian contingent prior to its assignment into combat. After all, the nation's leadership, both political and military, had worked long and hard to underscore Canadian independence particularly in the sphere of its military commitments, and it was loath to surrender that achievement easily. And so, the first hurdles were surmounted — political authorization for Canadian participation and the mechanisms for military integration were firmly set. As such, the nation was now firmly entangled in the Plough Project web. However, one of the greatest challenges still lay ahead — recruiting and selecting the "young, determined and energetic" Canadian personnel to fill the Canadian component of the FSSF.[42]

4

"HAZARDOUS DUTY":
Recruiting and Selecting the Force

[The First Special Service Force] will be a continental edition of commandos of the British Army. In selecting the men to make it up, emphasis will be placed on "youth, hardness and fitness.[1]

— Ross Munro, Canadian Journalist.

Now that the Canadian government decided, for political reasons, to participate with its American ally in the Plough Project, the next crucial step was to initiate, with the shortest possible delay, a speedy recruiting and selection process of Canadian Army personnel. Once selected, these men were to be sent to the U.S. for specialized training and integrated into the new American-Canadian formation now known as the First Special Service Force. The compressed time lines and pressure for immediate results left little time for a detailed, in-depth selection process. Innovation and expediency were the order of the day.

Training was to commence on 1 August 1942. Furthermore, Colonel Frederick was adamant that his personnel be ready for overseas deployment no later than 15 December 1942. The sense of urgency that permeated the creation of the FSSF was clearly evident in the extensive daily correspondence exchanged between Frederick and the senior Canadian officers of the National Defence Headquarters (NDHQ), in Ottawa, Canada, the Canadian Military Headquarters (CMHQ) staff in London, England, as well as the Canadian Military Legation, in Washington, D.C., throughout June and July 1942. All waited for Prime Minister King's final authorization to commence the recruiting of the Canadian contingent.[2]

This was received on 26 June 1942 and the development of the selection process commenced immediately.[3] Senior Canadian officers at NDHQ reviewed the FSSF selection guidelines drafted by Colonel Frederick. At first glance, it was evident that the Force was not going to be a regular infantry unit staffed by ordinary personnel. The

American commander sought a particular type of fighting man. Consistent with his ongoing selection of American personnel, Frederick made it clear that he preferred that Canadian volunteers also be chosen from the "lower ranks between 18 and 45 [years old], physically rugged and mentally agile, physically able and willing to take parachute training."[4] It became obvious to everyone concerned that superior physical fitness, experience, maturity, and youth were the cornerstones on which the FSSF would be forged.[5]

As a result, all potential candidates, regardless of rank, had to meet these prerequisites. The exacting nature of the upcoming mission meant that Frederick wanted his leaders at all levels to be young and energetic. To attain and develop this type of leadership, Frederick recruited some of his junior officers from the graduating classes of infantry and cavalry schools, a task he assigned to Captain Kenneth Wickham. "We based our selections upon our personal judgements of character and the quality of the men interviewed," explained Wickham.[6] Since these men had no previous service they could be trained, and moulded as the FSSF commander saw fit.

Recruiters sought candidates who showed "youth, hardiness and physical fitness."

Moreover, Frederick insisted that these young officers be supported by aggressive, dependable, and experienced NCOs who displayed initiative and leadership qualities. It was imperative that each man be able to work efficiently independently, or in small groups, regardless of the tactical situation or operational theatre. In recognition of the special task that the Forcemen would perform, as well as to attract the right type of individuals, Frederick directed that all other ranks (ORs) who successfully completed the unit's initial stage of training would automatically be promoted to the rank of sergeant.[7]

Frederick also amended his guidelines to ensure that the volunteers "possess in some degree the ability of a mountaineer, north woodsman and skier."[8] Carefully noting Frederick's directives, NDHQ drafted a message calling for this specific type of individual. The approved document was promulgated to, and posted in, all Army bases, training centres, camps, and officers' training centres throughout Canada, as well as the Canadian bases in the U.K. The carefully worded message did not reveal the nature of the mission, or the theatre of operation. It stated, however, that the Army sought personnel with outdoor and winter climate experience willing to undergo parachute training, and take part in "hazardous duty."[9]

The ideal candidate was described as "a mountaineer, woodsman and skier."

Lieutenant-General Kenneth Stuart.

The response was so overwhelming that Colonel L.M. Chesley, the director of the Directorate of Staff Duties (DSD) strongly advised the chief of the general staff (CGS), Lieutenant-General Kenneth Stuart, to implement stringent security measures to conceal the upcoming recruiting and selection process. "It would be possible for us to obtain this personnel [FSSF volunteers] at the same time we are raising personnel for the new parachute Battalion [1st Canadian Parachute Battalion (1 Cdn Para Bn)]," suggested a staff officer. "In this way," he explained, "we can possibly arrange to camouflage the Plough Project requirements."[10]

The CGS accepted this recommendation. Stuart ordered all those involved in the co-ordination and preparation of the Canadian and overseas Plough Project recruiting drives to proceed with the utmost discretion. On 12 July 1942, Stuart contacted Lieutenant-General McNaughton in the U.K. and ordered that all references to the Plough Project, as well as to the upcoming selection process, "be disguised by stating that the personnel are required in connection with the formation of a parachute battalion in Canada whose formation in Canada has just been authorized."[11]

As mentioned earlier, to expedite this process the CGS ordered that his previously released directive to organize, train, and equip one parachute battalion (1st Canadian Parachute Battalion), dated 10 July 1942, now be extended to include the organization of a second parachute battalion.¹² In the interim, the Canadian FSSF volunteers were to be referred to as personnel of the "2nd Canadian Parachute Battalion." Moreover, Stuart specified that for the moment this unit was to be considered "primarily for training purposes, and will consist entirely of Active personnel."¹³

During this period additional details of the FSSF's establishment were also forwarded to the CGS by the Canadian military attaché in Washington, D.C.; Stuart was notified that Frederick requested that both the Americans and the Canadians augment the strength of their contingents. This sudden change was prompted by the Norwegian decision to withdraw from this daring operation. After much consideration, the Norwegians feared their participation would inevitably lead to ruthless German reprisals on their countrymen.¹⁴

Frederick was unfazed by the latest setback. He simply took steps to replace the missing manpower. Moreover, the audacious commander used this momentary setback to his advantage. Frederick saw this as the opportune time to ask for additional volunteers to cover off wastage (personnel who did not meet the prescribed training standards and were removed from the unit) that would occur during the forthcoming training.¹⁵ His request was well timed because NDHQ had not yet commenced its selection stage. In the end, the CGS agreed to the increased demand for personnel. As a result, the new Canadian manpower quota was increased from the original 500 all ranks to 697 all ranks. As such, the Canadian contingent now included:

> Colonel (2i/c) — 1
> Lieutenant-Colonels, or Majors — 4
> Majors or Captains — 6
> Lieutenants — 36
> Other Ranks — 650 ¹⁶

Shortly after the promulgation of the 14 July 1942 CGS directive to raise a second parachute battalion, he created a 13-member committee responsible for overseeing all aspects of the establishment of 2nd Canadian Parachute Battalion, as well as expediting the various administrative requirements to select, assemble, and send the volunteers to the United States. High on the agenda of the committee's first meeting was the finalization of the selection criterion. On 16 July 1942, the committee unveiled the new Canadian criterion:

> A) Only active personnel will be accepted.
> B) Personnel must have volunteered for duty as parachute troops.
> C) Physical standards, as contained in Appendices "A" and "B" HQS 8846–1 (Pers. 1) dated 10 Jul 42, would apply.¹⁷
> D) Must be fully trained soldiers, both basic and advanced.

E) The combined qualities of mountaineer, northwoodsman, and skier, were very highly desirable; that is, they should have had winter training or be deemed suitable for training under winter conditions.
F) A knowledge of I.C. (internal-combustion) engines, leading to driver mechanics' qualifications, would also be desirable.
G) As the lowest rank in the unit would ultimately be that of Sergeant, the personnel selected must be considered as good N.C.O. material.[18]

Two days later, on 18 July 1942, one last clarification was made to the criterion. Home Defence personnel were permitted to volunteer providing that they were willing to go active. Additionally, the committee reiterated the importance of informing the volunteers that for the moment the lowest anticipated rank, in the Force, once all personnel passed their training would be that of sergeant.[19] Accordingly, NDHQ advised all training centres and unit commanders that the upcoming selection of OR candidates for this particular recruiting drive was to be extended specifically to warrant officers, non-commissioned officers or privates who were considered as good NCO material.[20]

Moreover, Colonel E. Line, director of personnel selection, provided the Army Examiners with three specific directives that were to be taken into consideration during the upcoming examination and interviews of the Canadian ORs. They were:

A) French-Canadian representation is desired, provided that such personnel are fully bilingual.
B) Minimum score of 140 upon Revised Examination "M" [IQ Test], together with a Grade 8 education.
C) Personality qualities desirable in an N.C.O. including sense of responsibility and some degree of initiative. There should also be evidence of qualities of aggressiveness, audacity and readiness to assume risks of physical injury.[21]

Following, the selection of the ORs all interview reports and Revised Examination "M" results were to be forwarded by the Army Examiners to NDHQ, no later than 22 July 1942, for final approval. Due to the specialized nature of the FSSF training program the director of personnel selection insisted that the assessment of these volunteers be "made with great care ... in view of the importance of the duty which they will undertake and the desirability of reducing to the lowest possible figure the proportion who may prove during subsequent training to be unsuitable."[22] All non-selected personnel were to be returned as quickly as possible by the District Depot, where the interviews were conducted, to their units of origin.[23]

Now that the contingent's selection criteria and establishment had been defined, the much-anticipated recruiting drive was officially launched on 18 July 1942, simultaneously

OF COURAGE AND DETERMINATION

The official selection requirements drafted for 1 Cdn Para Bn personnel were also used for 2nd Cdn Para Bn; namely, A-1 physical shape, quick witted, and nimble.

in the U.K. and Canada. Among the pressing issues still outstanding was the urgent need to appoint a commander for the Canadian contingent. As such, Lieutenant-General Stuart wanted an experienced man to lead this special unit. Due to the type of operational training that was currently being conducted by Canadian units with the British forces in the U.K., the CGS preferred that the officer be selected from the Canadian Army (Overseas).[24] Stuart contacted Lieutenant-General McNaughton and requested that he select this officer as quickly as possible.

The CGS explained that the commanding officer was to be, "young, energetic as activities will include parachute descent and prolonged subsistence off country in winter." Stuart also added that the officer "must have excellent qualities of leadership and preferably staff training ... and planning abilities as well as power of command."[25] Additionally, in order to fill the Canadian quota of FSSF personnel, Stuart ordered McNaughton to provide 10 percent of the Plough Project's manpower requirements, as well as half of the officer slate (23 officers).[26] To expedite the selection process Stuart sent McNaughton a copy of the physical selection criterion that had been developed earlier for the selection of 1st Canadian Parachute Battalion personnel.[27]

McNaughton immediately directed his staff to prepare a call for volunteers currently serving in the various Canadian field units, reinforcement units, and corps stationed throughout the U.K. Unit commanding officers (COs) were advised that the ideal candidates had to have "youth, determination, energy, initiative and skills with weapons."[28] Furthermore, those selected were expected to, "live under primitive conditions, and must be robust sturdy soldiers who can endure the worst physical ordeals."[29] Moreover, all candidates were to be volunteers, in A-1 physical shape, quick-witted, nimble, and willing to go undergo parachute and other types of tough training.[30]

While hundreds of soldiers eagerly responded to this call, their COs did not. Rather, they were angered by this 'urgent' call for "special" volunteers which they saw as nothing short of poaching their best personnel. The COs argued that this call for volunteers could potentially drain their units of their best fully trained soldiers and NCOs.

The soldiers on the other hand, many of whom had served in the U.K. since 1940, welcomed this unique opportunity to escape the long months of boring training and monotonous coastal defence duties on the English Channel. "I was tired of sitting around doing nothing, defending the coast with no ammunition," explained a disheartened Private George Wright, a member of The Hastings and Prince Edward Regiment, who had been posted in the U.K. since January 1940. "So," he added, "I volunteered for anything that came up in order to get out of there."[31] Similarly, Private Peter Cottingham who was serving with The Regina Rifle Regiment was fed up with the dreary daily regimen. As a result, Cottingham along with 200 others volunteered.[32] A few days later, he was informed that he was the only one of his unit to have been selected. "I felt that I had just won the Sweepstakes," Cottingham said. "I couldn't get into the air force but the paratroopers had to be the next best thing," explained the delighted soldier. "No more slugging it out with the infantry," he gloated, "I would ride into action in a plane."[33] Both Wright's and Cottingham's adventurous spirit and mindset reflected that of other soldiers who wanted to join this new secretive unit. To a man, they all desperately sought excitement and adventure. Bottom line — they wanted to go into battle as quickly as possible.

Lack of time meant the selection process turned out to be very rudimentary. Brigadier M.H.S. Penhale, a member of the CMHQ's General Staff, who was responsible for the oversight of the selection process and group's dispatch to Ringway, confirmed that "these candidates were assembled rather hurriedly."[34] It was a simple exercise. Basically, if a soldier volunteered, was physically fit, and had a satisfactory military record — he

Unit commanding officers were upset that the FSSF was poaching their best men.

Courtesy JFK Special Warfare Museum.

was accepted. "There were no interviews, testing or medicals," recalled Private George Wright. "My Company Commander called me in and said, 'they're putting together a suicide squad, and they are asking for one man per unit. Are you interested in going?' Before I could respond," explained Wright, "he told me to take the afternoon to think about it and come back and see him. That was the extent of the selection," recounted Wright.[35] Thus, the quickly selected FSSF volunteers now impatiently waited to be sent to the United States.

On 2 August 1942, as the selected personnel awaited their travel orders, McNaughton and Stuart received an urgent message from Major-General J.C. Murchie, the VCGS. Murchie informed his superiors that the FSSF planned to complete its parachute-training phase by 1 September 1942.[36] Thus, there was not sufficient time to send the U.K.-selected volunteers from the 2nd Canadian Parachute Battalion to the U.S. to undergo the parachute course. So, instead of returning the men to their units, Stuart suggested that the men be sent on a British parachute course, and upon qualifying be transferred to the 1st Canadian Parachute Battalion.[37] McNaughton agreed with Stuart's recommendation and on 24 August 1942, a total of 25 officers and 60 other ranks commenced their 16-day British parachute course at the Parachute Training School, Royal Air Force Station, Ringway, Manchester.[38]

Simultaneously, back in Canada, on 18 July 1942, the adjutant general, Major-General H.F.G. Letson, sent a message throughout Canada notifying all commanders that authority had been granted, two days earlier, for the immediate mobilization of the 2nd Canadian Parachute Battalion. Letson explained that the volunteers for this new unit would be drawn from every possible source including mobilized units, as well as reinforcements earmarked for trade training.[39] As for the recruitment of officers, the committee overseeing the organization of the battalion recommended that recruiters visit the officers' training centres (OTCs) in Brockville, Ontario, and Gordon Head, British Columbia, "as a quick source of aggressive young officers."[40]

The selection process conducted in Canada differed substantially from the one that was taking place concomitantly in the U.K.[41] First, all volunteers regardless of rank had to meet the same medical criteria as those required for the 1st Canadian Parachute Battalion. Secondly, during this process Medical officers were to be assisted by Army examiners of the Personnel Selection Section who would provide advice on the suitability of the candidates.[42] Thirdly, all candidates were to be interviewed, and undergo IQ tests. Lastly, in certain cases, officers who had been selected to join the Canadian contingent were asked to assist the recruiters with the interviews of other officer and ORs so as to expedite the screening phase.[43]

Hundreds of soldiers serving in Canada displayed an avid interest in the recruiting call.[44] For many of these bored and disillusioned soldiers, this seemed like the chance to escape the tedium of training to finally join in the fight against the enemy. After all, this is why they had joined in the first place. During the course of the interviews, many volunteers did not hesitate to voice their frustrations regarding their current status. "I was tired of operating a boat in Halifax harbour," explained Vern Doucette, "and watching troops sail off to war."[45] Donald Ballantyne echoed these sentiments. "I was bored with the routine work in Canada," asserted the veteran. "I was in a rifle regiment and all we did was dull guard duty on the West Coast and in Newfoundland."[46] A frustrated Lloyd D.M. Dunlop told his recruiter that he "joined to fight Hitler overseas. I've been here for over one year and we haven't gone anywhere. That's not why I joined the Army."[47] Another volunteer, Eugene Forward, confided that he wanted to join, "because he was fed up doing boring jobs." The dispirited soldier outlined the type of work he had been tasked to do during the course of the last months. "The lousy stinking job of digging up sod in the rain, like newly arrived immigrants, and doing things that had nothing to do with army training was depressing," he groused, "I really wanted to do something else."[48]

For other young soldiers, their motives to join this unit were very personal. "I was Jewish and I knew what was going on in Germany," revealed Sam Borditsky. "I met the people who came from Germany and related to me what was happening there. It was important to fight."[49] However, for the most part, the motivations and rationale of the volunteer recruited in Canada echoed those given by their U.K. counterparts. They sought adventure, better pay, advancement, excitement, escape from boring routines, and, most important, an opportunity to go into combat. Despite the best of intentions and the existence of a detailed selection criterion and medical examination process, the implementation plan was revised. The late authorization to organize this new battalion left the recruiters, medical staff, and Army examiners only 16 days to assess hundreds of volunteers; select and interview potential candidates; conduct medical exams and IQ testing, dispatch the chosen personnel to their assembly areas with the appropriate paperwork, ship them out to their training base in the United States. Reality dictated that short cuts be taken in order to comply with this unrealistic deadline.

Thus, prompted by this sense of urgency, the recruiters used their initiative and experience to find Frederick's soldiers. With regards to the medical part of the screening process for the FSSF, "emphasis was placed on 'youth, hardness and fitness.'"[50] While some candidates underwent rigorous physicals, others like Sam Borod recalled, "There was no physical testing."[51] As for Joe T. Jamieson, he just took his shirt off, and one look was enough. "I had worked in the hard rock mines, so, I was in pretty good shape," recalled Jamieson. "I got in quite readily."[52] Certain candidates like Eugene Forward were simply asked to go through the motions. "We had a quick medical," explained Forward. "It was a line and we were rushed through," he stated, "They looked us over very quickly, 'You're OK! You're OK!' That was it."[53] Another veteran, Vernon J. Doucette, chuckled as he recalled his medical exam. "They wanted a few good men," he laughed, "but they were in a hurry."[54]

While some medical officers were lenient with regards to their evaluations and testing, others were sticklers, and did not let anything go by. Certain volunteers, such as Captain Ralph Wilson Becket, who had previously served with The Essex Scottish

OF COURAGE AND DETERMINATION

Regiment in England, showed great initiative to pass certain parts of their medical examinations. Afflicted with poor eyesight, Becket explained his dilemma to the senior medical officer. The sympathetic officer handed him the eye examination chart and told him to memorize the last two lines. The next day reminisced Becket, "I read off the bottom two lines on the chart — hesitating a little once or twice to make it look factual."[55] Regrettably, there was another medical officer present. Suddenly, the officer moved toward the chart and pointed to a letter in another line. Unable to answer, Becket failed his test. The despondent officer mulled over the situation. His only chance to join the 2nd Canadian Parachute Battalion was to contact a friend who was on staff at NDHQ. Within 24 hours, Becket's commanding officer received an urgent telegram from Ottawa. It read, "Re: recent volunteer program, 2nd Can Para Bn, Captain R.W. Becket to be accepted irrespective of medical."[56]

Another officer, Captain J.F.R. Akehurst of The Algonquin Regiment also recalled his frustrating pre-medical examination. He recounted the exchange:

> Interviewing officer (IO): How old are you?
> Akehurst: Thirty-four.
> IO: Thirty-one is the limit.
> IO: How tall?
> Akehurst: Six foot two. (He was closer to six foot five.)
> IO: Six feet is the maximum for a paratrooper!
> IO: How much do you weigh?
> Akehurst: A hundred and eighty five.
> IO: If you weigh 185, I'll eat you. 185 is the limit. [57]

Disappointed, Akehurst saw his chances of joining this new unit dwindle rapidly. Luck, however, was on his side. "Where were you born and raised," asked the officer. "Northern Ontario," replied Akehurst. "You're in!" exclaimed the recruiter as he stamped the volunteer's form."[58] The surprised candidate left the room perplexed but nevertheless greatly relieved. The recruiter had duly noted NDHQ's directives regarding the selection of personnel who had lived in a northern climate, or worked in the outdoors, or snow-covered areas. As long as they had some type of outdoor experience these men were to be considered as prime candidates for the Force.[59] The interview process also varied greatly. It ranged from complex, to rudimentary to none at all. In certain cases, the interviews consisted of a few questions and no IQ tests were administered. Others were not so lucky. Some candidates were subjected to long interviews followed by written tests. "It was well after 12 o'clock at night and we were still filling questionnaires and doing tests," stated Eugene Forward. "They asked a great variety of questions," recalled the young volunteer. "Many were perfect for my way of thinking. They had to do with a lot of mechanical subject matters," explained Forward.[60]

During some interviews, several candidates took great exception to certain questions that were posed by the interviewers. William "Sam" Magee was taken aback when asked, "Do you love your mother? Would you sleep with her?" asked the examiner. "I almost killed the interviewer," clamoured an irate Magee. "But I wasn't charged — they were checking your reactions."[61]

During the course of these interviews, the young soldiers attempted to obtain some indications as to the unit's mission and deployment. But to no avail. "We were never told about the mission of the unit or its purpose," recalled Magee.[62] "They only said that it was for hazardous duty," added Vernon Doucette.[63] The obscure and vague questions varied from interviewer to interviewer and provided no clues as to the mission. Bill Story remembered being asked if he would "be willing to take orders from a superior in a foreign army." The puzzled volunteer "thought they meant Brits."[64] Donald Ballantyne stated, "All we were told was that it was a hush, hush unit." He added, "It would include mountain and parachute training."[65]

For others the lack of information really did not matter. William Wiber was just happy to have been selected. "I didn't know what in the world I was getting into," explained the elated candidate. "All I knew," commented Wiber, "was that it was new and exciting."[66] The prevailing aura of mystery and promise of adventure were the determining factors that prompted the volunteers to sign up regardless of the information provided. Later, when the selected candidates arrived from various parts of Canada and were assembled in Camp Sarcee, Alberta, volunteers asked all incoming newcomers if they knew anything regarding their upcoming training and mission. "We met a lot of people," affirmed Charlie Mann, "and tried to question them as to what the score was, and got the same dumb answers we were getting before."[67]

Throughout the entire course of the selection process, the interviewers were ordered to ask general questions and not provide any additional information that would jeopardize the mission. This line of questioning proved to be a complex and tactful process. "No mention could be made of the countries involved — no timings, no snow vehicles — but I did inform them," confided Captain Ralph Becket, "that this was to be a very special secret mission in a distant country, and that, landing by parachute there would be no way out."[68] For some volunteers, like Joe Glass, this warning was not a deterrent, but rather an additional incentive to join. "They said it was a suicide outfit, so you're taking an awful chance by joining," related Glass. "I thought, Gee! That would get me in combat pretty fast. I was very happy about that."[69]

More important, during the course of these interviews, the recruiters were instructed to observe and note the candidates' reactions and body language. Those who showed the slightest hesitation or nervousness or had a change of heart were disqualified. Lieutenant J.D. Mitchell, one of the selected volunteers, assisted in the evaluation of certain candidates. He remembered purposely using a line of questioning to unnerve the prospective applicants. He recalled:

> That evening some volunteers arrived from the Régiment de la Chaudière. Major Keen thought it would be a good idea if I interviewed them, so over I went and sat behind a desk as if I knew what I was doing. They came in one by one — some spoke English others didn't. I ploughed through in my limited French and always ended up asking if they would jump without a parachute; they all said, "Oui." However, the next morning, the spokesman returned to say that they had changed their minds and wished to return to their Regiment. Major Keene felt that it would be in everyone's best interest to do so.[70]

Becket who also assisted the recruiters with the interview process concluded his sessions by reiterating to each candidate the risks involved and "made it quite clear that there would be no shame whatsoever in deciding to return to their units."[71] No one was forced to stay, and anyone could leave at anytime.

By 28 July 1942, the selection of the 2nd Canadian Parachute Battalion personnel was in its final phase. The newly appointed commanding officer of the Canadian contingent, Major J.G. McQueen of The Calgary Highlanders was on his way to Canada. McNaughton recommended that this officer be promoted to the rank of lieutenant-colonel as quickly as possible, stating that McQueen was, "well qualified and suitable in all respects."[72]

In Canada, the volunteers were sent by train to two assembly areas. For the moment, the selected western volunteers, totalling 24 officers and 274 ORs, were sent to Camp Sarcee, Alberta. The eastern candidates, 38 officers and 376 ORs waited in Lansdowne Park, Ottawa, Ontario. They would soon join up with their future comrades in Camp Sarcee.[73] However, of the eastern contingent's projected total, 116 volunteers had still not yet completed their selection process.[74] At this time, however, this no longer constituted a pressing issue because NDHQ still thought that any upcoming unit deficiency could be made up with the volunteers who had been recruited in the U.K.[75] The Canadian soldiers now impatiently awaited to be sent to their next destination.

During their last few days in Canada, "we were given a little more information on the unit," recalled Patrick Smith. While some were pleasantly surprised by the challenges that lay ahead, others had a sudden change of heart. "Many decided that this training wasn't for them," explained Smith, "and requested to return to the west coast."[76] At this late stage, the loss of each man proved critical. In a last ditch effort to ensure that no other personnel wanted to leave, a group of officers re-interviewed 450 volunteers to confirm one last time that they would in fact undergo the upcoming training.[77] The men stood fast by their decision. "Everybody that I know was 'gung ho' for it," confirmed Lorin Waling. "It seemed that we all wanted the same thing, and that was, 'get to war.'"[78]

The recruiting drive to assemble the initial Canadian contingent for the FSSF was nothing short of a miracle, given how little time had been provided for the task. The 1 August 1942 deadline had been met. The first Canadian volunteers arrived at Fort William

Aerial view of Fort William Henry Harrison, Helena, Montana, U.S.A.

Henry Harrison, Montana, on 6 August 1942. Ten days later, a total of 46 officers and 649 ORs were on site, and many had already commenced their parachute training.[79] However, unbeknownst to the senior officers in NDHQ, and to the volunteers themselves, the FSSF's training regimen would be so severe during the course of the first few months that the FSSF very quickly was required to forward requests for replacements. These were sent to Ottawa as early as 24 August 1942, less than three weeks since the arrival of the Canadians.[80]

The month of August was a particularly difficult month for both the American and Canadian volunteers of the FSSF. It was during this period that an accelerated parachute-training course was conducted. Within these four weeks, a total of 176 Canadians were returned to Canada for various reasons such as: refusal to jump; training related injuries; medical reasons; undesirables; deserters; under age, and discharged personnel.[81] Among those returned was the Canadian FSSF senior officer, Lieutenant-Colonel McQueen. Regrettably, the CO had broken his ankle on his first parachute jump.[82] Such an unexpected large number of returnees required a new recruiting drive to fill the decimated ranks. However, with NDHQ now in the midst of preparing troops and units to reinforce its Army overseas in England, finding new replacements proved a difficult problem.

Nevertheless, Canada was still fully committed to the Plough Project. To facilitate and expedite this next recruiting drive, it was decided to limit it to Ontario, Quebec, and the Maritimes. The selection criteria were identical to those used during the testing of the initial group. This time, however, recruiting limitations were imposed. The recruiters were not permitted to draw upon all units. Moreover, personnel from trade schools were no longer eligible to volunteer. This restriction also applied to soldiers who were completing their final phases of advanced training. Furthermore, due to the fast paced FSSF training, Lieutenant-Colonel D.D. Williamson, the new officer commanding the 2nd Canadian Parachute Battalion, requested that all future officer replacements, be experienced officers who had served in units, rather than graduating officer cadets from the OTCs of Gordon Head or Brockville.[83] Quite simply, Williamson felt that service experience rather than youth was more valuable to the overall effectiveness of his officer cadre. All eligible volunteers were ordered to report immediately to Camps Borden (Ontario) and Debert (Nova Scotia) to undergo their medicals and interviews.

Regrettably, this second recruiting campaign was not as successful as the previous one. The number of volunteers had dropped off significantly. During this drive, the men posted in Camp Valcartier (Quebec) displayed very little interest for this type of training. Out of 200 men on parade, five volunteered, and were later rejected.[84] This, in part, may have been due to the preparation of Canadian Army units for imminent overseas deployment. Furthermore, rumours regarding the tough FSSF training regimen were being circulated by returned malcontents and personnel who had failed their parachute course.

Another problem that hindered this drive was the poor dissemination, either by design or otherwise, of the call for volunteers for special units. In the case of the 2nd Canadian Parachute Battalion, it was very important for both political and operational reasons that this unit attain and maintain its full establishment. As a result, Major-General Letson, issued Canadian Army Routine Order 2423, titled — Volunteers For Special Units:

> From time to time it is necessary to form special service units such as Parachute Battalions for which it is desirable to call for volunteers. In some instances it has been found that calls for such volunteers have not been fully circulated within Commands or units with the result that the unit personnel have not been given the opportunity to serve in these special units. Commanders and Commanding Officers will, in future, ensure that information from NDHQ is fully circulated within Commands and units in all cases where volunteers are called for. All applications are to be given suitable consideration where volunteers possess the necessary special requirements and qualifications.[85]

Clearly, these calls were very unpopular with unit and subunit commanders. Despite this hurdle, enough candidates eventually answered the second call, and were interviewed by Major Keane (Camp Debert), and Captain J. G. Bourne (Camp Borden), both FSSF officers, on 25 August. Again, time was of the essence. On 30 August, the two officers had exceeded all expectations. In less than five days, they had recruited five officers and 123 ORs.[86] These men were the last group of Canadian replacements selected for the Plough Project.

Although the selection process varied greatly, in the end, it was the tough training regime that became the ultimate discriminator. Nonetheless, Canada's contributions to the inaugural combined American-Canadian unit were eager, fit, and capable soldiers who would represent their nation well. Those who were selected and then went on to endure and persevere the gruelling training would set an enviable record of Canadian military prowess.

5

THE OTHER WAR:
The Bureaucratic Battle to Sustain the Canadian Component of the FSSF

> The administration of the Force was no doubt a headache to all concerned from top down, with the result that nothing was ever done to satisfactorily straighten out the problems that arose and what was done was always to the detriment of the Force.[1]
> — Lieutenant-Colonel J.F.R Akehurst, last commanding officer of the 1st Canadian Special Service Battalion, January 1945.

As Colonel Frederick and his Canadian officers began to create and shape their organization, their efforts were constrained by existing rules and regulations. The fact that the FSSF represented a totally new endeavour only made the task at hand more challenging. And, challenging it was, for bureaucracy is never an easy foe to vanquish.

Making matters worse, within the Canadian context the bureaucracy was formidable. Having fought hard in the First World War to establish the principle of command and control over its own troops, Canada was not about to back away from that principle now.[2] As a result, NDHQ created the Canadian Military Headquarters (CMHQ), based in London.[3] The mandate of this new headquarters consisted of overseeing all administrative matters relating to Canadian troops training and operating out of the U.K. Additionally, CMHQ was responsible for all co-ordination and communications between NDHQ, the British War Office, and Canadian field headquarters.[4] Moreover, to further improve and expedite the decision and reporting processes, NDHQ instructed CMHQ senior officers to work closely with, and report directly to, the MND through the CGS.

Concomitantly, as CMHQ personnel settled in their offices in the Sun Life Assurance Company of Canada building in London, Prime Minister King re-examined the current status of his government's Cabinet committees. The sudden shift of manpower and resources to the constantly increasing war effort necessitated a revision of the mandates of these committees.

OF COURAGE AND DETERMINATION

J.L. Ralston, the minister of national defence, shouldered the brunt of Canada's war efforts. In addition to his other ministerial responsibilities, Ralston also supervised all issues relating specifically to the Canadian Army. Within the first few months of the war, King quickly recognized that his minister needed assistance to manage the increasing requirements and commitments of his rapidly expanding department. To lighten Ralston's workload King authorized the appointment of two other DND ministers, one for the Navy and one for the Air Force. Also, two deputy ministers (Army) were added to the minister's staff.[5]

In addition, King felt it was important to bolster the nation's budding relationship with its southern neighbour. As such, in August 1940, Canada and the U.S. created the Permanent Joint Board on Defence to ensure there was a mechanism to study and recommend to the Canadian and U.S. governments solutions to mutual problems of defence.[6]

John Ralston, MND, visiting the troops overseas.

Later, in June 1941, the Canadian War Committee established the Canadian Military Mission (CMM) in the American capital. Initially, the United States, who at this time had still not entered the war, preferred that the entire Commonwealth war effort continue to be co-ordinated through Great Britain. However, Canadian senior army officers argued that the purpose of the CMM was, in fact, different. Its proposed mandate was to facilitate and expedite the direct exchange of military information and enhance the decision making process between Canadian Chiefs of Staff and the U.S. Joint Chiefs of Staff in order to maximize combined American/Canadian military efforts, specifically to demarcate spheres of military activities as they related to the defence of North America.[7] Nevertheless, it was also understood that this mission would continue to work very closely with the British Military Mission, in Washington, D.C., on other related military issues.

After months of deliberation and hesitation, the Americans finally saw the merits of this proposal. The rationale of the Canadian arguments coupled with the grim lingering reminders of the recent devastating Japanese aerial attacks on U.S. warships anchored in Pearl Harbour, Hawaii, on 7 December 1941, as well as subsequent Japanese military operations in the Aleutians off the Alaskan coast in May 1942, prompted the U.S., which was now officially at war, to re-evaluate the current status of its Home Defence stratagem. These bold Japanese military actions made it necessary for the senior military officers of both

THE OTHER WAR

countries to set up a close and effective co-ordinated military planning approach. In fact, the Americans assigned their Joint Staff Planners Committee the responsibility of liaison with the soon to be established Canadian Joint Staff Mission (CJSM).[8]

Shortly after receiving this excellent news, Lieutenant-General Stuart, the CGS, appointed Major-General Maurice Pope as chairman of the new CJSM. Stuart also informed Pope that he would act as the mission's Army representative. Pope's main responsibility consisted of representing the Canadian chiefs of staff during combined chiefs of staff meetings when questions affecting Canada were being deliberated.[9] Pope and his staff commenced their work during the first week of July 1942.[10]

The FSSF would soon be on their radar. As the Canadian recruiting and selection process began to churn out potential Forcemen, administrative and bureaucratic challenges quickly emerged. Moreover, due to the secrecy surrounding the Plough Project activities NDHQ preferred, for the moment, to limit the number of headquarters personnel selected to handle the project's records and documentation. Thus, to represent Canadian interests regarding this matter NDHQ appointed Lieutenant-Colonel Anderson, the staff duty 1 of the Directorate of Staff Duties at NDHQ, as the primary contact.

Major General Maurice Pope, chairman of the Canadian Joint Staff, Canadian Legation, Washington, D.C.

Unknown photographer, DND/LAC, e01075468.

Anderson travelled regularly to Washington where he attended Plough meetings. Upon his return, he briefed and advised the minister, the CGS, and a select group of officers from involved NDHQ directorates on the latest developments and their impacts on Canada's participation and anticipated contributions. However, by June 1942, NDHQ deemed that this reporting mechanism was no longer efficient. Additional staff had to be attached to this increasingly demanding project.

Reflecting on how to best resolve this pressing staffing issue Colonel Chesley, Anderson's superior, recommended to the CGS that it would be advisable to select an officer from Canadian Army's Pacific Command and appoint him as NDHQ's representative to the Canadian Plough Project planning team, in Washington.[11] Moreover, Chesley pointed out that the Americans indicated that the officer in question was also to become the FSSF's second-in-command.[12] Two weeks later, on 13 July 1942, Major Donald Dobie

(D.D.) Williamson of the Dufferin and Haldimand Rifles of Canada was nominated. He quickly reported to the military attaché, in Washington. However, the workload awaiting Williamson was so overwhelming that his superiors immediately agreed that he could not be expected to also take on the demanding responsibilities of being the FSSF second-in-command (2IC). This had led to the appointment of Major J.G. McQueen, as mentioned in the previous chapter, as CO of the Canadian contingent and FSSF 2IC.[13]

Time was always in short supply. The Americans fully expected that Canadian personnel be on site no later than 1 August 1942. Re-emphasizing the urgency of the matter, an impatient Major-General Letson, reminded all NDHQ staff that the, "CGS ... is very anxious that we should press on with these two units [1 Cdn Para Bn and 2 Cdn Para Bn] especially the 2nd Parachute Battalion."[14] As a result, NDHQ bureaucrats accelerated the administrative process to send troops to the U.S.

Lieutenant-Colonel W.A.B. Anderson.

No effort was spared to ensure that the recent selection board paperwork, as well as all existing personnel records for all selected candidates, contained complete and current financial, medical, disciplinary, promotions, honours and awards, and legal information as per Canadian Army personnel record keeping directives. Also, new identification cards were issued authorizing these volunteers to leave Canada and enter the U.S.

Furthermore, to protect and ensure the soldiers' well-being, it was imperative to compile and validate data required to confirm future pension rates, medical invalidity payments, and dependents' allowances in the event that personnel sustained career ending injuries, or died as a result of a training accident. Additionally, all records created during the volunteer's FSSF training phase in the U.S., such as new qualifications, exercise and course reports, current health and dental status, and instructional and administrative responsibilities conferred to Canadian personnel had to be duly documented and added to the volunteers' personnel service file. These new records were essential when later assessing the soldiers' military career advancement potential.

While NDHQ staff worked diligently on these personnel files, the Canadian government was adamant that an official Canadian-American agreement be prepared to clearly

THE OTHER WAR

document each country's administrative responsibilities as they applied to supporting and providing for the 2nd Canadian Parachute Battalion personnel requirements while training in the U.S. The Americans had already summarily constructed a possible course of action. However, Colonel Frederick knew that the implementation of their simple, yet practical, proposal would nevertheless raise serious Canadian political objections.[15] The fly in the ointment was the suggestion that the selected Canadian volunteers be discharged from the Canadian Army and take the U.S. Army's Oath of Service and Obedience. This radical suggestion, indeed, raised a series of concerns amongst the NDHQ bureaucrats.

From the very outset of this project, guarded Canadian politicians and senior army officers alike carefully monitored all American suggestions regarding the role and anticipated operational employment of the Canadian contingent. It was understood that these volunteers were, and would always remain, members of the Canadian Army.[16] Thus, NDHQ insisted on maintaining continued and total administrative control over its personnel. More important, it strove to ensure the preservation of the volunteers' Canadian Army status and identity.

Having already lost the British and Norwegian components of the FSSF, Frederick did not want to antagonize the Canadians. If the project was indeed to evolve from the planning to the operational stage, Frederick knew that he desperately needed these Canadian soldiers. Nevertheless, the commander of the FSSF fully understood NDHQ's concerns as well as the legal and political implications of having Canadian military personnel fully integrated during the training and future overseas deployments within the newly formed American combat unit. Thus, a judicious Frederick selected American Major Kenneth G. Wickham, and Major D.D. Williamson, the Canadian Army Plough Project representative, to prepare the Canadian-American agreement document.

Colonel Robert T. Frederick selected the isolated Fort William Henry Harrison as the FSSF home base because of its ideal terrain and climactic conditions for the Plough Project's summer and winter training.

OF COURAGE AND DETERMINATION

Wasting no time, the two officers met in Washington and consulted with staff of the office of the chief of finance in order to obtain input regarding the matter. On 15 July 1942, they submitted to Frederick a straightforward 13-point agreement detailing each country's administrative, disciplinary, financial, and organizational responsibilities as they applied to Canadian personnel selected to train with the Force. "Williamson and I," recalled Wickham, "had a very interesting time making necessary decisions."[17] Later that day, Colonel Frederick approved and ratified the document.[18] Copies were sent to both Canadian and American authorities for final approval.[19] The agreement emphasized that Canadian volunteers were not required to take the American oath of allegiance. As for regular disciplinary matters, it was recommended, for the time being, that all Force members be subjected to U.S. military regulations as laid down in the 1928 "Manual for Courts-Martial, U.S. Army." However, major breeches in discipline by any member of the 2nd Canadian Parachute Battalion, would, at the discretion of the CO, result in the soldier being returned to Canada for further disciplinary action. Additionally, all personnel judged unfit or not having the required temperament to undergo the rigorous training would be immediately returned to Canada. Moreover, funds would be advanced by the U.S. Army's chief of finance to ensure that Canadian personnel be paid in a timely matter. More important, the Americans agreed that a separate Canadian Army records keeping system, for the 2nd Canadian Parachute Battalion, be maintained by a Canadian paymaster, a pay sergeant, and a records sergeant to oversee all pay, dependents' allowances, and pension matters.

Whereas the U.S. Army preferred not to get involved in the unit's daily administrative issues and pay matters, it was, nevertheless, willing to assume all expenses relating to the provision of quarters, equipment, and uniforms. Additionally, the U.S. government agreed to defray all hospitalization and dental expenses. But, in the event that Canadian personnel were found unfit to continue training following their hospitalization, these soldiers would immediately be returned to Canada. Upon their repatriation, it became the Canadian Army's responsibility to continue to provide them with the required medical treatments during the course of their convalescence period.[20]

As for travel expenditures, the Canadian government was required to pay for the volunteers' initial transportation expenses from Canada to Helena, Montana. All subsequent transportation related disbursements were to be assumed by the U.S. government. Lastly, the Americans agreed to provide all rations with the understanding that the Canadian government be billed for repayment. Major Williamson was satisfied with the description and detailing of each country's responsibilities. "It gives us a definite working basis," commented Williamson.[21] It was a simple and straightforward agreement prepared by two army officers who basically wanted to return, as quickly as possible, to their respective pressing responsibilities. Frederick ratified this agreement and hoped that it would suffice and appease Canadian concerns. Copies of the Wickham-Williamson Agreement, as it was now referred to, were forwarded to NDHQ and U.S. Army headquarters respectively, for further deliberations.

THE OTHER WAR

The FSSF Colours were unveiled on 24 April 1943, while the Force was undergoing its amphibious training in Camp Bradford, Norfolk, Virginia.

Within days, each country's administrative responsibilities listed in this new agreement were carefully studied by NDHQ staff officers. Subsequently they drafted the 2nd Canadian Parachute Battalion (Serial 1354) immediate mobilization order. Sanctioned and approved on 16 July 1942, this order also detailed the unit's war establishment: one colonel; lieutenant-colonels, majors, or captains, 10; lieutenants, 36; and 650 other ranks.[22] Moreover, the mobilization order confirmed that the battalion was in fact, officially a unit of the Canadian Army.[23]

That same day, NDHQ Army Directorate representatives were convened to a special meeting to discuss the new mobilization order. Each representative confirmed their directorate's responsibilities regarding the organization, support, and administration of the 2nd Canadian Parachute Battalion. For the moment, all in attendance considered that the Canadian and American administrative and financial responsibilities listed in this order were acceptable. However, since the Americans were responsible for the planning and execution of the Plough Project, certain directorate representatives suggested that it, "be desirable to make the Americans responsible for the maximum possible administration."[24] Nevertheless, at the end of the meeting all in attendance agreed to allow each directorate representative to further review, with their respective staff, issues pertinent to their particular areas of administrative responsibilities as listed in this mobilization order.

OF COURAGE AND DETERMINATION

Over the course of the next few days, a 16-item agenda was drafted and distributed for the 28 July 1942 follow-up meeting. Of these items, two issues of concern were deliberated at length. The first pertained to the Canadian volunteers' current military status while training within a U.S. formation. All representatives concurred that it was imperative to emphasize to the soldiers that during the course of their training, in the U.S., they still retained their status as members of the Canadian Army and continued to be subjected to, and only to, Canadian Military Law and Regulations administered by Canadian officers. To ensure that this important issue was understood and agreed to by their American counterparts Lieutenant-Colonel G. A. Ferguson of the Directorate of Organization and Administration met with the judge advocate general to discuss the implementation of the Order-In-Council under the War Measures Act so as "to provide for reciprocal arrangements for the administration of Military Law in the U.S.A. and Canada," with regards to this new unit.[25]

The second concern dealt with the U.S. government's financial responsibilities relating to its expenses for the provision of hospitalization, medical, and dental treatment; quarters; transportation; travelling allowances; clothing; and equipment. D.G. Whittle, the Canadian Army's chief treasurer, remarked that the U.S. government would surely expect to be reimbursed. Therefore, it was imperative to further clarify and reconfirm both countries financial obligations. Additionally, from a financial planning perspective, it was also strongly recommended that NDHQ formulate a realistic cost projection detailing the funds required to cover off the unit's expenses during its stay in the U.S.[26] The staff forwarded these concerns to Lieutenant-General Stuart who in turn brought them to the attention of the MND.

Despite the staff angst, Stuart was not deterred by the minutia of these ongoing administrative concerns. The CGS reassured his American counterparts that the Canadian Army remained very committed to this project and flexible in working out problems. In the event that any additional unforeseen issues came to the fore, both Stuart and Frederick agreed, "that the method of their solution should be left to be worked out as they developed."[27] However, for the staff responsible to work out the issues, it became clearly evident that the administrative issues and legal ramifications surrounding the 2nd Canadian Parachute Battalion participation in the FSSF were far more complex than initially anticipated and that it would require vigilant monitoring and review.

Although the CGS was a supporter of the endeavour and agreed with Frederick's approach, Stuart nonetheless was cautious. He drafted a memorandum on 3 August 1942, advising the minister to officially define and confirm the 2nd Canadian Parachute Battalion's exact role and status within the FSSF. Stuart stressed that for the present, "the contingent was sent to the U.S. for training purposes only." The CGS also underlined the requirement that prior to any operational deployment of the battalion, Canadian government approval was required. Moreover, he also reminded the minister that once the FSSF deployed, a "detailed definition of the powers and responsibilities of each Government in controlling the operations of the Force" would have to be further discussed and agreed upon.[28]

Additionally, the CGS also requested the minister's approval regarding his administrative instructions drafted to assist and guide Lieutenant-Colonel McQueen in overseeing his daily duties, as the battalion's CO during the unit's training.[29] Stuart was adamant that McQueen "not commit any of the said personnel [2nd Cdn Para Bn] to any operational employment or to such dispatch until you have referred the matter to the Department of National Defence."[30] However, Stuart did authorize the CO to allocate 2nd Canadian Parachute Battalion personnel to the FSSF's subunits for training purposes only. In fact, this integration facilitated the provision of weapons, equipment, and clothing by the Force during the training. More important, the integration of Canadian and American volunteers was key to developing and fostering comradeship, trust, respect, and effective teamwork.

Furthermore, Stuart stressed that during this integrated training period Canadian personnel were to obey all lawful orders given by both American and Canadian officers. Despite this full integration, the CGS emphasized to McQueen that as the battalion's CO he still retained and exercised full legal military authority over all his personnel. All offences and infractions were to be dealt with under the existing Canadian Military Law, and the King's Regulations. In closing, Stuart also insisted that McQueen brief him monthly on all aspects of the 2nd Canadian Parachute Battalion's training and administrative activities. He directed that:

> You will be responsible for bringing and will bring to the attention of the Department of National Defence at all times any matter affecting the training, welfare, administration and discipline of Canadian personnel in the First Special Service Force which you may consider to be of interest or concern to this Department and you will submit regular monthly reports to the National Defence Headquarters on the 1st day of each month on all such matters. Copies of such reports will be made available to the Force Commander.[31]

To ensure that these monthly reports and other battalion-related documents arrived in a secure and timely manner, the CGS ordered McQueen to send these to the military attaché, in Washington who in turn would forward the files to NDHQ via sealed diplomatic bags.[32]

Now that the 2nd Canadian Parachute Battalion unit administrative reporting directives were established and formalized, the CGS focused his attention on another novel ongoing complex matter — that of accelerated promotions of Canadian personnel within the FSSF.[33] In his 5 August 1942 memorandum, addressed to the adjutant general, Stuart acknowledged that all Canadian personnel were eligible for promotion within the FSSF's war establishment. However, Stuart made it perfectly clear that all promotions awarded to Canadians during their training with the Force, "should be considered as an acting capacity only."[34] It was understood that certain promotions were in fact granted to cover off unfilled positions within the newly raised FSSF. Additionally, Stuart argued that these accelerated promotions did not reflect the true military career progression of the officers or ORs within the Canadian Army.[35]

Colonel Frederick, on the other hand, sought to ensure an equal representation of American and Canadian officers throughout all the FSSF's subunits, as well as establishing a proper chain-of-command prior to the beginning of the training. Thus, he elected to employ all incoming Canadian officers as he saw fit.[36] Frederick wanted to uncover as quickly as possible effective leaders who displayed initiative and resiliency. Consequently, all officers would have a chance to prove themselves. He asserted, "They are assigned to units regardless of nationality. The position to which an individual is assigned and the promotion given him is based solely of his ability — regardless of whether he is Canadian or American."[37]

During the initial training, all Canadian officers were notified that their appointments were to be considered as "temporary appointments" within the Force's establishment. These would later be confirmed as permanent providing that they performed satisfactorily.[38] In certain cases Canadian officers were also requested to temporarily cover off lower ranks until Frederick confirmed the Force's permanent officer slate.[39] Consequently, awarding acting ranks to officers and NCOs alike created additional administrative complications for NDHQ staff.

Upon learning of these new FSSF directives, 2nd Canadian Parachute Battalion personnel immediately inquired on how these temporary appointments impacted their salaries, pensions, and welfare of dependants in the event that they were killed or injured during the training.[40] These questions were forwarded to the director of organization and administration in NDHQ. Upon review, the director quickly reassured the CGS that battalion personnel who were in substantive rank, or acting rank, within the FSSF were covered under Section 14 of the Pension Act. As long as they remained with the Force, Canadian personnel retained their acting rank, pay, and benefits. In the event of injury or disability during this training period, the individual would be awarded a pension in accordance with the rank, or acting rank held at the time of any incident.[41]

Major-General Letson further added that all acting ranks granted to Canadians during the training phase with the Force would be revoked in the event that personnel sustained injuries preventing them to continue their training, or if they no longer wished to continue training with the Force. These men would be immediately returned to Canada, and revert to the rank they originally held with their former units.[42] So, for now, the complicated issue of acting ranks and ensuing benefits during the FSSF training period as they pertained to 2nd Canadian Parachute Battalion personnel had been clarified.

Adding to the myriad complications, McQueen's parachute injury as a result of an bad landing, as noted earlier, provided more complications. A 12-week recovery period was required to regain full use of his injured ankle and as a result, Frederick had to replace him as quickly as possible. To maintain the current training syllabus on schedule, as well as sustaining an ongoing proficient Canadian-American command and control structure,

THE OTHER WAR

The moment of truth.

Frederick insisted that McQueen's replacement be familiar with all aspects of the Plough Project, as well as with the Force's unique administrative requirements and training programs.[43] NDHQ subsequently directed McQueen to recommend a suitable replacement.

McQueen met with Frederick and reviewed the personnel files of the other Canadian majors currently training with the Force. From these, Majors Robert A. Keane and D.D. Williamson were selected as potential candidates. After further discussions, Frederick confided that he preferred Major Keane, "due to this officer's greater level-headedness."[44] However, a short while later Frederick was informed that Keane, who also suffered a parachute injury, was hurt worse than initially diagnosed, thus, eliminating him from the short list.

Wanting to resolve the situation quickly, Frederick insisted that McQueen's replacement be promoted from the Canadian officers currently serving with the battalion.[45] There was no time to select a new officer and bring him up to speed regarding all the Force's on-going training and administrative issues. During the course of the next few days, McQueen was in regular contact with Lieutenant-Colonel Anderson. While discussing this particular issue over the phone, McQueen seemed, "unwilling to nominate Major Williamson for this appointment."[46] To expedite the selection Major-General J.C. Murchie, wrote to McQueen stating that he agreed with Frederick's selection recommendations. Murchie then provided the following instructions regarding this matter:

> I am, therefore, to request your recommendation of any officer under your command whom you consider suitable for this appointment. If no such officer exists, may this Headquarters be advised most urgently, please, in order that the further necessary steps may be considered.[47]

With time being of the essence and having to select an officer already training with the Force, McQueen ran out of options. Thus, a few days later, McQueen drafted a letter recommending that Major Williamson be appointed as the new CO of the 2nd Canadian Parachute Battalion. "This officer is familiar with the project and problems of training this Force," wrote McQueen, "and is the officer who originally discussed initial arrangements with regards to training and administration of the Force with Colonel Frederick in Washington."[48] McQueen further added that Williamson displayed, "a great amount of drive and energy in his duties ... and is doing a most satisfactory job." However, McQueen cautioned that Williamson also had, "a tendency to be impulsive, but ... with added responsibility and experience he will overcome this tendency and I feel that his judgment is sound."[49] Without hesitation, NDHQ accepted McQueen's recommendation. Major Williamson was promoted, on 9 September 1942, to the rank of lieutenant-colonel and became the battalion's new CO.[50]

Prior to McQueen's departure from Fort William Henry Harrison, the CGS and Frederick agreed that, despite his limited service with the FSSF, McQueen had acquired valuable experience and as a result upon receiving ministerial approval, Lieutenant-General Stuart appointed McQueen as the Canadian Military representative on the U.S. War Department's planning staff for the Plough Project in Washington.[51]

The CGS provided McQueen with instructions detailing his new responsibilities:

> You will be responsible for bringing, and will bring, to the attention of the Department of National Defence, at all time, any matter affecting the development of this project or the training, welfare, administration and discipline of the Canadian personnel in the First Special Service Force which you may consider to be of interest or concern to this Department.[52]

More important, McQueen was now in position, "to discuss with the American authorities all matters of Canadian interest," specified Stuart, "thus relieving the Officer Commanding 2 Cdn Para Bn of much administrative detail in this regard."[53] Thankfully, McQueen's unfortunate mishap had been transformed into a positive development for the Canadians in the FSSF.

As McQueen familiarized himself with his new responsibilities, the CGS concurrently re-examined and revised the manner in which classified Plough Project documentation was being dispatched between Washington and Ottawa. Stuart decided that from this moment on all Plough documentation was to be channelled through the office of

THE OTHER WAR

Major-General Pope, chairman of the Canadian Joint Staff, Canadian Legation, in Washington. Trusting implicitly Pope's discretion, Stuart issued, on 9 September 1942, a directive briefing the chairman regarding his new administrative responsibilities regarding the Plough Project. More important, the CGS now also had to update Pope regarding the project's secret ongoing planning, Canada's participation in the mission, as well as McQueen's and Williamson's roles in the distribution of all related Plough classified records. Furthermore, the CGS instructed that:

> You [Pope] will be responsible for referring to the Department all matters of policy with respect to this project which may arise. In this connection you will note that Lt.-Col. McQueen and Lt.-Col. Williamson have been instructed to refer all such matters of Canadian concern to you. In the interest of secrecy, which is vital in the Project, I suggest that you entrust Lt.-Col. Williamson to direct all his correspondence intended to you to Lt.-Col. McQueen in the first instance. Lt.-Col. McQueen can then act as your Staff officer, thus retaining at a minimum the number of persons who are familiar with this Project.[54]

Lastly, on 12 September 1942, Stuart dispatched a seven-point administrative instruction to Lieutenant-Colonel Williamson officially informing him of his powers and responsibilities as the new CO of the 2nd Canadian Parachute Battalion.[55] These were, in fact, identical to those previously sent to McQueen, on 4 August 1942.

For his part, Williamson met with his officers and discussed the battalion's current status, daily activities, training progress, and concerns. During this meeting, two ongoing complex and frustrating issues that had developed during the course of the FSSF's parachute training phase were brought to his attention. The first problem concerned the difference in pay between Canadians and Americans. Soldiers wanted Canadian Army pay rates to be readjusted so that they would be in line with those of the American Army.

The second glitch dealt with the question of possibly awarding of U.S. Army parachute pay to the Canadian volunteers. These two situations quickly turned into a long drawn-out administrative tug of war between NDHQ and Canadian personnel in Fort William Henry Harrison. Throughout the course of the next few months, both sides presented and argued their cases and positions. From the outset, both Williamson's predecessor, and Frederick had repeatedly requested that NDHQ, and the paymaster general give serious considerations to grant the 2nd Canadian Parachute Battalion personnel the same pay rates as their American counterparts.[56] "I feel that in the interest of morale," remarked McQueen, "it is necessary for personnel of both armies to receive the same rates of pay."[57]

Following the Canadians' first pay parade, in August 1942, the soldiers were quick to point out that compared to the Americans they were grossly underpaid. "There was a bit of a rumble," recalled Force veteran Sergeant Charlie Mann. "We weren't very happy about it."⁵⁸ During the following weeks, these recurring pay issues were frequently debated at FSSF HQ meetings and regularly brought to NDHQ's attention by both Williamson and Frederick. Williamson also broached these issues in his first unit monthly report sent to NDHQ. "Morale hinges on the pay question, and I can't recommend too strongly," stressed the CO, "that equivalent rates of pay be adopted at the earliest possible moment."⁵⁹ This situation quickly turned into an "us" (i.e., Canadian component) against "them" (i.e., MND, NDHQ), and would remain that way during the entire course of the FSSF's existence.

Whereas NDHQ empathized with the officers' loyalty toward their men, several financial factors and regulations, nevertheless, had to be clarified before an equal pay scheme could even be considered or authorized. There were, in fact, many differences between the American and Canadian Army pay rates. First, the currency exchange rates had to be taken into account and assessed on a daily basis. And second, Canadian personnel's dependents allowances, income tax exemptions, and current acting rank pay would also have to be calculated and factored into each soldiers' pay scales. Last, to further complicate matters, the U.S. Forcemen were already drawing their parachute jump pay. American officers were given $100.00 a month, while ORs earned an extra $50.00 a month.⁶⁰ Concurrently, the paymaster general and DND Deputy Minister G.S. Currie were also discussing Frederick's request of awarding U.S. Army parachute pay rates to his Canadian personnel. However, all agreed that since NDHQ was currently in the process of formulating new Canadian parachute jump pay rates, which would be unveiled in the very near future, that there was now no further need to discuss the awarding of U.S. Army parachute pay to the Canadian volunteers.⁶¹

Simultaneously, Lieutenant-Colonels McQueen and W.A.B Anderson examined possible pay equalization schemes. Together they drafted and submitted two possible courses of action to Brigadier A.R. Mortimore, the paymaster general, for consideration. The first consisted of awarding American pay rates to 2nd Canadian Parachute Battalion personnel. In the event that this scenario was accepted, it was understood that the soldiers would be subjected to American income tax regulations, payable to the American government. However, personnel would continue receiving their Canadian Dependent's Allowances from Canada. To set up this new pay scheme, funds would have to be advanced by the American paymaster, and reimbursed to the U.S. by the Canadian government.

The second scenario proposed that Canadian personnel continue to receive their current Canadian Army pay rates, however, their salaries would be supplemented with the introduction of the new daily Canadian Army Parachute Pay, which the staff recommended would be exempted from income tax.⁶²

Brigadier Mortimore carefully studied both options and ultimately was comfortable with neither. The cautious paymaster general provided to Lieutenant-Colonel Anderson a detailed explanation of his reservations regarding these complex pay issues. He rationalized:

As you are aware this proposal is a complete departure from anything that has been attempted in the past, and in expressing an opinion it does not appear logical to endeavour to equalize the pay and allowances of the Canadian Army with those received by other Armies with which they may be called upon to serve, for if such a principle were established it is not unreasonable to assume that this could have a negative as well as an positive effect, e.g., when our troops are serving with a British Force where the rates paid to British personnel are lower. While it is understood that it is the intention to treat the 2nd Canadian Parachute Battalion with regards to pay, separate and distinct from other Battalions that may be organized, it is suggested that placing the 2nd Battalion in a preferred position by granting American rates of pay, the psychological effect on the other Canadian Parachute Troops serving elsewhere should be borne in mind, especially as American troops serving outside of the United States, receive additional pay equal to 10% of their base pay for officers and 20% for other ranks. It is suggested, therefore, the necessity for setting a rate of pay common to all Canadian Parachute Battalions wherever they are called upon to serve, would be desirable.[63]

Mortimore opted to adhere to the existing Canadian Army financial rules, regulations, and pay scales. Regardless of the Canadian volunteers' special training, and unique association with the U.S. Army, the paymaster general and other senior officers were staunchly opposed, from the outset, to confer any type of preferential financial treatment to the 2nd Canadian Parachute Battalion.

Upon reading the paymaster general's rebuttal, Lieutenant-General Stuart strongly disagreed with Mortimore's position regarding the battalion's pay issues. On 8 September 1942, the CGS submitted another equalization pay proposal for the minister's approval. Stuart recommended that, "Personnel of the 2nd Canadian Parachute Battalion be paid at American rates of pay and allowances for personnel without dependents, less the equivalent of American income tax on the amount of such pay and allowances, together with such dependents allowances" to which they may be entitled under Canadian Army regulations. "The effect of this proposal," argued the CGS, "will be that Canadian personnel will be remunerated for their military services at the same rates as their American comrades-in-arms, while their dependents in Canada will be provided for at existing Canadian rates."[64] While this proposal had merit, Ralston preferred to further reflect on the CGS's recommendation before handing down his decision.

By the end of September 1942, 2nd Canadian Parachute Battalion personnel became increasingly exasperated by NDHQ's inability to quickly resolve the second ongoing pay problem. For them it was a simple issue of "Equal pay for equal work." This lingering dilemma now affected the men's morale, and in certain cases discipline. In order to diffuse the escalating situation, Williamson met with all his personnel in the base auditorium and explained the complexity of implementing an equal pay plan. Even though the current regular pay situation was unfair, Williamson drew the men's attention to the paragraph relating to the battalion's pay matters as they were explained in the Declaration Form, and that had been duly signed by each volunteer. The paragraph stipulated, "I shall continue to receive pay and allowance, including dependants' allowance as provided under the Financial Regulations and Instructions for the Canadian Active Service Force, and such other allowances and emoluments as may, from time to time be authorized."[65]

This sudden reality check further upset the men. "They came into the theater singing and laughing," recorded the battalion's war diary chronicler, "but left a very sullen and sober group. There were very few complaints but their morale has been obviously, very shaken."[66] Following this difficult meeting, Williamson knew that his explanations and personal interpretation regarding the pay differences had not cleared the air. "In the main, however," reflected the unit's confident CO, "they took it very well and have adopted a watchful, waiting attitude."[67] On the other hand, the war diary chronicler was not as optimistic. "The Lord help us," warned the writer, "if this situation is not cleared up before the mid-month pay."[68] Still, Williamson thought it best to fully report to NDHQ the result of his presentation and the impact that the current pay differential had on his men's morale.

Upon receiving Williamson's September 1942 monthly report, Colonel L.M. Chesley noted the CO's concerns regarding the increasingly negative attitude of the men. Prior to forwarding the report to Lieutenant-General Stuart, a concerned Chesley penned a short note on the report's cover sheet. "C.G.S., You may wish to see, particularly para 13 [Morale]."[69] Senior leaders at NDHQ were not pleased with the recent developments at Fort William Henry Harrison, but regardless, they refused once again to alter their position.

Stuart, on the other hand, still found this situation unfair. He argued that this was the first time that Canadian Army personnel were fully integrated with the personnel of another Allied country's forces so as to form one cohesive operational combat formation. From previous discussions, Stuart also noted that the minister and other senior officers still did not understand the FSSF's uniqueness as a combat organization, or recognize the diversity, and dangers of its exceptionally demanding training program.

To further clarify this unit's uniqueness, Stuart drafted another memorandum on 9 October, reiterating yet again his position, to the MND, regarding equalization pay for 2nd Canadian Parachute Battalion personnel. In this detailed memo, Stuart brought forth additional information explaining why special pay considerations should be granted to this unit. He once again insisted that:

> I desire to draw again to your attention the factors which influenced me in making my original decision. The terms of service of the Canadian personnel in the First Special Service Force are different from those experienced by any other Canadian troops in the War. Although Canadian troops may

serve alongside British and American troops in a theatre of war without their pay equalized, they are not subjected to the same intermingling as goes on in the First Special Service Force. This Force is, as it were, one unit in which no regard is taken of nationality, and Canadians and Americans will sleep, eat, train and, it is anticipated, fight with their American comrades N.C.Os. and officers from both countries. Thus, the Canadian subaltern may be in charge of two sub-units; one commanded by a Canadian N.C.O. and the other by an American N.C.O. The composition of each of these sub-units would be composed of men of both nationalities.[70]

Regardless of the arguments presented by the CGS, McQueen and Williamson, the minister refused to alter his position. Despite numerous attempts to resolve these frustrating issues, the selected volunteers regrettably had to accept Ottawa's inflexible position and focus their efforts on surviving the upcoming challenging FSSF training regimen and develop a new unit *esprit de corps* with their American brothers-in-arms.

6

FORGING THE FORCEMEN:
Two Distinct Identities — One Common Legacy

> Gradually, the Americans and the Canadians assimilated one another and national pride gave way to pride of unit. The organization of the Force took shape.[1]
>
> — Donald Ballantyne

As senior American and Canadian military officers continued to resolve the intricacies of ongoing bureaucratic issues regarding their respective administrative responsibilities to support the soldiers committed to the Plough Project, Colonel Frederick and his staff focused their efforts on forging the Force into an effective unified fighting force. Due to the time constraints, this proved to be a challenging task. Aside from the training and administrative issues, they also had to examine American and Canadian army close order drill, customs, and protocols to determine how these elements could be incorporated into the formation's routine. The combination of all these components was essential in creating and quickly instilling unit pride, cultivating a unique identity, and fostering cohesion, particularly since the American and Canadian military systems had significant cultural and organizational differences.

Frederick realized that a key component to achieving his aim was finding a secluded army base where all efforts could be directed solely on developing and training this new formation without outside distractions or interference. More important, this base had to have all the geographical features and climatic conditions required to conduct the required training.

Frederick had narrowed down his choices to Camp Grafton, near Ramsey, North Dakota, and a little-used, isolated National Guard base, Fort William Henry Harrison, near Helena, Montana.[2] On 4 July 1942, he selected the latter. The factors that prompted his choice were: the base could accommodate 1,500 men; it could be easily expanded and winterized; it was located near Rogers Pass, which holds the record for the lowest temperature ever recorded in the U.S. (outside of Alaska); and it was in proximity to mountainous country where snow would be available for the Force's extended winter-warfare training.[3]

Following his decision, Frederick made arrangements with the commanding general, 9th Corps Area, to commence the needed additional construction work. Concurrently, Frederick dispatched Major John Shinberger, the Force's newly appointed training officer, to monitor the renovations. After a quick inspection Schinberger reported that "the selection of the training area was an excellent one."[4] As a result, throughout the months of July and August 1942, construction crews and military personnel coexisted within the confines of the rapidly expanding base. "There was dust everywhere, growing lines of tents, two great towers for drying parachutes and bulldozers everywhere," recalled Sergeant William Story.[5] Sergeant Charlie Mann added, "I would say that he [Frederick] knew the [military supply] system extremely well ... The stuff was just rolling in."[6]

However, within this incredible vortex of never-ending activity, there was one constant. "The confusion was unreal," related Lieutenant J.D. Mitchell.[7] This sentiment was echoed by Edward H. Thomas, an American officer. "As we entered the post, my sense of anticipation and apprehension rose. I was entering a new and unknown world," explained Thomas. "I was in unusual and unfamiliar surroundings, like none I had experienced so far in the Army."[8]

Frederick, on the other hand, was unperturbed by this atmosphere. On one occasion, he greeted a newly arrived officer and drew his attention to the considerable ongoing construction activities. A proud Frederick then turned and said, "This is the Force's home. Isn't it great!"[9] Unbeknownst to all concerned, amidst this on-going chaos, Frederick's melting pot designed to forge the Force was quickly taking shape.

As buildings mushroomed overnight, Frederick continued to formulate an approach on how to quickly integrate his American and Canadian personnel. Some of his officers suggested that, "we could really get these guys moving if we could get them competing, Canadians versus Americans."[10] The commander rejected this proposal outright. From the outset, Frederick made it very clear to all his officers that this formation did not comprise American and Canadian personnel. There would not be an "us against them" mentality. He was insistent that there would only be "Forcemen."

Furthermore, despite the fact that all training took place in the U.S., American volunteers were on the same playing field as their Canadian counterparts. They hailed from all parts of the continental U.S. from various military units — as a result, there were no pre-established cliques to deal with. As such, the first step of the integration process was a very simple and straightforward exercise. Frederick ordered that all personnel, within hours of their arrival, be posted throughout the FSSF combat echelon's subunits.

As noted earlier, the FSSF combat echelon, as of August 1942, comprised of the Force's headquarters; three regiments each consisting of two battalions (each battalion consisting of three companies of three platoons, with each platoon consisting of two sections of nine

Work hard, play hard!

men each). These subunits were commanded by either an American or Canadian officer. Their only role was to train hard and "fight like hell." Hence, upon being given their company and regimental designations, Frederick left it up to the soldiers to get to know one another and "work things out."

As the volunteers from both nations detrained, they were surprised to learn the identity of their final destination. Throughout the course of the selection process in both countries, the exact training location had never been disclosed. "We all thought we were going to Fort Benning," stated Story, "but instead we arrived in Fort William Henry Harrison, in Helena, Montana."[11]

Frederick's resolve for seclusion was immediately noted by the Canadians. "It [Fort William Henry Harrison] seemed to be out on its own," observed Sergeant Vernon Doucette.[12] Nevertheless, due to the various types of training that would be conducted, Frederick still found that the base was too close to the city of Helena.[13]

Within minutes, the culture shock began. "When we assembled off the train," recounted the puzzled Story, "we saw Americans with a variety of uniforms — shapeless coveralls, KP hats, cavalry hats, officers with cavalry attire, officers with green jackets and 'pink' trousers, and Colonel Frederick."[14] Ralph Becket, a Canadian officer, remembered the Americans' bewilderment when they saw the first group of Canadians marching into camp:

> Unlike the U.S. Army, the Canadian Army dressed in very different uniforms of its many regiments — all descendants of British regiments. Consequently we were marched in the three-column order peculiar to the British, in uniforms of the Guards, several different Highland regiments in their varying plaid kilts, the Fusiliers, the Rifles with their black buttons, and of course many different headgear. The Americans, officers and men, standing in the gate area, could scarcely believe their eyes.[15]

For the Americans, the "Canadian presence was a big surprise," revealed First-Lieutenant Edward Thomas.[16] "They were all slicked up in their tan uniforms," recalled Second-Lieutenant Mark Radcliffe, "with a piper marching them down the tracks. Right there I fell in love with the pipes."[17] The comportment of the Canadians was also quickly noted. "They were supposed to be the best Canada had," added Private Russell Wieneke, "They were well disciplined. When their sergeants spoke, they stopped — no matter what!"[18] The selection of the American volunteers differed somewhat. "Some were selected. Some were just sent," recalled William 'Sam' Magee. "Lots of them were drafted. Frederick was very upset."[19]

Once the initial administrative formalities were completed, each candidate was assigned to a specific company and regiment. They were then formed up and marched off to their living quarters. Second-Lieutenant Fred Hubbard, an American officer, recalled his first contact with Canadian personnel. "I called off their names and walked them back to my barracks," stated the young officer. "I had to get a Canadian Sergeant to lead them," admitted Hubbard, "because I didn't know the close order drill in the Canadian Army."

Following a short march, the soldiers arrived at their respective subunits and found very rudimentary living quarters. It was basically, "a tent, which was a square rig," laughed Magee, "with a canvas roof and a screen door."[20] It was within these primitive quarters that the integration process began. "First day we arrived we were paired off — two Canadians and two Americans to a tent," reminisced Magee."[21] This "was done to develop the concept of partnership," explained Sergeant Peter Smith. "You'd buddy up with an American for the entire training and future operations. That really worked out fine."[22]

Within the close confines of these tents, curiosity quickly triggered a series of questions. Soldiers inquired about each other's personal and military backgrounds, as well as the history of their country, customs, regional accents, expressions, and the particularities of their various uniforms. During these conversations, sensitive issues were uncovered, touched upon briefly, and dropped immediately. One veteran elaborated:

> We didn't take kindly to jokes about the King and Queen, nor did we enjoy being told Canadians were fools for continuing to be colonists and paying taxes to England. It took a day or so of discussion to educate our tent mates in British history following 1776.[23]

Prior to the arrival of the Canadians, confided Peter Smith's tent mates, who harkened from southern and western states, they had no clue as to what a Canadian looked like. He remembered:

> They were horribly misinformed on Canada. They didn't know one thing about us ... They had been taught that nothing existed north of the border. One guy said to his buddy, "Do you think that they will have their hair cut with a little strip down the centre and a feather in the back of the hair." They thought we were full-blooded natives.[24]

"They'd kid us, and pick on us a bit," recalled Peter Kroll. "But, we'd throw it right back at them, about the North and the South. That kinda straightened them out," chuckled the veteran.[25]

Canadians also quickly found out which subjects required a more diplomatic approach. "We learned not to make cracks about Franklin D. Roosevelt [FDR]," revealed Bill Story. "It was all right to talk about Mrs. Roosevelt, but not FDR." And, "we learned very quickly not to call an American who lived south of the Mason-Dixon Line a 'Yank.' These were sensitivities we got over quickly."[26]

Nevertheless, during the course of the first few days tempers flared, and fights broke out. Some individuals had crossed the line but learned quickly from their indiscretions. "We thought you guys were a bunch of sissies with those skirts [kilts] on," chimed, Tony Perry from New Jersey. "But when I lifted one of them up, I got the worst beating of my life."[27]

However, these incidents were an accepted part of the initial socialization process. "If there were problems," explained Private Eugene Forward, "a Canadian would fight an American and have done with it. The assimilation came quickly."[28] While all personnel were volunteers, originating from various units, some Americans were somewhat intimidated by the overseas service of certain Canadians.[29]

Within the first few days, Americans quickly picked up on certain Canadian habits and mannerisms. "Of course the Canadians had some funny ways," recalled an unidentified

American soldier. "When you passed them some food in the Mess Hall, they would let you hold the platter or bowl while they helped themselves. The only way we broke this habit," reminisced the veteran, "was to just let the dish drop in their lap. It worked!" [30]

Canadian idioms were another. "They picked up quickly on our manner of speech," explained Eugene Forward. "Are you going to do that, Eh? This was one of the first things they picked up," reminisced Forward. "Eh! Canada, we are going to have a lot of fun. Eh! Canada. There was a lot of good-natured ribbing," explained the veteran.[31] However, these quick periods of mutual indoctrination lasted but a few days. Friendships were struck and both groups grew to respect each other. From that point on, "the Canadians and Americans," recalled Charlie Mann, "jelled together just like Mummy and Daddy."[32]

The results were impressive. Joe Jamieson explained, "Within a month there was no such thing as a Canadian or an American."[33] Frederick was satisfied with the progress. "Each day it becomes harder to distinguish an American soldier from a Canadian soldier," noted Frederick. "The Canadians are picking up United States mannerisms and customs and the United States soldiers are picking up a few Canadian expressions and habits."[34]

Even visiting American officers could not distinguish an American from a Canadian.[35] On the whole, Frederick's first step regarding the "the one on one" integration process went smoothly. "The relationship between Canadian and American personnel is very congenial," confirmed Lieutenant-Colonel McQueen in his initial monthly report, "and is most satisfactory to both Colonel Frederick and myself."[36]

However, Canadian NCOs and officers did voice their displeasures with regards to rank privileges and customs that they no longer enjoyed. The NCOs regretted the fact that they did not have a mess of their own. The Canadian CO, Lieutenant-Colonel D.D. Williamson, smoothed over this situation by explaining, "the nature of the Force and the intense training doesn't allow for the usually accepted frills that go with the rank."[37] The Canadian officers also had to put in long hours to master American customs of the service, military courtesies, different mess practices, as well as to quickly adapt to their numerous and ever-increasing new training and administrative responsibilities. All the same, Williamson reported that his officers had accepted the "'when in

After a few days of training it became difficult to distinguish the Americans from the Canadians.

Rome, do as the Romans do' attitude and have admirably and efficiently taken the transition period in its' stride."[38]

Within days, the volunteers of both nations gradually parted with their previous unit allegiances and began to coalesce as an integrated formation. Nevertheless, despite each individual's best efforts, it became quickly evident that something had to be done to address the current confusion caused by the use of two different drill systems.

As a result, Force officers and NCOs quickly devised a new, much needed, FSSF drill instruction. Having no precedent to draw upon, the innovative Frederick, experimented with the blending of both U.S. dismounted and Canadian drill regulations. In certain cases, Frederick personally interceded to facilitate the acceptance and assimilation of particular drill movements. When certain Americans questioned as to why it was now necessary to swing the arms high, in British drill fashion, Frederick quickly proposed a compromise suggesting to swing them half way, stating that this movement would help them with their upcoming ski training.[39] Now that the Americans marched arms swinging, they no longer resembled "a bunch of constipated penguins," commented one pleased Canadian.[40]

Rather than waste time on developing extensive drill regulations Frederick elected to address and resolve the issues as they came up. Furthermore, he insisted that the FSSF drill be kept simple. "Stress should be placed on precision and unison of commands," explained Frederick, "and in marching in step with proper alignment. Commanders are reminded that the drill should reflect the smartness, efficiency and the highly select quality of the personnel composing this force." [41]

Even though Frederick drew from the drill regulations of both countries, he also maintained a flare for unique FSSF innovation. "One thing, that I liked was the marching cadence," explained Eugene Forward. "It was just like that of the Victoria Rifles, 140 steps a minute not 120 like the other units." [42] Also, because of the arm swing and the decision to march with weapons slung, "we looked different and somewhat smarter on parade," recounted Bill Story, "the Force really made an impact on viewers."[43]

In the end, adaptation was the word. Due to the very tight training schedule, drill indoctrination was, in fact, a "learn as you go" system. "There really wasn't time or interest in niceties of close-order drill," explained Story. "The main thing," he emphasized "was to get to and from activities without looking like a 'column of lumps.'"[44]

To further expedite matters it was agreed to adopt the American manner of saluting and use a higher percentage of American drill commands.[45] These changes forced Canadian personnel to pay extra attention to the sharply barked American marching orders that some Canadians described as sounding more like a fox hunt than drill.[46]

Nevertheless, habits were hard to break. Thus, when Canadian or American officers gave drills commands, "you always had to be alert," recalled Mann. "The Canadian officers would still give the Canadian commands."[47] However, as time passed all adjusted to the FSSF drill.

OF COURAGE AND DETERMINATION

However, despite the initial period of congeniality it became increasingly evident to the Canadians that American military customs and dress regulations would ultimately prevail. Colonel Frederick met with his officers and stated how pleased he was of the Canadians' willingness, "to fall in with the American ways," reported the 2nd Canadian Parachute Battalion's war diary chronicler, "especially since they were obliged to adopt more American customs than Americans had to adopt Canadian customs."[48]

More important, throughout the entire course of his command Frederick insisted on keeping the learning curve simple. His philosophy was further facilitated by "a mutual spirit of give and take," explained Lieutenant-Colonel Williamson.[49] Inevitably, there was a bit of grumbling, but in the end Canadian personnel accepted this fact and focused on the training. "Adapt and adjust," emphasized Gordon Sims became the FSSF's operative words of the day.[50] This unofficial motto was applied to all other unit training.[51]

The next important issue that had to be resolved was drafting and defining the Forces' dress regulations.[52] However, their implementation was hampered because

Evidence of Canadian dress disappeared within the first weeks of FSSF training.

FORGING THE FORCEMEN

Despite the Force's short stay at Fort William Henry Harrison a strong bond developed between the Forcemen and the citizens of Helena, Montana.

the supply system and base quartermaster were still being established during the first month at Fort William Henry Harrison and the issuing of uniforms was temporarily delayed. Thus, as an interim measure everyone was ordered to continue wearing what they had brought.

Concurrently, the CGS and his senior officers at NDHQ exchanged extensive correspondence with Major-General Pope, chief of the joint staff, in Washington, D.C., as well as Frederick, McQueen, and Williamson, regarding the new FSSF insignia, items of dress, and dress regulations. Stuart reminded all concerned that actions must be taken to ensure the preservation of the military identity of the Canadian volunteers.[53]

While keeping the Canadian dress and insignia concerns in mind, Frederick had already initiated the administrative process requesting designs of FSSF insignia. From the outset, Frederick wanted all FSSF insignia to be unique, distinct, colourful, steeped in tradition and honour, and to contain the national colours of both countries. "With these colorful, distinguishing marks, on the uniform," explained the formation commander, "it will not be difficult for one to recognize a member of this unique and proud Force."[54]

To expedite matters, Frederick contacted General Surles, Chief of the Bureau of Public Relations, in the War Department and requested his assistance in selecting a suitable distinguishing insignia. Surles replied, "he would put some qualified person with imagination to work on it right away."[55] Upon receiving a selection of shoulder insignia illustrations, Frederick and his team chose a spearhead motif. Frederick then ordered Major O.J. Baldwin, the Force's S-4 officer, to draft a letter to the commanding general of services and supply, requesting his authorization and approval of the submitted drawings of a proposed shoulder sleeve insignia (referred to as the Spearhead) and the cord, edge braid, for the unit's garrison cap as distinctive unit insignia.

The selected FSSF shoulder insignia consisted of a scarlet Indian spearhead with the words USA-CANADA stitched in white. The word CANADA was positioned vertically, with the letters USA positioned horizontally over it. This proposed shoulder insignia was agreed upon by Canadian officials as a suitable replacement for the shoulder insignia [worsted patches] bearing the word "CANADA" worn on the tunic's upper sleeves [shoulder area].[56]

As for the braid for the garrison hat, Frederick requested its approval to replace the various braids currently worn by the American FSSF enlisted men. He specified that this new braid would be worn by all serving FSSF personnel and would also be worn overseas when the unit was deployed. [57] In his request, Frederick's underlined that, "Both these insignia are desired for their morale building effect and as a means of securing homogeneity in a group selected from all branches of the armies of two nations."[58]

The request was forwarded through appropriate U.S. Army channels for authorization. In the interim, to further clarify this unprecedented request, Major Baldwin contacted Lieutenant-Colonel Comer of the HQ Services of Supply, Military Personnel Division, in Washington. Baldwin explained that the FSSF comprised of both U.S. Army and Canadian Army personnel. Furthermore, he stressed that Canadian regulations demand, "units having Canadian personnel have some distinct mark to indicate the presence of Canadians."[59] Both the sleeve insignia and the cap braid were immediately approved by Lieutenant-General Somerville, HQ Services of Supply, Military Personnel Division, on 12 September 1942. The general's authorization was then forwarded to the director, requirements division, who in turn forwarded the approval to the quartermaster general, heraldic section, for procurement and issue to the FSSF.[60]

Shortly after seeing the drawings for this new authorized unit insignia, personnel of the Services of Supply suggested to FSSF HQ that they may also wish to consider the use of the crossbow insignia, as a branch of service insignia. This insignia had been previously worn by the now inactivated U.S. Army Indian scouts.[61] In continuation with the current FSSF aboriginal theme this suggestion was readily accepted. FSSF officers would wear a set of these collar insignia in the branch area on their tunic lapels. When wearing the shirtsleeve order of dress, only one collar insignia was worn on the left shirt collar and the U.S. badge of rank on the right. "No other unit than the First Special Service Force will be authorized to this distinguished insignia," expounded Frederick, "and it will be with pride that we attach it to our uniforms and wear it in the near future."[62] Moreover, all NCOs and enlisted men wore on the left lapel of their dress uniform tunics a small brass disc on which were a set of raised crossed arrows. [63]

On 6 August 1942, the American under-secretary of war, Robert Patterson, announced to the public the creation of the First Special Service Force. Along with other information regarding this unit he also stated that the "Canadians and Americans will wear the same

FORGING THE FORCEMEN

"Any Players!" Forcemen unfold their "portable casino," a blanket around which eager participants congregated to play craps, a dice game.

uniform."[64] This announcement quickly caught the attention of Canadian and American journalists alike. R.T. Elson, an American journalist with *The Herald*, took a keen interest regarding this new unit as well as its Canadian personnel. Already, there were many rumours related to the FSSF's new unit insignia and uniforms. Elson reported that a spokesman from the Army's public relation bureau indicated that Canadian personnel would probably be authorized to wear a maple leaf or some insignia indicating their origin.[65] Ross Munro, a well-respected Canadian war correspondent postulated, "The Force will wear a special uniform distinct from either that of the Canadian or the United States Army, but its design has not been decided yet."[66]

The following day, further elaborating on the FSSF unit's insignia linkage to Native American history and artefacts, Elson speculated that the unit's insignia could be "crossed tomahawks to which the Canadians may be able to add the Maple Leaf." The journalist added that, "The Force will wear a special uniform distinct from either that of the Canadian or United Sates Army, but its design has not been decided yet."[67] In Fort William Henry Harrison there was much talk and speculation about the soon-to-be-revealed FSSF uniforms. "The new uniforms which will be our dress uniforms," explained Sergeant George "Red" Snider, "and will be a special shade of blue and it is rumoured will have on collar lapels crossed flags, the American Stars and Stripes and the Union Jack."[68]

As the rumour mill churned, another unique FSSF item of dress authorized in the fall of 1942 was unveiled. It was the three-color (red, white, and blue) unit lanyard or

OF COURAGE AND DETERMINATION

Two nations, one unit!

aiguillette made of dyed parachute shroud lines. During the course of a parade, Frederick unveiled the new unit lanyard, stating, "from now on, this is the only lanyard, I want to see." Then Frederick added, "and it will cost you ninety cents." A disgruntled Forceman grumbled, "You can't make us buy that thing!" Frederick replied, "True I cannot, but I will tell you nobody leaves this post unless he is wearing one." Shortly after, some of those who purchased this lanyard stated that when they went on leave in Helena, the women they met loved them. This comment alone was more than enough to convince those who had not yet purchased the lanyard to buy one immediately. [69]

The last dress item devised for the members of the Force was the oval cloth patch worn behind the U.S. Army Parachute Qualification badge. The outer part was stitched in gold thread. Positioned horizontally were three colors: Red on top; white in the middle, and blue at the bottom. Two small holes allowed the badge's posts to be slipped through the patch and through the tunic. It was then secured in place.[70] Thus, with the introduction of these new insignia and uniforms the U.S. and Canadian soldiers were slowly metamorphosising into one entity — the FSSF. Moreover, the uniqueness of these distinctive insignia, "contributed to making the Force a separate organization from the U.S. military," added Ralph Becket.[71]

From the outset, in his correspondence to, and conversations with, NDHQ staff, Frederick continually insisted that uniformity of dress throughout his formation was "most essential."[72] However, there remained a number of impediments. First, the FSSF Quartermaster stores were still being stocked. Second, there was a large number of personnel arriving and departing during the initial parachute training due to injuries; and third, NDHQ was very reluctant to allow Canadian personnel to wear U.S. walking-out uniforms rather than their Canadian uniforms.[73]

With regard to this last point Frederick argued, "the majority of Canadian soldiers have reported here with only one uniform for dress and therefore are finding it most difficult to have on hand a presentable uniform to wear when away from the post."[74] What is more, for security reasons, Frederick did not want the various and colourful Canadian uniforms to attract any attention to his formation. Rather, he wanted Canadian authorities to approve his request that Canadians wear U.S. Army uniforms and badges of rank.

After a series of discussions regarding the proposed FSSF dress regulations and the issuing of U.S uniforms, Lieutenant-Colonel McQueen drafted a report providing NDHQ with a detailed update containing a series of recommendations regarding possible dress options for Canadian personnel currently serving in the Force. Also, he needed NDHQ to authorize the provision of warmer battledress uniforms and proper Canadian military winter clothing or approve the wearing of American uniforms because fall and winter were fast approaching. While awaiting NDHQ's directives regarding these matters all Canadian personnel were fitted for the issuing of American uniforms.[75]

To accelerate the decision-making process, McQueen drafted a report in which he proposed the wearing of American Army clothing with the soon-to-be-issued new Force shoulder insignia; the wearing of brass Canada badges on the collars instead of the American collar badges marked U.S.; wearing of worsted Canada patches in the prescribed manner; and wearing of the Canadian badges of rank until special rank insignia for the Force is made available. Frederick agreed with McQueen's report.[76]

The CGS readily approved McQueen's recommendations and immediately forwarded the report to the appropriate NDHQ directorates for action. For the sake of expediency, and because it involved a relatively small number of personnel, Colonel H.A. Campbell, of the Directorate of Ordnance Services (A) agreed that 2nd Canadian Parachute Battalion personnel be issued with American uniforms.[77] Additionally, Lieutenant-Colonel Williamson initiated a proposal to manufacture locally a brass circular collar badge (disk) to be worn by Canadian ORs that bore the word CANADA and shared design features found on the U.S. collar badges worn on the right lapel of the American service dress tunics, also referred to as "Walking Out Class 'A.'"[78] The master-general of ordnance agreed and informed Williamson that his men were authorized to wear the spearhead patch.[79]

As time passed, Frederick's continued insistence that all Forcemen wear U.S. badges of rank irritated John Ralston the MND. Already frustrated by the fact that Canadian personnel wore American uniforms, an annoyed Ralston blasted the CGS:

OF COURAGE AND DETERMINATION

All new replacements also underwent the FSSF parachute-training course.

> I am not enamoured at the idea of wearing the U.S. uniform. I contemplated that as a composite force it would have a uniform of its own, i.e., neither Canadian nor U.S., but Canadian and U.S. personnel having some distinguishing patch or insignia, such as Canadians wear in the R.A.F.[80]

Within a week, Stuart informed the minister of the existence of the FSSF spearhead patch featuring the words USA-CANADA, and the "CANADA" collar badges (disks) worn by the Canadian ORs. Additionally, as a rebuttal to the minister's position regarding the creation a unique FSSF uniform the CGS wrote, "in my opinion it is too late to suggest a neutral uniform."[81] However, the CGS carried out the minister's stern directive that Canadian personnel continue to wear Canadian badges of rank. "On your concurrence," confirmed the CGS, "I will cause the necessary instructions to be issued, that Canadian officers and NCOs will wear the Canadian rank insignia." [82]

From the very outset the MND, NDHQ, and Colonel Frederick had very different views regarding the issue of dress and insignia. However, during the several months of lengthy deliberations over these matters, Frederick stood his ground. On 25 May 1943, Frederick and Williamson arrived in Ottawa and met with the CGS. One of the many issues discussed, at length, was the wearing of U.S. badges of ranks by Canadian personnel. Frederick and Williamson explained in great detail their rationale, specifically: to ensure security and uniformity of appearance; overcome difficulties in obtaining a supply of Canadian badges of ranks; and avoid having Canadian personnel arrested by U.S. military authorities because they were wearing Canadian badges of ranks.[83] Fredrick also reassured the CGS that the Canadian identity with regards to the FSSF orders of dress had been preserved. Subsequently Lieutenant-General Stuart reported to the MND:

> Both Cols. Frederick and Williamson pointed out that all personnel of the Force wear a red distinguishing device on the left shoulder. It is shaped somewhat like and Indian Arrowhead and contains in white letters "U.S.A" and "Canada." Canadian officers now wear a "Canada" badge in brass on both lapels of their jackets in the same manner as U.S. Officers wear a "U.S." badge. In a similar manner, Canadian soldiers of the Force wear a brass "Canada" badge on the collar of their uniform; the U.S. personnel wear a brass "U.S." badge. Lt.-Col. Williamson stated that Canadian personnel in the Force would have no objection the American badges of rank.[84]

The minister finally granted his approval on 3 June 1943, putting this long debate finally to rest.[85] As for the Canadian officers' dress code, Frederick and Williamson agreed that the officers were allowed to wear their Canadian Service uniforms with their Canadian badges of rank for special occasions.[86] However, when on duty Canadian officers would wear their U.S. Service uniform with U.S. badges of rank.[87] "All were sorry to give up the battle dress," reported the 2nd Canadian Parachute Battalion's war diary chronicler, "but agreed uniformity of dress was essential."[88] Nevertheless, "when time came for making the switch, there was some regimental pride and stubbornness on the part of some officers and other ranks," recounted William Story. "The Canadian Regimental system breeds great pride of unit."[89]

During a meeting with his officers, Frederick acknowledged the collaboration and understanding of the Canadians with regards to adopting the American uniform as the official FSSF uniform. He stated:

> I must compliment all the Canadians officers and enlisted men of the Force for the splendid way in which they have accepted the changes in customs, training and other phases of military life… I feel that there may be a slight possibility that the Canadian soldiers may have some reservation in taking pride in a uniform that is not Canadian. Let us consider for a moment that we are one Force; we have the same foe and we are in one fight, so there is no reason why we should not wear the same uniform. It is merely because the supply of the United States uniform was simpler than the supply of Canadian uniforms and because the United States agreed to furnish all equipment and supplies that the uniform that the men are now wearing is standard for the Force.[90]

OF COURAGE AND DETERMINATION

Bayonet training and other forms of close quarter combat were important elements of FSSF training.

The change, however, was easier for the first group of Canadians who arrived to Fort William Henry Harrison. The integration process was gradual and took second place to the fast-paced and gruelling training. For some, this imposed change went smoothly. "We all forgot our nationality — we were all FSSF," emphasized Gordon Sims.[91] Vernon Doucette arrived to the Force with an open mind. "When I went to the Force," explained Doucette, "I didn't consider myself a Canadian. We were all Forcemen."[92] As time passed, a new and distinctive formation identity defined the uniqueness of the FSSF. This was noted by Robert D. Burhans, a veteran FSSF American officer serving with the Force. "the Force character had evolved," observed the officer, "into something international in flavour."[93]

A few months later, as new Canadians volunteers joined the Force as replacements, the integration process came as more of a culture shock. Upon their arrival, they were marched to the FSSF quartermasters and within a few hours were outfitted with their new American uniforms and personal equipment. One of these new replacements, Herb Peppard, was quite apprehensive of this fast tracked integration process:

> I had a fierce pride in my family, my hometown, my province, and my country. Once we put on American uniforms, how long would our Canadian identity last? And the Americans, according to my prejudices, were all loud-mouthed braggarts and know-it-alls. How would they react to us?[94]

FORGING THE FORCEMEN

Peppard and his comrades were sent to the training regiment and quickly immersed into various basic training courses. Following successful qualifications, he was then posted to his company and regiment and integrated with the other Forcemen. It was during the next few days that his apprehensions of losing his national identity quickly subsided:

> After our small-arms training, we were integrated into the outfit, and I found out quickly how misplaced my "identity crisis" and fear of Americans had been. I was put in the first company of the first regiment as a member of the 60 mm mortar crew. The other three on the crew were O'Brien, Tratt, and Smitty. O'Brien was from Connecticut, Tratt from Montreal, and Smitty, or George Smith from faraway California. O'Brien and Smitty were as proud of their country and their hometowns as Tratt and I were of ours. The camaraderie that developed from learning a shared task together soon made us all best buddies.[95]

Bill Story added, "There was a magic induced by bringing Americans and Canadians together — learning how to get along."[96] Ultimately, Frederick achieved exactly what he wanted — one cohesive formation. His simple melting-pot exercise proved successful. Moreover, the camaraderie and teamwork would continue to grow during the following months of intense training.

7

NO ROOM FOR WEAKNESS:
Training for the Plough Project

I thought I was in pretty good shape until I got here.[1]
—Private Jack Callowhill

Due to the exigencies of Operation Plough, particularly the harsh climate, demanding terrain, and hazardous task, Frederick knew that it was imperative to forge his men into aggressive, innovative, cunning, and superbly conditioned combatants. Without a doubt, his unprecedented training regimen would ultimately prove to be the most demanding event of the military careers of those who dared to volunteer for the FSSF. After great preparation, Frederick had assembled a cadre of expert instructors and all the necessary equipment and weaponry required to hone the fitness and skills of his Forcemen.

Frederick's timelines were tight so he divided the Operation Plough training program into three distinct phases. The first phase, which took place between 3 August and 3 October 1942 focused on:

> Compressed parachute training;
> Intense physical training and conditioning throughout the duration of the entire training period;
> Demolitions;
> Unarmed combat;
> "Weasel" snow vehicle operation and maintenance;
> Weapons training on the Carbine, Browning automatic rifle, pistol, revolver, Thompson sub-machine gun, and Browning machine gun;
> Familiarization courses on German infantry weapons;

OF COURAGE AND DETERMINATION

Communications, map and compass navigation;
Chemical warfare;
Hygiene and first aid;
Scouting and patrolling; and
Small unit tactics including day and night exercises.[2]

Phase two, which ran from 5 October to 21 November, continued the core-listed training, and added specialty skills such as skiing, radio-communication, and mountain climbing. The final phase, scheduled from 22 November to December 1942, was to focus on honing skiing and rock climbing skills; living and operating in cold climates; winter warfare

Continual gruelling physical conditioning enabled the Forcemen to later endure and function with great efficiency under adverse and severe operational conditions.

exercises; and tactical training with the T-15 "Weasel" over-snow vehicle.[3] Frederick insisted that once the qualified Forcemen left Fort William Henry Harrison they would be able to operate efficiently in small independent groups, without support, in harsh winter conditions deep behind enemy lines.

To achieve these training deadlines, a strict timetable was devised. Training was conducted from Monday to Saturday. Reveille was at 0445 hours and sometimes earlier depending on the course or exercise. Following ablutions, cleaning of quarters, roll call, inspection, and physical training, the candidates were allowed a respite for breakfast. At 0800 hours all ranks embarked on a 2.5-kilometre obstacle course. Upon completion personnel then reported by regiment to their designated training areas. Course work went on until noon. Training resumed, after lunch, at 1300 hours and continued until 1700 hours. Additionally, evening classes were conducted four nights a week between 1900 and 2130 hours.[4] Significantly, to enable the FSSF combat echelon personnel to focus solely on their training all daily garrison tasks, work chores and guard duties were assumed by the Force's Base Echelon Service Battalion. This unit was composed exclusively of American personnel.[5] "This was great," recalled Sergeant Peter Smith, "all we did was train."[6]

Furthermore, to maximize the efficiency of the training schedule Frederick implemented four ground rules. First, punctuality quickly became a cardinal virtue and those who could not make timings were dismissed.[7] Second, all personnel, regardless of rank, underwent daily physical fitness training. This consisted of gruelling calisthenics and a run through the obstacle course. As usual, Frederick spared no expense when it came to providing his men with the very best training equipment. Lieutenant-Colonel Williamson was amazed when the FSSF obstacle course was unveiled:

> An obstacle course has just been completed and from personal experience, I feel quite safe in saying it is the "Grand-Daddy" of all obstacle courses. It takes a good half hour to negotiate which will give some idea of the difficulties one encounters during the passage ... This course included crawling, rope climbing, boxing, push ups, games, much doubling and running. In connection with running, each officer and man must be able to run a mile in less than ten minutes, and it's worth mentioning that the majority can do it in around seven minutes, some as low as five and one-half minutes which is our record so far.[8]

From day one, it was instilled into all Forcemen that the most important piece of equipment was, in fact, the individual Forceman. After all, individual stamina and endurance became key enablers to mission success. Ultimately, the superior physical conditioning of those in the FSSF quickly distinguished them from other Allied units and enemy troops. The severity of the FSSF's physical training regimen made quite an impression on

Williamson. "This [training]," he explained, "has been built to such a pitch that an ordinary person would drop from sheer exhaustion in its early stages."[9]

To complement the demanding physical training the Forcemen also had to develop mental toughness. This was achieved through the third ground rule — self-motivation. It was simply, "Go or Go!" stated Sergeant Joe Jamieson.[10] Those who were unwilling to take up the challenge were immediately returned to Canada. Sergeant George Wright explained that no one was forced to stay:

> It was a very easy outfit to get out of. If you didn't work you were gone. They only wanted dedicated fighters. It was important not to let the other guy down. If you felt you could not make it or continue, it was good-bye. This was an ongoing process. It didn't matter at what point of the training schedule you were at.[11]

Therefore, it was incumbent upon individuals to develop and nurture an attitude and state of mind required to overcome fatigue, hunger, hardships, develop an ability to block out pain, hone the will to persevere, and develop an unfathomable desire to succeed regardless of the cost. Consequently, all personnel realized that if they chose to remain with the FSSF, they had to excel daily and to prove themselves constantly to both their comrades and superiors.

Lastly, since Frederick felt that he had recruited seasoned personnel for this formation he elected to limit discipline to the strict minimum. He was not interested in garrison and parade soldiers. Lloyd Dunlop recalled this relaxed discipline. "The 'Top Kick,' he was the sergeant in charge of the company woke us up," recounted the veteran. "We formed up in front of our huts. He had a flash light and read off the names. The guys would yell out, 'Ho!' or 'Yeah!' They'd never said, 'Yes Sir!'"[12] Nevertheless, "the discipline was there," insisted Jamieson, "but they didn't exaggerate. We were told to do our jobs. If you didn't do it you were out."[13] Sergeant Paul Schoeler observed, "It wasn't like the Canadian Army." He explained, "You know, never ending marching, drill and exaggerated discipline. There was a certain nonchalance in the Force." Schoeler elaborated, "You knew what to do, and you did it! We worked hard and kept cool."[14] Canadians found this new approach a welcome change.

Regardless of Frederick's directives regarding discipline, Williamson continued to exercise strict control over the personnel of the Canadian contingent.[15] "Canadians were advised by senior Canadian officers," explained Gordon Sims, "that they should not even 'spit on the sidewalk,' we were ambassadors from Canada."[16]

So, within the first days at Fort William Henry Harrison all personnel had been briefed regarding these simple ground rules. "From day one we learned that there was no marching here," explained Private Forward. "Everything here was double time."[17] Each soldier learned to list directives and organize his time accordingly. "When pressed," conceded Sergeant Allen Lennox, "you could do a lot more than you thought you could."[18]

NO ROOM FOR WEAKNESS

As men adapted, the pace increased. "We ran everywhere," explained Donald Ballantyne, "we never walked."[19] No one wanted to fall behind. Personal pride and reputations were now on the line.

Since the mission hinged on the Force being inserted by air into occupied enemy territory, Frederick believed that the parachute jump course be given top priority. Other factors also came into play. First, due to the limited availability of required transport aircraft, it was imperative that all parachute training and qualification jumps be completed by the end of August 1942.[20] Second, the parachute training phase also doubled as a form of secondary selection process. In the event that personnel were unable to master their fear of heights, or sustained injuries that prevented them from proceeding to the next phase of training, they were immediately returned to their units of origin.

Frederick and his officers studied the current four-week U.S. Army parachute course given at the parachute school in Fort Benning, Georgia. All agreed that what was taught in this course far exceeded the operational requirements of the FSSF. More important, it could not be shoehorned into an already tight training schedule. Besides, Fort William Henry Harrison did not have, on site, the required parachute training devices such as the 250-foot High Tower, the 34-foot Mock Tower, or the myriad of other ground training apparatus to conduct a complete parachute course. Moreover, time and adequate transport resources were not available to shuttle FSSF personnel to and from Fort Benning or Fort Bragg. Therefore, it was imperative to modify the existing parachute course so that it could be given on site at Helena. To further save time two 1,066-metre runways and one

Learning the intricacies of parachuting.

parking strip were graded and prepared for the course. This allowed, all training to be conducted at the base.

Fredrick was also able to convince his superiors to approve and authorize his compressed course.[21] In the end, the new FSSF parachute course syllabus called for 10 days, averaging nine hours per day and it was given in three stages.[22] However, in practice, there was no set prescribed number of days for each of these stages.[23] Quite simply, Frederick decided that candidates' who mastered the training quickly could complete the course in a shorter period.[24] This streamlined the course even more.

In addition, the FSSF candidates, in contrast to their peers at the Fort Benning course, were not required to learn how to pack their own parachutes. This important task was judiciously carried out by riggers who were attached to the Force for the duration of the parachute qualifications. "These guys had to mark their chutes," explained Private Forward. "Each time there was a jump, one of the riggers was selected to jump also," he added, "This was done so the riggers wouldn't get careless."[25] With the arrival of the required aircraft, pilots, parachute instructors, and riggers everything was now in place to begin training the first week of August 1942.

Once briefed on the course requisites some volunteers had second thoughts. Many had never even set foot in an airport. To calm their apprehensions Lieutenant-Colonel McQueen did his best to reassure his men of the high quality of the American parachute training. "The instructors here," reported McQueen, "are reputed the best in the United States and I am convinced that every man that jumps is as well trained as it is possible to train him."[26]

And so, the men embarked on their fast-paced parachute training. Stage One consisted of physical training, tumbling, hiking, and jumping from two-foot high platforms. Gordon H. Baker provided the following insight regarding the objective of the initial platform training:

> The idea was to jump off and land rolling over to soften the sudden stops one undergoes during a parachute drop, which occurs at about the same speed. After doing that two or three dozen times one gets the idea.[27]

Candidates then proceed quickly to Stage Two. There, they were required to jump off four-foot high platforms, control and collapse their chutes in high winds, and take part in orientation flights. "Before the jump phase," explained the parachute candidate, "they took us out to the Helena airport and we went up on these orientation flights. They loaded us up and flew us around camp. The object of this ride," underlined Charlie Mann, "was so that we could get a feel for the aircraft."[28]

Furthermore, during the flight, the jumpmasters demonstrated the hook up procedures, how to respond correctly to in-flight commands and demonstrated the proper exiting techniques. Once back on the ground, candidates underwent additional suspended-harness drills, which taught them to control their main canopies during the decent and following their landing.

During Stage Three, candidates were taught proper exiting and landing techniques.[29] They practiced these drills by exiting from a large wooden built-to-scale mock-up representing the rear part of an aircraft fuselage. Throughout this stage the instructors repeatedly impressed upon the candidates, the extreme importance of executing these two drills in a flawless manner.[30] Upon completing all three stages each candidate underwent a final test. All that remained was the final confirmation — the actual jump qualification. Despite putting up brave fronts, instructors noted that the men's anxiety levels rose quickly.

To instil confidence, Frederick made it a point to lead by example. He immediately demonstrated that there was nothing difficult, or even extraordinary about parachute jumping. During one of the first parachute courses, the young commander, renowned for his lack of patience, just wanted to get on with it. He "submitted to a 10 minute description of how to twist in the harness," recalled a veteran, "and roll so as to absorb the shock of landing before he impatiently swung a parachute on his back and said, 'That's enough! Let's go!'"[31] He was amongst the first FSSF personnel to jump. Following his landing Frederick confessed that he had indeed been nervous. "No, more than a little nervous," added Frederick. "But my purpose was twofold," stressed the commander. "To lessen qualms others might have, and to let them know that I won't be sitting on my haunches."[32] Frederick's initial qualification jump set the tone for the Force's parachute training. "Seeing him do it," chimed Alan Blackwell, "made it difficult for the rest of us to refuse."[33]

During the initial and subsequent FSSF parachute training serials, Fredrick visited his men regularly and shared words of encouragement to set them at ease. "He [Frederick] told us that parachuting was just a small part of our training," recalled Herb Peppard. "He didn't want to spend too much time on it. He said it might just be another method of reaching an objective."[34] Sergeant Peter Smith added, "Frederick told us that this was just a means of travel from point 'A' to point 'B.'" So, that's why," explained the veteran, "in Fort William Henry Harrison, they didn't stress too much finesse about jumping. Basically, they told the parachute candidates that, "all they wanted to know was if you could jump and land safely."[35]

As the first group reported to the parachute hanger, Frederick interrupted them and for safety reasons ordered the temporary postponement of all qualification jumps until personnel were issued with a pair of U.S. Army parachute boots.[36] This new type of boot provided additional ankle support that was needed to soften the impact during landings. It was imperative to keep injuries at a minimum.

Once kitted, the anxious candidates then marched off to the makeshift airstrip. Each trainee was then designated to a "stick" (numbered groups of parachute candidates assigned to an aircraft) and ordered to put on their chutes. "They told us to strap them on tight," recounted Charlie Mann. "We put them on so damn tight, that we could hardly walk."[37] The reason for this was simple. "They had to be very tight," explained

Lieutenant J.D. Mitchell, "as you could give yourself a nasty burn if they were loose when the chute opened."[38]

Once loaded, the aircraft climbed to the prescribed altitude of 365 metres, the pilot then levelled off and set course for his approach to the designated drop zone (DZ). Heartbeats accelerated while all attempted conversations were drowned out by the loud drone of the aircraft's engines. Suddenly, the jumpmaster turned around and bellowed, "Stand -up, hook-up!" The candidates reacted in unison and now faced the moment of truth. As the aircraft approached the DZ, each man executed his last in-flight inspections drills. Suddenly, the next chilling command echoed throughout the aircraft, "Stand by the door!"[39] As the tense candidates shuffled toward the door the lead jumper adopted the prescribed exiting stance. The jumpmaster tried his best to alleviate the lead candidate's stress. While checking out the man's exiting posture he yelled out, "Don't look down, look at the skyline!" Lieutenant Mitchell recalled the jumpmaster's words when he was the lead jumper. He conceded, "That made it much better." The jumpmaster then screamed, "GO!" and the first jumper vanished quickly followed by the next jumpers. Those who could not bring themselves to jump were rapidly removed from the door, while their comrades stepped up and exited the aircraft.

All candidates who refused to jump were given a second chance. The pilot turned the aircraft around and proceeded once again toward the drop zone. Those who had initially balked now had to summon every ounce of courage to exit the plane. Even with a second opportunity, some candidates could not bring themselves to jump. "If a guy refused to jump you never saw him, or his equipment again," stated Vernon Doucette. "I think they took him down to a hotel. He was gone."[40] Sergeant Story added, "There was no shame involved, you just left."[41]

The ranks were further thinned out when some candidates, who had successfully logged their initial jump, stated that they did not want to jump ever again. Candidates who sustained minor injuries were given a few days grace to allow sprains and deep bruises to heal. All others were required to make their last qualifying jump within the next 24 hours.

With their first jump under their belts, the parachute candidates prepared for their second and final jump. Overall, Canadian volunteers had performed well. Nevertheless, the Canadian component sustained its share of parachuting and ground training injuries. As already stated, among the injured was Lieutenant-Colonel McQueen. Despite his injury, he was convinced the "training and instruction is of the highest quality and [the injuries are] in no way a reflection on the instructors."[42]

"We had lots of casualties at first with the parachuting," confirmed Sam Borod, "until we worked out a system."[43] The U.S. Army Parachute course was still in its infancy and changes were regularly made to improve the course curriculum. Sergeant Story explained the corrective training measures that were implemented during the latter part of the FSSF parachute course:

Paratroopers came in from Fort Benning, many that had been with the original test platoon. They taught us to land with our feet apart and stressed we shouldn't reach for the ground with one foot or the other foot in what they called pedaling. This method of keeping your feet and legs apart took away the support each leg can provide on a difficult jump. The army was concerned about the level of jump casualties. They actually filmed our descents and saw right away the problem was the legs were not supporting each other. The army later issued instructions to jump with feet together and the result was a dramatic drop in injuries.[44]

Not surprisingly, NDHQ staff became increasingly concerned by the number of volunteers who were returned to Canada.[45] McQueen drafted a report on 13 August 1942, explaining the challenges of this new training, as well as detailing the nature of the parachute injuries. He also reassured NDHQ that excellent medical care had been administered throughout all training and jump phases as well as during each man's sojourn in hospital. To further reassure NDHQ, McQueen concluded his report by stating:

> It must be realized that in this type of training casualties are bound to occur and while every effort is made to cut these to a minimum the fact must be realized and accepted. At the present time, the percentage is much lower than is accepted as normal.[46]

Frederick fully endorsed McQueen's report and added, "there was no deficiency of instruction or equipment in the training of Canadian personnel."[47] Nonetheless, during this period one officer and 175 ORs had been returned to Canada.[48]

While many Canadians and Americans volunteers left the FSSF during the parachute-training phase, those who remained worked even harder to earn the coveted U.S. Army Parachutist Badge. On 29 August 1942, 1,125 qualified parachute candidates formed up on the landing strip and took part in the much-anticipated "Wings Ceremony."[49] Of this number 35 Canadian officers and 436 other ranks, received their "jump wings."[50] It was an important moment in the FSSF's history and Fredrick insisted on personally pinning the jump wings on all qualified personnel.

Frederick was adamant "to make personal contact" with each of his Forcemen. He insisted on establishing this personal rapport with the rank and file because, "I won't always be there with the men," explained Frederick.[51] Despite the sweltering temperature and the inordinate length of the presentation parade the troops appreciated his gesture and for once the men did not mind standing patiently, on parade, under the blazing sun. "It was quite an important event," added a delighted Peter Smith. "He [Frederick] had a good word for everybody." While all were pleased to have received their American "wings," some, on the other hand, felt uneasy when they were referred to as paratroopers.

OF COURAGE AND DETERMINATION

Colonel Frederick insisted on personally awarding the "Jump Wings" to each candidate.

"We only had to do two jumps," explained Sergeant R.E. Blake, "I always felt that I was cheating, calling myself a paratrooper."[52] In hindsight, reminisced Sergeant Dunlop, "the parachuting was the easiest part of the training. The stuff that went on after the parachuting," he revealed, "was far tougher."[53]

Following the ceremony, Frederick took a moment to address his newly parachute qualified personnel. "He said that judging all the reports he received," recounted Smith, "that we were going to be the best trained soldiers in the whole allied force." The parachute training also had a very positive psychological effect on the graduates. During this gruelling training an additional selection process had taken place. It successfully brought together a group of men who mastered their fear. In doing so, it had separated "the sheep from the goats," stated a Forceman.⁵⁴ Furthermore, this initial training brought the Americans and Canadians candidates even closer together.

As the stressful parachute jumps faded into distant memory, they were quickly replaced by several new dreaded realities. The first was the rugged forced marches. Sergeant Mann described:

> The route marches were a continuous thing. Running, marching, and carrying heavy packs were all exercises made to build up endurance. We had route marches and forced marches. The difference between both was speed. You'd walk 120 paces a minute. Then you would double time. Double time consisted of marching and running. Both types of marches were done with full pack, helmet and jump boots.⁵⁵

As time passed route marches were extended from 20 to 40 to 60 miles and had to be completed in increasingly shorter timeframes. "When you thought you could not go any further," recollected Sergeant Jim Summersides, "they got you going double time."⁵⁶ If the men faltered the instructors yelled out, "Stamina, Stamina," to regain and maintain the hellish cadence.⁵⁷ The men were constantly pushed to the limit. Dunlop recalled:

> I remember one march I swear that I was sleeping as I was walking. I felt that I had walked four of five paces asleep. After marching 30 miles and as we were approaching the base, our company commander would straighten us up and we would march in as if we weren't tired at all. When we really got into the training we would have one of the marches at least once a week.⁵⁸

Yet, throughout these marches each man found a way to maintain his will and persevere. "What made the Force such an outstanding unit was the competitive spirit between the Americans and the Canadians," explained Eugene Forward. "It was not a negative thing by any means. "The underlying feeling was," recounted the Forceman, "that I'm as good as you are no matter what. This helped all of us perform better."⁵⁹

To relieve the boredom Forcemen such as Herb Langdon started to sing. "The Canadian led the way with many songs unknown to U.S. members," recalled an American Forceman. "I even learned 'Alouette.'"⁶⁰ As the long columns of Forcemen marched through the hilly terrain surrounding the base, Sergeant George Wright asserted that the men would now do anything to remain with the Force:

> I recall that we had a march competition between Regiments. We had a sixty mile march with packs and rifles. Colonel Marshall and 1st Regiment took it. We did it in 20 hours. Even if we were in shape your feet took a

OF COURAGE AND DETERMINATION

Maximizing time. Even during the summer months, some of the forced marches focused on the correct handling of ski poles in preparation of ski training.

> beating. They were all blistered. After the march our feet were aching. We soaked them, put on a pair of clean socks and put our boots back on quickly. We slept with them on. It was the only way to keep the swelling down and be able to walk the next day. I remember back in England with the Hasty P's[Hasting and Prince Edward County Regiment] we did a 100 mile march but it took us many days to complete it. [61]

This unmerciful and relentless training ensured that only the best candidates remained. "We lost a lot of Canadians who weren't up to the physical challenge," remembered Sims. They just couldn't hack it. We needed swinging bar room doors we were losing them so fast."[62]

These hardships increased the bonds of comradeship amongst those who survived. Comrades did not want to let their team members down. During one of the forced marches, Private Morris Lazarus sprained his ankle. "I had a bit of trouble coming in. Ross Earl, my sergeant, saw this and took my pack," recollected the veteran. "It was nice to see this kind of camaraderie." [63] Regardless of the toughness displayed by the Forcemen to successfully complete these various training exercises one officer nevertheless confided, "the emphasis on physical training was somewhat extreme."[64]

As weeks passed, it now became evident to FSSF headquarters that it was necessary to scale back certain forced marches over the mountain ranges to prevent needless injuries. "It had been decided that the original two day march was too rugged," wrote the

NO ROOM FOR WEAKNESS

Frederick insisted that all personnel be trained to handle and use German infantry weapons.

Forcemen spent hours honing their marksmanship skills on a great variety of U.S. Army weapons.

2nd Canadian Parachute Battalion war diary chronicler, "and the one day march over the range was sufficient."65

Simultaneously, personnel of all three regiments continued with their individual level training. These courses covered small arms training and range qualifications; demolition, unarmed combat, first aid, and hygiene; and navigation, operation, and maintenance of motor vehicles. The schedule dictated that all these prescribed courses be completed by 3 October 1942.

For the weapons training portion the Canadians were somewhat at a disadvantage because all selected weaponry was American. The aim of this multiple weapons training was to ensure every Forceman was capable of firing the vast inventory of weapons available. Notably, this included the field stripping and firing of the .30-calibre carbine, the .45-calibre pistol, the Browning automatic rifle, and the Thompson submachine gun.66 Once proficient in the effective handling of these weapons personnel then honed their marksmanship's skills. All Forcemen were warned that it was imperative to qualify on all of the weapons in order to remain with the Force. A man who could not shoot was a liability to others.

Despite the long hours spent qualifying on the various ranges, Canadians enjoyed this part of the FSSF training. Lieutenant Mitchell explained the differences in the FSSF and Canadian Army philosophies and attitudes regarding weapons training and range practice: "They [FSSF] were very generous in supplying us with ammunition," attested the Canadian officer, "and encouraged us to use the various weapons as much as possible." He revealed, "It was much different from the Canadian Army where ammo was issued in the most miserly fashion."67 Sergeant Joe Dauphinais was equally pleasantly surprised by the proactive weapons-training program in the FSSF. "When I was in Canada, we fired about five shots a year from a .22 caliber Enfield or .303 caliber Ross rifle," recollected the veteran. "When I got into the Force, they would let you take the guns out and shoot the hell out of them any time you wanted. When we didn't have any money to go down town, we would pick up a rifle and a few hundred rounds and go up in the mountains to shoot. There was no limit."68

Additionally, since the Force would be operating behind enemy lines Frederick insisted that his men also be proficient in field stripping and firing various types of regular and automatic weapons used by German infantrymen.69 During the range work, Forcemen compared them to their own weapons. They quickly acknowledged the deadly efficiency of these enemy weapons. "I really liked the Thompson sub-machine gun," explained Eugene Forward, "however the German Schmeisser was just as amazing. It fired three times faster." This weapon's rate of fire as well as its distinctive sound left a lasting impression on Frederick's soldiers. "When I later heard this German machine gun in combat," recalled Forward, "it made my stomach turn over."70

As the Forcemen expanded their knowledge and lethal repertoire of skills the men were then initiated to a rather unique style of unarmed hand-to-hand combat course.

NO ROOM FOR WEAKNESS

No expense was spared to equip the Force with the best available equipment.

Frederick had succeeded in hiring an excellent instructor. Following a conversation with Colonel Preston Goodfellow of the Office of Strategic Services (OSS) the officer recommended without hesitation 39-year-old Dermot M. "Pat" O'Neill.[71] This veteran law enforcement officer had many years of outstanding service with the Shanghai Police Force.[72] More important, he mastered various types of Chinese martial arts. Acting upon this recommendation, Frederick ordered Captain Burhans, his S-2 Intelligence officer, to immediately follow-up on the matter. "If he (O'Neill) is all right," instructed Frederick then, "arrange for his employment."[73] Shortly after, O'Neill was invited to join the Force as a civilian instructor.

It did not take long for O'Neill to impress the Forcemen. His introductory speech was short and to the point. "I'm not here to teach you to hurt," bellowed O'Neill, "I am here to teach you to kill."[74] These words immediately set the tone for this intense, fast paced, no-nonsense course. The brief introduction was followed by a series of impressive demonstrations during which unsuspecting volunteers were expediently and repeatedly introduced to Fort William Henry Harrison's hard packed ground. Despite numerous bumps and bruises the course became "very popular with the troops and great keenness and interest is shown," reported Lieutenant-Colonel McQueen.[75] Frederick who also participated in this training described it as "legalized assault, battery, and mayhem."[76]

The unarmed combat curriculum was simple. The lessons were spread over the course of the few weeks and totalled approximately 40 hours of instruction. All courses were held outside. Officers and men trained separately. Moreover, it was not O'Neill's intention to run a martial arts school. Instruction was kept at an elementary, but nevertheless lethal level. The course was basically, "a simple method, a kick and a poke, that any man could learn," described Captain Burhans. "The system was a simplification and improvement over Judo. It was twice as good and far more destructive to the victim."[77]

As such, at the beginning of each training session O'Neill explained and demonstrated the sequences of each exercise. He then observed and corrected the candidates throughout the lesson. Furthermore, he stressed the importance of understanding the sequence of each movement. The theoretical part was then reinforced by repetitive intense practice until each candidate attained

Instructor demonstrates unarmed combat techniques.

the required fluid execution of each movement. These techniques were further honed by giving the soldiers an understanding of additional vital complimentary elements such as speed, anticipation, surprise, relentlessness, and self-confidence. Moreover, to ensure that the candidates were on a constant state of alert, O'Neill occasionally threw dummy grenades or set off small charges to monitor the candidates' reactions.[78] The combination of all these teaching elements greatly enhanced the flow, speed, and execution.

Thus, hours of practice were spent kicking, punching, attacking, blocking, deflecting, counterattacking, and disarming opponents. Throughout the course, O'Neill explained the weaknesses of the human anatomy and how one could attack these points with fingers, fists, knees, elbows, fighting knives, bayonets, and basically anything that one could lay his hands on. "Plainly his job was to teach us dirty fighting — No Marquis of Queensbury Rules," observed Lieutenant Mitchell. He conceded, "this came in very handy as time went by."[79]

As the unarmed combat course progressed, the young soldiers attempted to best their instructor. However, this was easier said than done. "You'd see someone thrust at him with a knife, next thing you'd see was the guy flying one way and the knife the other," recalled an amazed candidate.[80] Moreover, O'Neill encouraged these challenges and even went so far as to promise weekend passes to those who could beat him. Many tried and all failed.

Frederick fully supported the training for operational reasons, however, the Forcemen found other venues where they could put their new skills to use. They had long memories and vividly recalled the infamous initial fight at The Gold Bar, in Helena, as well as numerous subsequent brawls in that and other establishments in Helena and neighbouring communities. Now, they returned to settle the score against local bullies, miners, and cowhands. Their new skills made short order of their adversaries. However, these fights spilled over into more serious clashes with military police (MPs) and local law enforcement officers. As a result, FSSF headquarters staff was required to work hard to defuse many complaints brought forward by the MPs and civilian police force.[81] The solution that came to all parties was a tacit agreement that it was best from now on to leave the Forcemen alone.

One FSSF officer, however, recommended that The Gold Bar be put out of bounds for Force personnel. Frederick quickly nixed the idea stating, "and do away with all that hand-to-hand combat training they are getting on their own time!" In order to keep the FSSF's good standing with the citizens of Helena, Frederick met with the bar owner and offered to pay for all the damages. The owner refused, explaining, "with the money those boys leave here on a Saturday night, I can afford the damages. They are welcome anytime."[82] Nevertheless, Frederick took measures to ensure that his personnel's excessive energy be drained in upcoming training.

One particular training activity that proved very popular with the troops was demolitions. As with all other training, Frederick left nothing to chance. Once again, he sought out the most competent instructors and the most up-to-date techniques and explosives.[83] Lieutenant Dan Ryan and his team of specialists from the U.S. Engineering Board, as well as Major Harvey, Royal Engineers, British Army, were selected to train the Forcemen.[84] The basic demolition course was given to all members during October 1942.[85] Due to the nature of the upcoming mission it was imperative that each solider be proficient, "in the use of demolition," explained Lieutenant-Colonel McQueen, "so that he would be capable of carrying out a task by himself if necessity arose."[86]

During these courses, candidates familiarized themselves with several kinds of explosives and detonators required to prepare and arm various types of charges. For some who had previous experience as miners it was *déjà vu*. They quickly showed off their skills by capping, "off the dynamite with their teeth … or playing a game of chicken with a stick of dynamite," chuckled Sergeant Dauphinais. "We had some close calls. What a fun bunch, I'm telling you. There was never a dull moment."[87] However, candidates who had never handled explosives were both impressed and intimidated by the destructiveness of these lethal charges. Sergeant Smith described the power and rapidity of the PrimaCord:

> We also used a lot of PrimaCord and became very familiar with blasting caps. You could take PrimaCord and put 20 wraps of it around a ten inch to two foot tree, light it and cut the tree right off. Everybody had to learn

OF COURAGE AND DETERMINATION

The much-anticipated arrival of the T-15 Weasel enabled the Forcemen to expand their operational abilities and movements over snow and ice.

how to crimp a detonator onto a fuse, and splice it into the prima cord. When it went off, it went off fast.[88]

Adding to this already deadly arsenal Lieutenant Ryan introduced a new type of explosive referred to as R.S. "It was a soft plastic material," explained, Ralph Becket, "it could be kneaded in your hands and stuck to things of almost any shape — something like Plasticine. In my opinion," summarized the officer," it was a considerably stronger explosive that TNT or dynamite."[89] Lieutenant Mitchell added, that the explosive had "tremendous cutting power, ideal for demolition of steel and concrete structures."[90] Ryan's preference for this type of explosive was noted by the Forcemen who nicknamed it "Ryan's Special."[91]

While it was important to handle these charges properly, it was even more important to instil confidence to all members of the Force in the handling explosives. Instructors noted that the men had concerns regarding the transportation of these charges into combat. To dispel these apprehensions they demonstrated to the men that enemy fire could not detonate these explosive. To prove his point, Ryan had his engineers fire several rounds into explosive charges. "They wanted to make sure," underlined Dauphinais, "that we knew it needed primer cord and a cap to set it off."[92] Now that the theoretical portion of the course was completed, the men were eager to apply their new-found skills.

As the Force had to be operationally ready by early December 1942, the fall proved to be extremely busy. And so, as the Forcemen continued to train for their hazardous mission, Frederick flew to England to confirm the final arrangements for Operation Plough.

8

WITHOUT HESITATION:
Creating a Potent Striking Force

Let our men know that we [FSSF officers] feel they are very special soldiers and that when they have finished their training here they will be the finest fighting men in the world.[1]

— Colonel Robert Frederick

With the FSSF training program well under way, Colonel Frederick met with Lieutenant-Colonel E.A.M Wedderburn, a British commando officer and winter warfare expert who had just returned from briefing the British prime minister and the chief of combined operations in England on the progress of Plough. Following this meeting, Frederick acted on Wedderburn's advice and decided to travel to London early in September 1942 to finalize mission planning. After all, there were some important details, such as aircraft availability for the insertion of the Force and its equipment, as well as liaison with the Norwegian government in exile and its resistance movement to finalize the target plan and gain any additional intelligence and co-operation that they could offer. Ominously, despite Churchill's continued enthusiasm, Frederick soon hit a wall.[2] Very quickly he felt a sense of impending doom.

His first hurdle appeared when he spoke to the intractable architect of Britain's strategic bombing campaign, Air Chief Marshal Charles Portal of the Royal Air Force (RAF). Frederick's request for the temporary diversion of 750 Lancaster bombers forecast for the middle of January was parried with finesse. "This is our best bomber," answered Portal. "If you can show us where Plough can accomplish more in its operation than one thousand Lancasters could do on the bombing runs," he continued reasonably, "we shall consider the plane for your uses."[3] Despite the seemingly fair and co-operative response, the underlying tone was not one of accommodation.

Frederick's next dose of reality occurred when the Combined Operations Command planners briefed him on the commando raiding program and, more important, the work of Brigadier Colin Gubbin's Special Operations Executive (SOE) and their Norwegian sabotage campaign.[4] Although the SOE had never even heard of the Plough Project, or the FSSF for that matter, they too had plans for sabotaging most of the targets that the Plough force was theoretically earmarked to destroy. Significantly, Gubbin's plan required very few aircraft and only two or three Norwegian agents for each target.[5]

Similarly, Colonel Frederick's discussion with Major-General Wilhelm von Tangen Hansteen, the commander-in-chief of the Norwegian Armed Forces, was fraught with impediments. Hansteen bluntly informed Frederick that the king and prime minister of Norway opposed the concept of the Plough Project. They were concerned that the large-scale destruction of power plants would create a greater hardship on the Norwegian people than it would on the Germans. Moreover, although they welcomed any assistance in ousting the occupying German forces, they did not wish to do so by destroying the vital industrial infrastructure that was key to Norway's economic well-being. Hansteen also stressed that Norway, "was not willing to take these sacrifices just for the propaganda value of something being done for the Western side in lack of a major second front."[6] As an alternative, he recommended that Frederick re-examine this issue with the SOE and the Air Ministry to select targets better suited to the "plough scheme."

With regards to operational matters, Hansteen explained that such attacks were best to be launched in very early winter. During these months, the nights were longer and weather-conditions hampered observation and enemy air operations. Furthermore, planners had to take into account that the projected area of operation was in fact open mountain plateaus. Consequently, without effective air-support, German fighter pilots could track and destroy the Force's snow-vehicles. Lastly, intelligence reports confirmed that for the past two years seasoned German ski and mountain troops were training extensively throughout Norway. As Frederick mulled over the comments of the commander-in-chief of the Norwegian Armed Forces he conceded that all these points were, in fact, logical and valid.

And so, with no apparent aircraft, no host country support, and competion from an organization that appeared to have a more efficient, more precise, and less resource intensive means of achieving the same goal, Colonel Frederick quickly realized that the Plough Project was doomed. And, any doubt he may have harboured was quickly dashed when he returned to London to meet with Lord Mountbatten prior to his flight to Washington, D.C. The chief of combined operations candidly explained to Frederick that the Plough Project was no longer a pressing issue. By this time, Combined Operations and the whole raiding concept was under siege by the War Office. The Allied effort, particularly as a result of American might and industrial capacity, was slowly beginning to turn the tide of war. Raiding and subversive activities, never fully supported by the mainstream military, were further marginalized as large-scale conventional operations, such as the invasion of North Africa, took shape.

Moreover, Mountbatten had no means of influencing the release of aircraft and conceded that SOE provided a more economical means of achieving the desired result, not

Entering a new dimension — amphibious warfare.

to mention at a more politically acceptable price for the Norwegian government in exile in London. As such, both men agreed to let Plough die. As a result, on 26 September 1942, Frederick sent an urgent message to Captain Burhans. The directive was short and to the point:

> Suspend effort on present line…New plan may be radically different and not concerned with hydroelectric or other industrial installations… Cease training on hydroelectric installations and … stress general tactical training, to include attack of fortifications, pill boxes, barracks and troop

concentrations. Change in weapons may be necessary to provide greater firepower, so suspend further small arms training pending a decision.[7]

Upon his return to the United States, in early October, Colonel Fredrick briefed General George C. Marshall, the American Army chief of staff regarding these latest developments. He then left his Washington office for Montana unsure whether the FSSF would be continued or disbanded. Consequently, it was now up to the American general staff to secure a political decision from both the American and Canadian governments on the future of the FSSF.

On 8 October 1942, Lieutenant-Colonel McQueen briefed the CGS, Lieutenant-General Stuart, regarding the cancellation of Plough. Later that day Stuart forwarded a telegram to Lieutenant-General McNaughton, Canada's overseas commander, informing him of the latest turn of events. The Canadians were now waiting for the Americans to make known their intentions prior to articulating their position.

However, the VCGS, Major-General Murchie's missive provided some telling clues regarding the future of the 2nd Canadian Parachute Battalion. He put forth four alternatives:

A. Continue with Special Service Force if Americans so desire.
B. Amalgamate with 1st Canadian Parachute Battalion.
C. Disband and Disperse Personnel.
D. Retain as an Ordinary Parachute Battalion For Service and Abroad.[8]

Importantly, Murchie highlighted the negative effects of options B, C, and D. He stated each has the "disadvantage of unwelcome publicity over cancellation of highly publicized Special Service Force as have B and C over apparent curtailment of our plans for Cdn [Canadian] Parachute Troops."[9]

In due course the Americans decided to maintain the FSSF.[10] On 17 October, General Marshall informed Major-General Maurice Pope, the chairman of the Canadian Joint Staff in Washington, D.C., that the U.S. Army decided to retain the FSSF as a special unit and considered possible employment in the Caucasus in early 1943. In order to maintain the Force's current fighting capabilities Marshall inquired if the Canadians would continue to support the FSSF before he initiated any discussions regarding this mission with the Soviet government.[11]

Concurrently, General Marshall directed that the FSSF training policy "will continue to be the readying of troops to endure hardships in the arctic and mountainous regions; to operate as saboteurs against vital industrial installations; to train personnel in the use of skis and snowshoes and in parachute operations; and to develop special equipment which could be transported either by air or ship, and which could negotiate terrain covered by snow and ice."[12] Although military intent and "will" to continue seemed to be present, the ultimate decision on whether it would be an international force was now in the hands of the Canadian government.[13]

The FSSF arsenal also included the dreaded flamethrower.

As such, the Canadian War Cabinet Committee discussed the issue on 28 October 1942. From a Canadian perspective, the existence of the "elite" First Special Service Force was considered by the government to be of marginal operational value after its original mission was cancelled. The *Minutes of the War Cabinet Committee* noted, "Though the future employment of the unit was doubtful, beyond its existence as a 'stand-by' force, acceptance of the U.S. proposal [continue unit's existence for special operations] was recommended as a token of intimate co-operation between the two countries."[14] Thus, the CGS was instructed to contact Major-General Pope, in Washington and clarify the following pressing issues: "Does the U.S. Army really want us to continue our association with the special service force?; that any operational projects contemplated be subject to approval by this headquarters; and what are the views of the Canadian commander in respect to continuing Canadian association with the Force?"[15]

During the course of the following two weeks discussions continued to address Canadian and American concerns. Then, on 11 November 1942, during a Cabinet War Committee meeting, Ralston announced, "after further consideration, that it had been decided to maintain Canadian participation in the special service force."[16] And so, for political reasons the FSSF continued to exist — the question was now to what end? For Frederick this was a major concern for it would determine the direction of his training and planning.[17]

Simultaneously, during this period the American general staff examined the best possible operational employment of the Force. This was not an easy task. The Americans informed their Canadian counterparts that the earlier considered Caucasus option was rejected because the terrain and tactical situation were deemed unsuitable.[18] Next, planners told Frederick that the FSSF would be deployed to New Guinea, but that too was cancelled. The Operations Division of the General Staff next considered using the FSSF in the Mediterranean area, specifically Italy, Sardinia, or Sicily. In addition, its use for the intended invasion of Kiska in the spring 1943 was thrown on the table, but apparently withdrawn when the planners deemed it too early to assign forces to that operation.[19]

Despite the uncertainty and variance in possible theatres of operation, Frederick and his Forcemen were required to continue training and prepare for an imminent deployment. Although higher direction was quick in coming, it was inconsistent and constantly changing. To Fredrick one thing was clear: regardless of the mission, they would ultimately be given, the Force would be prepared.

Meanwhile, on 21 September 1942, during Frederick's absence in the U.K., Lieutenant-Colonel Ridgely Gaither, with AFG HQ, had visited Fort William Henry Harrison to inspect and evaluate the FSSF training program.[20] Gaither met with Lieutenant-Colonel Shinberger, the FSSF training officer and other staff. While the initial meeting was friendly and cordial the Force officers were nevertheless, "extremely reticent to discuss their training mission or training objective," reported Gaither.[21] Moreover, Gaither's first impression of the FSSF officers was not a positive one. "The officers as a group," commented the officer, "did not present a very 'well turned out' appearance."[22]

Gaither then visited various training areas to observe the Forcemen. He reported that thorough demolition, scouting, and patrolling training were being conducted. However, the differences in AFG and FSSF training philosophies quickly became apparent. Gaither critiqued the FSSF's weapons training:

> The courses in the other weapons were to familiarize the soldiers with the weapons in case they were suddenly required to use them. This pistol marksmanship course consisted of firing five rounds with pistol and with the revolver. The rifle M1 course did not follow any of our standard courses; firing from the hip was stressed. It is my opinion that the marksmanship courses being conducted will result in the men having a general idea of all weapons, but I do not believe it will produce satisfactorily trained shots in any one weapons. Apparently no combat firing nor any team work in firing is contemplated.[23]

He also had reservations regarding the parachute course. Training had been reduced to the minimum and the reviewing officer pondered how the Forcemen would react in severe weather jumping conditions and mass drops. Moreover, Gaither strongly recommended that an Air Force liaison officer be attached to the Force to develop the pilot-parachutist teamwork necessary for enhancing unit airborne operations. In addition, the ongoing parachute test drops of the Weasel vehicles had proved unsuccessful and no alternate delivery contingency plan had yet been worked out.

WITHOUT HESITATION

Weapons training with the Browning .30-calibre machine gun.

As for the upcoming winter training syllabus, Gaither was not convinced of its approach and aims. "This is contrary to all our experience in teaching men to ski and operate in snow and mountains," related Gaither. "It is not believed that the winter training program for the force will be sufficient to give them any individual mobility in the snow, nor to acquire proficiency in operations in winter warfare."[24] Despite all these shortcomings, Gaither conceded that the FSSF officers were enthusiastic and morale was high. "And for this particular type of guerrilla warfare training that these officers purported to be teaching," mused the visiting officer "perhaps the training will suffice."[25]

So, Gaither left Montana and reported back to his superiors. AFG HQ staff resented Frederick's independent attitude, as well as his refusal to comply with current existing Army training doctrine and prescribed training practices. Moreover, they were not enamored by his reliance on Allied instructors, or the seclusion of the FSSF's training base.[26] However, these were precisely the reasons why Frederick wanted to train his men as he saw fit and keep the Army's stifling bureaucratic apparatus at bay so as to expedite the FSSF's rapid deployment. Finally, due to the secrecy of Operation Plough, Frederick could not, and would not, provide information to AFG HQ on the operation's aim, objective, or deployment date.

Despite these differences the visit did bring out three main recommendations on how the FSSF could further improve its training. The first suggested increasing collective tactical training at all levels. The second recommendation called for more time being allotted to testing personnel. The final recommendation stressed the development of an officer leadership program. The FSSF leadership conceded that corners had been cut and course matter compressed. However, these measures were taken out not due to lack of professionalism or interest but in to order to meet the operation's stringent deadline.

Nonetheless, as a result of the visit, while awaiting Frederick's return, the now newly promoted Major Burhans drafted a memoranda outlining new training standards for officers and ORs.[27] During the period, Burhans also received Frederick's 26 September directive regarding the cancellation of Operation Plough. And so, immediate additional changes had to be made to the FSSF training schedule to prepare the formation for its new role as assault infantry.

The war diary captured the transformation. From that moment, all efforts were placed on training the regiments to make them highly mobile assault groups capable of conducting the following types of combat missions:

a. Operate against vital military and industrial targets;
b. Operate as an overland raider force infiltrating, penetrating or encircling deep onto enemy territory to destroy important target;
c. Operate as a spearhead in forcing strongly fortified localities with the expectation of early support from friendly troops; and
d. Operate in cold or mountainous regions to accomplish any or all of the possible missions.

Furthermore, courses regarding combat principles were also expanded to now include a) Security, b) River crossings, c) Meeting engagements, d) Coordinated withdrawals, e) Attacking prepared positions, f) Night operations, g) Street fighting, h) Raids, i) Defense, j) Advanced demolitions, k) Rules of land warfare, l) Field exercises, m) Radio school, visual signaling, intelligence school, and air ground liaison.[28]

Moreover, the FSSF tables of organization were amended to increase the manpower and firepower of subunits:

a. The Weasel's original operational use was now limited to a support role;
b. The men would now operate as infantrymen at the section level, rather than T-15 crewmembers;

c. Sections were increased to 13 men, led by a staff sergeant now armed with a sub-machine gun; and

d. Section level fire power was increased with the addition of Browning light machine guns, rocket launchers, flame throwers and the recently acquired Johnson light machine gun.[29]

Also, not knowing the geographical location of their impending deployment Frederick ordered that ongoing efforts be continued to locate appropriate winter clothing and equipment, as well as communication equipment.[30]

While FSSF headquarters personnel fleshed out the new Force training schedule, the week of 28 September to 3 October was set aside to conduct refresher training. The following week personnel were tested on all subject matter. "The final results," explained Lieutenant-Colonel Williamson, "gave the platoon commanders a clear picture of the standing of each of his men."[31] At the end of this testing process, each regiment was given a detailed briefing explaining their weaknesses and the required corrective measures.[32]

In the interim, personnel continued with their prescribed individual and demolitions training, night exercises, and forced marches. Replacements, on the other hand, were sent to the training regiment to undergo the parachute course and other basic FSSF training. Upon completion, they were assigned to the combat echelon's three regiments. "So for right now," explained Captain R.W. Becket, the Force's assistant training officer, "it was straight ahead with our training, almost as if nothing had changed."[33]

However, the troops were not easily fooled. Even though the men had not been informed about the cancellation of Operation Plough, they knew something was amiss. "While some of us know that there was a serious change in the original planning," observed Becket, "very few of us knew the details and there was little, if any, discussion about it."[34] However, all knew that the FSSF commander was putting the final touches to a challenging new training plan.

On 20 October, Lieutenant-Colonel Shinberger unveiled the new four-week

Navigation training through dense bush areas.

OF COURAGE AND DETERMINATION

training schedule. Training started on 26 October 1942. The training officer also announced that new courses would be added to the FSSF training curriculum to provide specialist training to Forcemen who showed proficiency in mechanical work, communications, demolition, intelligence, medical, and air-ground liaisons.[35] Furthermore regimental commanding officers were directed to incorporate all previous training throughout all new applicable training and field exercises. The new training objectives for the FSSF were:

> a. Gunnery course consisting of qualifying personnel on the M-1 b. Rifle, qualifying two men per section on the Light Machine gun;
> c. Section leaders will be trained on the Thompson Machine Gun;
> d. Develop bayonet fighting skills to complement the hand-to-hand combat skills;
> e. Scouting and patrolling tactics at the small unit levels;
> f. Section and platoon combat firing drills during the course of deep infiltration, rear guard, street and mountain fighting scenarios;
> g. Combat principle (field exercises) involving tactical situations to monitor actions and reaction of personnel and officer;
> h. Development of combat leadership;
> i. Enhanced communication training for selected personnel;
> j. Motor instruction on the Weasel will be conducted in scouting and patrolling scenarios.[36]

In addition, to ensure a higher quality of instruction FSSF headquarters now monitored all regimental level training.

At the same time, officer training and development became a pressing issue. Frederick was disappointed by Lieutenant-Colonel Gaither's unflattering report. It reflected badly on the leadership of his officers, as well as their ability in command and control. Frederick conceded that for many of his young officers this was in fact their first posting to a combat unit since their graduation from various U.S. Army officer schools. Nevertheless, he was confident that these junior officers would rise to the occasion. With these thoughts in mind, Frederick met with his officers. In his address to them, he stated:

> In bestowing upon you your commissions, your governments have honored you with their highest trust and confidence. An army officer enjoys a position of responsibility and honor that he cannot regard lightly. Certain of you have abused this trust and confidence. An officer who cannot be trusted or who is irresponsible is worse than worthless, for he may easily do his government more harm than good. For the last time I shall caution you about these irresponsible acts, and I urge you to

Taking a much-needed break.

remember that you all enjoy a position that all must respect and in which you must govern yourselves as your governments justly require.[37]

Frederick reminded them that as officers they had to take control, hone their leadership skills, and be fully involved in all aspects of the training of their troops. Mistakes committed during training had to be corrected immediately. Additionally, Frederick was displeased with the men's appearance, deportment, cleanliness of quarters, care of equipment, and weaponry, as well as attention to detail during the training. Frederick stated that these matters could easily be corrected by establishing a better working rapport between officers and NCOs. He stressed that this bond was critical in nurturing teamwork. More important, he asserted that throughout training, officers and NCOs had to work closely to ensure their men developed confidence in themselves and a sense of unit pride.

Frederick went further. He also declared that it was imperative that they constantly remind their men that they had a special role as Forcemen, members of the one and only First Special Service Force. Frederick affirmed:

> Instill pride not only in the individual but have him take pride in his unit and the Force. Have the men realize that this Force they belong to is a very special Force, the only one of its kind in the world. All men are either volunteers or specially selected, and they are now taking part in a training program more extensive, thorough, and difficult that any attempted by any other unit.[38]

Frederick concluded his address with the following direction:

> We have tried to be reasonable and considerate in our demands on junior officers in this Force. Many of you came here with little experience as officers and we have given you time to get your feet on the ground, but more will be expected of you in the future and it's up to you to make good. You have been placed in positions of responsibility, and you owe it to the government that has given you this trust to do your duty properly, thoroughly and whole-heartedly.[39]

The gauntlet had been thrown down. It was now up to the officers to respond to this challenge. Leaving nothing to chance, Frederick personally ensured he developed and moulded his subordinate commanders into skilled, aggressive combat leaders. Furthermore, the mantra of the FSSF officers now became — "Lead from the front." If they did not, or were unwilling to do so, they would be replaced. In later operations, Frederick's attitude about leadership never wavered. He was always up front.

To further assist his officers, Frederick issued weekly training memoranda that articulated schedules, as well as training aims and objectives.[40] He also ordered his officers to attend the "FSSF officer school," which was held after regular training, to further enhance their knowledge and leadership skills.[41]

In addition, FSSF HQ issued periodic intelligence training memoranda that provided officers with the latest information on enemy and allied forces tactics, equipment, and organization.[42] In turn, Frederick ordered his officers to provide briefs on designated material during the weekly "officers" conference. Lastly, during the entire course of this training phase, Frederick invited allied officers to share their recent operational and training experiences.

Aside from professionally developing his officer cadre, Frederick now implemented the new training syllabus. Demolition training now progressed from the theoretical to the practical. In order to maintain a high level of realism Frederick provided his men with an excellent selection of targets consisting of abandoned concrete and steel railway bridges, buildings, mines, and smoke stacks. The FSSF demolition teams attacked these targets with great, and perhaps excessive enthusiasm. "We blew up half the bridges and shanties around Helena," exclaimed Sergeant George Wright.[43] "Most of the guys got a little carried away with it, really," admitted Sergeant Walter Lewis. "They blew up bridges, culverts, and everything around Helena, Montana. Good God! I had never seen anything like it."[44]

Not surprisingly, this unbridled enthusiasm led to a few regrettable mistakes. "We blew up a bridge … it was the wrong bridge. We blew up an old mine … we got the wrong mine," chuckled Private Robert Minto. "We blew the hell out of everything out here."[45] By the time the smoke cleared, there was nothing left save for giant craters, twisted steel, and shattered concrete. In certain cases, the blasts were so powerful that structural damage was caused to homes and windows in the adjacent town of Libby.[46] Later, Fredrick conceded that his exuberant Forcemen really "messed up part of Montana."[47]

As explosions continued to echo around Helena, other Force members began their M-1 Garand rifle training. Lieutenant-Colonel Williamson explained why the Force switched over to this new weapon. "The M-1 rifle has been substituted for the carbine throughout the combat force," reported Williamson. "This is felt to be a wise decision," he explained, "as it is much superior in range, hitting power, and proven ability to 'take it.' Also, it simplifies the ammunition supply."[48] The men agreed with the choice. They preferred the M-1 to the previous .30-calibre carbine. Peter Cottingham described this new weapon's superiority:

> These weapons we were issued with were all developed in the twentieth century unlike the old Lee-Enfield rifle that I carried in the Canadian Army. We were armed with the M1 Garand .30 caliber rifles which were semi-automatic and held a clip of eight bullets. It was an ideal combat weapon. All one had to do to fire it was to work the bolt to put the first round in the chamber and then squeeze the trigger. When the eighth round was fired the empty clip went flying into the air leaving the action open for you to insert the next clip with one swift movement.[49]

Notwithstanding the M-1's high rate of fire, Herb Peppard explained that properly aiming this weapon took some practice to maximize its lethal effect:

> In the Canadian Army we'd use only open sights, whereas the Garand had a peep-sight on the back — a flat piece of metal with a pinhole in it. You looked through the hole, lined the front sight on target, and fired.

OF COURAGE AND DETERMINATION

We trained by firing at targets at close range and moving them back as our accuracy improved. [50]

A bayonet could also be affixed to this weapon. Hence, Pat O'Neill was asked to expand his hand-to-hand combat courses to include bayonet training, as well as the proper handling of the recently received V-2 fighting knives.[51]

As the Forcemen continued to familiarize themselves with their new expanded arsenal, they also spent long hours on various weapon ranges to practice individual and group, day and night, firing drills, as well as anti-aircraft firing training. Since the Force now had to operate in an assault infantry role Frederick invited Captain I.H. Martin, chief instructor of the Canadian Battle Drill School in Vernon, British Columbia, to enhance the fire and movement tactics of FSSF subunits. [52] Martin and his staff gave a series of lectures and demonstrations on platoon and section level principles of fire and movement, which, in the Canadian Army, were referred to as "Battle Drill." The aim of this training was to accelerate the tempo of necessary action through the rapid execution of terse orders, based on practiced drills that are designed to address tactical problems.[53] Captain Adna U. Underhill, an American FSSF officer, described the Battle Drill demonstrations:

Chemical warfare training.

> The Canadians were understandably proud of this exercise which started out as a parade ground manoeuver of stylized flankings and turnings, but was based on the principle of covering fire and movement to take an objective. These could vary from machine gun nest to house-to-house fighting. As the basic concepts were learned, the training was moved to various designated field targets, and live ammunition employed.[54]

With the elaboration of these subunit tactics, live fire exercises were now also conducted to teach the men how to master their reactions under fire while manoeuvring in an organized manner toward their objectives. "We had to go through a ditch and under barbwire," recalled Lloyd Dunlop, "while live rounds were fired over our heads."[55] As the men became more comfortable, "the instructors then installed trip flares to set off small explosions," added Sergeant Wright. "This gave you a good idea," explained the veteran, "as to what to expect when you were fired upon."[56]

During the course of these field exercises time was also allocated to mountain climbing. Each Forceman was taught to climb steep escarpments using ropes, pitons, latches, and picks. Initially, many found this training intimidating. "It was scary, and a lot of fellows were petrified," revealed Dunlop. "However, we all parachuted, so after a while we got used to it," explained the veteran.[57] "The 'hairy' part of mountain climbing was in the scaling of almost vertical rock faces," added Cottingham.[58]

The elements added to the challenge. "It was November and pretty cold," recalled Eugene Forward. "I got about half way up and my fingers became numb. Ice had formed in all the cracks and crevices that you had to grab on to," recalled Forward.[59] As the men familiarized themselves with these techniques they were then taught to climb in groups of three or four using the same scaling rope. Unbeknownst to the Force, this training would pay great dividends during the assault of Mount La Difensa, in Italy, the following year.

As Forcemen perfected their mountaineering skills, Frederick sent a request to NDHQ for another 117 men to bring the Canadian contingent in line with the new FSSF Tables of Organization. Thus, the 2nd Canadian Parachute Battalion grew from 583 to 700 men.[60] With time running out NDHQ authorized that these men be selected from the 1st Canadian Parachute Battalion, which was currently training in Fort Benning, Georgia.

Captain Becket was immediately tasked by Frederick to visit this unit and recruit volunteers. A total of 97 paratroopers transferred to the FSSF and arrived on 10 December 1942. They were sent to the FSSF training battalion to undergo parachute and individual training .Afterward, they underwent ski and winter warfare instruction. Once qualified, the new Forcemen were integrated throughout the three regiments.

As well, during December, the FSSF was once again visited by AFG HQ to re-assess its operational readiness. The follow-up report revealed that the methods of instruction and the officer's command and control during field exercises had improved. However, room for improvement remained according to the reviewing officer:

> In general,… the training was energetic and determined. Physical condition of the force was excellent. All ranks seemed demolition conscious and were exceptionally well versed in that training phase. On the other hand, the training program is too broad and the instruction too general. Not enough attention is devoted to the perfection of details. Corrections

OF COURAGE AND DETERMINATION

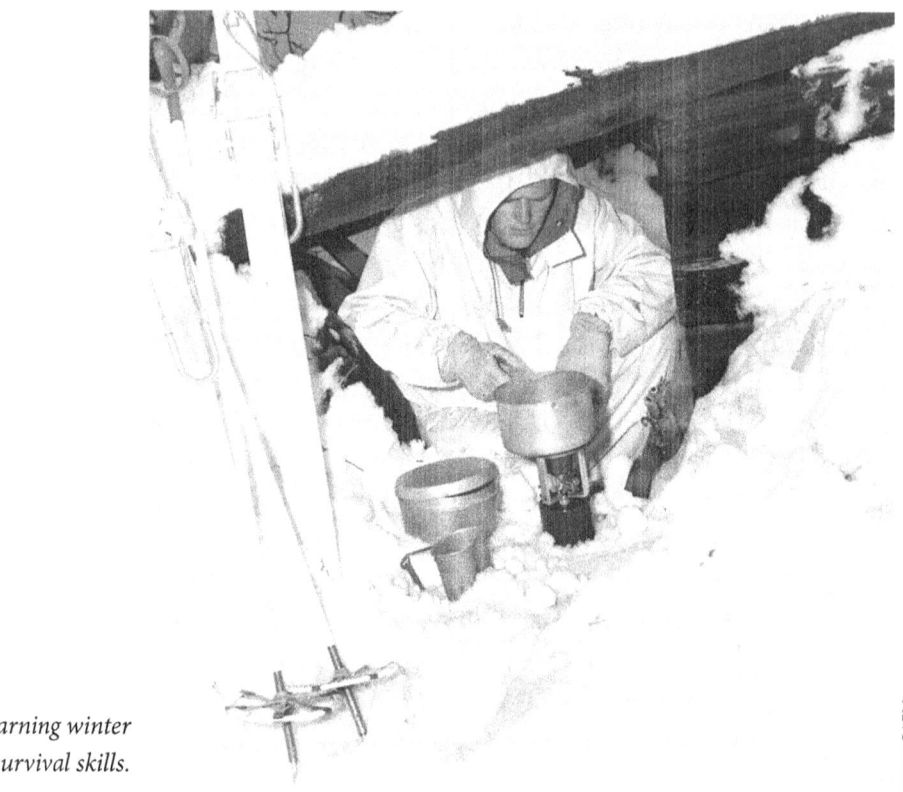

Learning winter survival skills.

of errors in training by instructors were too few. The latter indicates a need for more detailed training of junior officers. The tactics of the special vehicle (T-15) must be developed and more emphasis placed on security. In this connection, thought should be given to protection against enemy ski patrols and sentry dogs. Enthusiasm and morale of both officers and men were excellent.[61]

The FSSF commander found it difficult to accept comments from personnel who had never trained at such an intense and demanding level. Nevertheless, Frederick continued with his pre-established training schedule hoping for a quick deployment.[62]

As the reviewing officers returned to Washington, Frederick granted his Forcemen an eight day leave, by regiment, on a rotational basis. They had worked hard. Now, with deployment not far away, he wanted his men rested.

One area where Frederick remained concerned was ski training because a high percentage of his Americans had never seen snow. He hoped that the Norwegian ski instructors would quash his concerns. It didn't help that all personnel had to be qualified by 3 January 1943. To address this concern, during the second week of December, the men were sent, by battalion, to Blossburg, in Powell County, Montana, which sits at an elevation of 2,133 metres on the western slope of the continental divide.

WITHOUT HESITATION

The weather tested the Forcemen's endurance. Temperatures ranged from minus 28 to minus 42 degrees Celsius. Thankfully, the arctic clothing and equipment protected the men from the bitter cold and high winds. The living quarters were rudimentary, forcing the men to use their initiative and training to keep warm and comfortable. The quarters consisted of 26 boxcars with bunk beds and two small stoves, one at each end. Breakfast was prepared in two kitchen cars and was served at 0730 hours. Lunch consisted of a sandwich, apple, or orange. "You'd carry your lunch inside your parka," recalled Peter Smith, "so that it wouldn't freeze up."[63] The men then trained until 1700 hours and raced back to their base before dark for the evening meal.

Braving the elements, the Forcemen watched their Norwegian instructors demonstrate the proper use of equipment, as well as technique. After a few hours of practice, the men were ordered to form up in groups, shoulder their backpacks, secure their weapons, and follow the instructors. Throughout the training, the instructors stressed the tactical importance of effective trail discipline. Peter Smith recounted:

> They taught us to travel 200 to 300 men across a trail. They insisted that you plant your ski poles in the very same hole made by the men in front of you. Consequently, anybody that followed you wouldn't know if 25 or 400 men went by. There was just one set of tracks.[64]

As the men became more comfortable with the basic ski drills, the instructors increased the cadence. They also took them through forests to practice their mobility skills in confined areas. This training was followed be sessions devoted to climbing and descending various slopes. Initially, the descents proved to be the most difficult part of the training. After the first attempts, one of the Norwegian instructors shook his head and told the Forcemen, "When you're going downhill I don't think the enemy will have to catch you because you'll be hung up in trees, briers, and bushes."[65]

Despite numerous falls and crashes, the stubborn Forcemen gradually mastered their "torture boards." As the confidence level increased, the instructors initiated the men to the intricacies of downhill fire and movement drills. "We'd practice skiing downhill and dropping to firing positions," explained George Wright. "This was difficult because you had to position your skis flat of the ground, and with our heavy pack you had to find a way to get up quickly."[66] Once this drill was mastered, the instructors devised fire and movement scenarios. Peter Smith recollected:

> If you had a hill that wasn't too high they turned you around and had us practice advancing and fire support. We'd come down the hill in waves of 10 to 15 men. Then you heard a shot, you'd go into a flop position face first into snow and adopted a firing position. Then the next wave came in behind you and cover you, then you'd get up and race down the hill.[67]

Exercises were then expanded to incorporate the T-15 Weasels. Men and snow-vehicle crews co-ordinated their movements to practice hit and run raids. By the end of the week, the great majority of the Forcemen glided over the Montana snow and navigated with ease through the varied terrain. Captain Burhans was very pleased with the results. He reported, "The results amazed the Norwegian instructors. Captain Kiil's [officer commanding the Norwegian ski instructors] report at the end of February stated that in two week's training time 99 percent of the Force were competent skiers by Norwegian Army standards."[68]

Mountain warfare training.

Concurrently during the first three months of 1943, day and night exercises increased with the onus placed on closely monitoring combat leadership of the platoon officers. Furthermore, proficiency tests were conducted regularly to identify and correct shortcomings. As training wrapped up in March 1943, Lieutenant-Colonel Williamson met with his officers to discuss their concerns regarding what had transpired during the past few months. The main frustration centered on the fact that not many Canadian ideas pertaining to training had been adopted by the FSSF. Regrettably, this was the reality.[69] Despite the apparent indifference to Canadian training ideas, the Canadian personnel were treated well and those who showed leadership potential were promoted. In fact, on 18 March 1943, 98 Canadians were promoted to the rank of Sergeant.[70]

Then, suddenly, on 30 March 1943, Colonel Paul D. Adams, the FSSF executive officer, announced that all training was suspended. Moreover, the FSSF was ordered to relocate to another training facility. And so, as the last pieces of equipment were crated for transport, it was time to bid farewell to the citizens of Helena. On 6 April, outfitted in their dress uniforms, the impressive-looking Forcemen paraded through the downtown before cheering crowds. Many were sad to see the FSSF leave. Nevertheless, a strong bond remained between the citizens of Helena and the Forcemen. As this new reality sunk in, priests and ministers were kept very busy. Prior to leaving Helena, over 200 Forcemen married local girls. Then, on 11 April 1943, the FSSF entrained and headed for Camp Bradford Navy Operations Base (NOB), Norfolk, Virginia.

Once settled in, the FSSF commenced exhaustive amphibious training. The first part of their regimen entailed a series of basic courses (e.g., rubber boats handling, scaling nets), which the Forcemen were able to complete ahead of schedule. They then proceeded to the next phase, which entailed boarding transport vessels at sea. Once briefed on the necessary drills the men took part in a series of day and night amphibious training exercises. These were conducted by the U.S. Navy, onboard the USS *Thomas Jefferson* over a 12-day period off Solomon's Island in Maryland. The aim was simply to practice, in a tactical setting, all the necessary drills to conduct an amphibious landing from a naval transport ship. As such, the Forcemen had to scale nets, load vessels, navigate, and approach the shoreline in rubber boats and landing craft. Upon reaching the shoreline the men disembarked, reconnoitered the assigned landing zones, scaled cliffs, confirmed targets, and laid the required demolition charges. Once the targets were neutralized the Forcemen withdrew, paddled back to the transport ship and re-embarked.

It was during one of these night loading exercises (transferring personnel from transports ships via scaling net into awaiting assault craft) that the Force set a new record. A proud Burhans reported:

> The night loadings are the real test. The best Army division averaged about one minute per platoon load from the first man over to the time the boats pulled away. Of course, the Marines did it in about 52 seconds. That's the best we've ever seen … The Third Regiment … from the word go [did it in] exactly 33 seconds.[71]

Upon their return to port the Navy trainers reported that the FSSF was qualified to take part in amphibious operations. Frederick was very proud of his men's performance and rewarded their efforts. During a base parade presided over by Rear-Admiral Alan G. Kirk, commander of amphibious training of the Atlantic, Colonel Fredrick unveiled the FSSF's new colours. The 2nd Canadian Parachute Battalion's war diary chronicler provided a description:

> The Force colours made their first appearance, a good looking flag red background, a spread eagle in the centre with a shield on its chest with a dagger on it. One claw clutches an olive branch, the other a number of arrows. A ribbon underneath with [the words] the First Special Service Force, another in the eagle's beak for the Force motto when decided upon.[72]

Now that the amphibious training had been completed, extra time was allotted to practice swimming and rubber boat navigation, as well as to conduct a number of forced marches. On 19 May 1943, orders were issued to pack and move out the following day. The FSSF's next destination was Fort Ethan Allen, in Vermont.

Four days later, the Forcemen arrived and familiarized themselves with their new surroundings. Once again, a new training syllabus was introduced. Fredrick directed all

Blending into the environment.

regiments to review previous training and conduct exercises in order to reach the highest possible state of readiness for combat as an assault force.[73] As the men practiced their raiding tactics in the surrounding countryside, Fredrick and Williamson left for Ottawa and met with senior NDHQ officers, the CGS, and Prime Minister MacKenzie King to finalize details related to the 2nd Canadian Parachute Battalion's impending deployment.[74] Upon his return on 27 May 1943, Lieutenant-Colonel Williamson met with his officers and apprised them of the latest administrative developments. He also announced that the battalion now had a new unit designation — The First Canadian Special Service Battalion (1 CSSBN).[75]

During their sojourn at Fort Ethan Allen, the Force was visited, on several occasions, by 13th Corps inspectors to confirm the FSSF's combat readiness. The visiting officers observed that there had been noticeable improvements in command and control. Moreover, they reported that unit at all levels operated with a high degree of effectiveness and demonstrated great cohesion, particularly in exercises that were extremely realistic from an operational perspective. The AGF HQ inspectors concluded, "Yes, the First Special Service Force was ready for any job that had to be done."[76]

WITHOUT HESITATION

Despite these positive assessments, the Forcemen became increasingly frustrated. They wanted to see action. Sensing this growing dissatisfaction, Frederick met with his officers on 28 May 1943 and cleared the air. The war diary chronicler provided a synopsis of Frederick's address:

> Colonel Frederick explained the reason for the many changes in training had been the changing of the mission for the Force. He said that one day in Washington within 14 hours the Force had been assigned to 6 different missions. At present the Force was not assigned to any mission but it was sufficiently trained that it must expect to be alerted at any time and leave with little notice.[77]

Despite their frustration, deep down, they all knew that it was only a matter of time before the Force would be deployed. That day finally came.

Initially, the Force was to be sent to the U.K. and await further orders. Frederick then received new orders directing that the FSSF be sent to San Francisco. For the moment, all he knew was that the Force had been selected for an upcoming operation with the U.S. Navy somewhere in the northern waters in the vicinity of Alaska. Due to these new developments, on 14 June 1943, Major-General Pope sent a letter to Lieutenant-Colonel

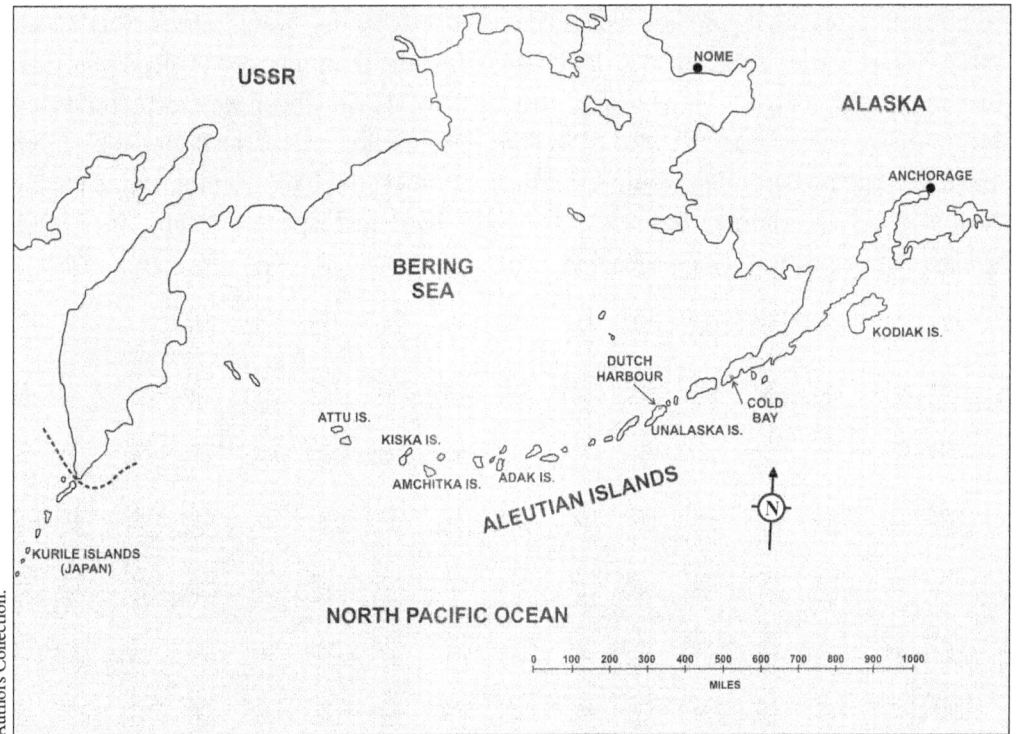

The Aleutian Islands.

Williamson informing him that the Canadian government had approved the deployment of 1 CSSBN as part of the FSSF to the Aleutians.[78]

The Aleutians were a chain of 300 volcanic islands extending over 1,900 kilometres from the Alaskan Peninsula to the Kamchatka Peninsula. Since 1942, Japanese forces occupied and fortified a few of these islands. After nearly a year of sustained U.S. ground, naval, and air operations in the Aleutians, the American government decided it was time to oust the Japanese invaders. However, for security reasons the exact location of the operation was not revealed to the FSSF.

Regardless, the jubilant Forcemen left Fort Ethan Allen on 28 June and arrived a few days later in San Francisco. There the FSSF joined other American units selected for the operation. A total of 32,000 men had been assembled to be part of General Charles Corlett's Amphibious Training Force No. 9 (ATF 9). Force personnel were immediately ferried to Camp McDowell located on Angel Island, near Alcatraz. While FSSF officers attended a series of restricted briefings, the men underwent medical exams and equipment checks, and were issued with cold weather and waterproof clothing. After being refitted the Force personnel were ferried to Pier 41 San Francisco and embarked on two Liberty ships, the SS *John B. Floyd* and SS *Nathaniel Wyeth*. On 11 July, these two ships and five other transports and four destroyers weighed anchor, passed under the Golden Gate Bridge, and headed out to sea.

Confined within the cramped living quarters the men soon battled bouts of seasickness. For the moment, the indisposed Forcemen hoped that they would survive this hellish cruise.[79] During the voyage the ATF 9's mission was finally announced to all combatants. They were tasked to take and neutralize Kiska Island. U.S. intelligence reports confirmed that this barren island was defended by well-entrenched elements of the Imperial Japanese Army. Finally, the Forcemen would see if their 11 months of hard training would enable them to match the vaunted prowess of the battle-hardened Japanese troops. The FSSF's baptism of fire was quickly approaching.

9

KISKA:
The Battle That Never Was

The guys hated Kiska. We always said that if the world needed an enema, than Kiska would be the ideal place to do it. It was so desolate. There wasn't one soul living there.[1]

— Peter Smith

As the days at sea passed, the Forcemen began to develop their sea legs. It took a few days, but the members of the FSSF overcome their seasickness, adapted to the continuous motion of the ship, and began to regain their strength. Moreover, circumstances dictated that they start focusing on their new mission. As such, the Force leadership cadre began attending daily briefings regarding Kiska.[2] They received reference material and maps to brief their men on such matters as Japanese forces, doctrine, and tactics, as well as Kiska's climate and terrain, and how to live and operate in the inhospitable and harsh Aleutian environment.

The Forcemen were also brought up to date on Japanese operations in the Pacific and specifically, in the Aleutians. Following the string of Japanese victories early in the war in Malaya, Siam, the Gilbert Islands, the Philippines, Burma, Hong Kong, Dutch East Indies, and North Borneo, the Japanese high command set its sights on the Aleutians. On 3 June 1942, Japanese air, ground, and naval forces attacked Dutch Harbour and landed on Adak. Three days later, they seized the islands of Attu and Kiska. The Japanese intent was to use Aleutians, as well as Midway Island, which they thought they would soon capture, to strengthen their defensive perimeter in the northern and central Pacific.[3] They also hoped these operations would draw the American fleet out of Pearl Harbour to protect the vulnerable American western Pacific. With this goal in mind, Admiral Isoroku Yamamoto deployed his fleet to intercept the U.S. Pacific fleet at Midway Island where he planned to destroy it.

OF COURAGE AND DETERMINATION

However, the battle proved to be a disaster for the Japanese.[4] The American victory at Midway on 7 June 1942, marked the shift in initiative. The Allies had finally contained the aggressive Japanese expansion. In turn, they launched a series of operations to reclaim the Pacific. Over the course of the following months as major land, air, and naval battles were being fought throughout the Pacific theatre, American forces also turned their attention to the Aleutians.

On 10 May 1943, the Americans stormed Attu Island. After 20 days of ferocious fighting U.S. troops finally wrested control of the island from the Japanese. But, the losses had been heavy. The Japanese had fought with a fanaticism that was incomprehensible to the American soldiers. If this was a sign of things to come, then the American planners knew that the upcoming Kiska operations would also prove very costly. Moreover, the terrain on Kiska provided the enemy with an abundance of natural concealment for their defensive positions. The island was 35 kilometres long and 10 kilometres wide. It featured many steep ridgelines at elevations of 365 to 520 metres, valleys, caves, lakes, streams, swamps, and dangerous coves. Vegetation consisted solely of long grasses, muskeg, and marshes. Furthermore, high winds, dense fogs, and heavy rains cloaked the enemy's activities, movements, and defensive positions.

As well, while the Japanese focused their efforts on defending the eastern coastline, most of Kiska's Bering Sea coastline, including beaches, located on the western side of the island, were dominated by steep 15- to 60-metre rock bluffs.[5] Thus, in order to offset heavy casualties, the Americans used every asset at their disposal to isolate the estimated 9,000-man Japanese garrison.[6] They ensured that Kiska would be cut off from the rest of the world.

Therefore, as of January 1943, elements of the U.S. Navy blockaded Kiska, while aircraft from the 11th U.S. Air Force and a number of U.S. destroyers bombarded Kiska and Little Kiska daily. As tons of ordnance were dropped on these two islands, Admiral Thomas C. Kincaid, U.S. Navy senior commander of the Kiska operation, awaited the arrival of ATF 9 to join up with the other ground forces designated to assault the enemy stronghold.[7]

As Japanese defenders withstood the continual heavy shelling, Frederick landed in Alaska and awaited the arrival of ATF 9. On 16 July, Frederick flew to Adak to inspect the FSSF's designated bivouac, as well as training areas. The FSSF commander was not pleased with what he was shown. First, the Force was completely separated from the other troops, who were all based on the other side of the island. This complicated communication and training co-ordination. Second, he deemed the proposed ATF 9 echelon support and supply system to equip and feed his troops to be inadequate. Third, Frederick did not agree with Corlett's proposal to have his men living in basic shelter tents. The Force commander knew that the upcoming operations would be gruelling. For this reason, he did not want his men to endure any unnecessary hardships or be sidelined due to illnesses or non-combat related injuries.

Last, Frederick could not justify wasting time and energy on building this bivouac, especially since the Force would be relocated to Amchitka within the following two weeks.

KISKA

Home is where you dig it — Amchitka.

Frederick believed that the FSSF's time would be better spent on training and learning how to operate in this harsh climate and terrain. So, the he sent a message to Corlett requesting that the Force set up its bivouac in Amchitka. This was quickly approved.

As Frederick finalized the new bivouac arrangements for the FSSF, the convoy transporting the Force dropped anchor, late in the evening of 22 July, in Kuluk Bay off Adak. Frederick boarded the SS *John B. Floyd* and briefed his officers of the 2nd Regiment and Service Battalion on the latest developments. Early next morning Fredrick went to the SS *Nathaniel Wyeth* and briefed the officers of 1st and 3rd Regiments. Two days later, the ships sailed for Amchitka, located 115 kilometres southeast of Kiska.

After 13 days at sea, the men were eager to disembark and start training. Loaded with 32 kilograms of equipment the Forcemen slogged through eight kilometres of marshy tundra. Captain Underhill remembered the trek:

> The last half mile, they cut across the beautiful green landscape. It took only 30 seconds to discover that it was beautiful to the eye only. Every step broke through the crust and plunged the strider into from six inches to a foot and a half of mud and water. The nearly two weeks of relative inactivity on ship board took their toll; everyone was puffing and sweating as they struggled to pull their feet from the sucking muskeg.[8]

OF COURAGE AND DETERMINATION

During the next forty-eight hours, the men struggled to set up the Force's bivouac. However, the inhospitable climate and terrain complicated this simple task. Thick fog rolled in enveloping, for hours on end, both men and equipment. Moreover, within the first hour everything was wet.[9] The men dug through thick layers of waterlogged muskeg hoping to reach a solid base on which they could erect their pyramidal tents. The Forcemen hoped that these excavations and the surrounding muskeg walls would shield the tents from the high winds and provide some protection in case of air attacks. While the men shovelled piles of muck, others prepared and manned a series of defensive positions and patrolled the bivouac's perimeter. "The fox holes so laboriously dug," explained the discouraged Captain Underhill, "were almost immediately half full of water."[10] Meanwhile, back at the beachhead, bulldozers graded beaches and a network of roads. Shortly after transport vehicles began hauling ammunition, equipment, supplies, and weapons to various holding areas. For the moment, items such as kitchen equipment and rations had to wait. This fact was not missed by the 1 CSSBN war diary, which captured that on their first day in Amchitka the Forcemen, "went to bed late and hungry."[11]

As the Forcemen finished their bivouac, they could hear, in the distance, U.S. fighters, bombers, and ships pummelling Japanese positions on Kiska. "Although the air forces have been active and have dropped a large quantity of bombs," pointed out Frederick, "they actually caused very little important damage." From aerial photo analysis and intelligence reports, the FSSF commander noted that "the bombing has been very inaccurate and the bombing through the overcast has been mere guess work, apparently with little effect."[12]

While the apparent ineffectiveness of the air strikes disappointed Frederick, they nevertheless sapped Japanese morale. Private Takahashi revealed:

> It's unbearable day after day. I think it would be grand if our fleet would hurry and land. I am going mad. Everyone is exhausted from their terrific bombing.[13]

And, as the Japanese garrison was continually pummelled American planners carefully analyzed the battle on Attu in an attempt to limit casualties in the upcoming fight.[14] The enemy's warrior code, which seemingly translated into a fanatical resolve to fight to the last man astounded the members of the FSSF.[15] A concerned Herb Peppard stated:

> [T]he Americans had taken Attu, the outermost island. The bad news was that only 31 of the 2,300 Japanese defending the island had been taken prisoner. The rest had either fought to the death or committed suicide! I was shocked and incredulous. What kind of people would [we] be fighting? Death seemed to hold no terror for them. In fact, it seemed that they welcomed it. This was against all my principles. My main objective in life was to stay alive. My morale plummeted at the news.[16]

KISKA

It was not lost on the Forcemen — they all knew that they would be in for one hell of a fight. "Now we were going against the real big boys" exclaimed Vern Doucette.[17] Pat O'Neill, the FSSF hand-to-hand combat instructor, who had spent many years in Japan, provided the Forcemen with his insights regarding their adversaries. "I've told you right along that the Japs are good soldiers. They've been at it for years, and they're tough," explained the officer. However, O'Neill reassured them that "our skills will be tested when we come up against those little men, but I think you can take them."[18] Regardless, all hoped that the daily bombing runs would inflict heavy losses on the enemy.

With the impending battle not far off, Frederick put in place a 10-day (5 to 14 August 1943), 12-hour day, customized invasion training regimen designed to prepare the force to meet both the anticipated enemy defences and tactics, as well as the topographical conditions.[19] However, the inhospitable Aleutian environment presented a series of daunting challenges. "The nights were really dark," recalled Jack Martin, "and you had nothing to let you know where you were or what direction you were going, so night patrol was a real challenge."[20] Forced marches were trying and exhausting. "Marching in the gumbo was extremely difficult," explained Lieutenant Mitchell, "as every step put you six inches into the stuff and released a swarm of mosquitoes; if we could make 5 miles a day, it was good."[21]

The angry sea also tested the men's resolve. During a beach landing exercise, a naval crew dropped the ramp too early. Surprised Forcemen fell into the icy heaving waves

Members of the 2nd Regiment on standby at the Amchitka airfield.

and some lost their weapons. Furthermore, frustrated Forcemen toiled to paddle, control, and manoeuvre their rubbers boats through these rough waters.[22] Adding to their misery were dangerous net-scaling debarkation drills. Herb Peppard recollected one hair-raising experience:

> [N]othing prepared me for the Aleutians, where the gigantic ocean swells around Amchitka Island made the manoeuvre very dangerous. It was a nightmare for me to reach the bottom of the rope ladder and find that the landing craft had fallen fifteen or twenty feet lower. I had many black-and-blue marks to prove the pain of it.[23]

The men quickly learned to adapt to their new surroundings. Greatly assisting the adaptation was the issue of additional warm and waterproofed clothing and footwear. More important, the quality of meals greatly improved. "Fresh eggs and meat made their first appearance [1 August]," reported the war diary chronicler. "Fried eggs for breakfast and beef steak at noon, a welcome change from dried and canned food."[24] Morale was on the upswing while stamina increased.

As the men trained, Frederick noted key deficiencies and continuing problems. As such, he ordered additional training to:

A. Increase ability for sustained operations in the field under adverse conditions;
B. Increase ability to operate over terrain typical of this locality;
C. Improve combat firing techniques;
D. Improve amphibious techniques.[25]

As the Forcemen continued to hone their skills Frederick's regimental commanders were being briefed on the latest intelligence. They quickly noticed that it appeared that enemy activities in the main camp, the harbour area, and the airfield near the Salmon Lagoon, seemed to have slowed down considerably from the earlier reports.

American intelligence officers continued to collect and analyze information during the course of the following days. Strangely, the latest data now revealed that many buildings had been disassembled, vehicles stripped and burnt, and certain gun batteries appeared to be covered.[26] A report dated 5 August 1943, stated that aircraft drew "sporadic small arms fire which varied from light to intense."[27] Despite this inexplicable lull in enemy activity, intelligence staff did nothing to further explore this new development.[28]

Frederick, however, refused to remain idle. The FSSF commander requested that reconnaissance teams be inserted into Kiska and obtain addition information regarding this strange situation. His request was denied. His commanders feared that if the patrols were captured they would compromise the invasion plans.[29] Instead, Fredrick was advised

KISKA

that a detachment of Alaskan scouts would be attached to the FSSF to assist the Forcemen with reconnaissance tasks following their landing.[30]

As the invasion date approached, General Corlett assembled all ATF 9 subordinate commanders. Frederick quickly used the co-ordination session to point out the poorly chosen exposed landing site for the 3rd Regiment. The latest aerial photographs revealed that the shoreline in the vicinity of Witchcraft Point, where the FSSF's 3rd Regiment was earmarked to land, was, in fact, very steep. Furthermore, on the high ground overlooking the beach there were foxholes, light automatic weapon positions, as well as possible Japanese anti-aircraft batteries on Robber Hill.[31] Frederick subsequently requested that the 3rd Regiment's landing site be changed to the left of their initial landing site on the shoreline directly in front of West Kiska Lake. General Corlett approved the recommendation.[32]

Finally, on 7 August 1943, Frederick received his invasion orders detailing the role of the FSSF in Operation Cottage.[33] The Force would be part of Landing Force 16.8.[34] Each of the three regiments was given a specific mission. More important, two of the three regiments were tasked to be the advance assault landing groups of the invasion force. "D-Day" was slated for 15/16 August 1943.

Kiska was divided into two operational sectors: north and south.[35] The FSSF 1st Regiment would operate in the southern sector under Colonel Edwin M. Sutherland. The 3rd Regiment

The seven-man, Landing Craft Rubber, Small (LCR[S]) used by the Force.

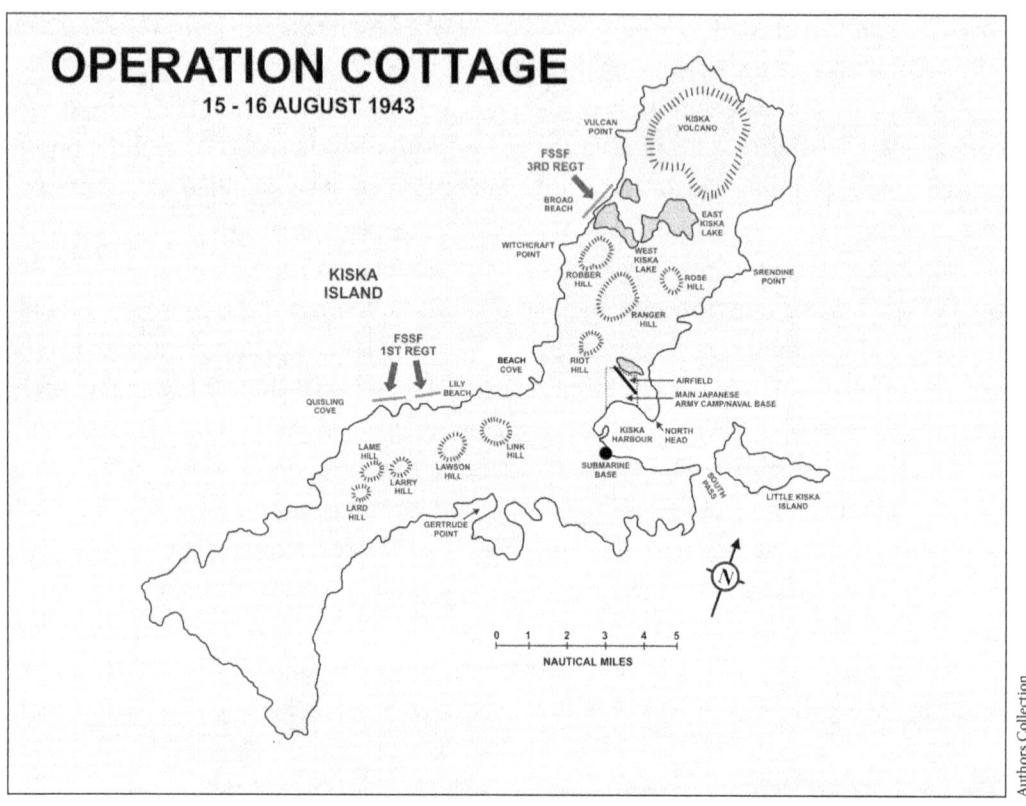

would operate in the northern sector under the command of Brigadier-General Joseph L. Ready, assistant commanding general of ATF 9. Depending on the operational developments following the landings of the 1st and 3rd Regiments, the 2nd Regiment was given two possible missions to be executed on order. First, the regiment was to remain in Amchitka as the FSSF airborne/seaborne standby reinforcement component. Second, if the main invasion forces did not need to be reinforced, then the 2nd Regiment was tasked to land on Little Kiska either by air or sea and destroy all enemy installations.[36]

So, as regimental commanders finalized their planning, FSSF personnel of all three regiments reported on 13 and 14 August to their respective assembly areas. There, the Forcemen checked their weapons and equipment and drew sufficient ammunition and rations to operate independently for a 24-hour period. "They gave us an allotment of ammunition," declared Vernon Doucette, "and we took half as much again. We were scared that the Japanese would come at us with Banzai charges."[37]

The men of the 1st Regiment would be the first ATF 9 troops to land on Kiska. In order to enable 1st Regiment to simultaneously accomplish all three of its objectives the regiment was reorganized, for this operation, into three battalions. The new provisional battalion, under the command of Lieutenant-Colonel Alfred C. Marshall, comprised the 1st Regiment's headquarters, the 1st and 4th Companies, and Air-Ground Liaison Team 184-1. The provisional battalion's objective was to land in the Quisling Cove and Lulu Hill

KISKA

area and then seize and defend Larry Hill. Subsequently, 1st Battalion, 1st Regiment (less 1st Company) along with Air-Ground Liaison Team 87–2, Artillery Forward Observer Party from Battery B, 601st FA, and attached Alaskan scouts would also land in Quisling Cove and secure Lame and Lard Hills. Lastly, 2nd Battalion, 1st Regiment (less 4th Company), and Air-Ground Liaison Team 87–3, Artillery Forward Observer Party from Battery C, 601st FA, and attached Alaskan scouts would land on Lilly Beach and secure Link Hill. Once all objectives and adjacent high ground was secured then the main invasion group could land unhindered.[38]

Then, finally on 14 August 1943, the 1st Regiment embarked on the destroyer USS *Kane* and a landing ship, tank (LST). Under the cover of darkness the ships sailed to their assembly area parallel to Beaches 9 Blue, 9 Yellow (Quisling Cove), and 10 Scarlet (Lily Beach) located on the western side of the island.

While the Forcemen of the southern sector's two advance-landing groups waited for the final order to leave, they decided to relieve the tension by playing craps. One chief petty officer could not believe his eyes:

> We've ferried a lot of people on a lot of invasions, and mostly the night before they write letters home or talk to their chaplains. But these crazy bastards[Forcemen]. Why, their officers had to go in and bust up their crap games when it came time to go ashore for the fight.[39]

Landing of main invasion force.

OF COURAGE AND DETERMINATION

At 0030 hours, 15 August 1943, at high tide, the two ships reached the designated assembly area. As the ships manoeuvred into their final disembarkation positions, Forcemen reflected on their upcoming baptism of fire. "We went through the full pre-invasion emotional spectrum," confided Don Ballantyne. "How will I react to enemy fire? How will I behave in combat?"[40] Upon the given signal, the 1st Regiment reported to their offloading stations. Under the cover of a thick fog the men, loaded down with between 31 and 45 kilograms of equipment and ammo, waited in total darkness as the LTS crew lowered the ramp. The Forcemen then dragged their rafts to the edge, got in and paddled out. Captain Becket recalled the difficulties encountered when leaving the LTS and embarking into the rubber boats:

> We had a rough time, and a wet time, in that sea as we disembarked one rubber boat at a time from the hanging and open bow of the LST [landing ship, tank]. We were endeavoring to form up so close to that pitching and rolling ship. With waves of some two to three feet and in almost total darkness it was not easy to manoeuvre those light rubber boats using paddles. The boat bobbed up and down and it took some twelve different infantrymen, acting as helmsmen to get their rubber boats beside the pitching ship so that their bowmen could grab the rope hanging alongside the ship then hang on to it. The ship and the tossing rubber boats were not going up and down at the same time nor for the same number of feet. Besides all this, the men in the boats had to receive and pass on to the boat behind, the other line[rope] that I was using to keep the battalion together as we went into the beach. But we did It! After some fifteen minutes of tossing about, soaking wet, we headed for shore and the Japs.[41]

Meanwhile, the ships of Landing Force Reserve located parallel to the 1st Regiment's position, but on the other side of the island, opened fire and feigned landing operations to distract Japanese defenders entrenched in the Gertrude Cove and Vega Bay areas, while other naval elements bombarded Little Kiska.[42] As the rounds crashed throughout the Gertrude Cove's shoreline, the 1st Regiment flotillas headed toward the landing sites. The men paddled hard for about 50 minutes and struggled to maintain their rubber boats in straight close columns.[43] Furthermore, the strong tide and wind now complicated matters. "Ice cold waves were breaking over the boat and there was a wind blowing against us," recollected Sam Barod.[44] The small craft were being pushed out to sea, forcing the frustrated men to paddle even harder. Suddenly, the clouds thinned out revealing a very bright moon. For a few moments, the men were fully exposed. Everyone froze. "Please God, push another cloud over it," prayed an anxious George Wright.[45] Within a few seconds clouds mercifully covered the moon.

KISKA

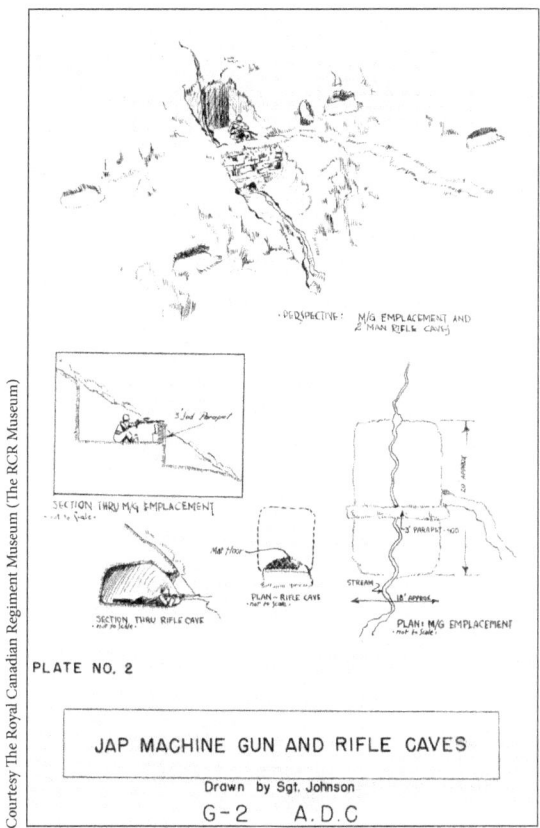

Intelligence graphics describing Japanese defences.

However, during this short nerve wracking instant, Captain Becket made the most out of this dangerous situation. "The sea lit up and suddenly we had amazing visibility," explained the officer, "enough to show me the volcanic peaks of my mountains objectives and moments later our tiny beach. I knew we were on the right course."[46] As the small flotilla approached the shoreline, heavy kelp which floated in abundance on the surface complicated the Forcemen's paddling and steering during the final hundred metres. Fortunately, the enemy had still not opened fire. The lead rafts finally nudged against the shoreline at 0120 hours. "It was an exciting moment," stated a relieved Becket.[47] "It was sure good to be on land," concurred Wright.[48]

As the first Forcemen disembarked quietly, 1st Battalion sent groups to mark the 9 Blue and 9 Yellow beaches in Quisling Cove and 10 Scarlet just north of Quisling Cove.[49] Concurrently, patrols were sent out on the western flank to reconnoitre and secure Lend Ridge. Other patrols were dispatched eastward to secure Lasso Hill and other high grounds overlooking the beaches. As the patrols advanced, an eerie silence prevailed. There was still no sign of the enemy. Once the immediate area around the beachhead was declared safe, the Alaskan scouts attached to the battalion disappeared quietly into the night to reconnoitre the ground prior to the Force's upcoming assault.

As the men of 1st Battalion prepared to move out of the beachhead area, 2nd Battalion completed the marking of Beach 10 Scarlet, located at the mouth of Lily Creek. Patrols were also sent eastward toward Lilac Hill and westward toward Lasso Hill. Concurrently, the 1st Regiment demolition team, headed by Lieutenant Dan Ryan, the Force's demolition instructor, laid charges throughout Beach 10 to clear rocks and obstructions to prepare landing lanes for the main invasion force.

Approximately one hour after the landing, the three battalions and attached personnel split up and moved inland toward their respective objectives. Under the cover of darkness, carrying heavy loads, the men inched their way through the high grasses and slowly ascended steep slopes in total darkness. "It was tough climbing due to the muskeg," recollected George Wright. "We didn't walk up, we crawled up. We were all wet."[50] Finally, the forward elements of 1st Regiment's three battalions reached the tops of Larry, Laird, Lawson, and Link Hills and Lame Hill Ridge. As they took up their positions, the next wave of Forcemen scaled the hills and navigated carefully along the treacherous ridgelines. Becket recalled the final moments of this dangerous ascent:

> The ridge that joined the peaks together and which we had to take to reach our furthest objective was unbelievably narrow — not more than two or three feet wide in most places. This meant that the Battalion had to proceed single file on that narrow ridge between Laird and Larry Hills. This would give us very little room to manoeuvre.[51]

When all defensive positions were consolidated, patrols were sent out, before first light, to probe the areas in front of 1st Regiment's position. As daylight broke, the Forcemen accelerated their advance and came across trails, caves, earthworks, and empty huts. These were checked carefully for booby traps and mines.[52] Again, there was still no sign of the Japanese defenders.

Meanwhile, back on Beach 10 the first explosions confirmed that demolition had commenced. Once completed, the FSSF HQ and Colonel Frederick came ashore after battling the receding tide. Shortly after, at 0630 hours, 15 August 1943, the main invasion force consisting of elements of the 87th Mountain Regiment, 17th Infantry Regiment, and other units came ashore. FSSF liaison personnel briefed the arriving troops and informed them of the absence of enemy forces. More important, they confirmed the locations of entrenched FSSF personnel with the hope of avoiding friendly fire incidents.[53] Nevertheless, elements of the main force were trigger-happy. Gunfire was heard throughout the day and night. A concerned Becket ordered his personnel to lie low and remain in their foxholes. "I was far from happy," related Becket, "I knew we were between a hard place and a rock — the nutsy 87th behind us and the Japs in front of us."[54]

Regardless of the number of troops now disembarking hourly, the Forcemen refused to let their guard down. They were still anticipating possible Japanese surprise attacks. As they scanned the landscape before them, landing craft shuttled from ships to shore unloading huge quantities of supplies. Bulldozers were then brought in to grade the holding areas to accommodate men, equipment, supplies, and vehicles.

Once the main force moved up to occupy the ridgelines and roads in the southern sector, Sutherland ordered his advance parties to move out in three directions: westward toward Lief Cove, eastward toward the Japanese naval base at Kiska Harbour, and southward in the direction of the enemy's installations on Gertrude Cove. During this advance the 2nd Regiment, still fogged in, waited impatiently on the Amchitka landing strip to attack Little Kiska.[55]

With the southern sector of Kiska Island now secured, Sutherland ordered the 1st Regiment to continue patrolling and to man its defensive positions. From all indications,

KISKA

Abandoned Japanese coastal gun.

it was now confirmed that the enemy had pulled out a few days before the landing. Little did the Americans know that during the night of 29 July 1943, Rear-Admiral Masatomi Kimura, commander of Imperial Destroyer Squadron One rescue fleet, slipped undetected by the American naval blockading force into Kiska Harbour.[56] The awaiting Japanese garrison quickly boarded the ships.[57] Leaving no one behind, Kimura then guided his ships out of the harbour and disappeared into the fog past the blockade. The Americans had been oblivious to this impeccably executed rescue mission.

As the Forcemen advanced through abandoned Japanese positions, it became increasingly obvious that the enemy had evacuated the island. One Forceman stated:

> After the beach was secured with the landing of the main force, we then moved from the ridge and searched for the Japanese, who had puzzlingly failed to show up. By that time the initial delight of having succeeded in making a surprise landing had turned into bewilderment. Where were they?[58]

Frustrated by this latest turn of events, Frederick sent a message to FSSF headquarters, "No yellow bastards in sight. Hoping for better hunting."[59] He then sent a message to Lieutenant-Colonel Williamson ordering the 2nd Regiment to stand down. Leaving the 1st Regiment behind on the island, Colonel Frederick and the FSSF HQ officers returned to the USS *Kane*. The FSSF commander now waited for the 3rd Regiment to land on the island's northern sector.

The following day, at 0000 hours, 16 August 1943, the second of the FSSF operational missions commenced. Under the command of Brigadier-General J.L. Ready, the FSSF 3rd Regiment, specifically, the 1st and 2nd Battalions, waited in silence in their respective LSTs to launch their rubbers boats.

As the small flotilla left the LST, the men felt as though they had been cursed. "Outside it was almost like daylight," recalled Lieutenant Mitchell, "and I thought that the Japs had lights on us, but it was the first clear moonlight that had occurred (so the meteorology section told us) in years."[60] The anxious Forcemen expected the enemy to open fire at any moment.[61] Regardless of this dire situation, there was no turning back. Following their prescribed battle procedures, each battalion aligned their rubber boats. Upon an agreed upon signal, the men paddled quickly, in formation, toward the rock blight separating the sea from West Kiska Lake. Upon nearing the shoreline, the men in the lead boats were stunned. They came up against huge granite boulders. "On this so called beach were rocks and boulders as big as my house," exclaimed a surprised Peter Smith. "They were white from seagull dirt that had accumulated there over many years. This is why they showed up as a beach on the aerial photographs."[62] Others such as Peter Kroll adopted a more philosophical approach regarding this latest SNAFU.

During our briefings, we were told that the beaches where we were supposed to land on were sandy beaches. They weren't and in a way I'm glad they weren't. It was all rock, so there was no way the Japanese could have mined it. If it had been sand, I don't think we could have gotten off the beach.[63]

Once again, the intelligence was wrong. However, this unexpected complication did not deter the Forcemen. The first rafts paddled along the boulders and eventually found an area where the rafts could be dragged over the rock to allow Forcemen to continue onto West Kiska Lake. Meanwhile a platoon was dispatched southward toward Witchcraft Point to mark the Broad Beach 14 Red and 14 Green for the main invasion force that comprised the Canadian 13th Brigade, the U.S. 184th Infantry Regiment, as well as other elements.[64]

Once the shoreline was secured, the Forcemen dragged their rubber boats and equipment over the boulders while the Alaskan scouts covered their flanks. "We had an awful time getting these fully loaded boats over these boulders and into Kiska Lake," recollected Lloyd Dunlop. "It was some struggle."[65] Gordon Baker was relieved that they were able to move away from these boulders and the ridgeline. "The Japanese had gone, fortunately, otherwise they would have mowed us down like hay," exclaimed the veteran. "The wall we crawled up," recalled Gordon "was honeycombed with holes the Japanese would have laid in and picked us off like flies."[66]

As the men organized their rafts on the West Kiska Lake shoreline, Major Thomas Gilday, CO of 1st Battalion, reminded all his officers and NCOs of the importance of

Abandoned Japanese equipment littered the island.

aggressive leadership and taking initiative in the event that the companies were separated and had to operate on their own. He stated:

> Do not wait for someone to tell you to do something you can do yourself. Keep your eyes out of your pockets. It is better to do something wrong than to do nothing. Control your men, lead them, guide them. You have received your orders use them as a guide, then use your head — it is a good one and I have every confidence in you and your men and know that decisions you make and will have to make on your own are the right ones. Don't be afraid to make them when the time comes.[67]

Upon the given signal, the men of 3rd Regiment embarked in their rubber rafts and paddled quickly on West Kiska Lake. They reached Robin Creek around 0300 hours. As the men abandoned their rafts, the Forcemen walked cautiously for another hour toward Ranger and Riot Hills. Once again, Kiska's geography challenged them. The Forcemen toiled with their heavy loads. Finally, they reached the top and occupied the high ground. "I was," exclaimed Sam Magee, "in tears at one point with the machine gun, climbing the hill. I was so exhausted. I was totally gone."[68] When the area was secured the 2nd Battalion, as well as the regimental command post, deployed to Ranger Hill. Once there, they extended the position to include Riot and Rose Hills. By first light, all objectives were captured without firing a shot. From their elevated positions, the Forcemen could observe the low ground in front of them. In the distance, one could make out the Japanese airstrip and harbour.

Despite an excellent landing and subsequent rapid deployment, the night operation proved mentally draining. The men had been on a constant state of alert, never knowing when Japanese soldiers would emerge from concealed positions. "We were told the Japs were very skilled and that they used spider holes dug into embankments," explained Sam Magee. "They would have a bamboo frame and they would live in there on water, rice and kelp and let you pass by and then slip behind you."[69] As a result, the Forcemen painstakingly scoured the areas between and around their defensive perimeters. At 0910 hours the first elements of the main force landed and made their way toward the forward positions of the 3rd Regiment.[70]

As the main force deployed throughout the northern sector, reconnaissance patrols inched their way toward the main Japanese positions located around Kiska Harbor. As the patrols approached their final objectives, measures were taken to ensure that they would not be mistaken for enemy personnel.[71] "When we walked near that base," explained Lloyd Dunlop, "we wore over our heads orange coloured mats. They were a couple of feet square. We put these on," explained the veteran, "so that our planes would recognize us as American soldiers."[72]

FSSF patrols reached the outskirts of the abandoned main Japanese Army camp overlooking Kiska Harbour around 1000 hours. During the final approach, "the guys were keyed. They were ready and anxious," reminisced Mann. "However, when we heard that nobody was home, everything fell apart." [73] It was a desolate scene. "There were damaged small submarines and aircraft," described Eugene Forward. "In other places there were abandoned artillery pieces, machine guns and loads of rifles."[74] Bomb craters, debris, damaged buildings, and equipment were the only remaining reminders of the Japanese occupation.[75] One Forcemen described the abandoned enemy positions. "In deserted dugouts we saw clothes hung on walls and even bits of food in plates on the tables; food that hadn't yet begun to mildew and looked as though it hadn't been set out for many hours."[76]

Despite the absence of enemy forces, the Forcemen proceeded with caution. "As we walked around," recalled Mann, "we were pretty leery because the Japanese were pretty

Japanese mini-submarine pens. The commander of the southern sector ordered Colonel Walker to guard and preserve the captured submarines.

good at setting booby-traps."[77] Nevertheless, soldiers could not resist hunting for souvenirs. As the main forces continued their advances and occupied both sectors, during the late afternoon of 16 August, Ready ordered the FSSF battalions to hold their positions and await further instructions.

As stores and material continued to be unloaded on various beaches no supplies had yet been sent to FSSF personnel. "We had a limited quantity of K-rations in our pockets," stated Doucette. "They did not last very long. Later, we had to go down to the beach and steal food. There was no resupply for us."[78] Colonel Fredrick was furious to see that his men were left to fend for themselves. "Even General Frederick went to the beach to get stuff," said Joe Jamieson. "He'd ask us, 'Did you get sugar?' and things like that. And if we didn't have any he'd find some," said the veteran. "He was the most marvellous man you could ever meet."[79] Soon the Forceman took matters into their own hands. Eugene Forward recalled:

> We had enough to survive on but we scrounged other units supply dumps. Boxes and crates were all stacked up and guarded by people who didn't know how to guard properly. We had fun going in and taking rations. It was good practice. On Kiska we made our reputation as scroungers.[80]

To add to the misery, the weather took a turn for the worst. "We were well equipped but we weren't equipped to stay there for an extended period of time. It was getting a little uncomfortable," recollected Jim Smith. "It started to rain then it just poured. It was a miserable time."[81] Rain quickly filled the foxholes and without proper shelters, the men were thoroughly drenched. Very quickly, the Forcemen had their fill of Kiska. As they waited on the exposed high ridges, Frederick received orders for two additional operations. The FSSF commander selected 1st Regiment for the tasks.

While 3rd Regiment under Lieutenant-Colonel Edwin A. Walker remained another day in the Robber Hill area, Lieutenant-Colonel Alfred Marshall's 1st Regiment, less one battalion, was pulled out on 17 August and ordered to attack Little Kiska. This well-fortified island was located at the mouth of Kiska Harbour. Its coastal defence guns and anti-aircraft batteries protected Kiska Harbor, the submarine base and the army camp.[82]

In contrast to the previous two amphibious landings, this was a daylight operation. On the afternoon of 18 August, Lieutenant-Colonel Marshall and his Forcemen disembarked from the USS *Kane* into rubber boats and paddled quickly toward Navy Cove. Confident that there were no Japanese defenders the Forcemen quickly stormed Beach 37, scaled the cliffs and captured a five-inch coastal defence battery and other anti-aircraft batteries. Patrols then combed the island and reported the all clear. Marshall then left Major J.F.R. Akehurst and his battalion to occupy Little Kiska. Once the island was secured, Frederick ordered the 1st Regiment to dispatch a platoon to guard the submarine base in Kiska Harbor.[83]

The remaining elements of 1st Regiment were assigned to take part in a second amphibious operation. Aerial photographs revealed the location of a radio station on Segula Island situated approximately seven kilometres northeast of Kiska. George Wright was among the Forcemen who landed on this desolated island:

> We headed right for this gravel beach. All the other landing crafts went right up onto the beach. The guy that operated our craft for some reason wouldn't bring it in. So, we had to get out in water up to our waist. It was cold and we were soaking wet. We spread out and headed toward the wireless station. When we got there we found out that it was an old dug in sod house covered with moss. A wire ran from this house to a pole. It had been somebody's cloth line. We also found an old smashed up

fishing boat, laying on a gravel shore. Later, we came upon two graves. From the inscriptions we assumed that one was a women and the other one was a child. We never found anybody else. That was it. That was our radio station.[84]

Once again, the intelligence provided proved to be inaccurate. Patrols confirmed that no enemy forces were on this island. The Forcemen then waded out to the awaiting landing craft and returned to the ship. The battle for Kiska was finally over.

Despite the absence of enemy troops, the Kiska invasion was not without cost. In total, the invasion force suffered 98 killed, 97 injured, and 130 sidelined due to trench foot.[85] During the course of the first day of the invasion, the dense fog unnerved many soldiers of the ATF 9. "It was all very mysterious," wrote a Forcemen, "and the mystery was not cleared any by the ghostly fog which at times almost completely blanketed the area." The Forcemen added, "In a small world of extremely limited visibility, suspicion raised dark monsters, and several shooting incidences occurred."[86] The FSSF sustained two injuries: one by friendly fire and the other during the handling of ordnance.[87] An upset Vice-Admiral Kincaid, the commander of the North Pacific Force, confessed that, "we had no way of anticipating our men would shoot each other in the fog."[88] On the other hand, a relieved Major-General Corlett stated, "I'm tickled pink we didn't have to fight." [89]

On 18 August, Frederick received a message from Admiral Chester W. Nimitz, the commander-in-chief of the U.S. Pacific Ocean Area, ordering the FSSF's immediate return to San Francisco. Both Major-General Corlett and Lieutenant-General J.L. DeWitt, commanding, Western Defense Command, were sorry to see the Force leave. In a letter to the War Department's adjutant general, Corlett praised the FSSF:

> In the occupation of the Island of Kiska, the FSSF was under my command. They performed all missions according to plan and even though no actual enemy was encountered, their missions were difficult and dangerous. They landed in rubber boats at unknown beaches during hours of darkness against what was presumed to be hostile shore. They moved across difficult terrain and positions where cleverly-concealed traps had been left by the enemy. They reached their objectives on schedule according to plan. To accomplish their mission it was impractical for them to carry packs to provide the ordinary comforts of soldiers in the field. As a consequence they were exposed to extreme discomfort for long periods of time. It is desired to commend all officers and men of the FSSF for their fine spirit and unselfishness. It is especially desired to commend Colonel Robert T. Frederick for his splendid leadership and devotion to duty. Colonel

Frederick has a force that should be of great value in almost any difficult battle situation.⁹⁰

DeWitt echoed Corlett's comments, "During the amphibious training phase and the actual operation, this organization displayed a fine spirit of teamwork and an unusually high offensive spirit." DeWitt added, "Its' combat efficiency is of the highest order and its readiness for immediate combat has been proven."⁹¹

Following the operation, Lieutenant-Colonel Williamson sent a report to NDHQ praising his men. "All ranks acquitted themselves very satisfactorily and their excellent work, performed under exceedingly difficult terrain and weather conditions was praised by Major-General Corlett, U.S. Army Task Force Commander."⁹²

Despite these accolades, the Forcemen had mixed emotions regarding this campaign. "It was a let-down," said George Wright.⁹³ "There was a disappointment that there was no enemy," added Lloyd Dunlop. "This was supposed to be our baptism of fire."⁹⁴ Others, such as Vernon Doucette accepted the situation. "Personally," confided the veteran, "I was relieved that there was no enemy in Kiska."⁹⁵

Nevertheless, their physical conditioning and extensive training had paid great dividends. "It was great training to show you what you could come up against," chimed Eugene Forward.⁹⁶ "And so," summed up George Wright, "Kiska turned out to be a dry run, but a great experience for the future. We found out what it was like out there in rubber boats not knowing what was waiting for you on the shore," explained the Forceman, "and how to deal with that fear that was always to be with you, when you entered into the unknown."⁹⁷ In the end, the Force had performed admirably during their first challenging operational deployment.

Kiska quickly became a distant memory. From 19 to 22 August the Forcemen focused on retrieving their equipment.⁹⁸ The Force departed for San Francisco from 23 to 24 August and arrived by the end of the month. On 1 September, they were ferried to Camp Stoneman, Pittsburg, California, where half of the Force was authorized a 10-day leave. The remainder entrained for Fort Ethan Allen, Arlington, Virginia, to commence their next round of training.

Not surprisingly, the Force underwent another tough training regimen. The focus remained on fitness and operational effectiveness. In addition, Frederick emphasized the improvement of discipline, military courtesy, and the correct wearing of uniforms. To ensure that these issues were corrected he directed his regimental commanding officers to carry out weekly uniform and equipment inspections. When time permitted, he himself conducted full field kit inspections.

As the Forcemen continued their training and leave rotations, Lieutenant-Colonel Williamson flew to Ottawa, on 12 September 1943, to met with NDHQ officers to discuss his pressing reinforcement issues. Sixteen days later, 65 additional men arrived at Fort Ethan Allen increasing the Canadian contingent to 38 officers and 615 ORs⁹⁹ Furthermore, upon his return Williamson learned that all FSSF regimental commanding officers were promoted to the rank of colonel.[100] And, the good news did not stop there. Shortly after, Frederick informed Williamson that the Force was about to deploy overseas for operations. Little did they know that the FSSF was about to write itself into military legend.

10

WHERE EAGLES DARE:
The Battle for Mount La Difensa

Our baptism of fire was one of the toughest battles of World War II — it was mountainous terrain, terrible weather (cold with both rain and snow), and against a clever dug-in enemy.[1]

— Donald Ballantyne

Finally, on 28 October 1943, the FSSF was dispatched from North America for special service in the Mediterranean area under the command of General Eisenhower.[2] The Americans had begun planning for this eventuality shortly after the Plough Project was formally cancelled.[3] Although the operation in Kiska provided a momentary distraction, U.S. planners had all along determined that "military developments indicate a very profitable possible use for the Force in the Mediterranean area. Special training in demolitions and in ranger operations especially qualifies the First Special Service Force for such an enterprise. Planning is now proceeding with a view to using the Force for early action in Italy, Sardinia or Sicily."[4] As a result, the Canadian government gave its approval for the American employment of the FSSF in the Mediterranean theatre on 14 October 1942.[5]

Five days later the Force left Fort Ethan Allen in Vermont to move to a coastal staging base at Camp Patrick Henry, which was approximately 19 kilometres north of Newport, Virginia. They left this location on 27 October and after an uneventful voyage on the *Empress of Scotland* reached Casablanca in French Morocco on 5 November. The arduous journey, however, had seemingly just begun. From Casablanca, the Force moved by train to Oran, Algeria — a slow, tedious two-and-one-half-day trip. From Oran, a five-days were used to move the entire Force by ship to Naples, which was completed on 19 November. The following day the Force moved 29 kilometres by road to a former German artillery barracks at Santa Maria Capua Vetere where they awaited their orders.

OF COURAGE AND DETERMINATION

WHERE EAGLES DARE

Originally, Eisenhower had earmarked the FSSF for deployment "as strong reconnaissance units for flank protection in the Apennines and for raids behind enemy lines and later possibly in the French Alps," as well as "for independent guerrilla and sabotage activities in Balkans and for support of groups."[6] But on 22 November, he assigned the FSSF to 2nd Corps, U.S. 5th Army, under Major-General Geoffrey Keyes, who in turn reassigned the Force, bringing it under operational command of the 36th Division under Major-General Fred L. Walker. Keyes and Walker had a very different idea of how to employ the FSSF.

The 5th Army, commanded by Lieutenant-General Mark Clark, was presently stuck. It had landed at Salerno, Italy on 9 September and managed to claw its way through a series of German defensive lines pushing the retreating German forces northward up the Italian peninsula driving them up the Volturno

The FSSF moved from Casablanca, Tripoli, to Oran, Algeria, in hot, tightly packed boxcars.

River valley and into the mountainous interior. But progress began to grind to a halt in October as the autumn rains swelled streams and rivers, flooding the countryside and turning the terrain into mud. Bridges were washed out; roads, where they existed, deteriorated; trails turned to slop and movement of any sort became difficult at best.

Moreover, the Germans now dug-in behind their "Winter Line," which was a network of fortifications/defensive lines that were anchored by natural obstacles. The primary defensive line within the defensive system was the "Gustav Line," which ran across Italy from the point just north of where the Garigliano River flows into the Tyrrhenian Sea in the west, through the formidable Apennine Mountains, to the Sangro River, where it empties into the Adriatic Sea in the east. However, there were also a number of secondary defensive lines that in total made up the Winter Line.

By mid-November, the 5th Army was abruptly blocked at the southern end of this defensive network, specifically at the Mignano Gap, a natural choke point leading to the Liri Valley and Rome. At Mignano, this component of the Winter Line was anchored on Mount Sammucro to the north and the mountain chain mass of Mount Camino–Mount La Difensa–Mount Maggiore to the South. From this formidable mountain redoubt, the

OF COURAGE AND DETERMINATION

The FSSF established its temporary quarters in a former German artillery barracks at Santa Maria Capua Vetere.

Germans were able to dominate the approaches with a commanding view of the surrounding area. They combined this observation with artillery fire and as a result were able to rain a storm of steel on anything that moved on the approaches to their positions. Repeated Allied attempts at attacking the mountain strongholds in November resulted in failure and heavy casualties. In fact, the ground was so exposed to enemy fire that many of the American and British dead were left on the battlefield as it was impossible to collect them.[7]

And so, with the arrival of the FSSF, generals Clark, Keyes, and Walker had already made plans for the employment of the formation. But, they had also arrived at some preconceived judgments. As such, the arrival in Italy proved to be somewhat disappointing for the Forcemen. Colonel Frederick, upon reporting to Lieutenant-General Clark, was met with the sarcastic observation by his new boss, "The Force is nothing but a bunch of overrated glory boys."[8] This sentiment seemed to have been rampant. One member of the Force recalled, "Major-General Geoffrey Keyes came by one day. He said, "I hear that you fellas are pretty good. But looking at you all I see are glamour boys."[9]

So, evidently, the FSSF was to be put to the test. On 24 November 1943, Keyes issued his orders for Operation Raincoat. The FSSF was soon to go into its first combat. The renewed 5th Army offensive was based on a simultaneous two corps attack against Mount

WHERE EAGLES DARE

Camino and Mount La Difensa. On the left, British 56th Division was responsible for assaulting Mount Camino, while Keyes gave the task of seizing Mount La Difensa to the FSSF. [10] The simultaneous assault was paramount as the failure to take one would jeopardize the other, because the German positions on either mountain dominated the approaches to the other. As well, for the Allies, punching through the mountains was of the greatest importance to rejuvenate the offensive and the drive toward Rome.

Clearly, their first mission was not an easy one. Mount La Difensa stood out as an unassailable wall against the Allied advance up the Italian peninsula. The 2nd Regiment was given the task of lead assaulting regiment. Colonel Williamson gathered some of his key staff and conducted an initial reconnaissance of the mountain on 24 November 1943. What they saw was disconcerting. "It is very high and rugged and promises real difficulties in getting up even without German opposition," noted the war diarist.[11]

Their dismay is not hard to understand. Mount La Difensa was a former volcano. The only accessible path to its summit was the southern slope that formed a natural ramp to the top. This ramp emptied out onto the former lava bowl that had long cooled off and now formed into a high altitude depression shaped like a saucer.

Initial forays seemed to reinforce the conventional wisdom, namely the only approach was the southern ramp. However, key to the process was the continuing efforts of Lieutenant-Colonel Tom MacWilliam, the CO of the 1st Battalion, 2nd Regiment, who

Scale model of Mount La Difensa for planning purposes.

OF COURAGE AND DETERMINATION

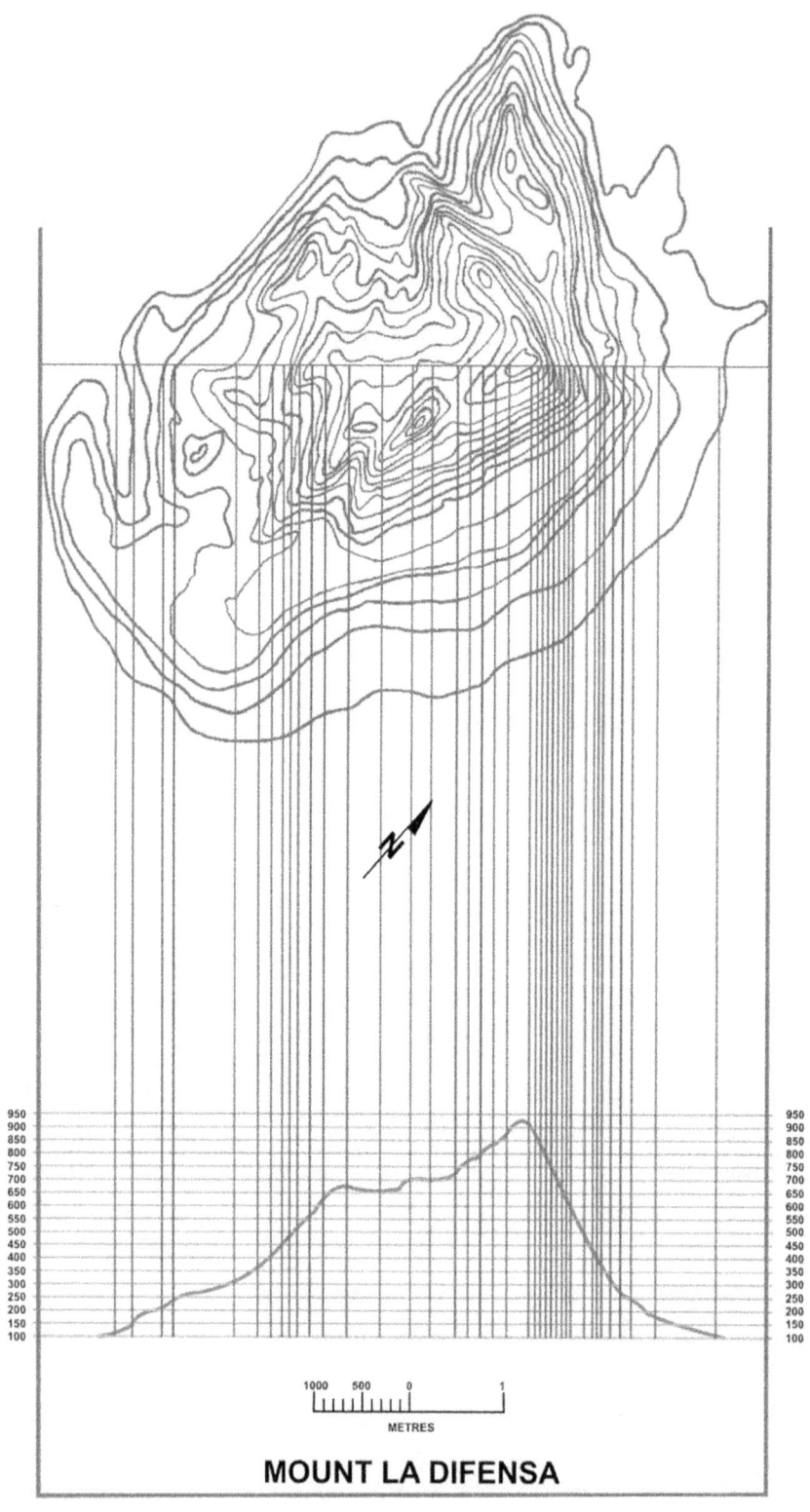

Monte La Difensa topographical profile.

Williamson tasked as responsible for spearheading the attack. He assigned a small team consisting of his deputy commanding officer (DCO), Major Ed Thomas, and 1st Company Officer Commanding (OC), Captain Bill Rothlin, as well as two scouts Sergeants Tommy Fenton and Howard Van Ausdale, to conduct a more detailed assessment.

At first, they made little progress in the thick bush and bramble at the foot of the mountain. But, Van Ausdale, a North American Native possessing an uncanny eye for ground and totally at home in the wilderness, seemed to find a possible solution. He was attracted to the large 60-metre cliffs on the north side of the mountain and the obscure little trail leading to their base. The northern route had its appeal. The approach was considered impassable, therefore, the enemy would most likely not bother to defend it. Moreover, the Forcemen all had mountaineering training so they should be able to scale the cliffs. It was risky, but offered to greatly surprise the enemy if they succeeded.

Williamson agreed with the plan and proposed it to Colonel Frederick. Before giving his approval, Frederick arranged for a Piper Cub aircraft to fly him over the objective to get a better look at the terrain. Seeing the ground from a bird's eye view he quickly realized the northern approach was the only viable solution to seizing the mountain without decimating his ranks.

The plan was now set. On the evening of 1 December, the Force departed Santa Maria at approximately 1600 hours and moved forward to a bivouac area at the base of the mountain. The ride to the front line was nerve wracking. "The sky lit up sporadically with great flashes of light as darkness fell," recalled Donald Mackinnon, "Guns, big guns deemed to be firing all around us." He remembered, "The noise was deafening and as the sky was illuminated we could see the surrounding mountains and lower clouds." What has always stuck with him was the fact that "There was a menacing feeling about it."[12] He was not far off the mark.

Once they off-loaded from the trucks at Presenzano, they had a 16-kilometre march through the mud to their bivouac area. The 1st Regiment, which was the divisional reserve, and the 3rd Regiment remained at the base of the mountain ready to support the attack on La Difensa. Frederick also tasked them with providing stretcher-bearers and transporting supplies up the mountain once it was secured. "Once we arrived at the base of the mountain," remembered Private Eugene Forward, "we were told to make ourselves as comfortable as possible and wait for further developments." He continued:

> During this time 2nd Regiment was making its way up the mountain. This waiting period was terrible. We were soaking wet. Our cigarettes, our Life Savers candies, and our tooth powder turned into mush. Everything we had was wet. We checked our weapons and we were told to make sure that our .45s were not stuck in the holsters.[13]

Another veteran had a similar recollection. He explained, "The base of the mountain was slop, reminiscent of a World War I battlefield."[14]

OF COURAGE AND DETERMINATION

For the 2nd Regiment, however, the march was not over. They now moved further on foot to a bivouac area on the eastern slope of Mount La Difensa. The march was slow and tedious in the heavy mud and the 2nd Regiment did not reach its destination until 0600 hours on 2 December 1943. Fortuitously, the day opened up with clear skies and a bright sun. This allowed the Forcemen to attempt to dry their equipment, cook a warm meal on a mountain stove, and clean their weapons. The enemy, however, remained active and the Forcemen had to exercise caution as the mountain approaches were under constant enemy observation and fire.

Finally, at 1830 hours, 2nd Regiment commenced its move into the assembly area. Not surprisingly, it proved to be a challenge in itself. Heavy fog, pouring rain, and deep mud made the move to the forward jumping off position an ordeal. Lieutenant Underhill recalled:

> Second Regiment continued to slog forward. The rain also continued, and the only light was the flash of artillery shells exploding above them on the mountain. Otherwise, it was pitch black. With every man carrying from 75 to 100 pounds and with footing varying from slippery rocks to six inches of mud, thoughts of personal injury faded from mind and were replaced with a dull determination to reach whatever objective was planned for the night.[15]

Mount La Difensa as it appears today.

At approximately 2200 hours, the 2nd Regiment reached the base of the cliffs and were in position to begin the ascent. At about the 610-metre level the mountain abruptly transformed into a sheer cliff. To the Forcemen it appeared as if the mountain rose "straight up in solid gray walls."[16] Lieutenant Mitchell recalled, "The mountain loomed over us and the echo of artillery through the mountains gave an eerie feeling. When our artillery shells exploded on the top, the smoke would drool down the face of the mountain and gave a spooky appearance."[17]

To soften up the enemy fortifications and cover the approach, a diversionary bombardment blanketed the German positions on the summit of La Difensa and Mount Camino. The bombardment was impressive by any standard. Approximately 925 guns from U.S. 2nd Corps and British 10th Corps hammered the objective areas. The quantity of ordnance dropped on Mount La Difensa, also known as Hill 960, prompted many of the Forcemen to call it "the million dollar mountain."

With the thunder of artillery in the background, the 2nd Regiment now stood in front of their last obstacle prior to engaging the enemy. The moment of truth had arrived — was there a passable route to the top? Scouts Van Ausdale and Fenton clambered off into the night followed by men carrying coils of ropes to string out and create two fixed lines that others could use to assist with the ascent. The scouts clawed their way up, their arm and leg muscles straining as they desperately sought hand-holds in the dark and forced their hands and toes into crevices and cracks in the wall face. Luckily, in places the sheer cliffs softened into steep grades that made the climb a bit easier. Van Ausdale also found a natural chimney in the rock formation that created a steep but climbable channel to the summit. After what seemed like an eternity, the two scouts reached the top. They had found a route that they believed would support the assault. They had also installed fixed lines to help the others with their climb.

The scouts now returned to report their success to Lieutenant-Colonel MacWilliam. Then at around 0100 hours, Frederick gave the 2nd Regiment the go-ahead. The scouts gathered up their weapons and equipment and proceeded to make their way up the mountain for the second time. On this trip, however, the remainder of the 1st Battalion followed. The lead assaulting battalion went in relatively light with only weapons, ammunition, and small packs. Their plan was to get all three companies up the cliff and then for all to shake out into extended line (1st Coy left, 2nd Coy in the centre and 3rd Coy right) for the actual attack on the German positions. The 2nd Battalion, in reserve, followed. They were less fortunate as they climbed with packs weighing anywhere from 35 to 50 kilograms consisting of additional weapons, ammunition, and equipment to consolidate the position once captured.[18]

At the bottom of the cliff, on a narrow ledge, Frederick had set-up his forward CP and anxiously awaited to hear reports on progress. Meanwhile, with the Allied bombardment blanketing the summit, the Germans quickly realized something was afoot and began to drop their own mortar and artillery fire on the approaches to the mountain hoping to catch the advancing troops. There fire, however, was far from the cliffs on the north side of the mountain.

Despite the weather and terrain, the assault was apparently progressing well. The scouts, particularly Van Ausdale, had chosen the route well. In the words of his peers "[Van Ausdale] got us to the top that night."[19] Major Thomas, a key proponent of the northern approach plan, described:

> The difficulty of the climb with combat loads was compounded by the dark night and the wet, treacherous terrain. Scrambling in the dark up the rocky trail with every foot and handhold doubtful demanded superhuman effort by men loaded with weapons, ammunition, radios and litters. To our ears, every rock displaced clattered downhill with sound magnified a thousand times and raised the question in our minds, "did the enemy hear this?, a not very comforting thought."[20]

Sergeant Bert Hopkins was less eloquent. He remembered:

> We climbed the back of the mountain. It was quite a cliff. We had ropes, we went up. It went well. It was raining, and it covered the noise. Sometimes rocks became loose and fell, but we got to the top unimpeded.[21]

The Force intelligence officer was another who captured the feat of the 2nd Regiment assault element when he explained:

> The difficulty involved in this move comes into sharp focus when it is remembered the cliff face of La Difensa begins at 2,000 foot level and extends upwards at a pitch of 60 or 70 degrees for approximately another 1,000 feet. This was the cleft that 600 riflemen, carrying packs which would have forced lesser men to the ground, negotiated without a sound. They groped for crevices with frozen hands while stretching their muscles to the aching point to keep from sliding backwards. like so many snakes, the sections crawled over the cliff face and, singly, broke over the rim.[22]

The progress made was laudable. After all, the difficulty of the terrain was only one of the challenges. The conditions were extreme. Rain and fog made everything difficult. One company commander gave simple final instructions. "In this damned fog," he declared, "we may miscalculate, but Jerry can't see any more than we can, and once the shooting starts, we'll know where he is. Lay down fire and move in with bayonet, grenades and Tommy guns."[23]

Once they reached the top of the cliff, they still had approximately 107 metres of rocky shale, which was buried under five to 15 centimetres of snow, to cross before reaching the summit. First Company cleared the rim at 0300 hours and spread out into skirmish line and slowly crept forward. By 0430 hours, although having lost contact with the 1st Company, 2nd Company was in position and radioed its headquarters to let them know the crest of the mountain was just ahead.

Moments later Colonel Williamson, who, with his CP party, had fallen in behind the 2nd Battalion on the way to the summit, passed the same message to Frederick at his forward CP. The importance of the message stemmed from the fact that the 142nd Regiment was waiting for word that the FSSF had seized the peak of La Difensa so that they could begin their assault on Mount Maggiore. When Williamson and his team were approximately 75 metres from the crest, word filtered back that the 1st Battalion had lost contact with its 1st Company in the gloomy pre-dawn darkness. At the same time, a German machine pistol fired into the night in the distance. Williamson apparently fearing that the plan was unravelling quickly decided to return down the mountain to report the turn of events to Frederick personally since he was unsure if the radios were working properly.[24]

Despite the absence of the regimental commander, the plan continued to play out. Only 3rd Company was still to reach its assault position. Then suddenly, at approximately 0530 hours, after the lead battalion reached the summit in entirety and prepared to position itself for the assault, in foggy pitch darkness, the tranquility on the mountaintop was shattered, as the Germans suddenly realized they were no longer alone. Beginning slowly with the crack of gunfire, they were soon directing a torrent of mortar, machine gun, and rifle fire at the attackers on the summit of La Difensa.[25]

Sergeant Hopkins asserted, "When we reached the top we regrouped in our platoons and sections. One of our recce teams went forward and came across some Germans. That got things going." He noted, "After the initial contact they [Germans] fought hard. They were entrenched in foxholes."[26] Don Mackinnon's recollection was similar:

> We [3rd Platoon, 1st Coy] reached the top without challenge. The Germans had not set up defensive positions above the cliffs assuming that this approach was unassailable. I don't recall great difficulty in the rope climb but it had to have been a very difficult task with the weapons and gear we were carrying. Knuckles, shins and knees took a terrific beating but fear and urgency gave us the adrenalin and strength necessary to keep moving up. Once on the top we started along a narrow rough and rocky path toward the German positions concentrated in a saucer-like area ahead of us. It seemed quieter now as we tried to make as little noise as possible. Second and third platoons were close behind us on the path. The whole company had reached the top without detection. We had got further than any earlier assaults and had achieved the element of surprise

so necessary to the success that followed. Suddenly the sound of rocks falling, a German voice challenging our two scouts. All hell broke loose! 5th Section dove behind a small ridge of rocks immediately in front of them. 6th Section sprawled to the left in a more exposed position. German machine gun fire was withering, hitting the rocks in front of us and spraying shale all around us.[27]

The CO of the 2nd Regiment, Lieutenant-Colonel MacWilliam, adhering to Frederick's dictum of commanding from the front, accompanied the advance platoon of 1st Company. When the firing began, he was already near the rim of the saucer. Despite heavy fire and a desperate, savage struggle against a tenacious foe, MacWilliam and his lead company seized the peak of the mountain. From a shell hole at the summit, at the forward most position of the assault, he now directed the attack against the remaining enemy positions. The situation was tenuous. The lead company had taken severe casualties in the chaotic struggle to take the summit. Adding to the confusion, MacWilliam had temporarily lost contact with 2nd and 3rd Companies during the arduous climb up the cliff. And, just to make matters worse, the newly taken position was subjected to heavy mortar fire and incessant sniper fire.

The "Bowl" at the top of Mount La Difensa.

Sergeant Chauffeur, a platoon sergeant remembered, "We were green. When we hit the first hedge above the cliff some mortars came in. The blast scared us and we froze. Then they really began to work us over. We crouched there and guys began going down on all sides of me."[28] Alan Blackwell remembered the visual effect of the battlefield as they prepared to assault. "I can honestly say," he wrote, "it was like walking into hell."[29]

The initial assault allowed the 2nd Regiment to gain a solid foothold around the north rim of the saucer. The fighting was confused and savage in the early morning murkiness. "Visibility continued to be close to zero," recalled Lieutenant Underhill, "Unless a breeze scattered the fog, it was almost impossible to distinguish objects more than ten feet away."[30]

Individuals and small groups slowly clawed their way through the German positions. One veteran recalled, "As Lieutenant Karl D. Kaash led his platoon into the gloom, two more enemy machine-guns were rattling to the front with such volume that he ordered the platoon into a firing line for support. Taking two men he advanced on the guns. Caught on the flank, the first machine-gun crew surrendered intact, similar tactics caught the second crew still firing when a hand-grenade silenced the gun. Few enemy were found alive."[31]

The 3rd Platoon, 1st Company, now confronted what seemed like the highest point of the mountain plateau. Here the Germans had built a complex of fortifications in caves and pillboxes that seemingly were left untouched by the Allied bombardment. From here, six enemy machine guns protected the northern approach. Sheets of flame indicated there were at least three machine gun positions busy firing out into the early morning murkiness. As the 3rd Platoon lay down a wall of fire, the remaining two platoons of 1st Company, as well as 2nd Company in its entirety, moved quickly into positions on the flank of 3rd Platoon and lent weight to their firepower. This forced the Germans out of their positions and they withdrew across the saddle to Mount Remetanea, which was also known as Hill 907.

Private Loring Waling explained, "It was a vicious battle for a short time, and after the battle there were a lot of counter attacks, the enemy used mortars terrifically."[32] It was not long before Frederick himself scrambled up the cliff and made his way to the summit where a pitched battle for the saucer-like top of the mountain was still raging. The bitter battle for control of the summit was waged by all ranks. Corporal Gordon Baker noted, "senior officers fought as savagely and unrelentingly as the enlisted men alongside of them."[33]

During the bitter struggle came a defining moment for the FSSF. As the popular legend goes, Captain Bill Rothlin and his troops had trapped a group of Germans in a gun emplacement. A German emerged carrying a white flag of surrender. As Captain Rothlin moved forward one of the other Germans in the group shot Rothlin in the face, killing him instantly. "Our group machine-gunned the rest of the enemy with all the firepower they had," acknowledged one veteran who was apparently present. It was from that moment, that many veterans insist that the FSSF adopted a "take no prisoners" policy.[34]

OF COURAGE AND DETERMINATION

Yet, Joe Glass, who was reportedly beside Captain Rothlin when he was shot provides a different account. Glass insists that Captain Rothlin and Syd Gath crawled up to his position. Glass promptly told them that there were white flags going up everywhere but one German, who had pinned Glass down, was not surrendering. Before Glass could warn them to keep their heads down, both peered up over the rock and were instantly shot by the German who refused to capitulate.[35]

By 0700 hours, the summit belonged to the FSSF. Despite the chaos, MacWilliam calmly moved about consolidating his newly won position against the inevitable counter-attack. Once he gained sufficient control of his unit, he quickly organized an assault on Mount Remetanea. He wanted to strike out while the Germans were disorganized before they could consolidate in a new defensive position. However, as he stood up to lead the way a sudden mortar barrage seemingly targeted his command group killing him and wounding others in his party. Major Thomas, the DCO, assumed command and cancelled the follow-on attack. He was concerned about the shortage of ammunition, the weakened state of the 2nd Regiment and the uncertainty of the enemy strength. Colonel Frederick, who had left his forward CP when his radios failed, agreed with the decision, and passed a message through his CP to higher headquarters that the attack would be delayed until the arrival of ammunition, reinforcements, and resupply.[36]

This did not mean, however, that Frederick was content to sit idle. He ensured the 2nd Regiment consolidated their position and sent out patrols to determine the enemy's whereabouts.

Colonel A.C. Marshall and his 1st Regiment on the mountain.

On the mountaintop, Frederick began to build the legend of his courage. Pat O'Neill described, "With bullets raking the air, Frederick moved from unit to unit, sending out patrols and placing men in outposts, to gradually widen the piece of territory we held."[37] Sergeant Gray, a Force scout remembered, "I always thought I got as far in front of the fighting lines as anybody. But, no matter how far ahead I got, the colonel was always farther. He was always closer to being shot that anybody."[38]

Although the day had started well for the Allies, they were not out of the woods yet. The FSSF held the top of Mount La Difensa. The British had managed to seize a portion of Mount Camino and the 142nd Regiment had eventually captured Mount Maggiore. However, all was tenuous as the Germans still held the saddle between La Difensa and Camino, as well as Mount Remetanea and were using their positions to pulverize the Allied soldiers holding the recently won mountaintops. By end of the day, the Germans had also pushed the British off the Camino heights and had retaken the monastery.

The 2nd Regiment continued to send out patrols to probe both approaches and defences around Hill 907, as well as to clear out pockets of German marksmen who were sniping and causing increasing casualties among the Forcemen on the summit. The patrols reported strong enemy dispositions south of the Remetanea Ridge. In light of the continuing shortage of men and ammunition, Williamson, who had made his way back up the mountain, proposed to postpone the attack on Hill 907 until the following dawn.

Frederick approved the delay. However, he was also taking pressure from his immediate boss, the commander of the 36th Division. The failure to take Hill 907 meant that the Germans could continue to fire on Mount Maggiore and endanger the 142nd Regiment's continued occupation of that objective. Moreover, the enemy could use Hill 907 as a jumping off base to launch counterattacks against La Difensa as well. Despite the heavy casualties the Germans suffered, Frederick and his commanders fully realized there were still a large number of German forces assembled close by. As such, he directed Williamson to ensure strong patrols were dispatched to keep the enemy pinned down and to use maximum artillery fire to prepare the objective for the upcoming assault and disrupt German efforts to fire on friendly forces.

By 1700 hours, the first of the ammunition resupply arrived. The effort to keep the troops at the summit of La Difensa resupplied for continuing combat became a battle within a battle. Sergeant R.E. Blake noted, "We just carried packs no weapons, just food, water and ammo. It was a very difficult trail." He lamented, "We couldn't use mules because it was too steep for them. We became the mules."[39] Lieutenant Mitchell recalled, "We had our pack-boards loaded with supplies and we could hear the fireworks at the top. It was solely an infantry action — man to man and no one could do anything for support."[40]

But if the steep, wet, narrow trails and heavy loads were not enough of an obstacle, the remaining German positions still had complete observation over sections of the resupply trails. Not surprisingly, they used their mortars and artillery to good effect to continually

Map by Amy Pierrson.

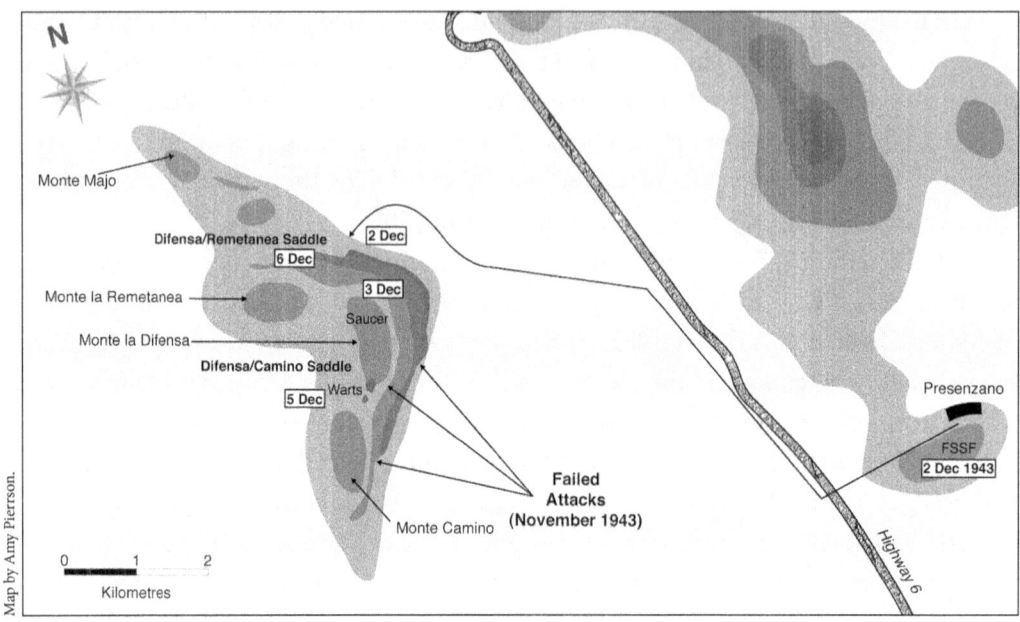

Monte La Difensa operations 2–6 December 1943.

Photographer Fredrick G. Whitcombe, DND/LAC, PA 115709.

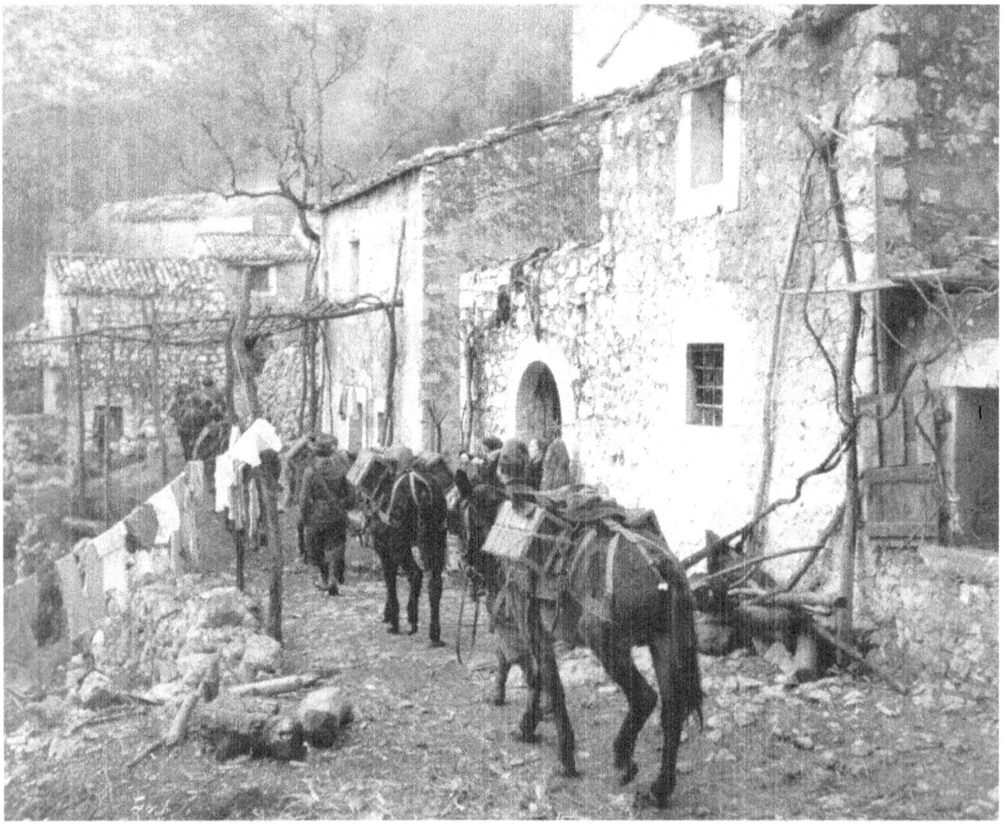

Mule team carrying supplies to Forcemen on the top of the mountain, 1944.

hammer the resupply effort. Mitchell wrote with some understatement, "We had to climb that mountain every night to keep them supplied ... the dash across that zeroed area [by German artillery] with a load on your back, was tiring to say the least."[41] Sergeant Wright explained, "the Germans were applying a sweeping fire from one end of the trail and then swept back. As they were pounding that trail, they were also bombing both ends of it to cut off the escape routes. Their shell and bombs were being guided by snipers who were firing tracers to direct their fire."[42]

By the morning of 4 December 1943, the Allied situation was under control but still tenuous. The night had brought pouring rain and a bone-chilling fog. For the exhausted troops manning the perimeter, under constant mortar and artillery fire, and with insufficient clothing and blankets, it was a long miserable night. Major Gerald McFadden recalled, "Dawn broke on a horrible scene. First light came through a dripping fog, which was a God-send [sic] for us. I tried to get in touch with other officers of the company, and rally their platoons. They were scattered all over."[43]

That morning the 2nd Regiment was reinforced by the 1st Coy, 3rd Regiment. Colonel Frederick sent the remainder of the 3rd Regiment back down the hill to assist with the transport of supplies to the top of the mountain. As well, since Colonel Marshall's 1st Regiment was still idle in divisional reserve, the 36th Division commander had released its 1st Battalion the previous afternoon to reinforce the 2nd Regiment prior to the attack

German PWs carry a wounded Forceman down the mountain.

on Hill 907. However, the battalion, led by Lieutenant-Colonel Becket, had still not arrived. It appeared they lost their way on the mountain in the dark.

As dawn broke, Frederick postponed the 0400 hours attack on Mount Remetanea. Interrogation of German prisoners the previous day revealed an enemy counterattack was planned. FSSF patrols seemed to corroborate the information when they discovered strong pockets of Germans massing just south of the Remetanea Ridge. Lieutenant-Colonel Robert Moore, CO of the 2nd Battalion (2nd Regiment), recalled, "In the process of moving, the rumor spread that a counterattack was being made by the enemy. On the basis of this, the attack was called off and the entire regiment remained alert until daylight."[44]

The plan was now to wait out the counterattack and then assault Hill 907 on the morning of the 5th. Strong patrols were sent out in the rain in attempt to work their way through the cloudbank that had settled on the top of the mountain and scour the entire area to locate the enemy. Throughout the day, the Germans pounded the summit with mortars and shellfire.

Patrols had captured German prisoners who were promptly questioned on the enemy's intent to counterattack. It became evident that the Germans too were suffering from heavy casualties and difficulties in resupply. Even so, they reported that a battalion-level attack was to occur at 0300 hours on the morning of 5 December. A report by an Allied artillery observer who saw approximately 400 enemy troops massing to the southwest of Hill 907 lent credence to the prisoners' statements. Moore recounted, "On the basis of this, artillery covering fire was called to our front to break up any possible assembly of force on the part of the enemy, and the regiment again maintained on the alert throughout the night. The planned attack [on Hill 907] was called off."[45]

The morning of 5 December showed some promise. The previous night several cases of whiskey accompanied the resupply run allowing each soldier several ounces of spirits. Moreover, Lieutenant-Colonel Becket and his 1st Battalion (1st Regiment) arrived. Frederick ordered them to relieve 2nd Regiment and take up their defensive positions so that Williamson's troops could prepare for a daylight assault that afternoon. The British seemed on the verge of finally clinching the Camino monastery and Allied patrols throughout the area reported an apparent thinning out of German forces. As such, Frederick felt confident that he could finally push the Germans from the adjacent mountain.

At approximately 1300 hours, Major Walter Gray, who replaced Major Thomas, who was wounded the day before, as the CO of the 1st Battalion (2nd Regiment) led a four-company battalion on the attack.[46] Halfway to Hill 907, the enemy poured a withering fire into the advancing troops forcing them to dig-in in a hasty defensive position on a knoll while they sent out patrols to determine the exact enemy positions.

With the 1st Battalion pinned down, Williamson deployed his 2nd Battalion, reinforced with 2nd Company (1st Regiment), to the southeast to clear the saddle of known German positions. They too quickly came under heavy fire and in a desperate, savage battle that was pressed from the flanks with bayonet and grenades, the Forcemen captured a series of "knobs" in the saddle that had been held by the Germans. As night fell, the FSSF was poised to drive home the attack the following day. Throughout the night, there were no signs of a German counterattack and it even appeared as if the enemy was in the process of a general withdrawal.

The morning of 6 December broke clear and sunny. The 1st Battalion launched its attack and advanced down the ridge to Hill 907. Its only resistance was long range harassing machine gun fire from Mount Camino. By noon, Mount Remetanea was seized with no opposition. Gray exploited the gain by sending two companies down the valley toward Rocca d'Evandro. Frederick captured the moment with a situation report to his higher headquarters:

> Situation at present [6 December — 1200 hours]: We have troops down to our left boundary at [the saddle] and have consolidated for defense of the area south of la Difensa. Our attack to the west against Hill 907 has progressed beyond the crest of 907. We are receiving much machine-gun and mortar fire from several directions, principally from the draw running southwest from la Difensa, from west foothills of Maggiore and from north slopes of Camino. We are endeavoring to place artillery support fire on the troublesome areas but it is difficult due to very low visibility and the British restrictions on our artillery fire.
>
> I shall push the attack to the west on past Hill 907 as far as condition of men will permit. Men are getting in bad shape from fatigue, exposure and cold.
>
> German snipers are giving us hell and it is extremely difficult to catch them. They are hidden all through the area and shoot burst at any target.
>
> Please press relief of troops from this position as every additional day here will mean two more days necessary for recuperation before next mission. They are willing and eager, but are becoming exhausted.
>
> Communication are heart-breaking. Mortar fire (and travel on trail) knock out lines faster than we can repair them. Every time we transmit by radio enemy drops mortar on location.
>
> German reinforcements approach up draw southwest of Camino, but I am unable to tell whether they are reinforcing or attempting to organize
>
> In my opinion, unless British take Camino before dark today it should be promptly attacked by us from the north. The locations we hold are going to be uncomfortable as long as enemy holds north slopes of Camino.[47]

That night the FSSF consolidated its gains and sent patrols out to ensure they maintained a dominance over the area. For their part, the British pounded the monastery at Camino and the next morning stormed it. By the morning of 7 December, British patrols linked up with the FSSF on the saddle. Although the German withdrawal became clearly evident, they had left behind a small rearguard that continued to snipe and harass with mortars. As such, the remainder of the day and night were spent tying in with the British and other 36th Division elements on the Camino–La Difensa–Maggiore mountain mass and clearing the last pockets of German resistance. Finally, on the afternoon of 8 December, the 142nd Regiment began to arrive to relieve the exhausted FSSF.

Although the summit of La Difensa was seized after only two hours of fighting, the struggle to capture the entire mountain mass dragged on. In the end, the Force remained on the top of the mountain summit for six days. Throughout they fought a tenacious enemy as well as the harsh environment. Battered by cold, wind, fog, ice, and rain and surviving off of limited rations and often muddy water, the FSSF soldiers appeared as apparitions as they descended the mountain on 9 December. One U.S. soldier remarked, "they all looked alike." He observed, "Their faces were gray, expressionless, and their clothes caked with mud and blood."[48] One of the veterans explained, "The impact of hell can only be felt by those who face it. Its description is only words."[49]

Colonel Williamson noted, "In the attack on Difensa everything was sacrificed to carry ammunition and supplies." He explained, "The men carried no blankets only ground sheets."[50] By 9 December 1943 the survivors of the battle returned to their base camp at Santa Maria. The cost had been horrific. The Canadian contingent lost two officers and 25 ORs killed or missing, and two officers and 84 ORs wounded. The Force in total lost nine officers and 71 ORs killed or missing, with another 11 officers and 339 ORs wounded. This amounted to a casualty rate of approximately 23 percent.[51]

Lieutenant-General Clark apparently changed his view of the FSSF. He praised their actions by awarding them a commander's commendation:

> The Special Service Force was given the task of capturing La Difensa, an extremely difficult piece of high ground in the Mt. Maggiore hill mass, the position of which was vital to our further advance in that sector. The mission was carried out at night in spite of adverse weather conditions and heavy enemy rifle, machine gun, mortar and artillery fire on the precipitous slopes over which it was necessary to attack. Furthermore, the position was maintained despite counter-attacks and difficulties of communication and supply. The fact that you have acquitted yourself well in your first action under open fire is a tribute to fine leadership and a splendid reward for time spent in arduous training.[52]

Clark was not alone in his praise. Major-General Keyes sent a note to Colonel Frederick that stated, "I am fully cognizant of the stubbornness of the enemy and the difficulties of weather and terrain encountered in this seizure of Mt. Difensa and Hill 907 [Mount

Remetanea], and of the bravery, fortitude, and resourcefulness with which your command overcame them."[53] Perhaps the greatest praise came from the British prime minister, Winston Churchill, who stated after the battle of La Difensa, "If we'd had a dozen like him [Frederick], we would have smashed Hitler in 1942. He's the greatest general of all time."[54]

The Force had demonstrated in its first combat that it had courage and determination. However, as events would shortly show, their time in the mountains was not over. There was still much suffering and dying to come in the mountains of Italy.

11

DEATH IN THE MOUNTAINS:
Mount Majo

Between the snow and the mud, it was a bitch fighting in the hills of Italy at any time.[1]

— Gord H. Baker

The men of the FSSF had proven themselves during the savage and bitter struggle for Mount La Difensa. Their risky approach up the back of the mountain had caught the Germans by surprise and they achieved in hours what the U.S. 5th Army had been unable to accomplish in weeks. However, there was little enthusiasm to celebrate their legendary feat of arms as the cost had been extremely high. In addition, there was little time to reflect on the victory as the fight was not yet over. As Lieutenant-General Mark Clark had promised them, when he visited during their memorial service on 12 December near Santa Maria, he had "bigger and better hills [for them] to climb."[2]

The FSSF was given 11 days to rest and recuperate. Meanwhile, the remainder of 36th Division was busy attempting to clear out the Germans that still clung to the dominating ground on the northern hinge of the Mignano Gap. No advance could be made on Casino or into the Liri Valley without first securing the remaining German mountain strongholds. By 22 December 1943, after vicious fighting, 5th Army had consolidated the southern hinge and secured a firm foothold on Mount Sammucro. However, the tenacious Germans still held on to Hill 720, a spur emanating from that mountain.

The reason this ridge was so strategically important was because it dominated the line of departure for 2nd Corps's final offensive to crack the Winter Line. The plan called for 2nd Corps, with British 10th Corps on its left flank, to push down into the valley. Major-General Keyes, the 2nd Corps commander, tasked the FSSF with protecting the right flank by seizing the high ground dominating the armoured approach into, and through, the valley. As such, its main objectives were Hill 1109 (Mount Vischiatro) and Mount Majo. Unfortunately, before the advance could begin, the enemy would have to be pushed off Hill 720. Keyes also gave this task to the FSSF.

As a result, on the night of 21/22 December 1943, the Force deployed from Santa Maria to Ceppagna village. The last minute task, however, necessitated some new orders. Frederick chose the 1st Regiment for the attack on Hill 720. Fortuitously, Keyes also assigned the Force some help, namely the 1st Battalion, 141st Infantry Regiment, to assist with the assault and subsequent occupation of the objective. The assault was set for 23 December, however, during the approach Frederick realized he had to delay the attack. The terrain was difficult, but the bigger threat was that the communication and co-ordination between the FSSF and the various supporting arms and assigned assault forces were ineffective. This had to be corrected.

As the necessary arrangements and planning was dealt with, the men sat shivering, wet, and cold on top of the mountain waiting. Finally, the assault was set for 2200 hours on Christmas Eve. But then another delay occurred as the assaulting units were required to firm-up co-ordination. This was not overly surprising since the overall 2nd Corps plan was complex as the FSSF attack was only one of several that would strike at a number of German positions in the area. Four hours behind schedule, shortly after 0200 hours on Christmas Day, the attack at last got underway. And, this time, the Forcemen were able to attack downhill!

Lieutenant-Colonel Jack Akehurst, CO 2nd Battalion (1st Regiment), was responsible for spearheading the attack. Although the Germans were on open ground they had created formidable defences using rock, concrete, railroad ties, and other solid construction materials. As Allied artillery slammed into German positions, the enemy responded in kind, combing the backside of Mount Sammucro where the Forcemen were assembled for the attack. One mortar round scored a direct hit on Akehurst's headquarters, wounding him and killing several others, as well as shutting down communications. Colonel Alfred Marshall, commanding the 1st Regiment, quickly moved down to take command of the battalion and lead the attack personally.

This latest turn of events imposed yet another delay as communications had to be re-established. Finally, at 0500 hours, the attack commenced. The bare rocky ground was unforgiving. Although a firebase pumped machine gun rounds into the German positions as fast as they could, the enemy still was able to sweep the ridge with a deadly fire. Casualties mounted quickly. Fighting turned to hand-to-hand combat as teams of soldiers had to use "well-pitched grenades and covering fire" to silence the German positions.[3] By 0700 hours the fight was over and 1st Regiment was firmly on its objective. At 1330 hours, the 141st Infantry arrived to relieve the Forcemen and the 1st Regiment, less a few patrols to assist with the mopping up of pockets of resistance in the area, marched down the mountain.

With the line of departure secure, the 5th Army could now continue with its plan of pushing through the Mignano Gap and breaking out into the Liri Valley. However, a brief pause was put into effect to allow the exhausted troops three days of rest prior to the big push. It was during this period that the Canadian component of the Force underwent a shock. Although Frederick had originally, on 18 December 1943, drafted paperwork nominating Lieutenant-Colonel Williamson, the senior Canadian in the FSSF, for the Legion of Merit with degree of officer for his part in the Mount La Difensa victory, by 1 January 1944, Frederick had not only scrawled by hand "withdraw" on the nomination paperwork, but he actually called Williamson in to see him to inform him that he had been relieved of his command. Moreover, Williamson was abruptly asked how quickly he could pack and leave the Force.[4] Williamson's adverse report read, "As a result of his performance during recent combat operations, personnel under his command have lost confidence in him and do not regard him with the respect a senior officer and combat commander must hold." Frederick concluded, "I feel that he [Williamson] is emotionally and temperamentally unfitted for combat duty."[5]

The main issue swirled around Williamson's sudden decision to descend the mountain as his troops were preparing to engage the enemy on the morning of 3 December 1943 and his subsequent behaviour on the summit. Williamson defended his actions as prudent and responsible. He claimed:

> I returned to report to Colonel Frederick at the advance CP because:
>
> (1) We were out of communications by radio with it and our forward elements.
> (2) Our 2nd Bn had lost contact with the 1st Bn, this was later regained.
> (3) The Colonel had informed me that the attack of the 142nd Infantry was not to proceed until we had secured La Difensa. I had already passed on to him an unverified report that we had taken La Difensa. On attempting to verify this by radio I found we could not do so nor by that time could I communicate with him at the CP. I was very disturbed over the situation and returned to report the facts personally. Having done so, I proceeded back up the mountain with the initial supply train. On arrival on La Difensa I took over from Lt. Col. Moore and ran the operation to its final success.[6]

The perception of those witnessing Williamson's behaviour, however, differed substantially. Affidavits collected weeks later by the Force adjutant told a story of a senior officer who demonstrated nervous, irrational, and, arguably, cowardly behaviour. Captain Eino Olson recalled, "Colonel Williamson was again very nervous and finally he dropped back, and it appeared that when we were able to see the top of the cliff above us he was extremely afraid of being fired on from the cliffs."[7] In the end, the headquarters staff went forward alone to set up the forward regimental command post (CP) without their commander.

OF COURAGE AND DETERMINATION

When he did arrive, he again demonstrated fright during the preparatory artillery barrage. Eino observed, "[he] was very nervous and afraid of shorts falling on us."[8]

During the approach march to the summit, the situation became worse. Williamson's CP party had fallen in with the 2nd Battalion on the approach. As they neared the summit, at one point, a German in the distance fired a machine pistol, the rounds going high over the heads of the Forcemen. Lieutenant Bill Story recalled:

> The next thing I knew the Colonel had his pistol out and had fired one shot. I asked him what he was firing at. He said he saw this sniper up there and pointed to the top of the mountain. Right after that he said that we had to go down and report to Colonel Frederick because it suddenly dawned on him that First Battalion had not taken their objective but that they had merely begun the attack and that he had to go down to warn Colonel Frederick that things were not going quite as he had expected. Colonel Williamson then fired six more shots in the general direction of the top of the mountain.[9]

Technician Fourth Class C.F. Rigg was another witness to the apparent breakdown of Colonel Williamson. He recalled that upon hearing word that the regiment lost contact with the 1st Battalion, "Colonel Williamson then became very excited and awfully jittery and couldn't quite speak properly."[10] Rigg opined, "He seemed like a coward. Even going down the hill he was continually telling me to stop and wait for him. He couldn't quite see me and his attitude was one definitely in my opinion of being thoroughly scared."[11]

For those witnessing Williamson's behaviour, his actions elicited some anger. First of all, there were strict instructions that there was to be no talking or shooting during the approach to maintain the element of surprise. Second, his weapon handling endangered those around him. On different occasions, he pointed his weapon at friendly troops thinking they were perhaps enemy.[12] Finally, he failed to live the credo and example set by Frederick himself, that officers were to lead from the front.

The members of the FSSF had come to form high expectations of their officers. Sergeant Joe Jamieson asserted:

> Our officers were with us. They didn't say, "You go here, you go there!" They were with us. They were in front. They just said, "Follow me." I had been in the Canadian artillery for two or three years and they would never even let us take a glass of water in the officers' quarters. Our Force officers trained with us, slept with us and ate with us.[13]

Sergeant Joe Wright agreed. He stated, "The relationship between the officers and men was different. They were with you. It was a closer association. You respected them. There wasn't all the pomp and fanfare. But when an officer told you to do something you did it, no question asked. If not it was good bye."[14] Donald Ballantyne remembered, "On the top of Difensa, I looked around and there was Frederick at my elbow. In the middle of hot fire fights Frederick was right there in the middle of it. He probably shouldn't have been there but he was — leadership by example."[15]

Little surprise then that Williamson's men found his behaviour unacceptable. Moreover, Williamson's subordinates didn't see their commander during the bitter combat on the mountain. Once he finally arrived on the summit, Williamson continued to show anxiety and fear. At one point Captain Eino peered into the CP and noted, "he was either under extreme fatigue or out of his mind.... My impression, however, in my own mind was corroborated when, even for his own comfort, he would not come out and on several occasions actually used a small hole dug at the door of his CP for relieving himself."[16] Major Walter Gray, the executive officer of 2nd Regiment, testified:

> I was in close contact with Colonel Williamson during the 4th and 5th of December 1943, and during that period he showed signs of extreme nervousness and indecision. In particular, he seemed very much frightened by shelling and intermittent machine gun or rifle fire coming over our heads. In order to push the attack and proceed with our mission it was necessary for Colonel Frederick himself to intervene, and it was also necessary for Lieutenant-Colonel Moore and myself to more or less take over and actually make decisions which should have been made by the regimental commander, Colonel Williamson.[17]

Colonel Frederick spoke with Brigadier A.W. Beament at the Canadian section at the general headquarters (GHQ) in Avellino to discuss the case personally.[18] In the end, the U.S. 5th Army "investigation" into the allegations concluded that events "Clearly indicate Williamson lost confidence of superiors and subordinates alike and unfit for active com[man]d."[19] This judgment was passed to the Canadian chain of command.

When Williamson was finally informed of the action against him on 1 January, Lieutenant-Colonel Akehurst, the officer now nominally commanding the First Canadian Special Service Battalion, recorded in the war diary:

> Colonel Williamson came in from the front this afternoon, he had been called into the Force Commander's CP in the morning, shown statements signed by some of his regimental officers, declaring lack of confidence in him as a result of the La Difensa operation four weeks ago. Not one officer said a word to him about it and he was given no intimation that they lacked confidence in his leadership until he was handed the declarations four weeks after. He felt that he might have been told. He was asked how

quickly he could be packed and leave as he had been relieved from his command, he had no opportunity to defend himself a most unfair way to handle the case and especially to treat the man who had helped create the Force and who has been at the helm through its many turbulent and trying times."[20]

Williamson did receive letters of support from some of his fellow Canadian officers, as well as some others, but they had little effect. Having been dismissed he was promptly sent to 14th Canadian General Hospital for a psychological examination. He was seen by Toronto neuro-psychiatrist Dr. (Colonel) Fred Van Nostrand, who believed that Williamson's behaviour was brought on by the stress of combat. Following the visit, Beament consulted with Lieutenant-General Harry Crerar, who in turn, based on evidence provided, supported the return of Colonel Williamson to Canada.[21] A report with recommendation was then sent to the Canadian Military Headquarters (CMHQ) in London . The recommendation was brutally frank — "Substance of report indicates clearly that Colonel Williamson has lost confidence of superiors and subordinates alike and obviously unfit for active command."[22] The message also clarified that "Van Nostrand also accepts evidence submitted that Williamson showed definite behaviour disturbance during first engagement with enemy and showed himself inadequate in his position of command."[23]

Although Williamson demanded a full inquiry, this never transpired. At the end of the day, the Canadian chain-of-command accepted the findings and recommendations of Frederick, the 5th Army, and the senior Canadian general officer in theatre. Moreover, the Canadian Army position was firmly entrenched that anyone being returned from a theatre of combat for any non-medical reason was not to be further employed in an operational role. As such, Williamson was returned to Canada and posted to 1st Canadian General Reinforcement Unit, with a TOS (taken on strength) of 21 February 1944.[24]

Williamson's dismissal was not the only key event to occur on New Year's day. The 2nd Corps commander issued new orders, but the FSSF mission remained the same, namely to secure the high ground on 2nd Corp's right flank and seize the towering 1,259-metre Mount Majo and subsequently Mount Vischiataro (Hill 1109). Frederick assigned the task to Colonel Ed Walker's 3rd Regiment, who planned to do a wide right flanking. However, to reach the starting point to capture Mount Majo, the Forcemen had to fight their way hilltop to hilltop until they reached the Viticuso–Cervaro Road at the base of their objective. As such, the assault was carried out in two phases. Phase 1 was the requirement to take the intervening ground and consolidate; and Phase 2 was the seizure of Mount Majo.

The route chosen by Walker meant that the Force first had to clear a number of objectives that dominated the approach. This responsibility was parceled out to the other regiments. The first obstacle was Hill 724 that dominated the small alpine village of Radicosa, which Frederick had chosen as his forward CP for the upcoming assault on Mounts Vischiataro and Majo. In the dark of night on 3 January, the 2nd Regiment

DEATH IN THE MOUNTAINS

Members of 2nd Regiment keep warm near Radicosa, 1 January 1944.

struggled through bitter temperatures and a howling windstorm to get to their objective. Trudging through ankle-deep snow and later, at higher altitudes, deeper drifts of snow, the Forcemen quietly ascended the mountain to launch a surprise attack. They had quickly learned that stealth and cunning saved lives.

This was once again the case. The Forcemen exploded onto the objective catching the Germans, who had been protecting themselves against the harsh elements, completely by surprise. Although the objective was taken easily, holding it became another question. The Germans on adjacent hills quickly lashed out with mortar fire that thoroughly hammered Hill 724, killing and wounding a number of FSSF soldiers.

Hill 724, however, now gave the Force a forward operating base. On the following night, the 1st Regiment deployed a fighting patrol that quietly eliminated a number of machine gun posts on Hill 675, which also dominated Radicosa. They had now completely outflanked the small alpine village. No surprise then, when, on the night of 5 January 1944, another FSSF patrol discovered that the Germans had completely withdrawn from Radicosa now that it had been outflanked.

The 3rd Regiment had not been idle, while the 1st and 2nd Regiments had been busy capturing Radicosa. Colonel Walker recounted:

OF COURAGE AND DETERMINATION

Two members of the FSSF defuse a booby-trap near Radicosa.

On the night of January 3rd, the [3rd] Regiment advanced in two columns — with mule pack trains following. The First Battalion on the right, Second Battalion on the left. Objective — across Ridge 850 to Ridge (950 and 1025), First Battalion on 1025, Second Battalion on 950 Regimental Headquarters with Second Battalion.

First Company had a very hard fight for 1025 just before daylight — many acts of courage in taking out machine gun positions. Third Company on their left, fought for their position on the left of 1035, with Fourth Company on their left fighting for 950. By 7:30 AM, the ridge was taken and fairly well consolidated. Stayed here for two days. The third night, the 2nd Battalion was ordered forward to take Mt Steffano, and Hill 750. Moved during darkness to Steffano, and Sixth Company to Hill 750. Enemy was forced to withdraw from high ground by daylight. But at that time occupied ground on three sides of this salient. It was very cold. Trench feet was bad. The enemy gave Fifth Company a tough time — machine guns and mostly mortar fire.[25]

That afternoon, on 5 January 1944, the remainder of the 3rd Regiment moved forward. They were now in a good position to launch the assault on Mount Majo. However, the weather

DEATH IN THE MOUNTAINS

and terrain were having a telling effect. Casualties mounted as hypothermia, exposure, and trench foot took its toll. The 1st and 2nd Regiments were down to half strength and the 3rd Regiment was down to two-thirds strength and losing more men daily. As a result, on 6 January, Keyes created Task Force "B" based on the FSSF. He assigned Frederick the 133rd Infantry Regiment, which was in corps's reserve, as well as "A" Company, 19th Engineers and some additional support troops. Then, Keyes ordered the attack on Mount Majo.[26]

The Force was ready. However, Frederick changed the plan. He now decided to launch a simultaneous two-pronged attack. He ordered the 1st Regiment to take Hill 1109 at the same time that 3rd Regiment advanced on Mount Majo. The 3rd Regiment crossed the road just below Steffano at 2000 hours that night. The enemy opened up with machine guns and mortars but it had little effect. The 3rd Company, the lead company of the assaulting 3rd Regiment, sent out an eight-man vanguard to clear the line of advance of snipers or other obstacles. It quickly came under a withering fire that threatened to hold up the entire advance. Sergeants John Rich and Ralph Swisher, immediately on their own initiative, attacked two separate machine gun nests simultaneously. Sergeant Swisher ran uphill and tossed a grenade into one pit killing two gunners and forcing the third to withdraw. Meanwhile Sergeant Rich crawled close to the other machine gun pit, fired his submachine gun until it jammed and then drew his pistol and leapt into the enemy position capturing it. Their quick thinking and courage alleviated a long delay and allowed the vanguard to seize a key piece of terrain.[27]

A Forceman with the Johnson light machine gun, Radicosa, 15 January 1944.

OF COURAGE AND DETERMINATION

The contribution of the vanguard force did not go unnoticed by the 3rd Regiment commander. "I anticipated delay," confessed Walker, "but the active work of Lieutenant Mitchell and his platoon cleared our route of advance with little delay."[28] Vanguard or not, Mount Majo was going to prove to be a hard nut to crack. Its topography alone was challenging. Rather than a single peak, the mountain consisted of a major summit connected by an exposed ridgeline to two adjoining peaks. As a result, the Forcemen would have to clear three objectives as the Germans surely occupied all three with mutually supporting machine gun positions.

And so, in the chilling cold and driving wind, the 3rd Regiment clawed its way to the summit. Walker planned to drive the 1st Battalion led by Lieutenant-Colonel Tom Gilday, straight for the main peak. He tasked the 2nd Battalion with flanking the summit from the left and enveloping Hill 1259 from the west. Walker described the initial attack:

> We had begun to climb the lower approaches to Majo. I went forward and found First Battalion Headquarters in position behind Third Company, which was in the process of clearing the ridge, which was a continuation of the left slope of Mt. Majo. Second Company had lost contact , but was on the way to the right to the main Mt. Majo feature. First Company had not appeared. Third Company was having a good scrap for the ridge, and from across the ridge about 300 yards where the enemy held both flanks a crossfire was falling between me and my headquarters, about 5,000 yards to the rear with Sixth Company.[29]

Lieutenant-Colonel Gilday, commanding the 1st Battalion (3rd Regiment), led the spearhead battalion advancing on the main peak. His commendation later read, "[he] led and fought his men over rocky snow covered terrain to the objective, and pushed the enemy out of their superior positions, inflicting a great number of casualties on them."[30]

The assault used stealth as much as possible, but in the end, it was a question of tenacity and courage. Private R.J. Summers recalled, "We were right under the German machine-guns before they opened up. Don't know how they missed us. Bright moonlight too. We went right in there and took them all out. About 28 men with three machine-guns."[31]

Part of their success was the indirect approach. Captain W.B. Perry's group "took a precipitous ascent on a route which was not covered by fire, as the enemy evidently thought it so unlikely for attack. They met fire only 30 yards from the summit of Majo, but pitched in with grenades, cleaned up four machine gun nests and consolidated their position."[32]

During the desperate struggle, Staff Sergeant Frank Harvey led his section in the assault when his group became pinned down by three machine guns and rifle fire. The terrain was barren and it afforded no cover. Darkness was their only protection. With a complete disregard for his own safety, Harvey rallied his men and charged up the mountain rushing

DEATH IN THE MOUNTAINS

Two members of the FSSF struggle with a tired mule in the mountains.

Forceman standing on the summit of Mount Sammucro.

the well-entrenched German positions approximately 200 metres away. Firing his Thompson machine gun from his hip, he led the assault.

When he was approximately five metres from the first trench, he tossed a grenade, wiping out the first enemy machine gun position. Without hesitation, although still under heavy fire, Harvey led his men on the assault of the second position once again putting it out of action. By now his section was scattered in the dark, each man fighting his own personal battle with the enemy entrenched on the mountain. However, the last German machine gun position was still firing continuously holding up the company assault.

Harvey's courage did not fail him. He quickly charged the final position.

He was within three metres of his objective when he was cut down, hit in abdomen and groin. Although mortally wounded and with his life ebbing away he completed the assault and knocked out the final German position, opening up the way for his company to capture Hill 1025.[33]

Staff Sergeant A.L. Wright, later commissioned to lieutenant, similarly stepped forward during the attack. During the night attack, "his company on an enemy-held mountain crest was halted by the deadly cross-fire of sixteen machine guns." Wright, who was commanding an assault platoon, proceeded forward alone to attack the enemy positions. "After crawling one hundred yards up the exposed, snow covered slope to within a few yards of the enemy position, he leaped to his feet and charged the gun emplacement firing his Thompson machine gun, killing one and capturing two of the enemy crew. After assembling a section of his platoon, he then personally led them in a charge against a second and then a third machine gun, putting them out of action and destroying three and capturing two more of the enemy."[34]

The main assaults were also aided by the actions of Captain Dan Gallagher, the OC of 1st Company. One reporter captured the essence of the combat:

> This intervening high ground consisted of several rocky peaks to test the skill and endurance of any experienced mountain climbers. There was a cold wind over the snow and all the climbing and moving had to be done in the dark. On one hill about 100 Germans with mortars and six machine-guns were taken completely by surprise by a force under Captain D.P. Gallagher ... They reached a point 30 yards from the summit ... and then put in their attack. The first the enemy knew about it was a lot of grenades bursting in their midst. Then there was fighting in isolated groups over the rough summit till practically every German was killed. Another force was taking a hill to the left but had to fight the whole way up. Nevertheless, after rock fighting from one end of the hill to the another the position was consolidated by daybreak.[35]

Gilday fought his battalion hard and they clawed their way to the top and seized the summit from the Germans through a large number of small courageous battles throughout the objective area. Gilday then quickly consolidated and "organized a defence that proved impregnable to at least 24 counterattacks before his battalion was relieved."[36] Sergeant Lloyd Dunlop remembered:

> We were right in the middle of the fire. We dug in nearly at the top of the mountain and were under constant German mortar fire. I remember trying to dig a fox hole. You couldn't dig very deep because it was all rock. So we piled rocks up to make a slit trench. Mortar bombs started dropping

in. I remember seeing guys desperately digging trenches on either side. I was praying that these shells wouldn't hit me. I was lucky. But, it did hit the next guy alongside of me. He was gone. Then, Captain Perry who was about 200 yards away had his leg blown off. He died before they could get him to the first aid station. The Germans were very persistent. They attacked and attacked and counter attacked. They wanted that mountain back, but we drove them away.[37]

The 2nd Battalion (3rd Regiment) was also successful, albeit at great cost and effort, at occupying the series of hills and knobs around Mount Majo. Colonel Walker explained:

It was 9 AM when a patrol from Second Company reached us, stating the feature had been cleared, but with difficulty. It was straight up into the face of the enemy — the enemy held the top and had every reason to want to continue to hold, as it was the commanding feature of all the surrounding country. The enemy proved this by their innumerable counter-attacks all the following day.... Mortar and artillery fire had begun to fall on our position and down the valley to the rear.... At about 0800, we had received, by radio and word, that the First Regiment on our left had been unable to advance from its original position of the night before, due to enemy resistance. We were out on a limb. We were low on ammunition. We borrowed from the reserve company. Troops being evacuated with trench feet. It was very cold at night. We were above the snow line. But it proved a life saver. No water — we drank melted snow for two days.[38]

The 1st Regiment had not fared so well. They had crossed the start line at 2130 hours. Their objective lay four kilometres distant over unforgiving hills. In the bright moonlight the Forcemen were badly silhouetted. Not surprisingly, they came under fire. The vanguard patrols were able to identify a defensive line on the first line of hills below Hill 1109. This imposed a six-hour delay as the assault companies destroyed a number of machine gun emplacements and flushed out snipers. As dawn broke, the exhausted and increasingly depleted 1st Regiment was forced to return to Stefano to reorganize.

The failure to capture Hill 1109 now meant that 3rd Regiment on Mount Majo became the focus of German attention, who alternated between pounding them with artillery and mortar fire and hurling vicious counterattacks against them. Alone on the summit, 3rd Regiment was unable to evacuate their wounded or concern themselves with the debilitating cold or frozen feet. Without food and running out of ammunition, the Forcemen tenaciously threw back 27 counterattacks during the day.

Unable to move because they were either under a withering storm of steel or beating back yet another German counterattack flowing over the lip of the summit, the

OF COURAGE AND DETERMINATION

Members of the FSSF pose on the top of Mount Majo.

3rd Regiment found themselves virtually cut-off and dangerously low on ammunition. Innovation and sound training quickly took over. Sergeant Wright explained:

> Once we had run out of ammunition, we used German ammunition and weapons. That turned out to be the best trick in the world. When a German heard a German machine gun firing, and you could tell the difference, they'd yell at us to stop firing thinking that they were being fired upon by their troops. They'd come out and that's when we got them.[39]

Courageously, the 3rd Regiment hung on to Mount Majo. By late afternoon on 7 January, the exhausted 3rd Regiment had consolidated and had a firm grip of their objective. Moreover, a patrol from the 157th Infantry, 45th Division, tied in on their western flank and held Hill 1130 providing additional security.

This now provided Frederick and the 1st Regiment with a definite advantage. They could launch their attack on Hill 1109 from Majo, giving them an approach that ran downhill. By late afternoon, 7 January, the 1st Regiment had reach its assembly point on Mount Majo. They then linked up with the 3rd Battalion, 133rd Infantry Regiment, which, as part of the newly formed Task Force "B," was now under Frederick's operational command. He had ordered them to deploy one company to relieve 3rd Regiment

DEATH IN THE MOUNTAINS

on Mount Majo; another would accompany 1st Regiment to seize Hill 1270, thereby protecting its rear; and the remainder of the 3rd Battalion (133rd Infantry Regiment) would assist with the assault on Hill 1109 and then occupy the summit once the objective had been taken.[40]

As the sun began to sink behind the horizon, Colonel Marshall and his 1st Regiment began their advance across the deathly quiet snow covered mountains. At midnight, the column halted in the valley between their objective, Mount Vischiataro and Hill 1270, as "L" Company, 3rd Battalion (133rd Infantry Regiment) struck out on its own to seize the high feature to the north of 1st Regiment's objective. At 0200 hours, 8 January, the tranquil night air was pierced by gunfire as "L" Company overran a lone outpost. Shortly thereafter Colonel Marshall received word that they had seized Hill 1270. He could now take his two remaining battalions and assault Hill 1109.

The valley where Marshall and his troops had halted was approximately at the same altitude as their objective. As a result, the approach was relatively easy. As they neared the open, flat summit, all remained silent. The two battalions, which had deployed for an assault, simply walked onto their objective without a fight. The German 2nd Battalion, 132nd Regiment, that had punished them so severely the night before had vanished. That morning, "K" Company, 3rd Battalion (133rd Infantry Regiment) occupied the objective and the 1st Regiment returned to Radicosa.

German fighting position in the mountains.

OF COURAGE AND DETERMINATION

As the FSSF fought its way through the mountains, 2nd Corps had slowly pushed its way through the valley along Highway 6. The German defences under renewed pressure began to buckle. Keyes now decided to use the FSSF Task Group "B" to pursue retreating German forces to the southwest. Within Frederick's area of responsibility were at least two German battalions that had been forced off the mountains. The FSSF was at Radicosa reorganizing and refitting after its constant diet of cold and combat. As a result, Frederick pressed his fresher elements of the 133rd Regiment to effect the immediate pursuit. However, this meant that on the evening of 8 January, the 3rd Regiment was required to return to Mount Majo and occupy it, while the 1st Regiment deployed to Hill 1270.[41]

Frederick ordered the 1st and 2nd Battalions (133rd Regiment) to attack Hill 689, Caparo Hill, on the evening of 8 January.[42] This would link Task Force "B" in the mountains with 2nd Corps elements on the Rapido Plain. The attack began at 0500 hours, and four hours later they were approximately half way to their objective. However, by noon they hit a wall of resistance and the attack stalled. Moreover, the enemy struck hard with counterattacks at the flanks of the battalions. Ominously, at 1330 hours, 9 January, a large German force had skirted Hill 1270 and attacked Hill 1109. The attack was halted just short of the summit.

Now pressed on two fronts, Frederick requested assistance from 2nd Corps. Keyes sent the 168th Infantry Regiment to assist with clearing out the pockets of resistance and Frederick ordered the 133rd Regiment to continue pressing its attack. By the late evening, the enemy pressure began to dissipate. Apparently, their offensive had been designed to buy time for the bulk of the German forces to withdraw behind the Gustav Line.

The following day, Frederick pushed his Task Force forward. The 133rd Infantry Regiment continued with its attack, however, the fog and rain made movement difficult. Contact with the enemy was finally regained on 11 January and the next day the 133rd captured Capraro Hill, but two days later were still unable to push any farther.

On 14 January, Task Force "B" was dismantled, however, Frederick still had the 100th Battalion under operational command due to the depleted state of the FSSF. The 3rd Algerian Division had relieved the Force on Mount Majo and Hill 1270 the day previous, so the FSSF was free for manoeuvre. Frederick now

Preparing a pack mule for a resupply run.

used his force to patrol and advance, clearing the FSSF's area of responsibility of remaining pockets of resistance. His regiments, by this time, were down to approximately two companies each.[43] Regardless they aggressively pushed forward. By 17 January 1944, they had linked in with flanking units establishing Allied control of the vanquished area. At noon, they boarded trucks and returned to Santa Maria.

The experience of the mountains was not soon forgotten. "We were up there 14 days," recalled Lloyd MacDonald, "We had no change of clothes, no socks, nothing. At the end, we were running out of water and praying it would rain."[44] Sergeant Paul Schoeler described:

> Life in those mountains was hell. You just had the clothes on your back, and they were usually wet from the rain and mist. If you were lucky you had a blanket. You'd curl up with a buddy to keep warm. You could only dig so far. We had to stack rocks to protect ourselves from those sweeping winds and shrapnel.[45]

Although the ordeal was horrific for the Forcemen, the impact they had on the 5th Army was impressive. Journalist Sholto Watt later wrote, "This force is an intensely dramatic embodiment of our common effort in a cause that commands the faith of all of us. It is North America in action — vital, efficient, spectacular — in a form that any man who sees may understand."[46]

International News Service correspondent Clark Lee reported that the exploits of the FSSF "captured the imagination of the entire Fifth Army and overnight made them almost legendary figures in a battle area where heroism was commonplace."[47]

The cost, however, was traumatic. By the end of the fighting in the mountains, of the 1,800 men in the FSSF combat echelon, approximately 1,400 had been killed, wounded, or hospitalized due to exposure, illness, and frostbite. This represented a 76 percent casualty rate.[48]

For the Canadians the casualties were significant. The Canadian government had made a decision earlier on to no longer reinforce the Canadian contingent of the FSSF due to the growing manpower crisis in Canada. As a result, the Force was becoming lop-sided since the Americans continued to send reinforcements. In fact, by the end of January 1944, the Canadian contingent in the combat echelon numbered 26 officers and 323 ORs, while the Americans numbered 33 officers and 781 ORs.[49]

The casualties were not surprising since Lieutenant-General Clark was using the FSSF, in the words of Lieutenant-Colonel Gilday, now the interim acting CO of the Canadian Contingent, "in a straight infantry role as shock troops for the Fifth Army."[50] Gilday bridled at the high casualties of such specialized trained troops. The recent mountain campaign had cost Canada six officers and 139 ORs killed and wounded.[51] Gilday reported that the strength of the 1st Canadian Special Service Battalion was down approximately 50

OF COURAGE AND DETERMINATION

Living conditions on the mountain, January 1944.

percent. And he did not anticipate recovering more than 25 percent of the wounded members due to the type of injuries they received.[52]

As the Force rested and refitted, Gilday reflected on the future of the Canadian representation within the Force. While the Americans were already bringing in new troops, CMHQ had still not provided a definitive answer on theatre reinforcement. Gilday feared that the influx of Americans would decrease the Canadian representation within the Force and lead to the loss of the Force's dual national character. In essence, Gilday feared the Canadian component would become marginalized. "Rather than have the Canadian element waste away," he warned, "I feel that the question of reinforcing the Battalion should be decided immediately."[53] Gilday was blunt and exceptionally clear on his recommended solution. He wrote:

> We have acquitted ourselves well in battle. There is a good feeling and many strong friendships between the Canadians and the Americans of the force. As new American reinforcements come in and Canadians become fewer in number it will be increasingly difficult to keep the friendly spirit and good relations that now exist. The Canadian element is liable to become a source of embarrassment to the Americans. It will also become increasingly difficult to keep the existing high morale when

> it becomes known that the Canadians are going to be allowed so slowly waste away.
>
> I strongly recommend that the Canadian element be withdrawn from the First Special Service Force while there is enough of it left to be of assistance to the Canadian Army. This withdrawal should take place immediately before the force is committed again in another phase of operations and while the force is undergoing re-organization after the present phase which is about completed.[54]

His recommendation was the catalyst for an arduous three-month debate between the senior Canadian general officers in Italy, in the U.K., and in Canada with regard to the thorny issue of perpetuating the Canadian component of the FSSF, namely the 1 CSSBN. Before committing additional troops to the battalion, however, the senior Canadian chain of command reviewed the entire issue examining the FSSF's initial role, special training, manpower, and evolution.[55] It was not lost on the CGS, Lieutenant-General Ken Stuart, that following the cancellation of the Plough Project and the Force's subsequent deployment to the Aleutians, the unit's operational role had changed. The FSSF was no longer a one-mission, quick-strike unit, it was instead "being used in a straight infantry role with the United States Army."[56] This significant change prompted many senior Canadian generals to re-evaluate Canada's future commitments to the FSSF. After all, at that very moment, the Canadian Army in Italy was in dire need of fully trained infantrymen and NCOs. Although Gilday strongly recommended that the Canadian element be withdrawn immediately, before the FSSF was committed to another operation, he did provide three options for the Canadian generals to consider. The first was to shore up the Canadian contingent to its full strength, including reinforcements, totalling 48 officers and 702 ORs. The second option was to remove the Canadian element from the Force and send the men as reinforcements elsewhere in the Canadian Army. The last option was to leave the remaining soldiers in the Force and let the Canadian element gradually waste away.[57]

By the end of January 1944, serious consideration was given to removing the Canadians from the FSSF. From the Canadian perspective, this course of action had merit. Furthermore, its immediate implementation would circumvent the need to set up an in-theatre reinforcement process. But, as the dithering continued, the Force received new orders. The decision would now be more complicated. Of greater concern, however, was the Force's new mission. They were once again being thrown into the furnace of combat.

12

ANZIO AND THE RACE TO ROME

In Anzio the fighting was tough. One minute you'd be talking to the person next to you. The next minute he was dead.[1]

— Sergeant Peter Smith

Finally out of the mountains, the FSSF had a little time to rest and recuperate. Although they had proven themselves as a first-rate combat force, the cost had been significant. After taking Mount La Difensa, the commander of the U.S. 5th Army continued to use the FSSF as crack assault infantry troops to dislodge a tenacious German enemy clinging to mountain strongholds. Although successful in the end, in many ways, the mountain campaign transformed the FSSF. The highly trained individuals that underwent gruelling specialist training back in North America became fewer and fewer. The deadly campaign in the Italian mountains designed to open the way for the 5th Army advance to Rome severely bled the FSSF. As a result, new reinforcements were required. None had the training of the originals. And neither would they be allowed the time to gain the necessary skills for the new challenge that awaited them.

With the U.S. 5th Army drive for Rome still bogged down in the mountains, Allied leaders decided to put additional pressure on the Germans. They now took Churchill's desire to strike at the "soft German underbelly" to heart. As such, they decided to gamble on an aggressive thrust into the German's rear area that would threaten the enemy lines of communication in the Alban Hills area southeast of Rome and cut off German forces in the Gustav Line. This, they believed, would force the enemy to pull out, or at a minimum, weaken their mountain strongholds. Churchill's intent for Operation Shingle, the code name for the new offensive, was simply to "hurl a wildcat ashore."[2]

OF COURAGE AND DETERMINATION

As a result, in the early hours of 22 January 1944, the Allies flung 6th Corps, approximately 36,000 American and British troops, as well as over 3,000 vehicles onto the beaches at Anzio, approximately 60 kilometres southeast of Rome.[3] Lieutenant-General Clark expected heavy German resistance. Not surprising then, his primary concern was more with establishing a stable beachhead than aggressively moving inland into the Alban Hills or advancing toward Rome. However, the Germans were caught by complete surprise. Aside from a few infantry companies, who were quickly overrun, the enemy had nothing locally available to block the Allied landing or thrust inland. By noon, 6th Corps engineers were clearing mines and cutting exit routes through the dunes to allow men and equipment to flow inland.

Unfortunately, Major-General John P. Lucas, the 6th Corps commander, took to heart his superior's concern and also became overly preoccupied with not overreaching. As such, he too focused his efforts on consolidating the beachhead and bringing ashore enough troops, munitions, and equipment to fight off any German counterattack that may materialize. The Allied timidity gave German Field Marshal Albert Kesselring ample time to move forces into the Anzio area to hem in the Allied salient.[4] By 0700 hours, 22 January, Kesselring had already ordered units from the 14th Army in northern Italy, as well as units from the Gustav Line in the south, to deploy to Anzio. By 1700 hours that evening, the first German troops began to arrive. By the end of the day, a thin defensive crust encircled the Allied beachhead. And, it would grow stronger with every day. Within 48 hours, Kesselring amassed 24,000 troops to contain the Allied assault.[5]

Anzio Beach.

ANZIO AND THE RACE TO ROME

By the beginning of February, it became obvious that the cautious and slow Allied approach had allowed the Germans sufficient time to recover and contain the beachhead. Churchill angrily decried, "I had hoped that we would be hurling a wildcat ashore, but all we got was a stranded whale."[6] By 12 February, Kesselring had approximately 120,000 troops arrayed against the reinforced Allied bridgehead.[7] The soft underbelly had been quickly transformed into an armoured shell. The quick and aggressive response was not lost on the Allies. An intelligence report conceded, "At no time since our landing has the enemy reacted other then aggressively in the Anzio — Nettuno area. He has constantly striven to maintain the initiative through the use of patrolling, reconnaissance and continual attack, even after being stopped in three all-out offensive efforts within three weeks."[8]

In fact, the German response was so overwhelming that the initiative was reversed. The Allies now feared the prospect of being swept back out to sea. As a result, Clark quickly worked toward reinforcing the besieged bridgehead.

Meanwhile, back at Santa Maria the FSSF was resting, re-equipping, and retraining. But this was short lived. Clark ordered them to the Anzio front to assist with holding the tenuous beachhead. At last light on 1 February 1944, the Force embarked on a number of LSTs and landing craft, infantry (LCIs) and sailed for Anzio. They reached the port the next morning and after a slight delay moved to a nearby assembly area. That night, 2 February, the combat echelon moved forward to relieve the 39th Combat Engineer Regiment along the Mussolini Canal. By 0330 hours, 3 February, the relief in place was complete. The FSSF had two regiments holding the front line and the third protecting the right flank of 6th Corps.[9]

But the FSSF was not the same formation that arrived in Italy months previously, or that assaulted Mount La Difensa. It had been greatly reduced in number. Captain Underhill acknowledged, "The First Special Service Force that landed at Anzio was considerably

Watching the Mussolini Canal.

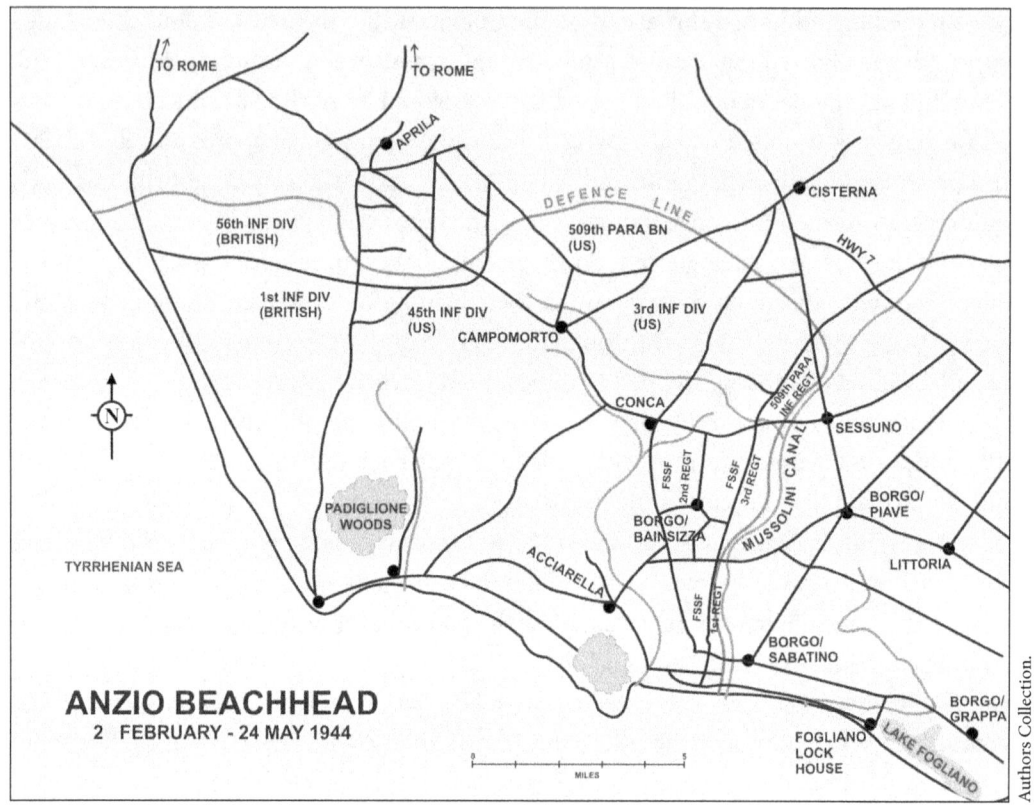

different than the Force that had landed at Naples some two months earlier."[10] Although a number of the wounded had returned to the Force, the reality was that a large number of the originals were dead or still recovering from wounds. As a result, the FSSF had no choice but to take in reinforcements that lacked the training and experience of the originals.

In addition, the FSSF had to reorganize. Reinforcements and replacements brought 3rd Regiment up to full strength. Colonel Walker recalled, "many troops were green — when we left by ship for Anzio beachhead on LCIs."[11] However, there were not enough reinforcements for the entire formation. As a result, the 1st and 2nd Regiments were still at half strength so they were reorganized into three battalions of three companies each.

Amazingly, with approximately 1,200 front-line troops, the 6th Corps commander expected the FSSF to hold one fourth of the beachhead, almost twice the area assigned to any other division. Lieutenant-Colonel Gilday asserted, "The portion of the Mussolini Canal which the Force holds is 11,000 metres long. This is very close to being 1/4 of the total front of the bridgehead. It is a very thin line to hold with 801 officers and men."[12]

Major Gerry McFadden, the CO of 2nd Battalion, 1st Regiment, recalled the dire position the Force found itself in. McFadden recounted:

> I had 69 men out of 300 and something out of a battalion. That is all that was left. And he [Regimental Commander] said, "here is the map here is

where you are going to go." I looked at the scale on the map, and I said, "My God! Jack, [Lieutenant-Colonel J.F.R. Akehurst] that's 1,200 yards. I only have 69 men!" He turned and looked at me, and said, "McFadden, if you can't do it I will find somebody who can." End of story.[13]

McFadden's concern was shared by others. Sergeant Donald Green exclaimed, "The canal was about twenty-five feet wide and about ten feet deep with varying sizes of embankments. I was amazed at the distance one platoon had to cover." He estimated, "The space between foxholes or dugouts was forty to fifty yards. I could judge our platoon covered nearly 400 yards."[14]

Anxieties, however, were brushed aside and the Force carried out its assignment. Lieutenant Conrad Legault recalled the occupation of their position:

> While the changeover [relief in place with the 39th Engineer Combat Regiment] was taking place, we could hear the Germans talk. Some of them even crept in close enough to dispose of their hand grenades and hinder our movement. We spent most of the night digging-in and waited impatiently for first light to have a good look at the terrain to our front and watch enemy movements. As soon as morning appeared, most of us peaked over the canal bank to reckon that the ground ahead of us consisted of 8 to 10 miles of flat ground back of which were fairly high hills providing the enemy with excellent observation over the whole beachhead area. There we were, sitting right in the middle of a large tray, wide open to air and artillery assault.[15]

Lieutenant Mitchell acknowledged, "They [engineers] didn't waste any time leaving — they didn't know where Jerry was so we had to find it out by ourselves. It was a different situation from the mountains where it might have been cold and miserable, but at least you could find cover quickly. Here it was flat and you could be spotted a long way off."[16]

The closeness of the Germans became an issue for none other than the Force commander. When the newly promoted Brigadier-General Frederick chose a farmhouse for his command post, the sudden noise and activity alerted the German outposts near the canal who immediately called for artillery fire to saturate Frederick's new headquarters location.[17] The FSSF commander deemed that intolerable and set in motion an aggressive patrol regimen designed to expel the Germans from "no-man's land" and push them away from the FSSF's front lines.

The new area of operation was challenging in its own right. Major Thomas explained:

> The Mussolini Canal was our key terrain feature. Between the dykes the channel of the canal was cut much deeper. Along the channel on either

OF COURAGE AND DETERMINATION

Primitive conditions on the front line.

> side were wide level banks allowing foot passage at normal water level. In flood stage they went under water. On both sides of the canal the terrain was flat, so flat that we felt we could see — and be seen — for miles. Since the [Mussolini Canal] project had been completed only recently there was little vegetation, particularly in the form of trees. The only terrain features that imposed themselves on one's vision were the "project" type houses, concrete block 2-story buildings scattered over the landscape.[18]

An official FSSF report reinforced Thomas's observations:

> Overall, the Mussolini Canal forms a natural barrier across the marshlands of the Littoria plain. The Canal in this area runs a slightly irregular course along the North-South line. At this season of the year the depth and swiftness of the water in the canal varies considerably and very rapidly, depending upon the weather in the immediate vicinity. At all times during this season it forms a natural barrier against mechanized armament. The terrain in this general area is flat, sandy farmland, crossed by an intricate system of small drainage ditches. The road network is good but virtually all traffic is confined to the roads, the soil in the open fields being too soft to bear vehicle traffic. The countryside is dotted with many farmhouses

which offer opportunities for observation and for ambush. Aside from the shallow ditches and fringes of trees along the roadside there is virtually no cover, and in clear weather all movement may be observed easily.[19]

And so, the Forcemen dug-in and began to adjust to their new surroundings. The initial days were cloudy and rainy, accompanied by German artillery fire and air attack. The rain and wind played havoc with sandy soil, causing slit trenches to cave in and foxholes to fill with water.[20] "Our positions in Anzio were rather primitive," recounted Sergeant Jim Summersides. He explained:

> They were deep holes. If you could beg, borrow, or steal something to cover the tops, you'd do it. Most of them had roofs over their heads and a lot of dirt over that. There were two people per foxhole. When we replacements came in, they paired us up with a veteran. So in each foxhole you had a greenhorn and a veteran. During my stay in Anzio I was paired up with two different veterans, one was a Canadian and the other an American.[21]

Ken McDougall wrote, "The country is flat as a pancake, with few trees and dull little farm houses scattered on it." He described how his company was deployed: "Our company inhabits a long earth bank on the edge of a field. It is just like a prairie dog colony. I stick my head out in the morning and the other heads pop up all down the row. One by one we come out into the open, stretch, walk about a bit, look at the sky."[22]

Despite the challenging topography, or perhaps because of it, Frederick set an important task for his Forcemen — push the Germans back and create a buffer, a "no-man's land" between the enemy and their own front lines. After all, the situation bordered on the absurd. Major Thomas exclaimed:

> We were surprised at the defense positions of the unit we relieved. It had set up its defense along the back side of the near dyke of the canal. Since from this position the far dyke blocked forward observation, the enemy could approach unobserved, and he did.
>
> We began setting up outposts on the forward dyke, then aggressive patrolling. We cut machine gun nests to provide interlocking bands of fire across our front and kept these positions manned 24 hours a day. We dug 2-man firing pits from which our men had forward observation so as to be able to cut down any enemy who dared approach our front in daylight. Every man had a firing position, either machine gun, BAR or rifle, to which he went in event of an attack.
>
> At night we set listening posts forward of the canal with radio communications. We dug our mortars in behind the rear canal bank, and

zeroed them in along our frontage so we could quickly respond to any enemy incursion. As usual, we had an artillery forward observer assigned to the battalion and he registered his battalion's guns in the same manner, only at a greater range. We strung accordion wire in front of the forward dyke and laid mine fields with clearly marked taped paths. These paths connected to passages we cut through the forward dyke, allowing patrols to pass through instead of over the top. This avoided their being silhouetted as they left the canal. For living quarters our men dug into the back side of the forward dyke, living like animals in burrows.[23]

The German main line of defence was approximately 1,500 metres to their front running roughly with the canal. Initially, some of the houses in the "no-man's land" between the two warring parties were still occupied by civilians, however, they were eventually evacuated as the fighting for control of the terrain increased. By the end of February, the Force had captured 145 enemy prisoners.[24] A FSSF report at the time indicated:

> During the first week of February the vigorous activity of our patrols forced the enemy to fall back a distance of approximately fifteen hundred yards, with the result that there came into being a kind of no-man's land between the two units. During daylight this no-man's land looked like a peaceful Italian countryside. As soon as darkness fell, the area became a place of manoeuvre for the numerous patrols sent out by both the enemy and ourselves. In the meantime both sides continued to improve their defensive positions along the respective main lines of resistance.[25]

Overall, the situation on the Anzio front failed to improve. Although surprised by the initial landing, the Germans continued to react aggressively and violently to the Allied landing behind their lines. By early February, the Allied position in the Anzio bridgehead seemed tenuous. On 11 February, *The Times* ran the headline "Fierce Efforts Against Beach-Head ... Heavy Fighting in Progress ... Danger to Allies in Beach-Head." The same day CBS correspondent Charles Daly reported, "The situation in the bridgehead is grim: we have been forced to give ground."[26]

Although shelling, probes by enemy patrols, and enemy air attacks were almost a daily occurrence in one form or another, the brunt of the German efforts fell on other sectors of the beachhead, particularly those held by the British. The war diary captured the situation. It reported, "Along the Force front Jerry seems to be digging in and laying mine fields and barbed wire against our patrols, the other fronts are meeting stiff German resistance."[27] However, on 16 February 1944, the Germans unleashed an attack against the FSSF lines. It was part of their larger offensive, code named Operation *Fischfang* (Fish Catch), designed to crush the Allied beachhead. For the Germans, this offensive was an all out effort.

ANZIO AND THE RACE TO ROME

The FSSF spent 99 days in the line at Anzio.

"All hell broke loose about 0600 hours," wrote Lieutenant-Colonel Gilday, "when the Germans let loose all their artillery and mortars and ours replied." He described:

> They [Germans] attacked all along our line, most strongly on the left flank held by 1st Bn., 3rd Regt. It was apparently a diversion for a main attack against the British, all attacks were repulsed and settled down to the regular artillery and air attacks. On the Force flank 4 hun tanks were knocked out and 3 probables being used as mobile artillery.[28]

The official FSSF S-2 (intelligence) report noted:

> Strong patrol action accompanied by tanks preceded a two company assault to seize and hold a CANALE MUSSOLINI bridgehead in vic[inity] re-entrant bend (C220). Four tanks and two SP guns were employed, 3 of the tanks and one gun being disabled by our artillery and rocket fire. An early effort to install a dug-in holding line 400 metres E[ast] of bend was abandoned early in the day.... 2 Enemy planes strafed 3d Regt forward area at 1000 hrs. Artillery and mortar fire was heavy prior to action.

> During the day enemy artillery quieted down to intermittent harassing along the sector front.²⁹

The overall German aggressive thrust continued and two days later, on 18 February, they pierced the Allied line penetrating almost 3,000 metres in the 45th Division area, which was close to the FSSF lines. However, by the afternoon of 19 February, the German offensive had run its course. They could not push the Allies back into the sea. Both sides now settled into a stalemate waiting for the Allies to build the necessary strength to break out.

This, however, did not mean that the front became quiet. The Germans continued an aggressive patrolling and shelling program. The war diary reported, "At the canal the Force is continually subjected to enemy artillery, they throw everything they have at our men for a few minutes and then quit while the Force get busy getting artillery support in for an infantry attack that does not develop." The result was not surprising. "The men," noted Gilday, "are beginning to get a bit tired and jittery as they have been in nearly 3 weeks with little sleep and continuous night patrolling."³⁰ Sergeant Summersides recalled:

> When you were in the front lines you never knew when the German would send a few shells over. It was unnerving sporadic fire. We were never pinned down for any length of time. They seemed to know where we were, just as we knew where they were. During the day, all movement was kept to the minimum.³¹

By the end of the month, the toll on the Forceman became evident. "The men are very tired," revealed the war diary, "as they are either digging or fighting 24 hours a day. The main question is 'when will we be relieved?'"³² Lieutenant-Colonel Gilday summed up the state of affairs:

> We maintained the initiative by active patrolling all along the front. The 1st Bn., 3rd Regt repulsed two very strong enemy attacks. Our orders are to "Hold the Canal." We have not enough strength to push past it and have to hold it by sitting on it and patrolling to the front. The enemy has high ground all around the bridge head and can see all our ground, shell all our roads from at least two sides. The boys have done a wonderful job.³³

Despite the success the FSSF was achieving, the canal fight was further depleting already limited manpower. Although some American reinforcements had been absorbed by the Force, the issue of Canadian reinforcements had still not been resolved. On arrival at Anzio the Canadian contingent numbered a paltry 39 officers and 493 other ranks, of which 12 and 154 respectively remained behind in hospital, meaning that only 366 Canadians were serving on the front.[34] The dissatisfaction was aptly captured in a 1 CSSBN war diary entry — "Another month comes to a close with no decision regarding reinforcements or British awards for our personnel. The lack of action on these two subjects is felt very keenly throughout the battalion."[35]

Back in NDHQ, Canadian commanders and staff were still wrestling with Gilday's earlier recommendation to pull the Canadians out of the FSSF. Although his idea had merit, it also provided some unsettling consequences. Some were concerned that such a unilateral decision would severely weaken the FSSF's in-theatre operational capabilities and possibly lead to the disbandment of the Force. They also feared, from a "political" perspective, such a decision could place undue strain on the Canadian-American relations.[36] Major-General Maurice Pope, Stuart's man in Washington, D.C., was quick to warn, "Any proposal to break up this combined unit, which is not only in a theatre operations but is actually engaged against the enemy, would prove embarrassing to a degree and might be construed as hardly playing the game." He concluded, "it would certainly be difficult to put across and as certainly would not enhance U.S. regard for us."[37]

The disbandment option, however logical and seemingly inescapable, was once again placed on the backburner. Senior Canadian commanders decided that at the moment it was essential to demonstrate Canada's continued commitment to the FSSF, particularly since the formation was currently in a theatre of operations holding a significant front line assignment. As a result, NDHQ quickly brought focus to bear on generating an effective reinforcement program that would deliver the right type of Canadian soldier for reinforcing the FSSF.

A subsequent study of the necessary qualifications required by reinforcements quickly revealed potential problems. The Forcemen were trained in such specialty skills as mountain operations, skiing, and amphibious training, as well as extensive training in demolition, parachute training, patrolling, communications, and mechanics.[38] No such pool of soldiers existed in the Canadian Army, much less in the infantry reinforcement depots currently being established in Italy. Nevertheless, Lieutenant-General Stuart was anxious to resolve this situation as quickly as possible. Therefore, he ordered Brigadier-General A. Warwick Beament, the chief of the Canadian Section headquarters, 1st Echelon, 15th Army Group, Italy, to determine what type of volunteer the Americans were currently sending as reinforcements to the FSSF.

Beament quickly determined that the American soldiers that were sent to the Force were, "good husky type infantry reinforcements." He also elaborated that currently no parachute or specialized training was required.[39] Furthermore, he confirmed that the Force would only be employed in an infantry role. Consequently, if the Americans sent infantrymen to the FSSF, Stuart recommended that the Canadians follow their lead. As a result, the CSG proposed that volunteers be selected from general infantry reinforcement pools to bolster 1 CSSBN.[40]

On 9 February 1944, Lieutenant-General Stuart met with General "Ike" Eisenhower, Supreme Allied Commander Allied Expeditionary Force, and reaffirmed Canada's commitment to the FSSF. Eisenhower was apparently quite pleased with this turn of events.[41] Nonetheless, from the Canadian perspective, the continuing participation was only driven by political concerns not operational requirements.

Important to note is that it was not only Gilday and other Canadian senior military decision makers who had issues with the continuation of Canadian participation in the FSSF. On 19 February 1944, Frederick wrote his immediate superior with reservations. "Upon completion of the current phase of operations," he penned, "it will be necessary to know the basic decisions that have been made for the future of the First Special Service Force." He revealed, "The combat strength of the force has been so reduced that the force cannot again take any major part in an operation, nor can it execute minor actions for any long period." Frederick further counselled, "To continue the force with its characteristics is not possible under existing conditions." He explained:

> The successes the force has achieved in combat have been the result of special training and the development of certain qualities and spirit in the officers and enlisted men. This training and development required a comparatively long time under favourable training conditions. Comparable results in combat cannot be accomplished by the force if its casualties are replaced with men who are not specially trained, nor without its full complement of officers who have been indoctrinated with the spirit and combat methods of this command.[42]

In addition, although on the surface the experiment of a joint Canadian-American formation seemed to work, there were clearly undercurrents of friction. Frederick himself acknowledged, "While the amalgamation of personnel of two armies into a single unit has worked successfully, it is basically unsound and difficult, and it has worked only because those intimately associated with the administration and supervision of the arrangement have made it work."[43] Frederick concluded, "For the sake of United States and Canadian relations, it may be best to let this unit pass out of existence while it is still in its prime, rather than to sustain it through a period when it will be remembered only for its faults and defects."[44]

Reservations aside, for the time being, both nations agreed to continue feeding the FSSF with reinforcements. Although there were a number of details to work out, finally, by 4 March 1944, a way ahead was reached.[45] NDHQ now authorized Brigadier Weeks to reinforce the Canadian element of the FSSF through the Canadian overseas reinforcement channel with infantry personnel.[46] Six days later, he tabled the new selection criterion for Canadian FSSF volunteers. For the moment, the new candidates were to be drawn from Canadian infantry reinforcements currently available in the Central Mediterranean Force (CMF). NDHQ also decided that battle casualties were to be replaced by infantry reinforcements from the U.K. and from facilities established in Camp Shilo, Manitoba.[47]

With the administrative requirements put in place all that remained was to find the actual replacements. After the initial call for volunteers in the CMF, Brigadier Weeks reminded the recruiters, prior to the upcoming selection phase, to ask all the volunteers if they were actually willing to comply with the 1 CSSBN conditions of service. In the event that they refused, they were to be rejected outright. Those who were accepted, were ordered to read and sign a revised "Special Declaration" form outlining the conditions of service.[48] All new personnel were eligible to receive parachute pay even though they were not required to undergo parachute training at this time. The volunteers were to be advised that they would wear American uniforms and use American equipment and weapons. Those who were selected would undergo intensive special training prior to joining the Force. It was also stipulated that no officers above the rank of lieutenant and no NCO would be accepted as volunteers for the FSSF. Lastly, in the event that parachute training was to be conducted, the candidates would be trained, in theatre, at the Cairo Jump School, in Egypt. Finally, all candidates were ordered to report for selection to the headquarters of 1st Canadian Base Reinforcement Group, no later than 10 March 1944.[49]

The response to the initial call was overwhelming. John Rowe, one of the many volunteers, recalled the incredible number of soldiers who showed up. He revealed:

> I was in the Canadian Depot in Avellino, Italy. There were notices posted everywhere stating that they wanted volunteers for the First Special Service Force. The next day, they had a huge parade. I would say that there were at least 3,000 guys that had volunteered. The officer in charge of the depot looked at the men and said, "No way! We want half of you guys." He then walked along the first line and cut the group in half. One half was dismissed and I happened to be in the other half. That's how I got into the Force. I just wanted to get on and do something.[50]

In less than six days a total of 52 officers and 728 ORs demonstrated their willingness to serve with the FSSF.[51] Whereas this was good news for the FSSF, Canadian infantry COs were concerned by this sudden unexpected recruiting drive. They quickly realized their ability to receive quality reinforcements had been comprimised. The perceived preferential treatment of the FSSF grated commanders in 1st Canadian Corps (1 Cdn Corps). "This practice is highly repugnant," stated the officers in a report to Brigadier Weeks, "as promising officers and potential NCOs are thus diverted from the fighting units of the 1 Cdn Corps."[52] Despite the protest, the decision stood and the reinforcements were sent to 1 CSSBN.

Sergeant George Wright, a Force veteran, met the new reinforcements as they arrived at the FSSF's training depot. "These fellows had come to us from [Canadian] units that had been in combat. The Force wanted seasoned troops rather than only greenhorns," explained Wright. "They didn't have a clue what type of an outfit they were coming too," revealed the battle-hardened veteran. One of the new volunteers who had previously served with a front line infantry unit "thought we were a unit that had just come from the States," recalled Wright. "He thought WE were greenhorns."[53]

What was clear was that the Canadian reinforcements were long overdue and those selected seemed to fill the bill. "They are a good looking body of men," remarked Lieutenant-Colonel Akehurst, the CO of the Canadian contingent.[54] The resolution of the Canadian reinforcement issue ensured, for the moment at least, a continued Canadian presence and identity within the Force. However, due to an increasing number of American reinforcements the Canadians were losing ground rapidly. On paper, the American component totalled 56 officers and 1,361 other ranks while the Canadian component totalled 47 officers and 585 other ranks.[55] Furthermore, the Americans had decided to increase the Force's size. In order to maintain the 50 percent Canadian ratio within the combat element of the Force, Akehurst requested additional troops. The reply from his Canadian chain-of-command was clear and non-negotiable — only battle casualties would be replaced.[56]

And so, finally, on 1 April 1944, a group of Canadian reinforcements numbering 15 officers and 240 enlisted men reported for duty. By the end of the month, the Canadian contingent stood at 53 officers and 676 other ranks, with an effective strength of 49 and 595, respectively. The American combat echelon totalled an effective strength of 56 officers and 1,361 enlisted members, with an additional eight and 288 respectively in hospital. The FSSF support echelon numbered an additional 750 Americans.[57]

"Night Raiders of Anzio" — *Painting by Roger Chabot.*

ANZIO AND THE RACE TO ROME

While the commanders and staffs were waging the bureaucratic struggle, the Forcemen remained on the front lines at Anzio and continued the daily drudgery of static warfare. They endured miserable conditions, constant shelling, and a deadly version of "cat and mouse" as both sides aggressively patrolled in an effort to control and dominate "no-man's land."

For the FSSF, patrolling became a key component of their tactical plan. Through constant aggressive patrolling, they would be able to keep the Germans off balance and on the defensive, and maintain an up-to-date picture of German disposition and intent. The task would be an exhausting and dangerous activity that took on a life of its own. One junior officer admitted, "Night patrolling is one of the most nerve-wracking operations and after a few weeks of nightly outings and roaming through mines, booby-traps and trip-wires, one is bound to feel the tension and enter into a state of extreme nervousness."[58] Sergeant Paul Schoeler explained:

> Each patrol was a war in itself. I was part of a company level fighting patrol. Our mission was to distract the German so that elsewhere along the line other patrols could get through. That night, I was sixth in line. I was about ten feet behind the guy ahead of me. Suddenly there was this tremendous explosion. As I dropped to the ground, I said a Hail Mary. I saw the guy in front of me way up in the air. He crashed into a ditch. We raced over. The ditch was full of water, he was drowning. We jumped in and pulled him out. One leg was badly twisted and the other was off at the knee. We gave him first aid and they took him back. The next night we were in the same area. We found his boot with the leg still in it. It was about 100 yards away from where we had been the night before. We dug a hole and buried it.[59]

Schoeler added:

> At night, that's when we did our damage. We had to man numerous night patrols to push the Germans further back and keep them honest. These were hard on the nerves. There were a lot of mines. You never knew when you'd step on one of these damn things. It was sheer hell. You'd get use to it, but you were always very tense.[60]

Corporal Gordon Baker observed, "When it gets dark some of the nervous ones think that every tree and shrub has just moved and fire at it. One shot and the patrols position is known to the enemy and right now the patrol is fighting for its life."[61]

It became a Darwinian process of survival of the toughest and fastest to learn. Sergeant Wright acknowledged, "For patrolling we learned as we went along." He described, "The blackening of the face and hands, you carried nothing unnecessary, just your ammunition and weapons. Stealth was the big thing. The more you did it, the better you got at it."[62]

And, there was no shortage of practice. Sergeant Donald Green commented, "Everybody was sure of at least one patrol every second night."[63] The Forcemen soon became experts. Ken McDougall believed, "We were like a lot of thugs sneaking along the hedgerows in the moonlight." He explained, "We had blackened our hands and faces, wore our oldest clothes, and carried rifles, knives and hand grenades in our pockets."[64]

Not surprisingly, they soon began to sow terror in the minds of their opponents. A captured German prisoner, *Jaeger* Erwin Ehlers from the 4th Coy, 7th *Luftwaffe Jaeger* Battalion revealed his unit was "much impressed with the aggressive attitude of the American troops on this front." He conceded that the patrolling conducted by the FSSF "keeps the Germans on alert status at all times."[65] Moreover, a Luftwaffe officer of the Herman Göering Division wrote in his diary, which was captured, "Every time we come into the line, the black devils with the baggy pants are all around us and we never hear them coming."[66] A directive from the German High Command that was taken from a prisoner provided a graphic enemy appraisal of the FSSF. The note read, "You are fighting an elite Canadian-American force. They are treacherous, unmerciful and clever. You cannot afford to relax."[67]

A FSSF unit newsletter captured the theme of the fear that the FSSF was instilling in their enemy. One article wrote, "'The men with the funny pants and the dirty faces' that come out of the night and hit them put the fear of God in the Kraut. Prisoners told [the interrogators] that the enemy soldiers didn't want to stay and fight us, they wanted to pull out. Our enemy here is afraid of the night because when darkness comes, so do the 'Black Devils.'"[68]

FSSF calling card — "The Worst Is Yet To Come!"

The war of patrolling dragged on for months. Lieutenant-Colonel Gilday asserted:

> We couldn't move forward. But our boys wouldn't stand for the Germans breathing down their necks, so they took out after the enemy lines every night by patrol. That's when we did our best work. The Germans were frightened to death of us because they didn't know who we were. We'd come in as a secret force and had these special uniforms that they couldn't identify. Our outfits didn't look like Canadian or American uniforms. We had specially made baggy pants that had originally been

intended for the snow in Norway. They were very comfortable and had lots of pockets.

At first, the Germans used to call us "The Men in Baggy Pants." Then it became "the Black Devils," because we used to blacken our faces and move in on them at night. Colonel Frederick had little stickers made for our men. We'd move on the Germans at night and kill them silently. Then we'd put one of these stickers on their heads or helmets, which said, "[*Da Dicke Ende Kommt Noch*] The Worst is yet to come."[69]

Major Stanley Waters noted that within the 99 days at the front, the average officer and soldier participated in approximately 40 separate and distinct patrols, some doing as many as 75.[70] Despite the endless patrolling and all the deprivation in Anzio due to terrain, weather, and enemy activity, the situation became worse. By the beginning of March, another factor made itself felt. Though the soldiers didn't know it yet, preparations for the Normandy landing were well underway. On 6 March 1944, the newly appointed commander of 6th Corps, Major-General L.K. Truscott, issued to all his subordinate commanders a long memorandum explaining how important it was to conserve munitions, equipment, and supply.[71] He stated, "Due to the necessity of diverting landing craft to other theatres where offensive operations against the enemy are in process or will soon be launched, the number of craft available for the supply and build-up of the troops in the Anzio Bridgehead is extremely limited and the greatest care must be taken to insure that they are used with the utmost efficiency."[72] As a result, shipments of ammunition, fuel, vehicles, and equipment were rationed and new shipments into the beachhead curtailed.

This was not the only annoyance to the Force. Another issue that began to brew was the resurfacing of the old problem of how CMHQ would deal with the Canadians in the FSSF. The issue was clearly explained by Lieutenant-Colonel Akehurst:

> Major Biscoe returned from Naples at noon. He was advised that the battalion was to be administered by C.M.H.Q., effective 1st June 44 and was to be brought into line with administration of all Canadian units overseas. This opens up all the old problems that we had hoped had been settled for good before we left the States. Higher authority persists in wanting to compare this unit with other Canadian Units. The Force has been formed for nearly two years and we have never yet come in contact in any way with other Canadian troops. The lives of officers and men of this battalion are tied in 100% with American troops and since the Force is American this condition is unlikely to change, and comparison with Canadian troops is most unfair. If we are to receive our lire at Canadian rates the already large difference in rates of pay will be still further increased and if on top of this we are subject to restricted pay,

it means the Canadian Pte has eight Canadian dollars to spend to the American Pte $110.00 per month.[73]

But the administrative issues had to wait. The time had finally arrived to break out of the Anzio beachhead. The 36th Engineer Combat Regiment commenced the relief of the FSSF from the frontlines along the Mussolini Canal on 9 May 1944 and finished the following morning. However, the 2nd Regiment, FSSF, maintained an aggressive patrolling schedule to ensure the Germans remained unaware that the Force had been withdrawn. From 10 to 21 May, the entire combat echelon of the FSSF conducted training, specifically infantry-tank combined operations, in preparation for the breakout. Then, on the night of 22 May, the FSSF moved forward to an assembly line to prepare for the big offensive.

It had been a long time under fire. Due to the length of front to secure and the shortage of troops, the FSSF had remained in the frontlines without relief for 99 days. During this period, they had suffered 114 killed, 702 wounded, and 65 missing. They had also captured 603 enemy prisoners.[74]

That was all behind them now. The advance to Rome was about to begin. There were three operational plans. The first was Operation Grasshopper, which entailed a drive to the east of the beachhead toward the south of Italy and a link-up with forces moving north. The second option was Operation Buffalo. This centred on a drive to the northeast of the beachhead to take control of the hill masses around Mount Arrestino and the interdiction of Highways 6 and 7. Finally, the third option was Operation Turtle. This entailed 6th Corps advancing northwest to capture Rome without any link-up with the advance of 5th Army from the South.[75]

In the end, General H.R. Alexander, the commander of the 15th Army Group, in line with Prime Minister Churchill's directive, ordered Clark to strike north to Valmontone, thereby allowing for the potential of cutting off the German retreat and encircling the German 10th Army in the South. Accordingly, Clark fixed his main point of effort at breaking through the German defences south of Cisterna.

Clark set 23 May 1944 as D-Day and 0630 hours as H-Hour for breakout. The FSSF had no problems moving into their attack positions. Lieutenant William Sheldon, 3rd Platoon commander in the 4th Coy, 1st Regiment, recalled:

> We marched for two hours or more with frequent stops finally arriving at a shallow ditch (the commonest cover on the flats of the Beachhead) at 3:00 a.m. — the ditch which was to be our position at H-Hour (6:30 a.m.) and some 150 yards in back of the exact frontline. The men were heavily laden with ammunition and weapons — a full combat load — and were tired when we reached our jumping-off point. Many of us dozed off for an hour or so. The front was about the same as usual — sporadic

Frederick and Clark consult on next moves.

machine gun fire and occasional shells. A few bullets passed over our heads, but no shells landed near.[76]

Then, at 0500 hours, Allied artillery opened up a ferocious bombardment. At 0630 hours, both the 1st and 3rd Regiments, supported by FSSF mortars and accompanied by tanks and tank destroyers, advanced on a broad front along the banks of the Mussolini Canal to the right of the 1st Regiment.[77] "Then all hell broke out," described Lieutenant-Colonel Becket. "The enemy opened fire," he recalled, "on prearranged heavy machine gun lines of fire."[78] He further explained:

OF COURAGE AND DETERMINATION

Our main wave slowed up a little to allow smaller units to work in with their grenades and their backing [depth] sections would move in and mop up. Then the Force advanced and by 8 AM 1st Regiment had reached halfway to Highway VII — they had made about a mile in three hours — very good going.[79]

Corporal Baker recalled, "By 8:00 o'clock First's [1st Regiment] drive was halfway to Highway 7: one mile gained. Resistance now became as tough as the initial machine-gun fire. The enemy was laying on vast quantities of mortar shell in an almost impenetrable curtain while farther back, the 88s were bulking up the mortar barrage with well placed salvos of high explosive and timed fire."[80]

Clearly, the enemy was not about to give in. Expertly placed mortar fire quickly engulfed the 1st Regiment. Colonel Marshall quickly advanced to escape the shelling. By 1000 hours, he had crossed Highway 7 and ordered his regiment to dig-in. He had achieved the Force's

FSSF PUSH TO ROME
23 MAY - 4 JUNE

Authors Collection.

first objective. At noon, German infantry and armour lashed out in a counterattack. However, Allied artillery quickly smashed the enemy advance. An official report documented:

> Extremely heavy fighting ensued initially by sniper, mortar and direct artillery fire. By 1100B our troops were resting on Hwy 7 with frontal resistance considerably relaxed but heavy fire coming from both exposed flanks. Artillery fire from both the Cisterna and Littoria areas created a particularly punishing crossfire. An enemy counterattack of armor, supported infantry, observed forming in the woods at 1130B was broken up by artillery. Early in the afternoon our TD [Tank Destroyer] defense was knocked out and the enemy brought the fires of 12 Mk VI tanks and an unknown number of SP [self-propelled] guns to bear directly on our forward elements who had crossed Hwy 7 and proceeded to the RR [railroad] tracks. A withdrawal was necessary as our flanks were not yet sealed nor was relief by 133d Inf immediately apparent.[81]

The 1st Regiment was not out of the woods yet. Its flank was left totally exposed. An ad hoc provisional grouping called "Pollack Force" from the 3rd Division failed to tie into the 1st Regiment on Highway 7. The Germans quickly exploited this error. A vicious artillery barrage became the opening salvo to yet another counterattack. This time, the attack was supported by a large number of tanks, including 12 Tigers.[82] Lieutenant Bill Sheldon remembered:

> Suddenly things began to happen. My men spotted a big German Tiger (Mark VI) tank approaching beyond the tracks — then another and another — 17 in all. Fifth Coy on our right was pinned down by fire, and began to withdraw. We were then forced to withdraw just to the other side of Highway 7 where we began to dig in. Then things really got hot. Jerry began methodically knocking out our tanks and TD's (Tank Destroyers) shooting with fearful accuracy. The discouraging thing was to see our TDs make a direct hit with their .75mm on the Tiger and the shells seemed to bounce off with no effect. Five of our TDs were knocked out in about as many shots and so were several tanks. One TD behind a house was pierced by a Jerry anti tank .88 mm after the shell had passed through a thick cement wall of the house. Suddenly we were without armour support. We held nevertheless in a shallow ditch and began to dig in with tank 88s and mortar landing all around us. Our battalion radio and HQ was knocked out so we lost communication with Regimental HQ. Just before it was knocked out, we had found it necessary to call down our own 155 "Long Tom" artillery on our positions.[83]

OF COURAGE AND DETERMINATION

German prisoners.

Major Thomas recalled, "The ground over which we attacked had little cover and intense enemy fire began almost immediately. Through the morning our progress was slow but steady." Then Thomas's lead company commander reported the presence of enemy tanks. "I ordered him and my other company commanders to withdraw because we had no weapons with which to deal with these tanks," explained Thomas. He also called for armoured support. Thomas lamented:

> Response came as pairs of our tanks and tank destroyers came up. They were ducks in a bucket for the Tiger tanks confronting us. A dozen of our tanks and tank destroyers came onto that battlefield and were destroyed. I was close enough to one them to hear the screams of the crew as the vehicle burned.[84]

Lieutenant-Colonel Ken Wickham described, "We had six tank destroyers assigned to us. As they approached flat ground to our front, I saw them all cut down and burning within 2 minutes when a group of German Tiger tanks wheeled in and took them under fire."[85] George Wright lamented, "I have never seen anything so terrible. The German tanks were equipped with 88s [88-mm cannon]. They were guns with a high muzzle velocity. The armour piercing [rounds] were going right through the American tanks and setting them on fire."[86]

Lieutenant Mitchell had a similar recollection. "Jerry tanks," he wrote, "the big Tigers with the 88s, arrived and knocked off the 5 tanks supporting us in short order; so, with no tanks 1st Regt was pinned down in a shallow drainage ditch."[87] Sergeant John Rowe asserted:

> On our push off from Anzio there was a tremendous artillery barrage that started 30 or 45 minutes before daylight. The only way you could communicate was by putting your mouth to a guy's ear. We followed tank tracks across the mine field and we got a lot of fire from the screaming Mee Mees (Nebelwefer). Our first objective was a railway line that we had to capture by two PM. We got there one and a half hour earlier. We were on our objective when we spotted a Tiger tank 300 yards on our left flank. They had captured a section of our men. Lieutenant Sheldon, ordered us to retreat. We had to run across this field and get into a bush. Another Tiger tank came along and raked the field with machine gun fire. I watched the bullets hit the ground around me. When they got real close, I just fell to the ground and heard the bullets go over my head. Luckily I got into the bushes. Not far away from us were three American Tank Destroyers. One of them pulled up and prepared to fire on the German tank. The Tiger fired first and took him out immediately. The next one pulled up almost in the same spot and the same thing happened. The third one pulled up and the same thing happened again. Three in a row. Then a forth one pulled up and got behind a stone house. The Tiger tank sent an armour piercing shell right though the house and took him out.[88]

By mid-afternoon, the pressure became too great and the 1st Regiment pulled back and dug-in once again. Lieutenant Sheldon stated, "The basic weakness of our position was that our left flank was wide open ... finally, the order came to withdraw, and it was truly a wise move."[89] As a result, the 1st Regiment pulled back 500 metres to tie into the Pollack Force which had finally arrived and now provided the necessary flank protection. By 2100 hours the 1st and 3rd Regiments were pulled back to regroup and the 1st Battalion, 2nd Regiment held the front line on the Highway 7 canal bridge.

Overall, the breakout had been very successful. Both American and British forces had punched through the enemy defensive line and pushed the Germans back to Cori on the edge of the mountains. After a brief pause, the FSSF resumed its advance. At 1600 hours, 25 May 1944, Colonel Walker's 3rd Regiment quickly seized Mount Arrestino. Under the overwhelming pressure, the German army began to disintegrate. Cori quickly fell and the Force pushed on through Rocca Massima to Artena.

Movement became difficult over the rugged mountain terrain. To assist the Forcemen, 6th Corps assigned them a company of Sardinian mules. In addition, local Italian muleskinners volunteered their animals to assist and some locals, caught up in the euphoria of the German withdrawal, also volunteered to act as backpackers. Even with the help, the mountain trek remained arduous. Sergeant Green remembered:

> Everything seems to be SNAFU. We don't know if we're going or coming. For three days now we've climbed up and down mountains. The going was rough and the boys with heavy equipment such as radios were having a tough time of it, and were begging, buying or stealing mules. We finally came to a mountain before the town of Artena and we stayed there for thirty-six hours. Highway No. 6 was directly in front of us and a line of resistance had been formed there by the Germans.[90]

Although the mountainous route was difficult, it was also mostly undefended by the enemy. The FSSF after action report noted, "That this [enemy] delay was necessary to cover withdrawal of 10th Army up Hwy 6 from the South was obvious, but as the beachhead defense had been stripped of all army reserves in favor of the strongest possible defense on the Adolph Hitler line, there was nothing left to hold the mountains once the thin initial line had been routed."[91]

Some enemy resistance was encountered as the FSSF neared Artena, however, it was fleeting. The city itself was quickly cleared by 3rd Division troops that had approached from farther north on the Anzio beachhead. As a result, the Force relieved elements of the 3rd Division on 27 May 1944. "We dug in deep at Artena as it was proving to be a very hot spot. Several German tanks were occupied in trying to shoot down every building in town and they were really whizzing 88s very close to us."[92] Sergeant Green observed, "Highway No. 6 was a good place to keep off, and the area around Artena was only comparatively safe when you were five feet in the ground."[93]

As the Force dug in at Artena, the enemy was busy massing north of Highway 6 in the Colle Ferro and Valmontone area. The Germans had set up a defensive line based on a group of tanks along a wooded rail line north and east of Artena. Lieutenant-Colonel Becket remembered, "[they] were giving us a helluva a hosing down."[94]

Not surprisingly, higher headquarters ordered the FSSF to attack the new German position. That afternoon the assault commenced with the 1st Regiment left of the Artena-Valmontone Road advancing across wide-open grain fields and the 3rd Regiment on the right of the road deploying toward the railroad station. Then, the Forcemen hit a brick wall. The Germans concentrated all their firepower — infantry small arms, tank, and artillery fire — all focused on the 1st and 3rd Regiments, which were deployed on a relatively narrow front. "The tracer fire coming across those grain fields — both theirs and ours," described Becket, "was unbelievable."[95] The results were devastating as the Force incurred heavy casualties.

Nonetheless, by midnight both regiments had achieved their objectives and tied in with flanking units. The FSSF remained in the Artena area and fought off a number of strong counterattacks. Once again, the strength of the Force was depleted. Lieutenant-Colonel Becket estimated that the 1st Regiment was at approximately half strength and the 2nd and 3rd at about two-thirds strength.[96]

Events now began to unfold rapidly. The same day, the 5th Army finally broke through the Adolf Hitler Line and seized Fondi. The road now appeared open for a swift advance up the Liri Valley. This added pressure to the German defence. On 31 May, 5th Army HQ pressed its attack. In turn, 3rd Division was ordered to seize Valmontone, which would cut traffic on Highway 6, while the FSSF was directed to take Colle Ferro, a large town that the Germans had been using as a launching pad for their counterattacks. The attack, scheduled for 1 June, involved principally the 2nd and 3rd Regiments.

The FSSF pressed forward and maintained pressure on the retreating enemy. "Attack proceeding as planned against stiffening resistance," noted the daily FSSF operations summary on 1 June 1944.[97] That morning the 3rd Regiment repulsed an enemy counterattack, but not until after a heavy firefight. The Germans were trying to avoid encirclement and were fighting a bitter rearguard to buy time.

But the German defence began to break down. Casualties mounted and the pressure applied by the enormous Allied advantage in men and material manifested itself. In fact, an intelligence summary noted, "the Herman Goring Division continue to offer strong resistance. [However,] losses in PWs and casualties are diminishing this number to the point that rear echelon troops are now appearing with forward elements. Cooks, bakers, teamsters, and other service personnel, will, as their number increases on the fighting line, greatly reduce combat efficiency."[98]

In the early hours of 2 June, the 1st Regiment, which was back in Artena regrouping, deployed a number of patrols to gather information. The 2nd Regiment, supported by armour, captured Colle Ferro shortly after noon against light resistance, while the 3rd Regiment advanced to block Highway 6. By mid-afternoon, the Force began to occupy the town and it linked up with French Spahis troops. Fifth Army elements advancing from the south and those which broke out of the Anzio beachhead had now linked-up.

However, the occupation of Colle Ferro was to be short lived. Frederick received an important call that fundamentally changed their task. Lieutenant-General Clark now ordered the FSSF to return to Artena to prepare for an immediate advance on Rome. Contrary to the orders of Clark's immediate superior to push north to Valmontone to complete the encirclement of the German 10th Army, Clark redirected his primary focus on an advance to Rome. He felt that he and the U.S. 5th Army had earned the honour of liberating the "Eternal City."

OF COURAGE AND DETERMINATION

Two Corps now attached Colonel Hamilton Howze's Armoured Task Force (Task Force Howze) and the 6th Armoured FA group (effective 0915 hours, 3 June 1944) to the FSSF. Fifth Army headquarters intended that the armoured task force "were to attack enemy during daylight each day and FSSF to attack during darkness each night until the capture of all objectives on highway 6."[99]

The 1 CSSBN war diary recorded the hectic events of 3 June 1944. It revealed, "Force is supposed to be out for a two day rest, but on arrival at Artena found everyone busy packing, ready to take off after dark for another push toward Rome. Force C.P. and medics are moving up highway six to Del Finocchio, it is not expected the hun will try to defend Rome."[100] As a consequence, the FSSF moved from its bivouac near Artena to the rear of Task Force Howze's position. That night, at 2000 hours, 2nd and 3rd Regiments passed through the tanks and attacked the enemy, securing their objectives by 0800 hours, 4 June 1944, the next morning. They were now on the threshold of Rome, stopped at Tor Sapienza, a suburb on the outskirts of the city.

The excitement of liberating Rome began to reach a zenith. During the night, at 0106 hours, Major-General Keyes ordered Frederick to secure the bridges over the Tiber River above Northing 68 within the City of Rome. The race was now on.

With the 2nd and 3rd Regiments already engaged, the task went to the 1st Regiment. As such, before first light, at 0400 hours, Colonel Marshall assigned two infantry companies to mount tanks of the 13th Armoured Regiment and eight armoured cars from "A" Coy, 81st Reconnaissance Battalion to advance west along Highway 6 to secure six bridges across the Tiber River in Rome.[101]

At dawn, the composite force advanced up Highway 6 bypassing German troops who were captured and sent to the rear under a thinly manned escort. At 0630 hours, Colonel Marshall's force entered the outskirts of Rome and hit its first real opposition in the form of an anti-tank gun behind a fortified stone wall.[102] The Forcemen and their supporting armour met stiff resistance and fighting lasted into the night. The enemy had deployed numerous tanks and self-propelled guns in support of their parachutists in a tenacious delaying battle. Captain Gus Heilman, commanding 2nd Coy, 1st Regiment, explained:

> At approximately 0630 hours the head of the column arrived at a large sign marked, "Roma," located on Highway 6 at 809644. At this point the two leading tanks of the column were knocked out by German anti-tank weapons. The infantry deployed and heavy fighting continued throughout the morning. At 1100 hours my company moved forward from its deployed positions in an attack to clear the enemy from the sector north and west of the road junction.[103]

Similarly, Lieutenant Sheldon described:

ANZIO AND THE RACE TO ROME

The advance to Rome, 25 May 1944.

Allied push to Rome.

OF COURAGE AND DETERMINATION

> We were suddenly told our immediate mission was Rome! After all the rumors and counter-rumors of the past 24 hours, it was hard to believe anything. Rome was 20 miles away, and we were to spearpoint the drive, but our Regiment again was supposed to be in reserve. We piled in trucks (wonder of wonders!) and began to drive towards Rome. Valmontone had fallen, and as we drove past Hill 301, it seemed incredible that the fighting had been so intense there but 36 hours ago. We passed through Valmontone — a shattered town — and started up Highway 6. German vehicles and corpses littered the roadside and the traffic was heavy — bumper to bumper. It looked like a race for the city ... At 4:30 a.m. our company and 2nd Coy (1st Bn) were awakened and told we would board tanks and be the first troops into Rome. No opposition was expected. This was exciting and the men's spirits were soaring. At 6:00 a.m. we clambered on board the tanks — the men singing as we started off trucks and jeeps passed us.... Without further event we got within 100 yards of the city limits. Then lightening struck. Our victory ride into Rome stopped very certainly and very suddenly.[104]

Sheldon observed, "These Jerries are a different breed of cats than the Beachhead Krauts. They fight doggedly and courageously, and must be attacked very aggressively to be dislodged."[105] He recalled:

> Shells were falling just ahead of me, and two of our tanks were hit and burning. Action was intense. I reached the burning tanks and in the smoke-filled air and on the debris-littered street, a tank commander told me I would have to flank to the right because Jerry big guns were shooting down the road and had to be knocked out.[106]

Frederick later provided a succinct synopsis to the press:

> At 2 a.m. Sunday I was ordered to secure seven bridges across the Tiber on the west side of Rome. I organized two companies of infantry and some tanks. Moving up the Via Casilina, we went across the city limits at 6:20 a.m. Two minutes later my two leading tanks were blown apart by German self-propelled guns. We pulled back outside the city. A reconnaissance disclosed that the Germans had at least four self-propelled guns, five tanks and 350 infantrymen. We tried to get our tank destroyers around for shots at the enemy armor, but the Heinies' stuff was too well screened. So we went farther north along the edge of the city and got in again by another road. We managed to clean up some of the enemy by hitting his rear and flank, stopped his counterthrusts and sent back

ANZIO AND THE RACE TO ROME

Jim Pringle, 4th Coy, 2nd Regiment, in Rome, Italy.

information which enabled the other troops on Via Casilina to crack him and finally finish him up in that sector.[107]

The hope of the Forcemen and others that the Germans would not oppose the liberation of Rome was quickly dashed. The Germans fought a tenacious rearguard action. As the Forcemen advanced further into the city, enemy defensive action increased and it became an infantry-dismounted clearing operation.

Meanwhile 2nd and 3rd Regiments assembled in Tor Sapienza in anticipation of a deployment into the north end of Rome in an attempt to cut off the withdrawing German forces that were crossing the Tiber River bridges and using Highway 7 to conduct their retreat. At 1300 hours, Frederick ordered a co-ordinated attack. 2nd and 3rd Regiments, supported by armour from Howze's Armoured Task Force, were to attack to the west, with the 3rd Regiment right forward on the assault, working toward a link-up with the 1st Regiment attacking to the north.

The official record of the FSSF noted, "Entrance of our troops into the city of Rome proper was made at approximately 041600B and was the first permanent entrance of Allied Troops to Rome."[108] Lieutenant Sheldon recalled, "Italians with rifles began to throng out and join us; our men were taking Jerry prisoners, crowds of people — it was fantastic — all utter confusion with so many people and with my company spread out over two blocks, control was almost impossible."¹⁰⁹ Captain Underhill wrote, "I can never describe how it felt, moving through a large strange city and seeing heads pop out of doors and windows — suddenly we would be recognized — the cry of 'Americani' would go up — people would throng out kissing us, cheering, clapping, and weeping, pressing us with bottles of wine — all this amidst constant small arms and some artillery."¹¹⁰ Sergeant Donald Green added, "We passed through the gates into the city. Up to this point there were just a few smiling Italians waving their hands to us from doorways but the further we got into the city the larger the crowds got."¹¹¹

But the euphoria was premature. Green recalled:

> We proceeded up the street toward the bridge. It was just getting dark now but we could still see where we were going. A section of each platoon were on one side of the street with the other section across from them. I was paying more attention to the store windows than to where we were going, when suddenly two machine guns opened up on us. We tried to take cover in the store doorways but found that all of them had huge iron gates with padlocks on them. One feels very large and helpless trying to press his body into a concrete building with someone firing right down the street at him. The first burst of machine gun fire had hit seven men on the right column.¹¹²

The 1 CSSBN war diary revealed, "There was considerable hun rearguard activity by small groups well armed with tank support and the men found themselves being embraced whole heartedly by the populace one minute and engaged in heavy street fighting the next."¹¹³

During the co-ordinated FSSF attack, as the 1st Regiment reached Acque Bollicante, Colonel Marshall moved on foot to re-establish contact with one of his depth subunits that had lost radio communications. As he started back through the streets of Rome, he had travelled scarcely 100 metres when a German 20-mm Flak-wagon cut him down, killing him instantly. His body was not discovered until the next day.

By 1800 hours the lead elements of the 2nd Regiment, advancing from Via Prenestina made contact with the 1st Regiment, and passed through them to carry on the attack through the city. Throughout, the enemy had fought doggedly. The official report captured, "Withdrawing elements of the 4th Parachute Div[ision] fought with extreme tenacity and were aided in some instances by civilian Fascists. Bridges across the Tiber River were defended by well-emplaced MGs [machine guns] and snipers."¹¹⁴

Nevertheless, the FSSF swift thrust through the city prevented damage being done to the bridges. An official report noted, "Rapid penetration by FSSF and attached armor of Task Force Howze denied the enemy sufficient time for demolition of bridges."¹¹⁵ By 2100 hours, the battle began to wane. The German tanks were destroyed, or had pulled back over the bridges that were still held by their rearguard forces. Two hours later, the Force had seized six of Rome's 16 Tiber bridges.[116] However, casualties were once again heavy.

The following day, 5 June 1944, the FSSF took over responsibility for the security of two more bridges. Frederick gave the task of securing the bridges to the 2nd Battalion, 3rd Regiment, with the support of a number of tank destroyers. The remainder of the FSSF regrouped at Tor Sapienzo to await further orders. On the night of 6–7 June, the 2nd Battalion, 3rd Division relieved the Forcemen at the bridges in Rome and the Force was pulled from the front lines.[117]

By 8 June, the Force in its entirety had set up along the shore of Lago Albano to rest and reorganize. The strength of 1 CSSBN was now 48 officers and 588 other ranks, of which 16 and 192 respectively were in hospital.[118] All told, the Canadian component now made up only approximately 34 percent of the Force.[119]

On 25 June 1944, the FSSF underwent shock as Brigadier-General, soon to be promoted again, Frederick bade farewell to the Force. Although not known at the time, Frederick was appointed to command the 1st Airborne Task Force (1 ABTF) and prepare for the invasion of southern France. At 37, Frederick became the youngest major-general in the U.S. Army.[120]

The loss of Frederick hit the Forcemen hard. They had come to love and respect their formation commander. Sergeant Ballantyne insisted, "Anybody in the Force would have laid down his life for Colonel Frederick because he led from the front. He was always present. He was one of the boys."[121] Another veteran commented:

> Colonel Frederick was a toughie. The guys worshiped the ground he walked on. He always set the example. He was always front and centre. He took no pre-training, he just went up and jumped. He always just seemed to turn up.[122]

Finally, Private Waling revealed, "A tough bunch of soldiers stood up and there were few that weren't wet eyed when he [Frederick] came to say good-bye. He was wounded nine times. He was a soldier that you could not help but follow."[123]

The task of leading the FSSF now fell to West Point graduate, artilleryman, and 3rd Regiment commander, Colonel Edwin Walker.[124] The new commander surely had big shoes to fill. And, he would soon get the opportunity to do so. On 1 July 1944, the FSSF left Lago Albano and boarded two Liberty ships at Anzio to sail to Naples. Yet another mission awaited the Forcemen.

13

TO THE BITTER END:
Operation Dragoon and the Fight Through Southern France

The "long march east" was no "march" — it was a war. I have no exact numbers of 3rd Regiment's casualties going across Southern France, but I lost many fine men; dead or wounded. I believe that none of our men were taken prisoner. The Force's advance to the Italian border was no "Champagne Campaign" — to those who did not return — and not to those who did.[1]
— Lieutenant-Colonel R. W. Becket

As the FSSF took a well-deserved rest at Lago Albano, the Forcemen used the respite to reorganize and take advantage of their close proximity to the "Eternal City." Compared to Anzio, Lago Albano was paradise. However, the bureaucratic war continued. Lieutenant-Colonel J.F.R. Akehurst, the Canadian-contingent CO, travelled to Naples and pushed higher headquarters for reinforcements for his depleted battalion.[2] "The Canadian element," revealed a concerned Akehurst, "[is] only about 30% of the American …"[3] Moreover, since there was very little time to train any new reinforcements, Akehurst pushed for replacements that already possessed advanced infantry training.

This was not surprising. Germany was reeling under the Allied juggernaut and everyone knew that the Allied Command would keep the pressure on. Therefore, it was just a short matter of time before the Force was once again tossed into the fray. As such, refresher training began once again on 12 June 1944. Eleven days later, Canadian reinforcements arrived, four officers and 206 ORs in total, and began the intensive FSSF indoctrination training.[4]

Prior to leaving, Brigadier-General Frederick had commented on the calibre of the newly arriving Canadian replacements and had stated that they "were of a most satisfactory type." Other American FSSF officers remarked that, "the Canadian reinforcements are not only of a good physical type but appear to be well trained as infantry."[5] Upon completing their training, the Canadian replacements were integrated throughout the Force.[6] Despite the recent additions, the lack of sufficient Canadian reinforcements remained a pressing issue.[7]

OF COURAGE AND DETERMINATION

Preparatory training.

On 30 June, Colonel Walker received a letter from Lieutenant-General Clark informing him that the Force was no longer attached to the 5th Army.[8] The FSSF was now placed under the command of Lieutenant-General Jacob L. Devers, commander of U.S. 6th Army Group, also known as Southern Group. Later that afternoon, Walker received orders to relocate to Santa Maria di Castellabate, a small seaside village located approximately 80 kilometres down the coast from Salerno.

As the men set up their bivouacs in the new location, Colonel Walker used the time to put his personal stamp on his new command. He met with his officers to discuss his concern with the poor discipline that existed within the Force. "He then went into a long talk giving constructive criticism on many points," captured the 1 CSSBN war diary, "particularly discipline in which the Force has been notoriously lax. The officers were asked to set an example and to look for breaches in discipline and not shy away from them."[9]

But his concern for discipline became a secondary concern as an intensive six-week amphibious training program began on 5 July 1944. Within a short period, the Forcemen, as well as attached naval beach marking parties and naval shore-fire-control parties, practiced rubber boat embarkation drills from destroyer escort transports (APDs). Subsequently, there were towing drills by LCIs to designated landing areas.[10] Operation Bruno, which included a full-scale amphibious landing, was conducted as a confirmatory exercise.[11]

Staff from 7th Army headquarters assessed the FSSF and was fully satisfied. Shortly after, on 11 August, the FSSF received its warning order for its upcoming operation. The

Force then sailed to Propriano, Corsica, and erected its temporary pre-invasion base. Most realized the only logical invasion target was Southern France.

Once settled in, FSSF HQ was briefed on Operation Dragoon, an American/British/French amphibious-airborne invasion commanded by Lieutenant-General Alexander M. Patch, commander of the 7th Army.[12] Devers ordered Patch to establish a beachhead between the towns of Cavaliere and St. Raphael, located on the French Mediterranean coastline, and engage and destroy elements of German Army Group "G" operating in this area.[13]

Major-General Truscott commanded Patch's amphibious force. This component consisted of the 3rd, 36th, and 45th Divisions of the U.S. 6th Corps, the FSSF, French commandos, and various U.S. and British vessels. Following this landing, the French 2nd Corps under the command of General de Lattre de Tassigny, would land and deploy on the left flank of the invasion force.

Also taking part in the assault was the newly formed airborne division, 1 ABTF, which comprised American and British independent parachute and glider companies, battalions, and regiments, led by Major-General Frederick.[14] The airborne component would be inserted by parachute and gliders in the Le Muy area, north of St. Raphael. Once on the ground, the airborne forces had the task of cutting all enemy communications and blocking German units deploying to counter the amphibious landings. Meanwhile, the amphibious force was responsible for securing all beachheads on the French Mediterranean coastline.

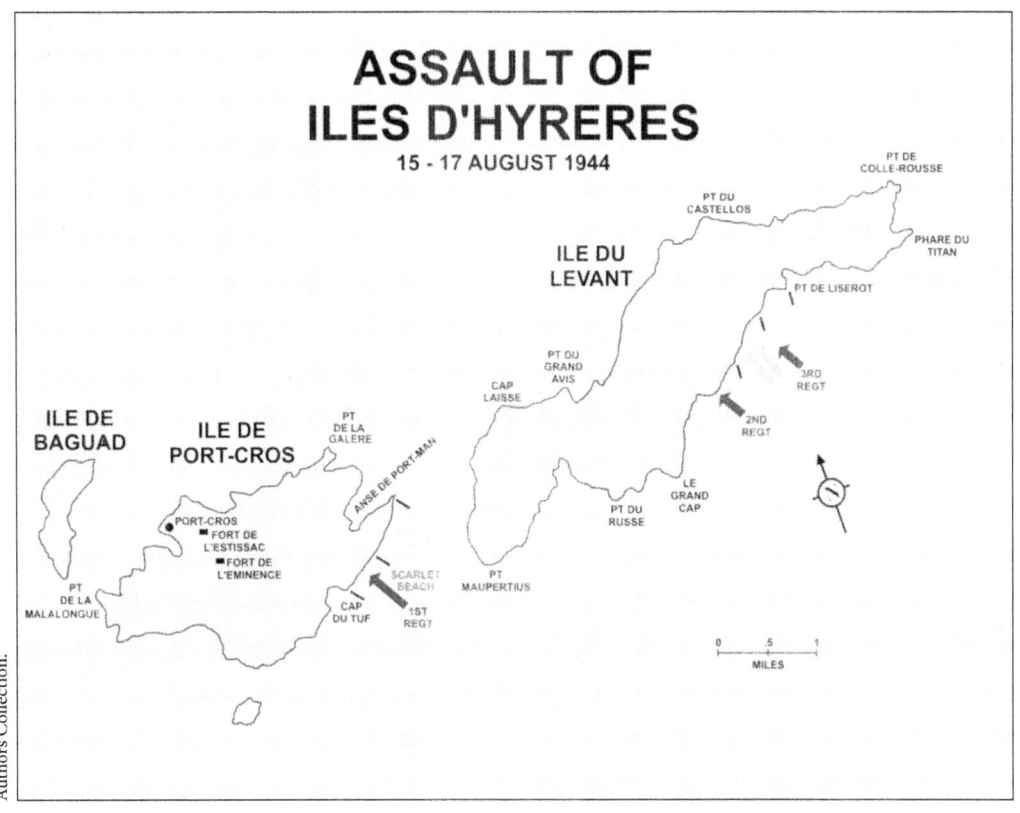

OF COURAGE AND DETERMINATION

Once consolidated, Patch would then reorganize his forces into two major components; one would advance north and attack General Friedrich Weiss's 19th Army, while the 1 ABTF would push eastward along the coast toward the French-Italian border.

During the amphibious operation, the FSSF was part of the SITKA assault group. This group was responsible for protecting the left flank of Patch's main invasion force and capturing two islands that were part of the Islands d'Hyeres located off the French Mediterranean coast between Toulon and the town of le Lavandeau.[15] The FSSF was given two missions. The 1st Regiment was tasked to capture Ile de Port-Cros, while 2nd, 3rd Regiments, Force's HQ, and Force's Headquarters Detachment would seize Ile du Levant. On 14 August 1944, the Forcemen boarded their ships and sailed off to their respective invasion staging areas. Their final campaign was about to begin.

At 2300 hours that night, the Forcemen embarked into their rubber boats and assembled into their assigned landing groups. One Forcemen described the beginning of the operation:

> Troops dropped their rubber crafts over the side of the ship and as crew members of the LCAs (Landing Crafts, Assault) steadied them to ship side, they scrambled down the nets burdened with the tools of their trade. Quietly, then, they paddled up to their pre designated LCA's standing nearby. As soon as each LCA had hooked up its nine rubber craft, it

Coastal battery at Port-Cros.

pulled off to the port side of the ship and slowly executed long circles under the starlit sky…. Finally when the entire battalion was afloat in their proper formation, it moved off toward shore, resembling somewhat a well-disciplined colony of water bugs.[16]

As the LCAs approached the shoreline, the sailors signalled the Forcemen to unhook their towlines. The men then paddled quickly toward their respective beaches.[17] In the meantime, shortly after midnight, the beach marking parties, who had already landed, marked the beachheads and installed ropes to scale the cliffs. The 1st Regiment, 1st Battalion, landed on Scramble Emerald Beach and 2nd Battalion landed on Scramble Scarlet Beach located on the eastern shore of Port-Cros Island. Wanting to leave the beachheads as quickly as possible, the anxious Forcemen grabbed the ropes and climbed the cliffs. "I was about half way up when somebody dropped a metal ammo box," recollected John Rowe, "It just banged and crashed all the way down. The guys were cursing."[18] Everyone froze. Thankfully, there were no enemy troops in the immediate vicinity.[19] Once on top, the Forcemen regrouped and awaited their orders to move out.

The 1st Regiment's two battalions then advanced under the cover of woodland and thick underbrush. "The Maquis [thick bush] as it is locally known," explained a Forcemen, "is a foliage so dense that it is nearly impassable and grows to height of up to 10 feet, literally covered the island."[20] The two battalions forged ahead and reached their respective objectives.[21] Within the first hours, 1st Battalion cleared the Port Man area, capturing eight defenders. By 0900 hours, 15 August 1944, 1st Battalion had secured its initial objective.

Meanwhile, 6th Coy, 2nd Battalion, headed south toward Fortin de la Vigie, a small fort, built on the island's highest point. As the Forcemen approached, the defenders opened fire. After a short firefight, the Forcemen hailed the garrison requesting their surrender. As one enemy soldier came out, others opened fire, and the battle raged on. By 0815 hours, 15 August, the Forcemen captured the fort, rounded up the prisoners and tended to a wounded Forceman.[22] As 6th Coy consolidated its position, 4th Coy pushed ahead and came upon Fort de l'Eminence, the island's largest enemy defensive position. "The walls were so thick and so wide that you could have driven a jeep on the top of those walls," described an impressed John Rowe.[23]

The vigilant defenders immediately opened fire, killing and wounding several Forcemen. Refusing to back down the Forcemen unleashed a heavy barrage of machine gun fire and salvos of anti-tank rockets. Despite their aggressive attack, the Forcemen realized that rocket-launchers and grenades did little damage to the fort's massive structure. As a result, officers ordered their men to fall back to a safer location and developed a new plan of attack. In order to limit needless casualties, Lieutenant-Colonel Akehurst requested air strikes and naval fire support.

Meanwhile, as 4th Coy personnel dug-in around the fort, a series of reconnaissance patrols pushed ahead toward Port-Cros harbour located on the western shore of the island. As they made their way toward the harbour, the patrol members observed enemy activity in the vicinity of their other objectives, le Chateau and Fort de Lestissac. By 2030 hours, the Germans evacuated the town of Port-Cros and relocated to Fort Lestissac. Shortly after, 3rd Coy with 2nd Coy in reserve entered and occupied the town. As the sun set, platoons from both 1st and 2nd Battalions patrolled the outer perimeters of the chateau, Forts de l'Eminence, and de Lestissac to ensure that the enemy troops were confined to these three fortified positions.

By the next morning, 16 August 1944, 2nd Coy was prepared to attack the chateau. It would prove a daunting task. The approaches to their objective were barren, covered with boulders and rubble providing the Forcemen with very little protection. Furthermore, the chateau's walls ranged between 1.5 to 4.5 metres in height.

Even so, an assault was required. The plan was simple. 2nd and 3rd Platoons would provide cover fire while 1st Platoon raced toward the chateau and scaled walls. Then, at 1120 hours, upon the given signal, the Forcemen unleashed a deadly barrage of bazooka, mortar, and machine gun fire. The surprised enemy attempted to return fire as the men of 1st Platoon scaled the walls and peppered the inner courtyard with heavy automatic fire. By 1140 hours, the chateau fell to the attackers. Nineteen prisoners were marched out carrying their dead and wounded. The FSSF suffered one killed and six wounded.[24]

Now, only two objectives remained. However, they were the most formidable of the Port-Cros defence system. A 1st Regiment reconnaissance report noted:

> Lestissac at 100 meters dominated the village area. The terrain surrounding the fortress had been completely cleared of all foliage; and an extensive barbed wire and mine field covered this area. The Fort itself was star shaped — the outer wall about 15 feet height and once protected by a wide dry moat. There was on entrance though this wall, shuttered by an iron gate. It appeared that an inner wall existed inside which was the main bastion. The outer diameter was about 75 meters. Previous enemy fire indicated that the Fort's defenses were alert and planned.[25]

The enemy was certainly waiting. As patrols approached the fort, they immediately encountered deadly machine gun and mortar fire. Colonel Walker ordered his Forcemen to pull back and requested an air strike. Finally, at 1800 hours, on 16 August 1944, Martin B-26 Marauder medium bombers roared towards the designated targets. The first aircraft, "came right over our positions," stated Jim Summersides, "and fired their .50 caliber machine guns to mark their targets. They came in low and the empty casings clunked down all around me."[26] John Rowe also observed the attacks on the two Napoleonic fortifications:

> I watched them come in. They were trying to drop a bomb so that it skipped on the ground and hit the fort to take the wall out. There were

six planes carrying two bombs. They all made their two runs and weren't successful. At that time, I didn't know what they were trying to do. I thought to myself, "Boy! You guys are terrible! You should go back for some more training."[27]

As the smoke cleared the onlooking Forcemen were disappointed by the results. Despite their age, the fortifications withstood the pounding of the ordnance.

Since the air strikes had not yielded the anticipated results, the USS *Augusta* was brought into the fray. The cruiser unleashed a few salvos against the fortifications. Despite the bombardment, the Germans continued to hold out. The 1st Battalion took up positions once again near Fort Lestissac and prepared to storm the stronghold. The CO selected the 3rd Coy to lead the night attack, while 1st Coy remained in reserve and 2nd Coy occupied the nearby Chateau. Captain William Merritt, OC, 3rd Company briefed his men. They would approach the fort from the west and charge toward the entrance while the remaining platoons provided covering fire.

At 2230 hours, Merritt gave the signal and his men raced through the open terrain drawing heavy enemy fire, which now confirmed the location of the enemy's firing positions. As a result, the supporting platoons quickly opened fire. From his precarious position, Merritt ordered his bazooka teams to take out the fort's front gate. The rockets roared toward the target and exploded. As the main gate collapsed, the lead Forcemen rushed the entrance and laid down heavy fire. As they stormed the inner courtyard, they came under heavy fire and sustained casualties. Despite their hazardous position, they did not fall back. Mercifully, a few minutes later the German garrison commander ordered his 22 men to lay down their weapons.[28]

Meanwhile, the German troops garrisoned in Fort de l'Eminence continued to keep the Forcemen at bay. Under the cover of darkness, on 16 August 1944, the men of the 6th Coy, 2nd Battalion, supported by the 5th Coy, attempted to breach the fort's gate with anti-tank rockets. Their spirited attempt failed as the defenders targeted their positions with continuous deadly mortar and machine gun fire. Akehurst then ordered his men to pull back and called in naval support fire. Shortly after, at 1300 hours, on 17 August, HMS *Ramillies* moved into position and unleashed her 15-inch guns against the fort.

The last isolated German defenders endured the barrage. Following the bombardment, two Forcemen were sent with a German prisoner requesting the garrison surrender. Seeing that their situation was hopeless the 48-man garrison capitulated at 1345 hours.[29] The 1st Regiment had finally secured Port-Cros and was then relieved by French troops. During this operation, the Forcemen captured one officer and 109 enemy soldiers.[30] Lieutenant-Colonel Akehurst and the men of 1st Regiment were ordered to pull out, boarded their vessels, and sailed for Port Croix.[31]

Simultaneously, the 2nd and 3rd Regiments were also involved in a series of operations against German forces stationed throughout Ile de Levant.[32] The FSSF commander

OF COURAGE AND DETERMINATION

The rugged coastline of Ile du Levant.

tasked Lieutenant-Colonel Moore and his 2nd Regiment to locate and destroy enemy installations in the southwest area of the island. Meanwhile, Lieutenant-Colonel Becket and his 3rd Regiment were given the responsibility of destroying enemy positions in the northeastern part of Ile de Levant. Additionally, each regiment designated a battalion that could be used as reinforcements in case the other regiment needed assistance with its tasks.[33] Following their orders groups, the men left the transports ships and embarked into their rubber rafts. They were then towed by landing craft for a distance, and paddled the rest of the way toward their respective beaches.

The 3rd Regiment, Force HQ, and Headquarters Detachment landed on Green and Purple Scrambles beaches while 2nd Regiment landed on Blue (1st Battalion) and Red (2nd Battalion) Scrambles beaches.[34] "The cliff was sheer," recalled Captain Underhill, 2nd Regiment, "but only between 80 to 100 feet high. What made it difficult," added the veteran "was the shale surface which was loose in places."[35] The 3rd Regiment's landing site also presented its challenges. Sergeant Peter Smith recalled his final approach to the beachhead:

> In the distance, I heard the water pounding the shoreline. I had been around water all my life and it sure didn't seem like it was hitting a beach. The spot that we were supposed to land was now about 300 to 400 yards

away. Once again, here we had big rocks on the coastline. We had an awful time getting over these. The swell would bring you up and would then pull you back down almost immediately. It was tough to get off the rafts. When we did get out we now had to walk over the big round slippery moss-covered rocks. The footing was treacherous. We had to tie all our weapons to the cross support pieces inside the rubber boats and drag them in.[36]

Once off the beachhead, the companies reformed and advanced on their respective objectives.

The 1st and 2nd Battalions of Lieutenant-Colonel Becket's 3rd Regiment, made their way toward the eastern point of the island. Their objective was to capture a German coastal artillery battery before it could engage the left flank of the 7th Army's amphibious landing force. The advance was slow as the men's mobility was hampered by thick underbrush. "It took us some two hours to cut through that maquis and reached the road," stated a frustrated Becket.[37] The 3rd Regiment finally came upon the road leading to the coastal battery.

As the Forcemen moved into positions along the road, reconnaissance teams inched their way toward the objective. From their concealments, they observed a small hut, the Phare du Titan lighthouse, and a coastal battery. Becket noted that there was something wrong:

> They were damn funny-looking cannons. I stood up, walked closer and saw that all those "guns" were nothing but large trees, all trimmed down

The difficulties of resupplying the Force.

to logs — set up on cartwheels and covered with strips of metal from tin cans, each small piece nailed on ... I was amazed, then angry and then a wee bit relieved and amused. The ruddy Huns had fooled us all — including our submarine reconnaissance party — and the whole Seventh Army.[38]

After uncovering this subterfuge 3rd Regiment quickly secured all its objectives by 0730 hours on 15 August. Meanwhile, the 1st Battalion of Moore's 2nd Regiment moved along the island's roads along the northern coastline, while 2nd Battalion advanced along the southern coastline. As they approached Fort Arbousier and an abandoned penitentiary, German troops opened fire. After a series of firefights, these two positions fell to the Forcemen. Regrettably, many of the defenders had escaped and joined up with other enemy forces where they waited for the FSSF in alternate camouflaged positions.

As the Forcemen pursued the fleeing enemy, they once again drew heavy enemy fire. "It was quickly apparent Jerry had laid out defensive positions with pre-aimed automatic weapon fire, wire and mines," confirmed Captain Underhill.[39] Further down the northwestern coastline in Port de l'Avis, well-entrenched German troops also engaged the Forcemen from various fortified machine gun and mortar positions. Heavy enemy fire forced 2nd Regiment to pull back and adopt a hastily fortified defensive position.

Tiring of this "cat and mouse game," Colonel Walker ordered Becket to dispatch one of his battalions to reinforce 2nd Regiment. Becket selected Lieutenant-Colonel J.G. Bourne, 2nd Battalion, to assist Lieutenant-Colonel Moore. At 2200 hours, 15 August 1944, all three battalions opened fire on the last German positions. The enemy immediately returned heavy fire. "We hit this crossroad," recalled a Forceman, "I was in the lead. Then a couple of mortars shells dropped in. That's what they always did. They'd pull out, knew the positions, waited till we got there and fired on us."[40] Mortar rounds landed among the advancing 2nd Regiment. One unidentified Forcemen described the deadly effect of the enemy's mortar fire. "Major E.H. Thomas signalled his men to sweep through this dense bush," recalled the Kroll. "We all hit the dirt as the mortars whined and broke across the roadway... Shouts from the bushes indicated that men were hit and into the dirt road, still menaced by the mortar fire, staggered a group of men."[41]

During this chaos, bazooka teams made their way toward the entrance of the main German underground bunker. Once in position the teams fired several rockets at the main bunker's reinforced doors. Although failing to breach the bunker, the repeated explosions demoralized the isolated defenders. With no hope of being relieved, 100 Germans troops marched out and surrendered at 2300 hours.[42] Ile Levant had been captured. In total, the FSSF captured a total of 1 officer and 114 German enlisted men.[43]

Once again, the Forcemen had risen to the challenge and had successfully accomplished all their missions. Nevertheless, the losses during the Ile d'Hyreres operations upset the Forcemen. Lloyd Dunlop decried this operation:

TO THE BITTER END

The cliffs of Ile du Levant.

> What I was upset about was the fact that we lost about 40 men on these two islands. If proper reconnaissance had been carried out we could have bypassed the island, not taken any useless casualties and gone straight to the main land and moved onto Marseille.[44]

Furthermore, continual front line action wore down the Forcemen. Underhill disclosed that at this point casualties increasingly affected the men's morale:

> After almost nine months of combat and the loss of hundreds of comrades, the loss of one more could hardly be considered a surprise. Yet these men had been through so much together and had such love and admiration for one another that each new fatality became a personal loss.[45]

It was during these operations that civilian observers and the new FSSF reinforcements noted the stubborn refusal of FSSF originals to back down from any challenge. United Press (UP) correspondent Clinton Conger wrote, "They fought ferociously with ridiculously light weapons to reduce three century old forts whose walls withstood eight-inch naval guns…"[46] Canadian Major W. Winston Mair who joined the FSSF in Santa Maria di Castellabate and was assigned to 1st Regiment as the assistant executive officer questioned the Forcemen's warrior spirit:

> The men were too courageous. They had a mistaken concept that courage and physical fitness were all that was necessary. For example, a group of the Forcemen were surrounding ravines in which there were a number of Germans. All they had to do was shoot down into the ravine and toss in a few hand grenades, and sooner or later the krauts would have surrendered. Instead, after tossing in a few grenades, they rushed into the ravine, taking some prisoners, but suffering unnecessary casualties themselves. It was unnecessary and foolish courage. Another thing, if a boy got himself hurt in a minefield, the problem was not to get someone to rescue him, but to hold back a multitude.[47]

Still, it was this incredible and unique bond that continually motivated the Forcemen to persevere and overcome any challenge.

On 18 August, the FSSF was relocated to Sylvabelle, near Cavalaire Bay, south of St. Tropez to prepare for follow-on operations. As the men rested, FSSF and 1 CSSBN HQ staff took advantage of this short rest period to resolve new and ongoing administrative problems. Because of Canadian Army operations in Italy, it became increasingly difficult for 1 CSSBN to request reinforcements. Moreover, the battalion's frequent moves in Southern France complicated the establishment of effective communication between 1 CSSBN HQ and the Canadian Army's echelon in Italy. Additionally, with the FSSF training unit based in Santa Maria Capua Vertere, Italy, it was difficult to receive updates regarding the status of the readiness of the reinforcements.[48] Last, Lieutenant-Colonel Akehurst continued to experience difficulties tracking wounded personnel who had been admitted to various U.S. Army hospitals in Italy.[49] Some hospitalized soldiers were still missing and their whereabouts unknown.

Unfortunately, due to the Force's new mission all administrative tasks had to be, once again, put on the backburner. On 20 August 1944, the Force was ordered to move eastwards to the small coastal town of St. Raphael. The Force was once again to move into the mountains.

While the Forcemen prepared to advance, General Patch's Seventh Army was engaged in a series of offensive operations against the German 19th Army. Meanwhile, 1 ABTF continued to regroup following its massive parachute drop and glider landings in the Le Muy area.[50] They were ordered to relieve 6th Corps units and protect the 7th Army's right flank as it advanced toward Cannes. To the north, U.S. armoured units reached the Durance River and then pushed ahead toward Grenoble. However, on the left flank, the Germans based in the Marseille and Toulon areas were putting up fierce resistance.

To maintain continued pressure on the retreating German forces operating along the French coastline and the Maritime Alps (between Cannes and the Franco-Italian border), Frederick requested that the FSSF be attached to his task force. As a result, on 21 August, after Frederick issued his orders to Colonel Walker, the FSSF deployed to

The capture of Fort l'Eminence, Port-Cros.

The rough terrain of the Maritime Alps compelled the Forcemen to haul much-needed ammunition, supplies, rations, and water to their mountaintop positions.

the right flank of 1 ABTF and relieved British 2nd Parachute Brigade operating in areas west of the Siagne River overlooking Valbonne.[51]

Simultaneously, Walker established communications and confirmed the FSSF's operational boundary lines with the 509th Parachute Infantry Combat Team operating on the Force's right flank, as well as the 517th Parachute Regimental Combat Team operating on the FSSF's left flank along the Mediterranean coastline. As the FSSF awaited its orders to commence its advance toward the Franco-Italian border, Walker tasked the 1st and 3rd Regiments to man the forward positions, observation posts, and roadblocks. He designated the 2nd Regiment as the Force reserve and they also carried out rear area security tasks.[52] As the Forcemen scanned the mountainous and wooded terrain they knew that, for the moment, the well-concealed German rearguards forces held the upper hand. It would be yet another gruelling operation.[53]

An intelligence report confirmed the Forcemen's intuition:

> PW's report that 44 Div mission being to hold Grasse "for the honor of the Fatherland," i.e., at all cost. Such a position offers good natural defence possibilities, being uphill from the Siegne River on the southern slope of the Maritime Alps. A marked lack of communications, the prevalence of prominent ground, and the uneven terrain all are favourable factors for defense. In considering German capabilities for the offensive if one or more divisions are added, the enemy will always command high ground in an advance to the south.[54]

So, on the surface, the FSSF mission seemed simple — pursue and maintain contact with the enemy rearguards, force them to fall back in a disorganized state thus preventing them from establishing and manning effective defensive positions. However, the terrain and the enemy would make it anything but simple. The skilled German rearguard tactics consisted of impeding the Forcemen's advance by setting up roadblocks surrounded by barbwire entanglements and booby traps; using harassing artillery, mortar, and sniper fire; defending demolished bridges, laying mine fields, and destroying road systems located in critical junctions, tunnels, and mountain passes. Knowing the challenges that lay ahead, Frederick assigned 1st Platoon, B Company, 645th Tank Destroyer Battalion, two platoons of the 887th Airborne Engineer Company, and the 601st Field Artillery Battalion to support the FSSF.[55]

Then, on 21 August 1944, the 1st and 3rd Regiments commenced their advance. FSSF patrols reached the Siagne River the following day. However, maintaining constant contact with enemy forces proved challenging due to the limited number of vehicles available and the warm weather. Regardless, the Forcemen advanced on foot. Furthermore, in order to maintain pressure on enemy rearguards Forcemen carried rations, water, and ammunition to last for several days.

Within hours of their initial advance, Lieutenant-Colonel Becket, CO, 3rd Regiment, encountered his first roadblock. The Forcemen pushed through and continued their advance fighting through a number of abandoned German obstacles and enemy rearguards. One report noted:

> Our pursuit was made on foot. Contact was not always easy to maintain. Roads were blown; trails were mined in many cases. The enemy was confused and poorly led. He did not fight a time-delaying action but, rather made long disjointed withdrawals, fighting where he could gather his strength and with widely varying determination. His opposition was sporadic, unexpected and difficult to foretell.[56]

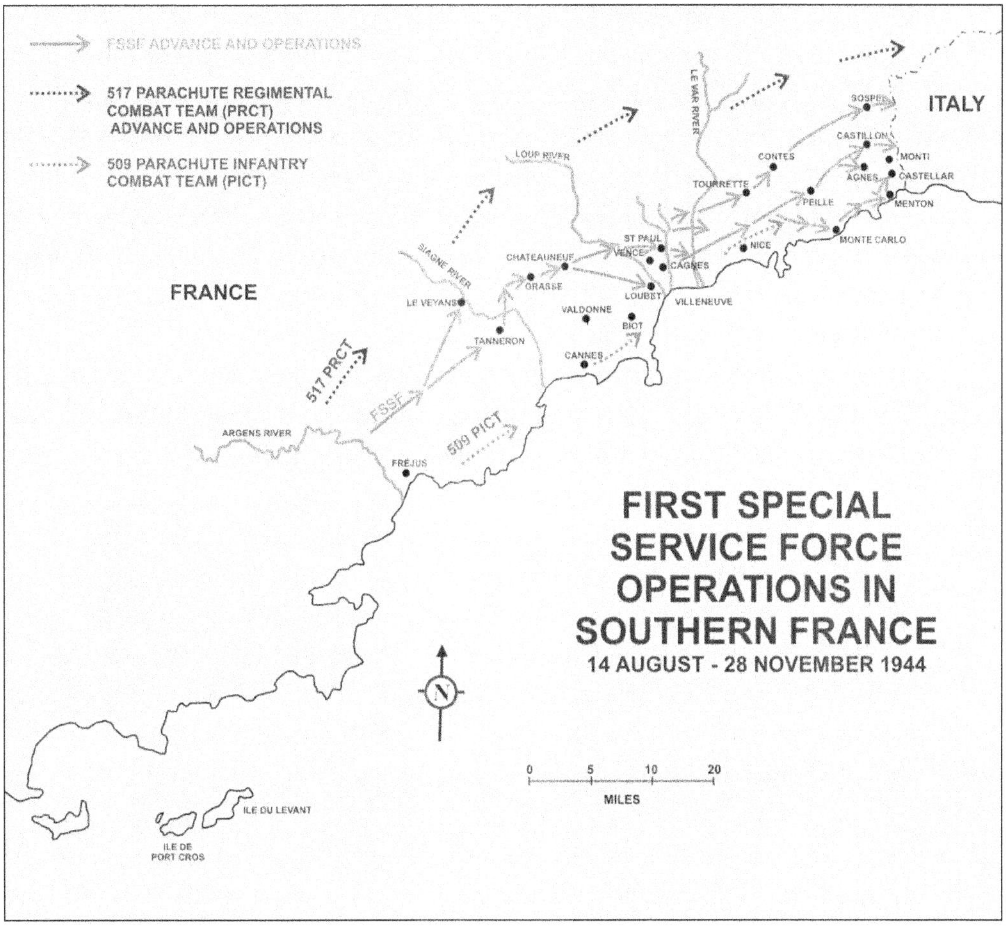

TO THE BITTER END

FIRST SPECIAL SERVICE FORCE OPERATIONS IN SOUTHERN FRANCE
14 AUGUST - 28 NOVEMBER 1944

"The action varied from place to place," explained Charlie Mann. "Sometimes there was nothing for miles. Then you'd hit a tough pocket of resistance." In order to limit casualties enemy positions were quickly neutralized by artillery and naval fire or by the FSSF's Cannon Company.[57] In addition, the Force's Intelligence Section worked closely with naval fire support to maximize the efficiency of the supporting fire.

Army mules were pressed into action to haul heavier loads.

Following these bombardments, the Forcemen stormed into action. "We'd either shoot it out or flank it," stated Mann. "The objective was to never stop and always push ahead." By 24 August, FSSF intelligence reports confirmed that the enemy, "continued hasty withdrawal to the East with only scattered, disorganized resistance and a lessening in local mine-laying."[58] Joe T. Jamieson noted that the FSSF's constant pressure disrupted the defenders' delaying tactics. "The mines," observed the veteran, "were now just being tossed here and there."[59] However, it was the dreaded Shu-mines that caused most of the mine injuries. This deadly device was, "the size of a small honey box," explained Donald J. Green, "filled with explosives to blow off a foot or part of one."[60]

Following each action, prisoners were sent to holding areas and interrogated by FSSF HQ and intelligence staff. New information enabled the Forcemen to further assess the identity and combat efficiency of their adversaries. Captain Finn W. Roll reported:

> PWs state that the 148th Inf Div consists of at least 80% Poles with German officers and NCOs in charge. Personnel is very young (17–20) or over-age (35–45) … Training throughout the Division is not high. Weapons used by the Division are Belgian, Italian, Czech and Polish made and PWs state difficulty is often encountered in their operation. PWs were told that no weapons re-supply was available. The 148th Inf Div is considered a second-class division and adequate transportation has never been provided.[61]

To maintain constant pressure on the enemy's rearguard forces, Walker rotated his regiments as vanguard. Throughout the advance, newly arrived reinforcements were immediately spread amongst all three regiments.[62] Regrettably, the new troops had very little time to adapt to their new surroundings and comrades. Officers and men alike were pressed into action. Four young officers reported to Lieutenant-Colonel Becket during the first days of the advance. Becket recalled meeting them:

> They were fine looking, keen young men, no older than 20 and all 2nd Lieutenants … Off they went. I never saw any of them again but I checked on their individual stories. I was shocked. One of those young men was killed the same night. Two were wounded within a few days and the fourth was hospitalized out within a week with a nervous breakdown — what we used to call "shell shock."[63]

Among the reinforcements were also a number of Forcemen who had recently been released from hospital. Whereas wounded colleagues were welcomed with open arms and their will to fight was never questioned it quickly became evident that the gruelling daily tempo and hot weather proved too much for the recuperating Forcemen. "There is no place in our combat echelon," reported an unidentified company commander, "for men who are troubled with old wounds or ailments of physical kinds. It is far less troublesome to keep a man in a rest area rather than in combat when you are counting heavily on him."[64]

Problems also plagued the enemy's effectiveness. The FSSF's aggressive and persistent pursuit eroded the defenders' resolve to fight. Prisoners revealed that the Poles serving in German units now attempted to desert at every opportunity. To counter this systemic problem German officers and NCOs were abusing these soldiers and executing deserters.[65] Nevertheless, rearguard units were now ordered to hold their positions and delay the FSSF, as long as possible, so that a series of defensive positions could be consolidated in the Maritime Alps. Furthermore, they had to use every means at their disposal to ensure that escape routes were kept open for the continuing evacuation of German troops and vehicles.[66]

And so, as Lieutenant-Colonel Moore's 2nd Regiment approached Villeneuve-Loubet, on 26 August 1944, the well-entrenched enemy forces were waiting. This town had to be held at all cost because it was the quickest evacuation route for the German troops to escape into Italy.[67] As the 2nd Battalion neared the outskirts of the town they encountered the largest enemy force to date. Following a series of heated firefights, 2nd Regiment captured 72 prisoners, killed a large number of defenders, and wounded another 100 Germans.[68] Despite the enemy's determined defence the Forcemen had successfully shut down their escape route.

Forcemen attacking a German position in Bazemore.

OF COURAGE AND DETERMINATION

By 30 August 1944, the Force had liberated 22 towns, inflicting heavy losses on the German rearguards while capturing 398 PWs.[69] However, the cost was ever-mounting casualties. The losses totalled, 21 killed in action, 152 injured, 217 admitted to hospitals for various ailments, as well as 21 non-combat related injuries.[70] And there was no immediate end in sight. By the beginning of September 1944, the Force and its supporting organizations now fought along a 10-kilometre front between L'Escarene, Peillon, and Laghet. The Force's resources were further stretched when Frederick ordered Walker to send 2nd Regiment to relieve the 509th Parachute Infantry Combat Team, which operated on the Force's right flank, along the Mediterranean coast. All three regiments were now on the front lines pushing the enemy toward the Franco-Italian border.

On 6 September, 2nd Regiment set up positions in Monaco. A few hours later patrols reported the town of Menton had been evacuated.[71] Efficient use of naval gunfire continued to facilitate the FSSF advance. One report confirmed:

> Our advance along the sea coast from Monaco to Menton and our holding operation along the Italian border in which we are now engaged, has been greatly aided by Naval gun fire especially in the coastal areas. This fire was closely coordinated with the fires of land batteries by the Naval Liaison Officer who remained in close contact with Naval Forward Observers in forward observation post and with the ships.[72]

As German gunners engaged the advancing Forcemen, deadly naval barrages forced them to abandon their positions. As the Forcemen pursued and entered the towns and villages hundreds of civilians and French Forces of the Interior (FFI) personnel flooded the streets and celebrated their liberation. Whereas the French population greeted their liberators with great enthusiasm, wine, and flowers, they were not so kind to those who had collaborated with the Germans. Donald J. Green vividly recalled an incident which took place in the town of Biot:

> We slept for a few hours and were up in time to see the Frenchmen shave the hair off six girls who had been intimate with the Germans. We didn't approve of their punishment but had enough sense to mind our own business. It was interesting to watch their different reactions. Several cried hysterically and pleaded their innocence. The next one broke away from her captors and made a break to get out the door. One of them pulled a pistol and fired several shots after her, but she was finally dragged back half naked and her head was shaved. The next two seemed resigned to their fate. They had defiant smiles on their faces and offered no resistance. When the job was done they pulled bandanas out of their pockets, put them on their heads and walked out of the shop amid a

chorus of hissing and booing and several peoples trying to snatch off their bandanas.[73]

On another occasion, Lieutenant-Colonel Becket dispersed a raucous crowd and put a stop to another hair-shaving session. With the Germans only a few kilometres away and the town still within range of their artillery, Becket imposed an immediate curfew. The Forcemen had enough to do without having to police the towns they liberated. FFI personnel complained to Colonel Walker but to no avail.[74]

On 8 September 1944, despite the difficulties of operating in the mountains, the three regiments occupied all the high ground from Castellar to Castillon. Two days later, Walker halted the advance. He then had the Force consolidate their defensive positions. In addition, he ensured they maintained an aggressive patrolling posture to keep pressure on the Germans.

The difficulty of the terrain now made itself felt. The mountains, valleys, and long distances disrupted the FSSF lines of communication. The Force felt increasingly isolated and cut off. More powerful radios, greater quantities of telephone wire, and batteries were pushed forward along a very strained supply chain.

Increasingly though, it sunk into the Forcemen that they were once again engaged in a static war, where the Forcemen had to man observation posts and endure deadly artillery fire. The 1 CSSBN's war diary chronicler described the effect:

> Artillery still scattered along front lines and taking its toll on our personnel. Looks like the Force is getting another Anzio deal, being given a very large front to hold by active patrolling with its high rate of casualties. The Force is completely committed with no reserves and for that matter there are no troops to speak of between here and Marseilles, but the Hun seems to be fighting a holding war though he has more troops than we and some really fine forts (built by the French as the southern portion of their Maginot Line).[75]

Additionally, the stress of being under constant fire was now also taking its toll on the Forcemen. "It is quite noticeable," observed the war diary chronicler, "how many of the original men are cracking, they have been through too much of this sort of thing, 99 days without a break at Anzio, over a month already here and no prospects of relief."[76]

This problem was also noted by Akehurst. In his monthly report to NDHQ, the CO wrote that, "a noticeable increase in cases of psychoneurosis, especially among the original men. They have been through a lot of heavy and trying fighting."[77] Regardless, the Forcemen stood their ground, endured the elements, the rough terrain and continued with their daily operations. By the end of September, the Force had captured 316 enemy combatants.[78]

OF COURAGE AND DETERMINATION

By October, the FSSF mission had not changed. Forcemen continued to defend a difficult mountainous 16-kilometre front; they patrolled the outer perimeter of Castillon and engaged the enemy.[79] Meanwhile, as the 7th Army pushed steadily northwards, the increasing distance now made it impossible to adequately support the 1 ABTF, and hence the FSSF. As a result, Frederick's task force was detached from 7th Army and attached to 6th Army Group. For the moment, Frederick agreed that he would continue to support the Force during ongoing operations in the Castillon area. The German forces, for their part, still refused to give up Fort Castillon despite enduring daily heavy artillery, naval, and mortar fire. By 22 October, the 2nd Chemical Battalion and the 602nd Field Artillery were removed from the FSSF while 463rd Parachute Field Artillery Battalion was attached to provide much-needed fire support.[80]

Long periods of waiting while manning defensive positions frustrated the Forcemen. "Our lack of offensive action," explained an annoyed FSSF intelligence officer, "was the sole guarantee of the enemy's effective defence."[81] Nonetheless, the Germans finally evacuated the fortifications in Sospel and Castillon during the night of 27/28 October 1944. The next day the FSSF moved quickly through these locations and immediately occupied all the high ground overlooking the border. Major Murray D. Kirkwood, CO of 1st Battalion, 2nd Regiment described the terrain in his battalion's area of responsibility located between Castellar and Castillon:

> My Battalion's right flank began at about 2,500 feet altitude and my line continued to twin peaks with an altitude of almost 4,000 feet. The high one Comes Restaud, the other Roc d'Ormea — the section line before the final rise to the twin peaks ran along the tops of a shear wall almost perpendicular on our side of the line. The closest road from which to reach this area terminated in the small village of Castellar. It was about two miles from Menton and at an altitude of about 1,000 feet, and that meant many switchbacks to make the climb.[82]

By now, the fighting had slowed down considerably and only 24 PWs had been captured.[83] While the Force set up its new defensive positions overlooking the Franco-Italian border, Lieutenant-Colonel Akehurst became exasperated with the increasing complications of maintaining effective communication with NDHQ and CMHQ. There was no Canadian Army administrative support system available for his battalion in southern France. What's more, air courier and cable services required to forward reports, documents, and requests to CMHQ, in a timely manner, were not available. As well, no information could be obtained to confirm the burial sites of his deceased personnel. Now, even the battalion's simplest administrative daily tasks could no longer be accomplished.[84]

To further complicate matters, discipline within the 1 CSSBN was breaking down. During the course of October and November 1944, a total of 35 field general courts-martial cases were tried. Furthermore, there was an increasing number of personnel who were absent without official leave (AWOL). In defence of the Forcemen, the war diary chronicler wrote, "Although no excuse for breach of discipline the men are getting pretty fed up and tired sitting up in the mountains day after day. It is over a month now and nearly two months steady fighting."[85] In addition, CMHQ informed Akehurst that the battalion would no longer be reinforced.[86] In sum, it was not surprising that morale plummeted. "The feeling of dissatisfaction," wrote the war diary chronicler, "within the Force is again increasing both among Canadians and Americans. The Canadians still feel their country has let them down and written them off to the U.S. Army. They did not volunteer to become American soldiers but to join in a 50/50 outfit. There is little Canadian about the Force."[87]

Furthermore, the working relationship between Akehurst and the Force commander, Colonel Walker, also deteriorated. "He [Akehurst] could not see eye to eye with the Force Commander," revealed the war diary.[88] On 8 October 1944, Walker approved Akehurst's request to return to the Canadian Army. However, since the battalion's days were numbered, Akehurst stayed on as the 1 CSSBN CO until the end.

The inevitable conclusion was drawn by CMHQ and NDHQ senior staff who could no longer see the value in reinforcing or maintaining the 1 CSSBN. Brigadier Weeks agreed. He stated:

> Reinforcements for 1 Cdn Spec Serv Bn must come up to the specifications laid down for Canadian paratroops. The standard is very high and consequently the cream of the infantry reinforcements go to the 1 Cdn Spec Serv Bn. From that point of the GOC 1 Cdn Corps, the Divisional Commanders, etc, this practice is highly repugnant as promising Officers and potential NCOs are thus diverted from the fighting units of 1 Cdn Corps.[89]

The CGS agreed with Weeks, adding that since "effective Canadian administrative control is quite impossible. I would point out also that this unit appears now to be submerged to such an extent with the U.S. Forces that the value to Canada of its retention is no longer apparent." Thus, on 7 October 1944, Stuart recommended to the MND that "the Canadian element of the Special Service Force be disbanded and that the personnel be returned to the U.K. for reallocation."[90]

Concurrently, the commander of the Mediterranean Area recommended to the U.S. War Department that the FSSF be disbanded. However, no official communication had yet been released by the War Department.[91] Thus, American and Canadian military bureaucrats were ordered to draft the disbandment directives for the FSSF and 1 CSSBN.

So, as the cool and wet November weather settled in on the Forcemen, they remained in their defensive positions facing the Germans and continued to protect the 6th Army

OF COURAGE AND DETERMINATION

Group's right flank. The men were getting increasingly disgruntled with their role. "It was almost impossible to keep the men sharply alert," remarked Captain Underhill, "and carelessness or relaxation could lead to a mortar round casualty or sneak attack on an outpost."[92] Eugene Forward added:

> Even though the fighting was not fierce as in our other campaigns we were nevertheless still losing men left and right. Some guys had become sloppy. Just because this was the "Champagne Campaign" you could still get killed. The easiest way of advance was not always the safest. One group was walking on the highway and an artillery shell landed among them. Many had been killed.[93]

As FSSF casualties continued to mount, bitterness and frustration over what was perceived as needless casualties grew amongst the Forcemen. "That's the sort of thing [that] happens to an outfit like this when it's put in a static position," asserted Dave Langly. "Over forty of the deaths have been while we were sitting on our asses here on the f****** border."[94] The 2nd Regiment's officers and NCOs also criticized the use of their personnel in this defensive stratagem. "If selected troops are to maintain an aggressive spirit," observed the officers and NCOs, "a will to attack and close, they should be used for that and spared the attrition on personnel and breakdown in morale which goes with holding a line under bad weather conditions and under continual harassing fire."[95] The numbers were not trivial. From 11 September to 30 November 1944, 1 CSSBN casualties alone, incurred during defensive operations totalled 11 killed and 69 wounded.[96]

By the end of November, the remaining German forces crossed the border into Italy. Nevertheless, the Forcemen remained wary. "I've learned never to underestimate the enemy," stated an unidentified 2nd Regiment NCO. "No matter what his condition, he is always capable of putting up a good fight. In realizing this we are just giving the devil his due; and it might help to keep us alive and see the end of this thing."[97]

The enemy's resistance, however, became increasingly sporadic. Higher headquarters now decided to relieve all units attached to the FSSF and send them to other fronts. By 17 November 1944, airborne units of the 1 ABTF who took part in the push to the Franco-Italian border were being replaced by infantry units. Two days later, General Jacob Loucks Devers, commander of 6th Army Group sent a message to 1 ABTF HQ stating that the FSSF would undergo a reorganization and that Canadian personnel were to be returned to the Canadian Army.[98] Colonel Walker received orders, on 21 November 1944, informing him that the FSSF was no longer attached to 1 ABTF and would now operate under the command of the 44th Anti-Aircraft Artillery (AAA) Brigade.

The following day Lieutenant-Colonel Akehurst left for England and met with senior CMHQ officers. The CO was informed that his battalion would shortly be disbanded.

Nevertheless, Akehurst argued that the 1 CSSBN, as a distinct Canadian entity, should be retained. "The strength of the unit is such that even if it were necessary to take away the parachute status," explained the CO, it "could operate as a commando battalion with great effect. There is only one Para Bn in the Canadian Army," underlined Akehurst, "and there is only one Special Service Bn. Could not both be kept alive?"[99]

Regrettably, the recommendation for disbandment had been approved and authorized by the MND. All agreed, however, that the battalion had served honourably in many challenging operations. Thus, senior Canadian officers instructed that, "maximum consideration to be given to maintaining morale of all concerned and to ensure that individuals do not, repeat, do not, suffer by disbandment."[100] Lastly, DND ordered that disbandment proceed quickly and without publicity.[101] So it was that a dejected Lieutenant-Colonel Akehurst brought these directives back to his battalion on 30 November. Upon arrival, he shared this news with a select group of officers.

During Akehurst's absence, on 28 November 1944, the FSSF was finally relieved by the 100th Infantry Battalion and the 442nd Regimental Combat Team (RCT). Tired and drained, the Forcemen descended the inhospitable mountains. After four months of continuous fighting the FSSF's "Champagne Campaign" had come to an end. The Forcemen were relocated to a bivouac area in Villeneuve-Loubet. As the men rested, Akehurst and Walker quietly prepared for the disbandment ceremonies.

14

DISBANDMENT

> It happened crudely. They disbanded the Force because we were no longer required for combat. The guys were very upset. The disbandment ceremony was very cold. That's the way it was. It wasn't a happy occasion.[1]
> — Private Morris Lazarus

On 28 November 1944, after four months of gruelling operations along the French Mediterranean coast and in the Maritime Alps, the FSSF was withdrawn from the mountains overlooking the Franco-Italian border. The drained Forcemen were relocated to a bivouac near Villeneuve-Loubet. As the men relaxed and enjoyed day passes to Nice, rumours quickly circulated postulating possible missions in Germany. One rumour that caused a great deal of concern was the speculation that the FSSF would be deactivated. This scuttlebutt soon became too real. Regrettably, the Force had outlived its operational usefulness. "Allied High Command had decided that Light Infantry raiders were no longer needed," explained Captain Underhill, "the German Forces would be smashed with regular infantry and armoured divisions — broad swords and battles axes, not rapiers."[2]

NDHQ had also determined that the experiment had run its course. As a result, NDHQ directed CMHQ to arrange the return of 1 CSSBN personnel to the Canadian Army as quickly as possible. To expedite this process, Colonel Michael A. Dunn, the officer in charge, Canadian Section, GHQ, 2nd Echelon, Allied Armies Italy (AAI), arrived in Menton, on 28 November 1944. Dunn met with Colonel Walker and Lieutenant-Colonel R.W. Becket, the acting CO, and briefed them on the decision to withdraw 1 CSSBN from the FSSF.[3] Walker was shocked by this sudden turn of events. "The removal of Canadians from his Force," he declared, "would certainly seriously cripple his units as an operational force." Nevertheless, NDHQ's decision was irrevocable.

OF COURAGE AND DETERMINATION

Once the battalion was removed from the FSSF, its personnel were to be divided into two groups.[4] The first group consisted of 35 officers and 274 ORs, all parachute qualified personnel, who would be returned to the U.K. They would have the option of serving with the 1st Canadian Parachute Battalion.[5] To mitigate any undue hardship due to the disbandment, CMHQ proposed that the paratroopers be taken on as a distinct company in that battalion.[6]

The second group consisted of personnel who had originally been recruited by Akehurst from a Canadian Army infantry reinforcement depot in Italy. These 13 officers and 404 NCOs were to be sent to the 1st Canadian Brigade, Allied Army in Italy, and used to reinforce Canadian units currently operating in that theatre.[7] In his discussions with CMHQ officers, Lieutenant-Colonel Akehurst did his best to convince the commander of 1st Canadian Corps to keep the 1 CSSBN men together. He suggested forming them as a company and sending them to an infantry battalion. In the event that this proposal was not feasible then Akehurst recommended that the soldiers be returned "to the reinforcement of that particular unit from which they were taken to come to the 1 Cdn Spec Sv Bn."[8]

Significantly, Dunn advised that every effort be made to track down all the unaccounted 1 CSSBN personnel still recuperating in various U.S. Army hospitals in Italy and France. He also made sure everyone understood that, for security reasons, NDHQ did not want any publicity regarding the battalion's disbandment.[9]

On 30 November 1944, Lieutenant-Colonel Akehurst returned from London with the CMHQ disbandment directives.[10] Upon his arrival at battalion headquarters, Becket immediately briefed his CO on the information provided by Colonel Dunn. For the moment, both officers agreed that it would be best not to inform the men of the disbandment order. They wanted the troops to enjoy their last days with their American comrades.

On 4 December 1944, FSSF HQ issued a directive to all regimental commanders instructing them to have all their personnel form up the following day at 1450 hours, by

Force deactivation parade, 4 December 1944, Loup River Flats, Villneuve-Loubet, France.

DISBANDMENT

regiment, on the Loup River flats, on a field west of the 3rd Regiment's bivouac area.[11] The parade format called for each regiment to form a 12-man front. The first rank of each regiment was to be formed entirely of American personnel. Company officers were to form two ranks in front of each regimental formation. Then, battalion commanders with two officers were to form up two paces in front of the company officers. Lastly, regimental commanders with two staff officers were to form up five paces in front of battalion commanders. Importantly, Canadian regimental and battalion commanders were to ensure that they were to be relieved in their position by the next ranking American officer in their commands when the command "Fall out Canadians" was to be given.[12]

The following day, at 1400 hours, all Force personnel were formed up. As they awaited the arrival of Colonel Walker, the men speculated as to the nature of this parade. Most of them still did not know what was about to happen. At 1500 hours the buglers announced the arrival of the Force commander. Colonel Walker took his place in front of the Force as the regimental commanders called their men to attention.

The Colours were then marched on. Subsequently, Colonel Walker called upon Lieutenant-Colonel Akehurst to address the Force. Akehurst stated, "the Canadians were now returning to the Canadian Army, that they had enjoyed their being with the Americans and hoped the Americans would remain as a unit and continue to carry the Union Jack and the Stars and Stripes as our thoughts and good wishes would always be with them."[13] This unexpected announcement caused much grumbling amongst the troops on parade. The men looked at each other in disbelief. Some choice words could be heard throughout the ranks. The Canadian were very upset. "I had tears," confessed Sergeant Peter Kroll.[14]

Akehurst then returned to his position within the parade formation. Colonel Walker called the men to order. His message was also heartbreaking. Walker pronounced, "there was now no longer a First Special Service Force, that he was sorry the break-up had to come but that it was far better to break-up with a really good reputation rather than be wiped out like the American Rangers and that Special units were being broken up all over."[15] The American Forcemen were dumbfounded. The Force commander gave the men a few minutes to vent their frustrations. He then called the men to attention. The Forcemen stood in silence. Some could not contain their tears.

Walker then called the Force chaplain, Captain O.E. Liggett. The chaplain proceeded to read the invocation. This was followed by the reading of the Roll of the Fallen. After a moment of silence, the chaplain pronounced the memorial prayer. The buglers then sounded the taps. "The lump in my throat nearly prevented me from finishing," wrote Corporal Otis C. Crabbe Jr., one of the buglers.[16] As the last notes echoed throughout the field, the chaplain gave the final benediction. This was followed by the playing of both national anthems. The FSSF Colour party then advanced. The Force Colours were slowly lowered and sheathed. The troops remained at attention until the Colours left the field.

Then, at the command of "Canadians Fall Out," Canadian personnel turned left, exited the ranks, and proceeded to a designated assembly area located on the left side of the field. There they were quickly formed up into three companies. Sergeant Peter Smith still vividly recalled this moment:

> Many were crying. The parade was like a wake. When we were told to get out of the ranks I was surprised. Some men who had stepped out with me I thought for sure were Americans. I remember particularly one guy from Windsor, Ontario. I had pegged him for an American because he was a real scrounger. As time went by you didn't know who was who. It was very sad.[17]

As the 442nd Regiment's band began to play, Lieutenant-Colonel Akehurst gave the order for the 1 CSSBN to advance in column formation. The men of 1 CSSBN reverted back to the Canadian drill and marched proudly past their American comrades and left the field. "You never saw a bunch of men march so well in all your life," beamed Sergeant Vernon Doucette.[18] "A lot of us cried," expounded Sergeant Charlie Mann. "A lot of us were sad, that we were losing our buddies, our friends, our brothers. It was over."[19] Many now felt like lost souls. "We had been integrated for so long," lamented Sergeant Bert Hopkins, "that we had lost our nationality. We were first and foremost Forcemen."[20]

Meanwhile, as a sign of solidarity and respect, the American Forcemen did not cover off the places vacated by their Canadian brethren. The spaces remained empty. After the

Force de-activation parade.

DISBANDMENT

Canadians exited the field and went to their assembly area, the Americans received the final dismissal. This last order signalled the end of an incredible adventure. Colonel Walker then headed toward 1 CSSBN. Accompanied by Akehurst, Walker walked through the ranks of all three companies. "He shook hands with all the Canadians," recalled Donald Green. "He carried a handkerchief in his left hand. I don't suppose it will ever happen again, a full colonel and a Texan to boot, with tears in his eyes."[21]

It was a very difficult and sad occasion. "The news of the breakup of the Force was met with mixed feelings," stated Akehurst. "It was a surprise to all and it can only be estimated that 50% were glad and 50% sorry to leave."[22] Sergeant John Rowe, pondered on this sudden turn of events. "In a way," reflected the veteran, "I was happy that it was over. It was good to get out of the never ending fighting."[23] Others, such as Sergeant O.C. Beacon, were furious. "Why would anyone break up the First Special Service Force?" expounded an irate Beacon. "The Army's made many SNAFUs but they would never go this far! Why break up a unit that has achieved every task it was ever give? Why break up a winning combination?"[24]

The next day 1 CSSBN personnel received their pay, packed their kits, and prepared to move out. The last hours were heart wrenching. Americans and Canadians spent the afternoon and early evening reminiscing, exchanging addresses, and wishing each other well, hoping that one day they would be able to meet again. At 2000 hours, on 6 December 1944, the Canadians headed toward a large convoy of awaiting trucks in Villeneuve-Louet. Under the tearful eyes of their accompanying American friends, the Canadians boarded

FSSF Colour Party — final parade.

36 trucks. For the next minutes, the slamming of the trucks' tailgates being closed resembled to a death knell. Americans who congregated around the trucks joked, and handed out cigarettes and chocolate bars to their comrades. Upon the given signal, at 2315 hours, the engines roared to life and mufflers spewed thick black smoke. As last farewells were exchanged, the truck headlights came on and there was the normal grinding of gears. Then, the lead truck started to move, slowly followed by the rest, one after the other.

As the vehicles accelerated, Americans continued to run alongside the trucks. Within minutes, they could no longer keep up. The exhausted men stopped and silently watched the convoy disappear into the darkness. As the Americans returned to their bivouac they immediately noted that the atmosphere had changed. "Their departure," explained an unidentified American Forceman, "left the Loup River encampment half vacant and many sad and empty feelings. For us, an era had ended." [25]

Meanwhile, as the convoy headed toward Marseille, the Canadians sat in the dark reflecting silently on the past two years. The convoy finally arrived in the city, and a few hours later, the Canadians boarded the *Ville D'Oran* and left the port at 1400 hours, on 7 December 1944. After a short two-day trip, the Canadians landed in Naples. The men were then split into two groups, entrained, and sent to Nola. There they transferred onto waiting trucks and headed toward Avellino.[26] Upon arrival, they received a warm welcome from the Canadian barracks personnel.

The next few days were hectic. Personnel from 1 CSSBN were sent to the quartermaster stores where they turned in their American clothing and received Canadian uniforms. They then reported to awaiting administration and pay staff. The clerks worked feverishly reviewing the men's paperwork to ensure that all documents were up to date. "Everyone in this section should be gray haired by night," observed the war chronicler.[27] Akehurst looked on and appreciated the hard work and thoroughness of the clerks. The battalion's administration had always been a great source of frustration explained Akehurst:

> The period was a hectic one between moving from place to place and closing out battalion affairs in Italy and the U.K. The administration of the Force was no doubt a headache to all concerned from top down, with the results that nothing was ever done to satisfactorily straighten out the problems that rose and what was done was always to the detriment of the Force. The chief problems can be broken into two groups; 1) Pay, and 2) Honours and Awards. Such a Force composed of Americans and Canadians could be handled more satisfactorily if the administration was handled by one or another country, but a joint administration did not work.[28]

Once the administrative and clothing matters were completed, Akehurst issued a company level conversion training directive. The objective was to commence training on 14 December and convert all ranks to Canadian methods of warfare, drill, discipline, and

DISBANDMENT

A last look.

training by 23 December 1944.²⁹ However, on 17 December 1944, battalion personnel were divided into two groups in accordance with the CMHQ directive.³⁰ At 0830 hours, Lieutenant-Colonel Akehurst met with the group slated to return to the 1 Canadian Base Reinforcement Group (1 CBRG), Italy. Akehurst wished them well, "and hoped they would continue to give a good account of themselves," reported the war diary chronicler.³¹ This final meeting had proven difficult for Akehurst. "Those left behind in Italy," explained the CO, "were certainly bitter, they had volunteered to become parachutists but never got the chance and felt they were being ditched."³²

However, Lieutenant-General P.J. Montague, the chief of staff, CMHQ, made sure that their unique FSSF experience and specialized training would be put to good use. He informed Lieutenant-General Charles Foulkes, GOC, 1st Canadian Corps, that these highly trained soldiers and combat veterans would be made available to him to reinforce his units. A delighted Foulkes replied:

> Looking forward to receiving well-trained and operationally experienced soldiers of high category from disbandment of SSBN. Feel this will add to morale and efficiency of Inf Bns Corps as a whole. Would like to spread this advantage throughout corps and therefore I am accepting your suggestion group allotted to us be posted to first available vacancies in former units in their present ranks on completion of refresher courses

rather than first alternate of inserting complete coy in one BN. I am suggesting to Formation Commanders that where possible these individuals be employed in tank hunting and scout platoons for which they would seem most desirably suited. Will see that this personnel is given every consideration and hope that satisfactory arrangements will be made concerning pay.³³

Foulkes then immediately informed Major-General H.W. Foster, GOC, 1st Canadian Infantry Division, and Major-General B.M. Hoffmeister, GOC, 5th Canadian Armoured Corps, of this latest development:

> The reinforcements which have been provided to 1 Special Service Battalion by 1 CBRGp since the arrival of the Battalion in Italy are being returned to 1 CBRGp for service in this theatre this amounts to 14 officers and 404 ORs, all of whom were originally intended as reinforcements for infantry in 1 and 5 Cdn Divs … It is very satisfactory to receive this considerable quantity of highly trained and experienced soldiers in view of the present reinforcement position. It is true, that due to the high proportion of NCOs that careful arrangements may be required to post them in their confirmed ranks. However, in view of the excellent services they have rendered operationally in the mountains of Italy, at the Anzio beach-head, and the landings in the south of France, it is most important that all ranks receive considerate and equitable treatment…This group will be posted wherever possible to the units which they were originally intended to reinforce, and I suggest to you that many of them may be desirable material for tank hunting and scout platoons.³⁴

In the interim, 1 CSSBN personnel who remained in Italy embarked on their conversion training. During the training, 1 CBRG instructors noted that these men, even though having been issued with Canadian uniforms, still wore jump boots and FSSF shoulder insignia. Colonel J.H. Christie, commanding officer of 1 CBRG, being a stickler for dress and comportment did not appreciate these dress code infractions. However, after contacting higher authorities Christie issued the following dress clarification:

> Boots — I was informed by DAA and QMG HQ 1 CBRG, late yesterday afternoon, that the Group Commander is willing to allow those members of the S.S.F. Bn who have purchased their Jumping Boots, to retain them. All members of the S.S.F. BN who have been remustered back into the C.I.C. will, however, be issued with ONE pair of Boots, Ankle with Laces, and will wear them, and NOT their jumping Boots, while on strength

DISBANDMENT

of 1 CBRD or when proceeding forward to 4 BN. Flashes — I have also been informed by the DAA and QNG HQ 1CBRG that the Commander 1 CBRG had authorized the S.S.F. Bn remustered personnel to wear their red "USA–CANADA" flash on the right sleeve of their Battle Dress and Great Coats. The flash of course, will be worn below the Divisional patch.[35]

Meanwhile, the U.K group was transported to 2nd Canadian Non-Effective Transit Depot (2 Cdn NETD), Forino where they stayed from 17 to 27 December.[36] "The men of the U.K. draft," remarked Akehurst, "were very eager to get to England and to find out what was in store for them." [37] In the meantime, the parachutists continued to practice Canadian Army drill, underwent Canadian weapons refresher training and range work. On 27 December, at 0745 hours the U.K. group were transported to Naples where they boarded the awaiting *Arundel Castle* at 0930 hours. Shortly after, the ship left the crowded port and joined up with a convoy heading to Scotland. That same day Lieutenant-Colonel Akehurst flew to England to make the necessary arrangements to set up his men in quarters provided by the 5th Canadian Infantry Training Regiment.[38]

As CMHQ prepared for the arrival of Akehurst's personnel, Brigadier W.H. S. Macklin, the deputy chief of the general staff, explored various options as how best the Canadian Army Overseas could benefit from the 1 CSSBN personnel. Macklin recommended that the 1 CSSBN's senior officers attend a company commanders' course given at the School of Infantry. After completing the course these officers could then be sent to an infantry training battalion for reorientation. Some of the junior officers slated to join 1st Canadian Parachute Training Company (1 Cdn Para Trg Coy) were currently waiting to attend a junior leaders tactical course at the Canadian Training School (CTS) before being sent to the training company. The balance of junior officers were to attend conversion training at 3 Wing, Canadian Training School.

As for the other ranks, Macklin suggested that the men be retained as a group and sent to a training battalion to undergo a six-week conversion training course. Upon completion, suitable personnel would be recommended for transfer to an officer cadet training unit (OCTU). Privates would also be given the option of remustering to the Canadian Infantry Corps or transfer to the paratroops. Those opting to continue as paratroopers would be sent to the 1st Canadian Parachute Training Company to undergo parachute conversion training at Ringway. Finally, those wishing to continue as instructors in reinforcement depots could do so.

On 6 January 1945, the *Arundel Castle* dropped anchor off Gouroch, Scotland. Shortly after Lieutenant-Colonel Akehurst came aboard to greet his men. 1 CSSBN personnel were then split up into two groups. This first group disembarked in Gouroch while the second was sent to Greenock. Both groups then entrained and arrived in Aldershot the following day. There the men were then loaded onto trucks and sent to Warburgh and Wilkens Barracks and to the reception depot.

OF COURAGE AND DETERMINATION

Major-General E.G. Weeks, CMHQ, meets with the soon-to-be disbanded 1 CSSBN personnel.

The following day, 1 CSSBN personnel woke up early. The weather was dreary and depressing. As luck would have it, a heavy blizzard descended on them. Regardless, Weeks arrived at 1100 hours and addressed the men. He announced:

> On parade this morning I informed the officers and men of 1 Cdn Spec Serv Bn that their parachutist pay would cease effective 10 January 1945 ... With respect to badges and formation patches, I find the personnel wearing the hat badge of the SS Force and the formation flash. As personnel of this unit are about to undergo conversion training I decided that they should be permitted to wear their present badges and flashes until they were reposted to a new unit. I think this is sound as some may go to Infantry and other to 1 Cdn Para Bn, and until the training is completed it is nothing more than a guess as to where the individuals will eventually be posted. With regards to the parachutist badge I told them that they could continue to wear it as long as the individual complied with the routine order published I believe in 1943....[39]

Furthermore, Akehurst pointed out that Major-General Weeks requested that the men not discuss or write about their unit's disbandment:

DISBANDMENT

> [Weeks] thanked them on behalf of the Chief of Staff for the work they had done, that he was sorry their exploits had of necessity always been cloaked in security but some day the story could be told and they would get their dues.... He also stressed the need for security in so far as mentioning the disbandment of the Force in letters.[40]

Following the short address the men were formed up and the CO led the 25 officers and 275 NCOs on their final march past.[41]

After the parade, Akehurst supervised the transfer of 1 CSSBN personnel to No. 5 Canadian Infantry Training Regiment (5 CITR).[42] On 10 January 1945, the battalion was officially disbanded.[43] Over the following weeks, Akehurst finalized the unit's disbandment administrative details. Effective 5 February 1945, Akehurst was given the command of the 7th Canadian Infantry Training Brigade (7 CITB). It was definitely a change of pace, and not to his liking. Akehurst confided:

> In the early part of last year both Lieutenant-General Clark U.S. Army and Major-General Weeks told me that on return to the Canadian Army, if the Force is broken up, it would be to an officer's advantage rather than disadvantage to have served with the FSSF, and so far, I have not found this to be the case.[44]

Meanwhile ex-1 CSSBN personnel wishing to serve with the 1st Canadian Parachute Training Company were sent to Bulford. The balance remained at 5 CITR and underwent conversion training. "It was almost like being back in basic training," lamented Sergeant Wright. The ex-Forceman explained:

> What really shocked us was the poor quality of the field training. They took us on patrol to take out this dummy pillbox. That's where we laughed. It was so out of touch with reality. We had to learn all these hand signals, double time and all that, and verbal signals. I think the first question we asked the sergeant was, "What do you think the Germans will do when you are waving your arms?" We had a good laugh. It was a joke. You don't have all these hand signals when you have to do the real thing. In the Force, we trained hard. When we got into a situation every member of the group knew his role, what to do, and that's what you'd do. Once in the field or under fire, you didn't change plans. I didn't like this unrealistic training.[45]

Upon completion, some opted to return to their former units, others remustered, a few elected to go to infantry training depots as instructors. As well, a group was sent to the

OF COURAGE AND DETERMINATION

Lieutenant-Colonel J.F.R. Akehurst leads the 1 CSSBN in its final march-pass. Major-General Weeks takes the salute.

training brigade in Vernon, British Columbia, as American weaponry instructors for troops selected to participate in possible operations against Japan.[46] Those who were still hampered by nagging injuries and wounds were given the option of applying for a medical discharge.

The transition to Canadian Army life proved difficult. The FSSF unique training and operational challenges, as well as the special camaraderie, were greatly missed by all Forcemen. Many found it very difficult to adjust to their new roles. "They finally sent us out as instructors to other camps," stated Sergeant Wright. "There were a couple of us at this camp and after leaving all the guys you had been through so much with, it was hard to take, to be stuck with a bunch of Zombies [Conscripts]. The two of us were down in the dumps."[47]

Sergeant Peter Smith missed the action. "In England, I was then sent to teach young soldiers how to build bunkers against shell bursts. I didn't like it," bemoaned the veteran. "I wasn't interested in instructing. So, I volunteered with Wally Porchak for the 1st Canadian Parachute Battalion."[48] It became quickly evident to these veterans that nothing could replace the Force. "It just wasn't the same anymore," concluded a nostalgic Sergeant Joe Jamieson.[49]

Back in Ottawa, all remaining 1 CSSBN unit files located in NDHQ's records branch were closed and archived. On 23 April 1945, Lieutenant-General J.C. Murchie, CGS, sent a draft to the MND office seeking the government's approval of the disbandment

DISBANDMENT

of 1 CSSBN.[50] The submission was approved by former general McNaughton, now the MND, on 25 April 1945, and forwarded to the Clerk of the Privy Council.[51] That same day General Order 203, Disbandment — Active Units confirmed that the Governor-General-in-Council authorized the disbandment of Serial 1354, 1st Canadian Special Service Battalion, CIC of the Canadian Army, effective 10 January 1945.[52]

As for the American ex-Forcemen, a total of eight officers and 345 enlisted men volunteered as parachute replacements for the 82nd and 101st Airborne Divisions. The remainder were formed into the new 474th Infantry Regiment (Separate) commanded by Colonel Walker. The regiment was activated on 6 January 1945 and operated as an independent formation not attached to any current U.S. Army division. The European Theatre of Operation (ETO) headquarters directed Walker to train for an upcoming operation in Norway and to act as a coastal defence force between La-Hay-du-Puits and Cherbourg against possible attacks from German forces still stationed in the Channel Islands.[53] To enable Walker to prepare for these two operational tasks, the regiment's manpower was increased by adding the 99th Infantry Battalion, composed of Norwegian-Americans. The 474th Infantry Regiment establishment now comprised three battalions totalling 160 officers and 3,080 men.

Upon completion of its training, the 474th was deployed with the U.S. 3rd Army, on 1 April 1945. The regiment participated in a series of security missions during the 3rd Army's advance into Germany. On 9 May 1945, the day following the official declaration of Victory in Europe, Walker was ordered to deploy to Norway and join Task Force "A." The task force was responsible for disarming and repatriating 300,000 German troops back to Germany. The regiment also participated in cleaning out, "remaining pockets (of resistance)," explained Corporal Otis C. Crabbe Jr., as well as rounding up, "collaborators and such, and guard over the Norwegians until they have their own government set up."[54] On 15 October 1945, the regiment boarded a Victory ship called *Dominican Victory*, in Oslo, and arrived in New York, 10 days later. The 474th Regiment was disbanded on 27 October 1945.[55]

During its short history, the FSSF had carved its name in military legend. The Forcemen had achieved great success, whether in defence or in the attack. They had earned the respect of both friend and foe, and through their determination and courage had achieved great feats of military action. The cost, however, had been high. The casualties suffered by the FSSF during the course of their five operational deployments were staggering. The Force sustained more than 2,300 casualties including over 400 killed and missing.[56] Amongst these were 272 officers and men of 1 CSSBN who were killed, or died of wounds, as well as countless wounded.[57] The unselfish sacrifice and acts of bravery had not gone unnoticed. In total, 17 British and 70 American awards were bestowed upon the Canadians. [58] The Americans were awarded 222 decorations.[59] These awards were a testament to the determination and courage of the Force.

15

EPILOGUE

Although the FSSF was in existence for only a little over two years, its impact was long lasting. In fact, it resonates with Canadians and Americans to the present day. Not surprisingly, its influence was particularly felt by the veterans who served in the formation. Sergeant Charlie Mann asserted:

> The Force had, and still has, a tie that binds. It has a spirit that just won't quit. They have a loyalty that you won't believe. I think that the First Special Service Force was the finest unit that North American put together.[1]

He was not alone. "No one had the esprit de corps such as the FSSF," attested Staff-Sergeant Gordon Sims. "We were tighter than family," he stated, "It changed my life."[2] Sergeant Brett Hopkins was another of many who agreed. He proudly commented:

> It was a tight knit outfit. I think that the difficulty of the training had a lot to do with it. The integration also had a lot to do with it. Different people and different backgrounds. I was very proud to be part of this outfit.[3]

The sentiment of belonging and achievement was shared by virtually all who served in the FSSF. "I never encountered anything quite as rewarding as the relationships there, the confidence that each man had in each other," acknowledged Private Lorin Waling.[4]

Part of the magic appears to be the fact that to most of those who served, the Force was not coloured by nationality, but rather duty and service to one another. Sims explained, "We all forgot our nationality — we were all FSSF."[5] Sergeant Vernon Doucette conceded, "When I went to the Force I didn't consider myself a Canadian. We were all Forcemen."[6] Sergeant Joe Glass recalled, "The esprit de corps was excellent. You never knew who was Canadian and who was American."[7]

In the end, the outcome proved to be an exceptional formation that became a military legend. Staff-Sergeant Bill Story believed, "I always felt that the amalgam of Canadians and Americans in the Force produced a sharper type, and better type, of soldier than either the two separately."[8] Sergeant Joe Jamieson clarified:

> It was great. Each man was trained to work in small teams or independently. Each man knew what to do, and he did it. It was an unbelievable outfit. Everywhere we went, we never gave an inch, we never backed up. It was an outfit that will never be forgotten.[9]

And, its members were certainly imprinted for life. "The whole thing was a growing up process," explained, Sergeant George Wright, "You came in as a kid and suddenly, you became a man with experience." He added:

> You never believed that you'd ever acquire this type of experience. The friendship was unique and the camaraderie was incredible. It was more than friendship, it's as if we were brothers. As one of the fellows once said, "There wasn't anybody that wouldn't give his life for a friend. Guys would take the bullet rather than see their friend get hit."[10]

It was not only the members of the Force who recognized their uniqueness. Newspapers also picked up on the FSSF. The *Montreal Daily Star* is but one example. They noted, "Canadian and American troops of the 1st Special Service Force are the toughest and most versatile fighting men of North America."[11] But again, this came at a high cost. Major-General Frederick later revealed that the casualty rate for original Force members was between 250 and 300 percent. "Throughout the campaign," he insisted, "they did the impossible."[12]

With an emotional attachment that runs that deep, predictably, there would be a reunion. The first was held after the war in Helena, Montana, in 1947. Remarkably, one has been held almost every year since then, alternating between Canada and the U.S. Only age and a dwindling number of veterans has threatened to bring an end to the events. Arguably, there is no greater proof to the deep attachment and lasting bonds that were created than this.

However, the uniqueness and special character of the FSSF has also spawned dozens of books and articles, re-enactors, documentaries, and even a Hollywood blockbuster

EPILOGUE

film. But most important, the formation that existed for only a little over two years has been remembered by both militaries in Canada and in the U.S. By September 1945, all of Canada's special operations forces (SOF) organizations and units were disbanded and the Canadian government focused on a massive demobilization of its military capability.[13] However, a small group of former members of the SOE, FSSF, and the 1st Canadian Parachute Battalion developed a plan to resurrect a distinct Canadian SOF entity. Their methodology was as shadowy as the unit they intended to build.

As the Army worked feverishly at demobilizing and at the same time creating the structure for the post-war Canadian Forces (CF) the commanding officer of the small Canadian Parachute Training Centre in Shilo, Manitoba selectively culled the ranks of the disbanded FSSF and the 1st Canadian Parachute Battalion. Quite simply he chose the best from the pool of personnel who had decided to remain in the Active Force to act as instructors and staff for his training establishment. Devoid of any direction from Army headquarters, the CO and his staff focused on making contacts and keeping up to date with the latest airborne developments. These prescient efforts were soon to be rewarded. It was the perpetuation of links with Canada's closest allies, as well as the importance of staying abreast of the latest tactical developments in modern warfare, specifically air-transportability, that provided the breath of life that SOF advocates were searching for.

To this end, with the aim of using manpower and resources efficiently, NDHQ directed that the parachute training and research functions reside in a single Canadian joint Army/Air Force training centre. As a result, on 15 August 1947, the Joint Air School (JAS), in Rivers, Manitoba, was established. The JAS became the "foot in the door." It was responsible for the retention of skills required for airborne and, with some ingenuity, special operations, for both the Army and the Royal Canadian Air Force (RCAF). More important, the JAS, which was renamed the Canadian Joint Air Training Centre (CJATC) on 1 April 1949, provided the seed from which a SOF organization would eventually grow.[14]

The hidden agenda of the airborne cadre quickly took root. Once the permanent structure of the Army was established in 1947, they quickly pushed to expand the airborne capability within the JAS by submitting a proposal in the spring for a Canadian Special Air Service company.[15] This new organization was to be an integral subunit of the Army component of the JAS with a mandate of filling Army, interservice, and public duties such as Army/Air tactical research and development; demonstrations to assist with Army/Air training; airborne firefighting; search and rescue; and aid to the civil power.[16] Its development, however, proved to be quite different as its name implies.

The initial proposal for the special subunit prescribed a clearly defined role. The Army, which sponsored the establishment of the fledgling organization, portrayed the Canadian SAS Company's inherent mobility as a definite asset to the public at large for domestic operations. A military appreciation written by its proponents argued the need for the unit in terms of its potential benefit to the public. It explained that the specially trained company would provide an "efficient life and property saving organization capable

OF COURAGE AND DETERMINATION

Canadian Special Air Service (SAS) Company paratroopers emplaning for a practice jump, 1948.

of moving from its base to any point in Canada in ten to fifteen hours."[17] Furthermore, the company was framed as critical in working in support of the RCAF air search-rescue duties required by the International Civil Aviation Organization agreement.

The proposed training plan further supported the benevolent image. The training cycle consisted of four phases broken down as follows: First, tactical research and development (parachute related work and fieldcraft skills); second, airborne firefighting; third, air search and rescue; and forth, mobile aid to the civil power (crowd control, first aid, military law).[18] Conspicuously absent was any evidence of commando or specialist training, which the organization's name inherently implied. After all, the Canadian SAS Company was actually titled after the British wartime Special Air Service that earned a reputation for daring commando operations behind enemy lines.

In September 1947, the request for approval for the subunit was forwarded to the deputy chief of the general staff. Significantly, it now had two additional roles added to it — public service in the event of a national catastrophe and provision of a nucleus for expansion into parachute battalions. However, the proposal also noted that the SAS company was required to provide the manpower for the large program of test and development that had been undertaken by the Tactical Research and Development Wing, as well as demonstration teams for all demonstrations within and outside the CJATC.[19]

As support for the subunit grew, its real identity began to emerge. An assessment of potential benefits to the Army included its ability to "keep the techniques employed by [British] SAS persons during the war alive in the peacetime army."[20] Although this item was last in the order of priority in the list, it soon moved to the front.

EPILOGUE

NDHQ authorized the subunit with an effective date of 9 January 1948. Once this was announced, a dramatic change in focus became evident. Not only did its function as a base for expansion for the development of airborne units take precedence, but also the previously subtle reference to a warfighting, specifically special forces role, leapt to the foreground. The new terms of reference for the employment of the SAS Company, which was confirmed in April, outlined the following duties in a revised priority:

a. Provide a tactical parachute company for airborne training. This company is to form the nucleus for expansion for the training of the three infantry battalions as parachute battalions;
b. Provide a formed body of troops to participate in tactical exercises and demonstrations for courses at the CJATC and service units throughout the country;
c. Preserve and advance the techniques of SAS [commando] operations developed during WW II 1939–1945;
d. Provide when required parachutists to back-up the RCAF organizations as detailed in the Interim Plan for air Search and Rescue; and
e. Aid Civil Authorities in fighting forest fires and assisting in national catastrophes when authorized by Defence Headquarters.[21]

The shift was anything but subtle. The original emphasis on aid to the civil authority and public service–type functions, duties that were attractive to a war-weary and fiscally conscious government, were now reprioritized if not totally marginalized. It did, however, also represent the Army's initial reaction to the Government's announcement in 1946, that airborne training for the Active Force Brigade Group (regular army) was contemplated and that an establishment to this end was being created.

The new organization was established at company strength — 125 personnel all ranks. It was comprised of one platoon from each of the three regular infantry regiments, the Royal Canadian Regiment (RCR), the Royal 22nd Regiment (R22R), and Princess Patricia's Canadian Light Infantry (PPCLI). All members were volunteers, most with wartime airborne experience, who were carefully selected. They were all bachelors, in superb physical condition, who showed initiative, self-reliance, self-discipline, mental agility, and an original approach. Captain Guy D'Artois, a wartime member of the FSSF, and later the SOE, was posted to the subunit and became the acting officer commanding.[22]

D'Artois trained his subunit of carefully selected paratroopers as a specialized commando force. His intractable approach and trademark persistence quickly made him the "absolute despair of the Senior Officers at Rivers [CJATC]." Veterans of the Canadian SAS Company explained that "Captain D'Artois didn't understand 'no.' He carried on with his training regardless of what others said." Another veteran recalled that "Guy answered to no-one, he was his own man, who ran his own show."[23]

But the issue was soon moot. To date, the continued survival of the JAS and its limited airborne and SOF capability, as represented by the Canadian SAS Company, was largely due to a British and American preoccupation with airborne and air-transportable forces in the post-war period. In essence, a nation with paratroopers possessed a ready sword. This was critical in light of the looming 1946 Canada/U.S. Basic Security Plan (BSP), which imposed on Canada the requirement to provide one airborne/air-transportable brigade, and its necessary airlift, as its share of the overall continental defence agreement. By the summer of 1948, the Canadian SAS Company represented the sum total of Canada's operational airborne and SOF capability. Clearly, some form of action was required.

As a result, the CGS directed that training for one battalion of infantry for airborne/air-transported operations be completed by 1 April 1949. After all, the BSP dictated that by 1 May 1949, the Canadian government be capable of deploying a battalion combat team prepared to respond immediately to any actual Soviet lodgement in the Arctic, with a second battalion available within two months, and an entire brigade group within four months.[24] This was the death knell for the SAS company.

South of the border, FSSF accomplishments kindled an effort to resurrect the concept, or at a minimum, the legacy. As a result, in 1960 the FSSF's Colours were retrieved from the museum at West Point Military Academy and, in a formal ceremony at Fort Bragg, were presented to the U.S. Special Forces, commonly known as the "Green Berets," along with the FSSF battle honours and history.[25] This was in concert with a larger-scale reorganization. Specifically, on 30 October 1960, all special forces groups were reorganized into a regimental system. Accordingly, 1st Special Forces Group was redesignated the 1st Special Forces Group (Airborne), First Special Forces, with roots that went straight back to the FSSF.[26]

During the 1960s, 1st Special Forces Group (1 SFG) activities focused largely on operations in the Republic of Vietnam. By 1963, the group numbered 1,258 personnel. However, with the withdrawal of the U.S. from Vietnam and the subsequent downsizing of its military, the 1st Special Forces Group (Airborne) was one of many organizations cut from the order of battle. It was officially deactivated on 30 June 1974, at Fort Bragg, North Carolina.

Even as the U.S. cut ties to the FSSF, its legacy inspired action in Canada. By the early-sixties, the notion of an Army rapid-reaction and special-forces capability gathered momentum in Canada, largely fuelled by the American involvement in Vietnam. In 1966, Lieutenant-General Jean Victor Allard, the new commander of Force Mobile Command (FMC [i.e., the Canadian Army]) decided that the Canadian Army would develop a similar capability. Specifically, he aimed to have a completely airportable unit, with all its equipment, that could be deployed to any operational theatre in as little as 48 hours. Therefore, on 12 May 1966, Paul Hellyer, the MND announced, "FMC would include the establishment of an airborne regiment whose personnel and equipment could be rapidly sent to danger zones."[27]

EPILOGUE

For Lieutenant-General Allard, the new airborne regiment represented flexibility and a higher order of professionalism and soldiering. The Army commander clearly believed that "this light unit is going to be very attractive to a fellow who likes to live dangerously, so all volunteers can go into it." His creation was to be open to all three services and manned exclusively by volunteers. "We intend," he asserted, "to look at the individual a little more rather than considering the unit as a large body of troops, some of whom might not be suited for the task."[28]

In the spring of 1966, General Allard, now the CDS, took the next step and discussed the formation of what he fondly labelled the new "airborne commando regiment." Colonel Don H. Rochester was appointed as the commander-designate and he was given a further year to refine the "Concept of Operations," organization, and structure. The prospects seemed unlimited. The "exciting thing about General Allard's concept," recalled Rochester, "was that this unit was to be radically different. Except for aircraft, it was to be self-contained with infantry, armour, artillery, engineers, signals and supporting administration." Furthermore, he explained, "all were to be volunteers and so well trained in their own arm or service that they could devote their time to specialist training."[29]

The Canadian Airborne Regiment (Cdn AB Regt) was officially established on 8 April 1968.[30] It consisted of an airborne headquarters and signal squadron (80 personnel), two infantry airborne commandos (278 personnel each), an airborne field battery (80 personnel capable of providing two three-gun troops of pack howitzers, or two groups of six medium [82-mm] mortars), an airborne field squadron (81 personnel), and an airborne service commando (i.e., combat service support and administration — 89 personnel).

The regiment's mandate was impressive if not overly optimistic. It had to have the capablity to provide for the defence of Canada; a U.N. "stand-by" role; peacekeeping operations; missions in connection with national disaster; SAS-type missions; coup-de-main tasks in a general war setting; and responsibility for parachute training in the CF. The respective Canadian Forces Organizational Order (CFOO) stated, "the role of the Canadian Airborne Regiment is to provide a force capable of moving quickly to meet any unexpected enemy threat

The Canadian Airborne Regiment's regimental Colour.

OF COURAGE AND DETERMINATION

Members of 3 Commando, the Canadian Airborne Regiment, training in the Canadian Arctic, 1980s.

or other commitment of the Canadian Armed Forces."[31] In addition, the new Army commander, Lieutenant-General W.A.B. Anderson, ordered the Canadian Airborne Regiment planning team to visit both the U.S. Special Forces Centre and the British SAS Regiment to gather the "necessary stimulus and factual data upon which to develop your concept."[32] Moreover, he directed that an element of the airborne regiment must be proficient at: high-altitude, low-opening (HALO) team parachute descents; deep penetration patrols; underwater diving; obstacle clearance and laying of underwater demolitions; mountain climbing; and "Special Service Forces"-type team missions.[33]

Although outwardly a conventional airborne regiment, by design it was clear that the Canadian Airborne Regiment, both officially in accordance with its CFOO and through direction given by the CF chain of command, was intended to be capable of special operations. The emphasis on "SOF" like capability was also enshrined in the Operational Concept, as well as in the later doctrinal manual, *CFP 310 (1) Airborne: The Canadian Airborne Regiment.* Under the heading "Special Operations," a long list of tasks were included that were clearly SOF in nature. Specifically, the document stated that the "Canadian Airborne Regiment is to be prepared to carry out the following operations for which it is specially trained: disruption of lines of communications, destruction of critical installations; psychological warfare operations; special intelligence tasks; recovery tasks; deception operations; internal security operations; counter-guerilla operations; and support of indigenous paramilitary forces."[34]

EPILOGUE

The emphasis on special operations was not lost on the airborne's leadership, which focused at times almost exclusively on daring direct-action commando-like raids. Moreover, as a number of former commanding officers noted, if something happened (e.g., terrorist incident) they knew they would get the call so they attempted to train individuals in the necessary skills required for those kinds of special operations.

The quality of the original individuals was incontestable. Official recruiting themes stressed the superior attributes of the new genre of warrior. They insisted that the new paratrooper be to be an excellent athlete, an expert at small arms, and a survival specialist. Furthermore, the candidates need to be robust, courageous, and capable of a high level of endurance. Not surprisingly, the Canadian Airborne Regiment received a larger percentage of the more ambitious, determined, and energized individuals. They skimmed the cream of the Army. Only experienced officers, non-commissioned officers, and soldiers were accepted. All riflemen within the commandos were required to be qualified to the rank of corporal. This meant that the respective individual had previously served within a regular rifle battalion. As a result, they were already competent and experienced in the basic drills of soldiering. Equally important, they were on the whole older and normally, more mature. This allowed the regiment to direct its training effort toward specialized training such as mountain and pathfinder operations, patrolling courses, skiing, and unarmed combat.

The regiment quickly forged a reputation for undertaking tough, demanding, and dynamic activities. It set new standards for physical fitness and training realism. In keeping with its status as a strategic force capable of global deployment, the regiment travelled throughout Canada and the United States, and went to exotic locations such as Jamaica, to practise its lethal craft. It conducted training and exchanges with the British SAS, American Rangers and special forces, and the French Foreign Legion. By the early-seventies, the Canadian Airborne Regiment was at its zenith. It had the status of a mini-formation, direct access to the commander of the Army, and an increased peacetime establishment of 1,044 all ranks.

The Canadian Airborne Regiment was formally linked to the FSSF. In fact, it perpetuated the Force and carried the FSSF Battle Honours on its regimental Colours. This was a significant benchmark for the legacy of 1 CSSBN. According to CF doctrine:

> Perpetuation is a uniquely Canadian system that provides a means of preserving military operational honours for successive generations. The system was developed by the Army and used extensively to safeguard the record of service of Canadian expeditionary force units during the First World War. The system has changed little over the years. Only combatant units that have gained an honour and/or distinction in the field may be perpetuated and only serving combatant units with a proven link to the previous one can claim and be awarded the honour of perpetuation. [35]

And so, the Canadian Airborne Regiment carried on the tradition of the FSSF. It also participated annually in Menton Day ceremonies with its U.S. special forces and Ranger colleagues to celebrate the memory and traditions of the FSSF.

The airborne regiment deployed to Montreal, Quebec, during the FLQ Crisis in October 1970 and four years later was dispatched to Cyprus during the Turkish invasion of that island.[36] However, in all cases the regiment functioned solely as conventional infantry. On 26 November 1976, the regiment was moved from Edmonton, Alberta, to Petawawa, Ontario, and its formation status was stripped.[37] It now became a simple unit within the newly re-roled Special Service Force (SSF), which provided the Army with a relatively light, airborne/airportable quick-reaction force in the demographic centre of the country which could be moved quickly to augment either of the flanking brigades for internal security tasks, to the Arctic, or to U.N.-type operations.[38] The SSF, also, made great efforts to articulate its intimate association with the FSSF legacy. For example, its emblem included the famous V-42 fighting knife.

Brochure marking training activity between JFK Special Warfare Center, Fort Bragg, and the Canadian Airborne Regiment.

However, the restructuring inflicted additional wounds. The Canadian Airborne Regiment was dramatically pared and it lost its preferred standing within the Army for both manning and exemptions from the mundane taskings that other units endured. Out of necessity, it began to accept more junior members across the board (i.e., officers, senior NCOs, and men), and suffered the corresponding degradation of capability. Moreover, it faced an increasing number of attacks from senior CF leaders who were not favourably disposed toward "special soldiers," particularly during a period of constantly shrinking defence budgets.

Adding to the frustrations of the members of the regiment was the fact that despite its CFOO and international stand-by status it was never deployed. Senior CF leadership argued that deploying the regiment would strip Canada of it strategic reserve. More realistically, the problem centred around the make-up of the airborne unit itself. It lacked the necessary mobility (i.e., armoured and wheeled vehicles) and the support infrastructure

EPILOGUE

Member of Pathfinder Platoon, Canadian Airborne Regiment, practicing HALO insertion, 1990s.

needed if it was to deploy for extended periods of time. Accordingly, it was easier to send conventional units to do the operations, which were all conventional in nature anyways.

Continued downsizing of the regiment to battalion status in 1992 further degraded both the status and capability of the Canadian Airborne Regiment . Nonetheless, in December of that year, the regiment deployed to Somalia on a peacemaking operation under Security Council Resolution 794. Unfortunately, it experienced disciplinary problems in theatre that detracted from its overall actual stellar performance.[39] The regiment pacified its sector in less than three months, earning the praise of Hugh Tremblay, the director of humanitarian relief and rehabilitation in Somalia, who stated to all who would listen, "If you want to know and to see what you should do while you are here in Somalia go to Belet Huen, talk to the Canadians and do what they have done, emulate the Canadians and you will have success in your humanitarian relief sector."[40] Nevertheless, in the media and the public consciousness the mission was ultimately defined as a failure due to the poor leadership and criminal acts of a few. The inexplicable and lamentable torture killing of Shidane Arone, a Somali national caught stealing within the regiment lines, became the defining image of the Canadian Airborne Regiment's operation in Africa.

The public outcry and criticism of DND that followed an attempt to cover up the incident at NDHQ, as well as later revelations of hazing videos within the regiment, created a crisis of epic proportions and senior political and military decision makers desperately sought a quick and easy solution to their troubles. They swiftly found one. During an official press release on the afternoon of 23 January 1995, David Collenette, the MND, announced, "although our senior military officers believe the Regiment as constituted should continue, the government believes it cannot. Therefore, today under the authority of the National Defence Act, I have ordered the disbandment of the Canadian Airborne Regiment."[41] With that decision, the CF's link to the FSSF seemed to be broken.

In the interim, a resurgence of American interest in the Asia-Pacific theatre spelled a return of the American military's connection to the FSSF. On 1 September 1984, the U.S. Army reactivated the 1st Special Forces Group in Fort Bragg. Its 1st Battalion was forward deployed to Tori Station, Okinawa, and the 2nd and 3rd Battalions were stood-up in Fort Lewis, Washington. The group operates out of Joint Base Lewis-McChord to the present day and continues to carry on the FSSF lineage.

In Canada, years before the Canadian Airborne Regiment was disbanded, Canada's next connection to the FSSF began to develop. A fundamental shift in the threat picture to Western industrialized nations erupted in the late 1960s. Political violence, or more accurately terrorism, became recognized as a significant "new" menace. Bombings, kidnapping, murders, and the hijacking of commercial aircraft became commonplace worldwide. In the Middle East, Europe, North America, and elsewhere, countries were thrust into a state of violence as both homegrown and international terrorists waged a relentless war that recognized no borders or limits. The murder of Israeli athletes at the 1972 Olympics in Munich, West Germany, became one of the defining images of the crisis, as did the 1975 terrorist assault on the headquarters of OPEC in Vienna, Austria.[42]

The problem went beyond a spillover of Mid-East conflict and politics. In Germany, groups such as the Baader-Meinhof gang (or Red Army Faction), created death and destruction. Holland was besieged by Moluccan terrorists, and Britain struggled with the Irish Republican Army (IRA) and the Northern Ireland question. In North America, foreign terrorists imported their political struggles and launched attacks against targets in Canada. A few examples include: the storming of the Turkish embassy in Ottawa by three Armenian men (Armenian Revolutionary Army) on 12 March 1985; the paralyzation of the Toronto public transit system on 1 April 1985, as a result of a communiqué sent by a group identifying itself as the Armenian Secret Army for the Liberation of our Homeland in which they threatened death to passengers of the transit system; and the downing of an Air India flight off the coast of Ireland on 23 June 1985, killing 329 people as a result of a bomb that was planted prior to its departure from Toronto's Pearson International Airport.

Not surprisingly, much like other countries around the world, Canada decided it needed a counter terrorist (CT) capability of its own. In 1986, with a number of high-profile terrorist acts having been committed on Canadian soil, the Government of Canada created its own CT force. Although initially the responsibility was given to the Royal Canadian Mounted Police (RCMP) under the title Special Emergency Response Team (SERT), Canada's first Hostage Rescue (HR)/CT organization was transferred to the CF in 1992.[43]

EPILOGUE

Lieutenant-Colonel Peter Kenward pins Canadian "jump wings" on to American special forces personnel, 1994.

Canadian Special Operations Forces Command Crest.

From the beginning, NDHQ slapped a cap on the size of Joint Task Force Two (JTF 2).[44] The maximum size of the unit was to be no more than 120 to 125 individuals. As such, the organization was based on two assault troops, a sniper troop and a number of specialists (e.g., demolitions), as well as a training cadre.

Once established, JTF 2 visited the SAS, Delta Force, and SEAL Team 6. In addition, the SAS sent a training cadre to Ottawa to provide assistance with the CT assaulter program. Very early, the CO realized that the unit would have to evolve. JTF 2, to ensure its relevance and utility to the greater CF, was required to develop a green (SOF) role. As such, the unit began to evolve in the mid to late-1990s toward a more military SOF orientation and capability; however, CT/HR remained JTF 2's primary focus. In 1994, the CDS approved growth for JTF 2, as well as a transition from a pure black CT role to other special operations tasks. With this mandate, the unit's role expanded to include responsibility for providing contingency planning assistance teams (CPATs), close protection party (CPP) tasks for senior political and military decision makers, and special reconnaissance. These tasks gave the new JTF 2 operators exposure to key governmental and military personalities as well as experience in such foreign locations as Bosnia-Herzegovina, Côte-d'Ivoire, Haiti, Kosovo, and Rwanda.

As the unit evolved, it also began to search for its military roots. As such, it informally began a relationship with Canadian FSSF veterans and the FSSF association. However, in the aftermath of the terrorist attacks in New York on the morning of 11 September 2001 (9/11), JTF 2 became pre-occupied with its deployments to Afghanistan in support of the American Operation Enduring Freedom (OEF). Specifically, JTF 2 deployed a special operations task force (SOTF), which consisted of an assault troop.

The SOTF was deployed as part of OEF and was under operational control of the American commander of the Combined Joint Forces Special Operations Component Command. Their tasks included direct action, special reconnaissance, and sensitive site exploitation.[45] The JTF 2 based SOTF was deployed in theatre from December 2001 to November 2002. When the SOTF first arrived in theatre, JTF 2 was largely an unknown quantity and the American SOF commanders were quite frankly reluctant to use them. By the end of the tour, the JTF 2 SOTF had become the designated coalition theatre direct action (DA) reserve force with American subunits allocated to it under tactical control (normally Rangers or 82nd Airborne and aviation assets). Moreover, it executed more missions than any other coalition SOF force assigned to the Combined Joint Special Operations Task Force — Afghanistan.

Unquestionably, its participation in OEF was a critical turning point in JTF 2's evolution. Its participation, or, more significantly, its impact in theatre bolstered Canadian credibility. "We had to shoulder our way into the international SOF community with reps from the British SAS and US Delta," explained Colonel Clyde Russell, the CO of JTF 2 at the time, "but once we got our seat at the table, now we can hold our own."[46]

Participation in OEF also ended debate back at the unit in Ottawa: JTF 2 was now a Tier 1 SOF organization. One JTF 2 detachment commander explained, "9/11 put us full throttle into the warfighting game and allowed us to pass a number of hurdles that would have taken years in a peacetime environment." Major-General Michael Day, one of the original SOTF commanders assessed, "We progressed the unit in maturity decades that first year [in Afghanistan]."

Despite the importance of JTF 2 participation in theatre, by 2002, the operational tempo had begun to stress the organization. In addition, the great utility of SOF forces in the new security environment had come to the attention of political decision makers who now directed JTF 2 to expand exponentially. In response, the unit had to take a tactical pause, so it pulled out of Afghanistan, as did the conventional CF contribution to OEF.

During this pause, JTF 2 increased its efforts to cultivate links to the FSSF association and in 2003 it publicly stated that "the unit wanted to build strong historical links to the Devil's Brigade" and it worked toward that end.[47] While JTF 2 had pulled out of Afghanistan, it still had a presence. From 2003 to 2005 it provided a Joint Liaison Team — Afghanistan (JLT-A). Then on 24 December 2004, the U.S. Embassy in Ottawa delivered a demarche to Foreign Affairs Canada requesting that Canada provide SOF forces to OEF in Afghanistan as early as possible in 2005. The diplomatic note affirmed that Canada's

EPILOGUE

previous SOF contribution to OEF in Afghanistan in 2001–02 "was highly valued by the US." Additionally, it confirmed "that relatively small numbers of special operations forces exert a disproportionately large operational impact."

The request was strongly supported by both the CDS General Rick Hillier and the deputy defence minister, D. M. Elcock. They explained, "The deployment of Canadian special operations forces to Afghanistan would make evident our ongoing commitment to an active engagement in the Campaign Against Terrorism and it would also demonstrate our direct burden sharing with our closest allies." The deployment was also in tune with ongoing strategic objectives for the CF in the global war on terrorism. The deployment would assist the government of Afghanistan in providing security and stability in the country and in supporting reconstruction activities; it would assist with the elimination of Al Qaida, the Taliban and other anti-coalition militants as continuing terrorist threats to international peace and security; and it would support efforts to address the humanitarian needs of Afghans.

The deployment of a JTF 2 SOTF to Afghanistan in support of OEF was authorized by the Canadian government on 1 June 2005. Its mission was "to conduct combat operations in the Afghanistan theatre of operations (ATO) in support of US-led operation Enduring Freedom (OEF) for a period of one year." Canadian Special Operations Forces (CANSOF) was back at war. Once again, the SOTF was deployed under operational control of the commander U.S. Central Command (CENTCOM). Its tasks focused primarily on direct action, special reconnaissance, and sensitive site exploitation. However, the SOTF was also tasked to be prepared to conduct other tasks, such as hostage rescue and close personal protection as ordered.

Concurrently, another important benchmark the development of a legacy of the Canadian/U.S. FSSF occurred. On 13 August 2005, Lieutenant-General Philip Kensigner awarded the U.S. Army Combat Infantryman's Badge to Canadian survivors of the FSSF at the Sheraton Eau Claire hotel in Calgary, Alberta. After 40 years of lobbying by the FSSF association, the U.S. Congress finally approved awarding the badge to Canadians in May 2005.[48]

As well, a major CF reorganization took place at this time. On 19 April 2005, General Rick Hillier, the CDS, declared that he was "bringing JTF 2, along with all the enablers that it would need, to conduct operations successfully into one organization with one commander." As a result, on 1 February 2006, as part of the CF's transformation program, Canadian Special Operations Command (CANSOFCOM) was created. The purpose of CANSOFCOM is to develop; generate; and, where required, employ and sustain SOTFs capable of achieving tactical, operational and strategic effects required by the Canadian goverment.[49]

An important link to the FSSF was now beginning to emerge. One of the new units in CANSOFCOM was the Canadian Special Operations Regiment (CSOR), which was located at Canadian Forces Base Petawawa, in Ontario. It was officially stood up as a new

OF COURAGE AND DETERMINATION

Canadian Special Operations Regiment operator conducting winter mobility training, 2010.

unit of the CF on 13 August 2006. It was created as a high-readiness, agile, and robust special operations force that was created as a vital enabler for JTF 2 to address a capability gap that existed prior to its creation. The regiment is capable of supporting and conducting a broad range of special operations missions (i.e., DA; search and rescue [SR]; defence, diplomacy military assistance [DDMA], and non-combatant evacuation operations [NEO]) at home and abroad. It was also to be the public face of CANSOFCOM. As such, actions to link it directly to the FSSF commenced.[50]

Of great significance, on 27 September 2007, the second meeting of the Battle Honours Committee met in NDHQ and unanimously recommended that JTF 2 and CSOR be afforded honour-bearing status.[51] On 4 February 2008, General Hillier, approved the status. At the same time, the CDS also approved the perpetuation of the 1st Canadian Special Service Battalion by CSOR. This meant that CSOR would perpetuate and carry the nine battle honours that 1 CSSBN earned from it service in the Second World War.[52]

As such, CSOR now carries on the proud traditions of the FSSF. CSOR currently has approximately 450 personnel. It is slowly growing with a goal of reaching a strength of 690 personnel. Not surprisingly, CSOR has already carved a name for itself on operations in Afghanistan, Libya, and Africa. In addition, it continues Canadian participation in Menton Days. In fact, the 67th annual Menton Week (conducted by U.S. SF) was held from 5 to 9 December 2011, at Joint Base Lewis-McChord, home to the 1 SFG. CSOR proudly took its place to represent the Canadian lineage. The deputy commander of 1

EPILOGUE

Canadian Special Operations Regiment and 1st Special Forces Group Colour Party, Menton Day, Fort Lewis-McChord, 2011.

OF COURAGE AND DETERMINATION

SFG, Colonel Brian Vines, stated, "Both of our units adhere to the values that the first special service force espoused, those of duty, honour and valor. We're honored to be here today to be a part of this event and remember those who've gone before us, both Forcemen, and members of our respective units who've made the ultimate sacrifice."[53] The Canadian captain leading the Canadian contingent asserted, "It's to honour the special relationship we've had with American special forces since World War II. I've worked with more than a couple of American special forces teams during my tours in Afghanistan and the camaraderie usually comes along quickly because of the mutual histories we've had."[54]

Aside from the military linkage, others also continue to push rememberance of the FSSF. In 2011, the FSSF was also honoured with the creation of an original Scottish tartan. The design was filed with the Scottish national tartan registry for the FSSF, an initiative spearheaded by the Shining Thistle Pipe Band, based in Helena, Montana, and the FSSF Association.[55] Moreover, on 29 February 2012, a gala event was hosted by the Canadian embassy in Washington, D.C., to support the initiative of a Montana-based congressional delegation, which was pushing for the award of the Congressional Gold Medal, the highest American civilian award that can be bestowed. Only about a half dozen units have ever received it.

In addition, on 27 January 2013, the MND recognized the military achievements of the FSSF one last time when he bestowed upon them the Minister's Award for Operational Excellence in Ottawa, Canada. The citation read:

> In recognition for extraordinary accomplishments and dedication to operations during the Second World War, their significant contribution to the Allied victory in Europe and in their role for establishing the foundation for Special Operational Forces in Canada and the United States.[56]

The FSSF existed for but a short period of time. Yet, its unique make-up, character, and legendary battlefield record have ensured it has stayed in the forefront of military and public memory in both countries. In the end, it's a story of courage and determination.

ANNEX A

CONSENT TO SERVE DECLARATION FORM (JULY 1942)

All volunteers posted to the 2nd Canadian Parachute Battalion were required to sign the following declaration form:

> I _____ hereby volunteer for service and duty with the Second Canadian Parachute Battalion of the Canadian Army and solemnly declare and agree to undergo training in parachute jumping and in warfare under winter conditions.
>
> I further solemnly declare and agree that while on service or duty with the Armed Forces of the United States within the United States of America, its territories and possessions, I will obey all lawful orders and commands given to me by superior officers in the said Armed Forces of the United States, as if such superior officers were members of the Canadian Army of relative rank.
>
> I further solemnly declare that I understand that, while on service or duty with the Armed Forces of the United States of America, within the United States of America, its territories and possessions, I shall continue to be governed by the Army Act, the King's Regulations and Orders for the Canadian Militia, and all other laws, orders and regulations

applicable to the Canadian Army in Canada and that if charged with an offence under the above-mentioned Act, Regulations, Laws or Orders, I may be tried by the authorities empowered so to do under the Army Act and King's Regulations and Orders for the Canadian Militia. I further understand that, while on service or duty with the Armed Forces of the United States within the United States of America, its territories and possessions, I am subject to the laws of the United States of America and if I am charged with an offence; under the said laws, I may be tried by the appropriate civil authorities of the United States of America.

I further solemnly declare that I understand that, while on service or duty with the Armed Forces of the United States of America, within the United States of America, its territories and possessions, I shall continue to receive pay and allowances, including dependents' allowance as provided under the Financial Regulations and Instructions for the Canadian Active Service Force, and such other allowances and emoluments as may, from time to time, be authorized.

I further solemnly declare and agree that my voluntary engagement for service and duty with the said Second Canadian Parachute Battalion is subject to the conditions above set forth and shall continue with the said unit so long as required by superior military authority.

Source: Form, "Declaration to be signed by all officers and other ranks (in triplicate) posted to Second Canadian Parachute Battalion," DHH, file 168.009 (D43), Organization and Administration of 1st Canadian Special Service Battalion, Jul 42/May 43.

ANNEX A

SPECIAL DECLARATION (REVISED 25 MARCH 1944)

All Canadian volunteers recruited in the Mediterranean Theatre and posted to the 1st Canadian Special Service Battalion were required to sign the following declaration form:

I, _____, (Number) _____, (Rank) _____, (Christian Names) _____, Surname, _____,

(a) Hereby volunteer for Special Service with a Canadian Special Service Battalion or Airborne Unit of the Canadian Army for so long as my services with that unit may be required and agree to undergo training in Parachute Jumping and in warfare under winter conditions and upon completion of such training to serve wherever required.

(b) I further understand that the Canadian Special Service Battalion is from time to time ordered to serve with the armed forces of the United States and that in course of such service it will be necessary for personnel of the Canadian Special Service Battalion or other Airborne unit to serve in units or in formations commanded by officers and NCOs of the United States Army and for personnel of the United States Army to serve under the Command of Officers and NCOs of the Canadian Special Service Battalion.

(c) I further agree that while on service under the conditions set fourth above I will obey all lawful orders and commands given to me by Superior Officers in the said Armed Forces of the United States as if such superior officers were members of the Canadian Army of relative rank.

(d) I further declare that I understand that while on service under the conditions set forth above I shall continue to be subject to the laws orders and regulations applicable to the Canadian Army and to be disciplined by Canadian Army Officers.

(e) I further declare that I understand that while on service under the conditions set forth above I shall continue to receive pay and allowances including dependents allowance as provided by the Canadian Army and such additional rates of pay as may be authorized for Parachute Troops and to be eligible for a pension if entitled under the pension act.

Source: Special Declaration, LAC, RG 24, Vol. 10404, file HQ Cdn 56/6/1 CSSBN/1, DHH, file designation, 2000A5.009 (D53), Correspondence, messages, policy procedures. The declaration form was to be completed in duplicate and forwarded to 2nd Echelon. One duplicate original was to be retained by 2nd Echelon, with the Officer or Soldier's documents, and the original forwarded to CMHQ for transmission to NDHQ.

ANNEX B

THE FSSF AND OPERATION JUPITER:
A Historical Clarification

There are some individuals who have written that the Plough Project and the FSSF were somehow intertwined with Operation Jupiter, the code name for a proposed plan to invade northern Norway. In fact, one book was actually titled *Snow Plough and the Jupiter Deception*. This premise, however, is disputed.[1] British Prime Minister Winston Churchill was the architect and protagonist for Operation Jupiter and he fought hard to convince his military staff and his American and Canadian allies to adopt it. Initially, he intended it not as a deception but as an actual operation. Churchill believed it could relieve pressure on the Soviets by creating a second front. In the early part of 1942, the German onslaught was such that the Allies feared the Soviets would be defeated, if they did not receive some assistance other than the massive quantities of supplies that were being provided. "With the Russians fighting on a gigantic scale from hour to hour against the main striking force of the German Army," asserted Churchill, "we could not stand idle." He insisted, "we must engage the enemy."[2] In fact, the Americans even proposed Operation Sledgehammer, an assault on the French coast, possibly against a port such as Cherbourg, to draw off German forces. All realized this was a last ditch, sacrificial effort that had little chance of success. But such was the concern for the Soviet ability to remain in the war.

Churchill also believed that Operation Jupiter would protect the northern resupply convoys and act as a bridgehead to expand south and eventually retake Europe. In fact his plan was:

> First, in "Jupiter" we can certainly bring superior forces to bear at the point of attack and in the whole region invaded; secondly, if successful, we get a permanent footing on the Continent of constant value to the passage of our convoys and capable of almost indefinite exploitation southward. In fact, we could begin to roll the map of Hitler's Europe down from the top. Once we have established ourselves with growing air-power in the two main airfields, we can attack by parachute and other means under air cover the airfields to the southward and make ourselves masters of this northern region, so that with the spring of 1943 other landings could be made, Tromso and Narvik taken, then Bodo and Mo, by combinations of seaborne landings under shore based air. No great mass of the enemy could be brought to bear upon them, except by inordinate efforts over bad communications. The population would rise to aid us as we advanced, and only as we advanced.... The distractions caused to the enemy's movements would far exceed the employment of our own resources.[3]

Both British and Canadian planning staffs laboured hard at making it work. "Our objective," they described, "is to capture and hold air bases in the Petsamo, Kirkenes and Banak areas." They aimed at "assaulting during the last week of September or very early October [1942]."[4] However, in the end the planning staff was forced to recommend against the operation since it "had only a 50% chance of success and a failure could be a military disaster of the first order."[5]

Despite his enthusiasm for Jupiter, Churchill did admit that Operation Torch, the invasion of North Africa, was the primary focus. "Though I hoped for both 'Torch' and 'Jupiter,'" conceded Churchill, "I never had any intention of letting 'Jupiter' queer the pitch of 'Torch.'" He explained, "the difficulties of focusing and combining in one vehement thrust all the efforts of two mighty countries were such that no ambiguity could be allowed to darken counsel."[6]

However, Churchill, who was always full of offensive schemes and who jumped at every innovative and novel idea, never fully abandoned the "Norwegian option" and believed, as a minimum, it could serve as a deception to force the Germans to keep resources pinned down in Norway. As such he continued to bedevil his staff with constant memos and notes querying status reports on projects and directing new initiatives.[7] The British chief of the imperial general staff, General Alan Brooke, lamented the "constant flow of proposals for operations and changes in operation with which he [Churchill] deluged his military advisers," the stream of suggestions the prime minister made with respect to choosing "particular individuals for particular responsibilities," and "the difficulties of convincing him that these matters should be left to his constitutional military advisors." Alan Brooke continually counselled Churchill that "he could not play a pawn on the 'chess-board of war' and expect it to be a queen."[8] Even this counsel had little effect on dampening Churchill's active and furtive mind.

Nevertheless, at no time was Jupiter directly tied to the Plough Project or the FSSF. Operation Jupiter was to be a conventional operation carried out by an estimated two to five divisions.[9] Its mission and objective was completely different and divorced from the Operation Plough/FSSF mission set. During the brief period that Operation Jupiter was under consideration American, British, Canadian, and Russian forces were all involved.[10] Churchill, however, approached the Canadians to take it on. "I thought," wrote Churchill, "that this operation [Jupiter] would give a glorious opportunity to the Canadian Army, which had now for two years been eating its heart out in Britain, awaiting the invader."[11]

Quite simply, neither the Plough Project, nor the FSSF were ever earmarked as part of the equation. The interface is fleeting and based on a narrow window of inquiry. The first nexus was a reference to "the new snow tanks" when Churchill spoke of defending the potential gains achieved in Norway during the winter.[12] Whether he was referring to the Weasel, which of course is not a tank but rather a personnel carrier, or some other vehicle under design is unclear. Nonetheless, the reference was in regards to a means of mobility and firepower not the employment of the FSSF.[13]

The only actual reference to any possible employment of the FSSF in Operation Jupiter was a self-imposed staff check ordered by Colonel Frederick prior to his visit to England in September 1942.[14] The document entitled "Memorandum on an invasion of Northern Norway," written by Lieutenant-Colonel A.D. Dahl on 12 September 1942, is the only document found on the subject. It had no follow-up and appears to be only a staff check to prepare Frederick should the topic arise during his upcoming trip to England. The document speaks to its providence. Dahl wrote:

> I have been asked by Colonel Frederick to give my opinion about a possible use of the Special Force in an invasion in Northern Norway. The very short time at disposal has not permitted me to go into the problem as thoroughly as one could wish. Nor have I any detailed information about the German Forces and enemy fortifications in Norway. What I can do is therefore just to give, briefly, some personal ideas on the subject.[15]

Days, later Frederick departed for Britain. He met with Lord Mountbatten, the commander of Combined Operations Command on 17 September 1942. During the visit, the Plough Project was discussed and Mountbatten reaffirmed that "it was agreed that the [Plough] proj[ect] would be American entirely."[16] Moreover, Brigadier Colin Gubbins from the SOE also attended the meeting to discuss deconfliction of possible targets. There is no indication that Operation Jupiter was discussed in any manner. Moreover, it demonstrates the intention to maintain the original objective of the FSSF.

OF COURAGE AND DETERMINATION

The following day Frederick met with Lieutenant-General Andrew McNaughton, the Canadian commander of Canadian forces overseas, who had been asked by Churchill in the early summer to examine the feasibility of Operation Jupiter. Frederick wrote:

> Gen[eral] McN[aughton] is keen and interested. He was quite familiar with the project and asked many questions about training and equipment. He suggested that I read his papers on a plan for the capture of Nor[thern] Norway. The plan envisages the use of five or six div[ision]s during the winter.[17]

Again, the meeting, discussion, and outcome underscore the fact that even though McNaughton was aware of the FSSF and the Plough Project, it was never factored in to the planning for Operation Jupiter. It also, reinforces the fact that Frederick had little knowledge of the larger operation.

Trying to find a bona fide linkage between the Plough Project/FSSF and Operation Jupiter is extremely difficult. However, evidence to refute any direct connection between the two is far more pervasive. First, as noted above, Churchill targeted the Canadian Army to undertake the Jupiter mission. He requested that McNaughton undertake the planning for the operation. Even during the initial planning stages all agreed that a byproduct of any announcement of McNaughton's role as commander of such a scheme and any visit to the Soviet Union for planning purposes would lead the Germans to believe something was being planned for Norway.[18]

Moreover, a note from British Combined Operation Command Headquarters to President Roosevelt on 27 July 1942, made direct reference to the Canadian Army role in deception tied to Operation Jupiter to cover for the preparations for Operation Torch. "The Canadian Army here [England]," wrote a senior naval officer, " will be fitted for Arctic service. Thus, we shall be able to keep the enemy in doubt till the last moment."[19] On a similar note, once Jupiter was officially scrubbed in August 1942, Churchill himself wrote a letter to Canadian Prime Minister Mackenzie King, on 25 September 1942, in which he revealed, "we are preparing British divisions in Scotland for Arctic service as part of cover."[20] Again, never was the Plough Project or the FSSF directly or indirectly implicated in Jupiter or the subsequent deception concerns to cover for Operation Torch.

The decision to push the operation on the Canadians further distances the Plough Project and FSSF connection. In fact it would preclude the FSSF as Canada had clearly stated that they would defer planning and operational control of the FSSF operations to the Americans.[21] In addition, there is no reference made in their detailed analysis or planning to the Plough Project or the FSSF. In fact, it was quite the opposite. Canadians undertook the analysis and need for Operation Jupiter quite seriously and viewed its possible adoption as implicating Canada and its Army in Britain for the conduct of the task.[22]

ANNEX B

Additionally, in their planning the British had already designated substantial forces to the operation in their appreciation of the task. All were either British or Empire troops. Specifically, the force structure consisted of: 49th Division (of which one of its three brigades, 146th Brigade was stationed in Iceland); 52nd Division; 1st Mountain Regiment; an airlanding brigade; a parachute brigade; and four commandos. In addition, the plan had also identified the allocation of special units, specifically, forestry corps, Royal Engineers, and Inland water transport.[23]

A later assessment, written on 22 September 1942, updated the force structure. It stated, "The maximum army forces that could be provided for Jupiter would be a corps of two divisions. These would be moderately trained in mountain warfare and virtually devoid of Arctic Training. From one to three brigade groups and up to seven commandos are all the troops trained in combined operations that could be found."[24] Again, absolutely no mention of Operation Plough or the FSSF was made in any of the top-secret planning documents. In fact, once again, it was quite the opposite. In studying the documents produced by the special planning staff, it becomes quite obvious they had no idea of Operation Plough or the training of the FSSF. Much of their estimate concerned the problems and lack of information on Arctic training, movement, and equipment.

Second, the time period in question when Operation Jupiter was actually under significant consideration was the same time that the FSSF was immersed in the stand-up of the Plough Project. Again, there is no reference at all made to Operation Jupiter. Importantly, the Canadian planning staff submitted the complete draft of Operation Jupiter to Lieutenant-General McNaughton on 6 August 1942, when the FSSF was in the cusp of being formed.[25] Operation Jupiter was cancelled in September, when Operation Plough and the FSSF were just getting started and still completely focused on their mission to attack specific hydroelectric stations and wage a guerrilla war designed to tie down German forces in the interior of Norway. Even in October when the idea of resurrecting Operation Jupiter surfaced, albeit briefly, again, no mention of Plough or the FSSF emerged.

Even when the Plough Project itself was cancelled, the question became now what? Again, no consideration from the American or Canadian planning staff or decision makers was evident with regards to maintaining the force in any shape or form as a deception requirement or as a means to reinvigorate Operation Jupiter. In fact, a memorandum drafted for General George Marshall on the "Employment of First Special Service Force" listed a number of possible uses of the Force with advantages and disadvantages. Again, no mention is made of a FSSF role in Operation Jupiter or as a deception force. Moreover, as early as 17 October 1942, General Marshall directed that the FSSF continue its training, "with a view to its possible employment in the Caucasus area in early 1943."[26] The focus area changed and the Canadian government gave its approval for the American employment of the FSSF in the Mediterranean theatre, on 14 October 1942.[27]

Third, other than the one staff check written by Lieutenant-Colonel Dahl, there is no mention of Operation Jupiter in the voluminous official records of the FSSF. Moreover,

OF COURAGE AND DETERMINATION

The First Special Service Force, written by Lieutenant-Colonel Robert D. Burhans, which has been the seminal history of the FSSF since the formation's disbandment, makes no mention of Operation Jupiter. Burhans was the formation's intelligence officer who was cognizant of all possible missions and intelligence matters. He never mentioned it, nor is there a single sheet of paper in his extensive personal records that even provides a hint of the operation. And for that matter, none of the numerous credible histories of the FSSF mention it either.

Finally, there were a number of other initiatives ranging from SOE operations, designated Arctic commandos, allied units and formations undergoing specialized winter and mountain warfare training, as well as naval and air operations in the Northern theatre of operations. Any and all of those provided Churchill with the means to continue his Norwegian deception once the decision was taken in September 1942 to scrub Operation Jupiter as a viable military option.[28]

More significantly, the FSSF was a formation under the order of battle of the U.S. Army, therefore under the command and control of the Americans. It was irrelevant what musing Churchill may have had, written or otherwise, with regard to the employment of the FSSF as they were not within his area of control. According to Lieutenant-General G.G. Simonds, President Roosevelt "came out strongly against the venture [Jupiter]."[29] Furthermore, the American commitment required for Operation Jupiter was limited in the assessment of the secret appreciation written by the special planning staff to "2 combat ships and 150 transport aircraft."[30] All ground forces were to be from Britain or its Commonwealth countries.

Quite simply, from the beginning, the Plough Project and the FSSF were created for a specific purpose. The mission aim, training, and focus never wavered and never were they tied to any other scheme or operation. Once Operation Plough was cancelled, the Americans moved quickly to find a viable task for the FSSF. They did not tie it to any Arctic deception.

Had the Plough Project continued as a mission, could it have been linked to a deception tied to Operation Jupiter? If Operation Jupiter had been initiated, would the FSSF possibly have been re-tasked to support the invasion of Norway? Perhaps, but that is counterfactual/"what if history" — conjecture. Historically speaking, the Plough Project and the FSSF had no official or direct linkage to Operation Jupiter or a prolonged deception thereof.

NOTES

INTRODUCTION

1. "The 'Black Devils,'" *Time*, 4 September 1944. Clipping, Department of National Defence (DND) Canadian Airborne Forces Museum, Canadian Forces Base (CFB) Petawawa (hereafter cited as CAFM) files.

CHAPTER 1

1. Hilary St. George Saunders, *The Green Beret: The Story of the Commandos* (London: Michael Joseph, 1956), 118.
2. See Williamson Murray and Allan R. Millett, eds., *Military Innovation in the Interwar Period* (New York: Cambridge University Press, 1996); John A. English, *On Infantry* (Westport: Praeger, 1984), 47–85; Len Deighton, *Blood, Tears, and Folly* (London: Pimlico, 1995), 160–204; and Len Deighton, *Blitzkrieg* (Edison, NJ: Castle Books, 2000).
3. Fifty-three thousand French troops were evacuated 3–4 June 1940, after the withdrawal of the British forces was complete on 2 June. The British Admiralty estimated that approximately 338,226 men were evacuated between 26 May and 3 June. The British left behind 2,000 guns, 60,000 trucks, 76,000 tons of ammunition, and 600,000 tons of fuel and supplies. Cesare Salmaggi and Alfredo Pallavisini, *2194 Days of War* (New York: Gallery Books,

1988), 4 June 1940; and I.C.R. Dear, ed., *The Oxford Companion to World War II* (Oxford: Oxford University Press, 1995), 312–13. See also John Parker, *Commandos: The Inside Story of Britain's Most Elite Fighting Force* (London: Headline Book Publishing, 2000), 15. See also A.J. Barker, *Dunkirk: The Great Escape* (London: J.M. Dent & Sons Ltd., 1977), 224.

4. Cecil Aspinall-Oglander, Roger Keyes. *Being the Biography of Admiral of the Fleet Lord Keyes of Zeebrugge and Dover* (London: Hogarth Press, 1951), 380.
5. *Ibid.*, 380.
6. Quoted in John Terraine, *The Life and Times of Lord Mountbatten* (London: Arrow Books, 1980), 83.
7. *Combined Operations: The Official Story of the Commandos* (New York: The Macmillan Company, 1943), v. He added "it can be won only when our armies have taken physical possession."
8. Winston S. Churchill, *The Second World War: Their Finest Hour* (Boston: Houghton Mifflin Company, 1949), 246–47. See also Colonel J.W. Hackett, "The Employment of Special Forces," *Royal United Service Institute* (hereafter cited as RUSI), Vol. 97, No. 585, February 1952, 28.
9. Colonel D.W. Clarke, "The Start of the Commandos," 30 October 1942, 1. Public Records Office (hereafter cited as PRO), DEFE 2/4, Records of the Ministry of Defence, Military Operations Records, Combined Operations Headquarters, War Diary Combined Operations Command, 1937–63.
10. *Ibid.* The word "commando" is Afrikaans meaning a "quasi-military party called out for military purposes against the natives." Hugh McManners, *Commando: Winning the Green Beret* (London: Network Books, 1994), 7. See also "Commandos," *Canadian Army Training Memorandum* (*CATM*), No. 20, November 1942, 20.
11. Patrick Cosgrove, *Churchill at War: Alone 1939–1940* (London: William Collins Sons & Co. Ltd., 1974), 95.
12. See Eliot A. Cohen, *Commandos and Politicians* (Cambridge: Center for International Affairs, Harvard University, 1978), 37–40; Maxwell Schoenfeld, *The War Ministry of Winston Churchill* (Ames: The Iowa State University Press, 1972), 124; and Cosgrove, 95.
13. Quoted in William Stevenson, *A Man Called Intrepid* (Guilford, Connecticut: The Lyons Press, 2000), 131.
14. David Jablonsky, *Churchill: The Making of a Grand Strategist* (Carlisle Barracks: Strategic Studies Institute, U.S. Army War College, 1990), 125.
15. *Ibid*, 92.
16. *Combined Operations*, 16; and Aspinall-Oglander, 381.
17. Clarke, "The Start of the Commandos," 2; and Saunders, *The Green Beret*, 22.
18. "Early History — Interview with Colonel Dudley Clark," 30 October 1942. PRO, DEFE 2/4, War Diary Combined Operations Command; Brigadier Peter Young, *Commando* (New York: Ballantine Books, 1969), 8; *Combined Operations*, 4; John Parker, *Commandos: The Inside Story of Britain's Most Elite Fighting Force* (London: Headline Book Publishing, 2000), 19–21; Brigadier John Durnford-Slater, *Commando* (Annapolis: Naval Institute Press, reprint 1991), 14; "Organization and Training of British Commandos ...," FSSF, 11 November 1942, 2; and Aspinall-Oglander, 381.

NOTES

19. Clarke, "The Start of the Commandos," 2.
20. Combined Operations, 5.
21. See Peter Wilkinson and Joan Bright Astley, *Gubbins & SOE* (London: Leo Cooper, 1997), 50–68; Parker, *Commandos*, 9–15; Young, *Commando*, 12; Saunders, *The Green Beret*, 22; and *Combined Operations*, 5.
22. Aspinall-Oglander, 381; Durnford-Slater, *Commando*, 14.
23. "Hand-out to Press Party Visiting The Commando Depot Achnacarry, 9–12 January 1943," 2. PRO, DEFE 2/5, War Diary Combined Operations Command; "Organization and Training of British Commandos," Intelligence Training Bulletin No. 3, Headquarters First Special Service Force (FSSF), 11 November 1942, 5. Department of National Defence, Directorate of History and Heritage (hereafter cited as DHH), File 145.3009 (D5), Organization and instructions for the 1st Canadian Special Service Battalion, July 1944 to December 1944; Young, *Commando*, 12; and Clarke, "The Start of the Commandos," 1–2.
24. "Hand-out to Press Party Visiting The Commando Depot Achnacarry, 9–12 January 1943," 2. PRO, DEFE 2/5, War Diary Combined Operations Command; Saunders, *The Green Beret*, 28; and Young, *Commando*, 12.
25. Durnford-Slater, *Commando*, 15, 20.
26. "Hand-out to Press Party Visiting The Commando Depot Achnacarry, 9–12 January 1943," 2. PRO, DEFE 2/5, War Diary Combined Operations Command.
27. Brigadier T.B.L. Churchill, "The Value of Commandos," *RUSI*, Vol. 65, No. 577, February 1950, 85.
28. Charles Messenger, *The Commandos 1940–1946* (London: William Kimber, 1985), 411.
29. *Combined Operations*, 7; Durnford-Slater, *Commando*, 15; Saunders, *The Green Beret*, 36–37.
30. Saunders, *The Green Beret*, 29.
31. "Role of the Special Service Brigade and Desirability of Reorganization," 2. PRO, DEFE 2/1051, Special Service Brigade, role, re-organization, 1943–44; "Organization and Training of British Commandos ...," FSSF, 11 November 1942, 7; and Durnford-Slater, *Commando*, 15.
32. "Role for the Special Service Brigade ...," 3, 10; "Hand-out to Press Party ...," 2; "Commandos," *CATM*, 29; Saunders, *The Green Beret*, 41; and Brigadier Julian Thompson, *Behind Enemy Lines* (London: Sidgwick and Jackson, 1998), 5
33. "Notes on Commando Training," 1 November 1942, paras 1–18; "Organization and Training of British Commandos ...," FSSF, 11 November 1942, 4; *Combined Operations*, 6–8; "Role for the Special Service Brigade and Desirability of Reorganization," 10–11; and Saunders, *The Green Beret*, 36–38, 41–42.
34. "Notes on Commando Training," 1 November 1942, paras 1–18; *Combined Operations*, 6–8; "Role for the Special Service Brigade ...," 10–11; and Saunders, *The Green Beret*, 36–38, 41–42.
35. Young, *Commando*, preface.
36. Julian Thompson, *War Behind Enemy Lines* (Washington, D.C.: Brassey's, 2001), 2.
37. Churchill, *Their Finest Hour*, 467. See also Saunders, *The Green Beret*, 29–30; and Aspinall-Oglander, 382.
38. "The Role of the Special Service Brigade ...," 13.

39. Quoted in Anthony Kemp, *The SAS At War 1941-1945* (London: Penguin Books, 1991), 12.
40. "Further Report on Discussion to Paratroop Training School, Ringway," 5 July 1941. PRO, AIR 29/520, No. 1 Parachute Training School Ringway, previously Parachute Training Squadron, July 1940 to December 1947.
41. "The Role of the Special Service Brigade ...," 13.
42. *Ibid.*, 14.
43. Churchill, *Their Finest Hour*, 165-66.
44. *Ibid.*, 466.
45. Churchill, *Their Finest Hour*, 467; Saunders, *The Green Beret*, 35; and Robert W. Black, *Rangers in World War II* (New York: Ivy Books, 1992), 8.
46. "Interview with Colonel Dudley Clarke."
47. Saunders, *The Green Beret*, 30.
48. Durnford-Slater, *Commando*, 32.
49. Quoted in *Ibid.*, 32-33; Parker, *Commandos*, 27; and Aspinall-Oglander, 383.
50. "Draft Directive to Director Combined Operations," 12 October 1940. PRO, DEFE 2/1, War Diary Independent Companies. See also Rear-Admiral J. Hughes-Hallett, "The Mounting of Raids," *RUSI*, Vol. 65, No. 580, November 1950, 581-82.
51. Letter, Roger Keyes to Anthony Eden, 7 October 1940. PRO, DEFE 2/1, War Diary Independent Companies.
52. *Combined Operations*, 26; Aspinall-Oglander, 383; and Young, *Commando*, 15.
53. Dear, 763; "Commandos," *CATM*, 31; and Thompson, 11.
54. John Terraine, The Right of the Line: The Royal Air Force in the European War 1939-1945 (London: Hodder and Stoughton, 1986), 559.
55. Terraine, The Life and Times of Lord Mountbatten, 85.
56. See "Amphibious Warfare Headquarters Small Scale Raids in Europe." PRO, DEFE 2/694. There were only four raids conducted in 1944.
57. Eric Morris, *Churchill's Private Armies* (London: Hutchinson, 1986), 163; Thompson, 340-42; Adrian Weale, Secret Warfare (London: Coronet Books, 1997), 63-64. and Buckley, 174-76.
58. See Saunders, *The Green Beret*, 50; and Parker, *Commandos*, 37.
59. Durnford-Slater, *Commando*, 54.
60. See Philip Warner, *The Special Forces of World War II* (London: Granada, 1985), 75; Durnford-Slater, *Commando*, 43-55; Saunders, *The Green Beret*, 48-50; Young, *Storm from the Sea*, 29-31; Buckley, 184-85; Weale, 65; and Parker, *Commandos*, 36-40.
61. Morris, Churchill's Private Armies, 200; Parker, Commandos, 42; and Young, Storm from the Sea, 32-35.
62. Parker, *Commandos*, 41-42.
63. *Combined Operations*, 65-70; Thompson, 293-95; A Wing Commander, "The Bruneval Raid," *Royal Air Force Journal*, Vol. 2, No. 5, May 1944, 159-60; "The Bruneval Raid," *War*, No. 32, 28 November 1942, 6-10; Weale, 65-67; and David Eshel, *Daring to Win* (London: Arms and Armour Press, 1992), 33-34.
64. *Combined Operations*, 71-100; Denis and Shelagh Whitaker, *Dieppe: Tragedy to Triumph* (Toronto: McGraw Hill Ryerson, 1992), 48; Parker, *Commandos*, 66-75; Saunders, *The Green*

NOTES

Beret, 82–101; Hughes-Hallett, "The Mounting of Raids," 583–84; Hackett, "The employment of Special Forces," 29; and Dear, 974. Although very successful, the cost was high. A total of 79 percent of the commandos and 52 percent of the naval force were either killed or captured.

65. 10th Panzer Division circular, "Sabotage and Commando Operations," 10 January 1943. PRO, DEFE 2/6, War Diary, Combined Operations Command.
66. Reproduced in Parker, *Commandos*, 2–3. See also Thompson, 127.

CHAPTER 2

1. Memorandum, Geoffrey Pyke, "Mastery of the Snows," reproduced in Lieutenant-Colonel Robert D. Burhans, *The First Special Service Force: A War History of the North Americans 1942–1944* (Nashville: The Battery Press, 1996), 3.
2. Not all would agree with Churchill's and Mountbatten's insight or penchant for the unorthodox. Historian Nigel Hamilton stated that Mountbatten, while serving as chief of combined operations, was a master of intrigue, jealousy, and ineptitude. Like a spoilt child he toyed with men's lives with an indifference to casualties that can only be explained by his insatiable, even psychopathic ambition ... a man whose mind was an abundance of brilliant and insane ideas often without coherence or consistent doctrine. Allied to the equally undisciplined, wildly imaginative Churchill — with whom Mountbatten would often stay for weekends — the two made a formidable and dangerous pair." Quoted in Will Fowler, *The Commandos at Dieppe: Rehearsal for D-Day* (London: Harper Collins, 2002), 27.
3. Geoffery Nathaniel Pyke was not so much a scientist as he was an individual with a vivid and uncontrollable imagination. When the war broke out in 1939, the War Office quickly recruited him to work in the Combined Operations planning cell.
4. Pyke, "Mastery of the Snows," reproduced in Burhans, 3.
5. Dr. Vannevar Bush, the lead scientist charged by the American President to run the Office of Scientific Research and Development, described Pyke as a "pseudoscientist." Bush stated, Pyke "was short on physics, especially short on engineering judgment, but he had lots of ideas, some of them superficially brilliant and intriguing." Vannevar Bush, "Churchill and the Scientists," *The Atlantic*, March 1965, 99.
6. See David Lampe, *Pyke the Unknown Genius* (London: Evans Brothers Ltd, 1959), 82–86; and Burhans, 3–4.
7. Lampe, 88–90.
8. Major J.W. Ostiguy, Army Historical Section Sketch, "The First Special Service Force," 14 March 1951, 1, DHH, File 145.3003 (D1); James Ladd, *Commando and Rangers of World War II* (New York: St. Martin's Press, 1978), 152; and Lampe, 90–91.
9. Burhans, 33.
10. *Ibid*, 33.
11. Pyke, "Mastery of the Snows," in Burhans, 3. See also "Notes of Interview with Colonel Williamson, 1 Cdn S.S. Bn, 1 Special Service Force," 1. DHH, File 145.3011 (D1), Organization; and Earl Maso, "Yanks Guard Targets They Were to Wreck," *Stars and Stripes*, 15 June 1947.

12. Pyke, "Mastery of the Snows," in Burhans, 3–4; C.P. Stacey, *Six Years of War: The Army in Canada, Britain and the Pacific* (Ottawa: Queen's Printer, 1955), 104–05; and Joseph A. Springer, *The Black Devil Brigade: The True Story of the First Special Service Force in World War II* (Pacifica, CA: Military History, 2001), xxviii–xxix.
13. Burhans, 27–28.
14. Pyke, "Mastery of the Snows," in Burhans, 3–4 and 29; Stacey, *Six Years of War*, 104–05; and Springer, xxviii–xxix.
15. Burhans 29–30. The intelligence assessments on the cost of operations against Rumania and Italy and the potential beneficial effect to the Allied war effort resulted in the decision to drop both from the Plough Project and focus exclusively on Norway.
16. Colonel Stanley W. Dziuban, United States Army in World War II. Special Studies: Military Relations Between the United States and Canada 1939-1945 (Washington, D.C.: DoD, 1959), 259–60. See also Lampe, 111.
17. Thomas Gallagher, *Assault in Norway* (Guilford, Connecticut: The Lyons Press, 2002 ed.), 3.
18. *Ibid.*, 3.
19. Heavy water or Deuterium oxide was vital to early experimentation since it has twice as many hydrogen atoms as ordinary water and is 10 percent heavier. The heavier weight acts as a slowing mechanism, "moderating the speed of the neutrons set free in an atomic reactor and permitting these elementary atomic particles to achieve a chain reaction that could split the nuclei of a fissionable element and cause an explosive release of atomic power." The focus on heavy water was somewhat overblown. Allied scientists later discovered that graphite would also moderate the speed and was in fact more effective. See Dan Kurzman, "Sabotaging Hitler's Bomb," *Military History Quarterly*, Vol. 9, No. 2, Winter 1997, 38; Gallagher, 8; and Nigel West, "SOE's Achievements: Operation Gunnerside Reconsidered," *Royal United Services Institute* (*RUSI*), Vol. 148, No. 2, April 2003, 77.
20. A cyclotron is an apparatus in which charged atomic and subatomic particles are accelerated by an alternating electric field while following an outward spiral or circular path in a magnetic field. Katherine Barber, ed., *The Canadian Oxford Dictionary* (New York: Oxford University Press, 1998).
21. Ian Dear, *Sabotage and Subversion: The SOE and OSS at War* (London: Cassell Military Paperbacks, 1999), 119; and William Stevenson, *A Man Called Intrepid* (Guildford, Connecticut: The Lyons Press, 2000), 113. Bohrs had already split the uranium atom with a release of energy a million times more powerful than the same quantity of high explosives." Stevenson, 55.
22. *Ibid.*, 55–62, 78, 416–41; Jonathan F. Keiler, "The Prospect of a Nazi atomic bomb is sobering but German scientists themselves doomed the project to failure," *Military Heritage WW II History*, July 2004, 28–31; and Kurzman, 38–47.
23. Author R.T. Ross states that Norsk-Hydro was Operation Plough's number one target. See Robert Todd Ross, *The Supercommandos: First Special Service Force, 1942-1944* (Atglen, PA: Schiffer Military History, 2000), 10 and 30. See also Ralph Wilson Becket (former commanding officer 1st and 3rd Regiments, FSSF), "The Stars and Jack" (personal narrative of his service with the FSSF), 1993, 21/305, DHH, BIOG B, File: Biographical file — Ralph Wilson

NOTES

Becket (hereafter cited as Becket manuscript); Peter Wilkinson and Joan Bright Astley, *Gubbins & SOE*, 106; and Burhans, 3.

24. Ross, 10; and Burhans, 4.
25. Burhans, 4.
26. Lampe, 111.
27. Robert Tyron Frederick was born in 1907. He joined the Californian National Guard at 14, by lying about his age. In August 1923, he entered Staunton Military Academy in Virginia. The following year he was accepted to West Point. He finished in the top half of his class academically, qualified as a rifle sharpshooter and pistol expert, served on a number of committees, and earned the appointment as a company commander. Upon graduation, he joined the Coast Artillery Corps. In the interwar years, he served in a number of command and staff appointments across the U.S. and in the Panama Canal Zone. In 1939, he was posted to the Projects Group, Operations Division, War Department General Staff in Washington, D.C., as the chief of Current Section, Logistics Groups, Operations Division. Department of Army, "Statement of Military Service of Robert Tyron Frederick 017 196," CAFM, Gord Sims fonds. See also Anne Hicks, *The Last Fighting General: The Biography of Robert Tryon Frederick* (Atglen, PA: Schiffer Military History Book, 2006).
28. Burhans, 8–9. See also Robert H. Adleman and Colonel George Walton, *The Devil's Brigade* (Philadelphia: Chilton Books, 1966), 16–18 and 27–29.
29. Lampe, 122–23.
30. Adleman and Walton, 30–32; Lampe, 122.
31. See Adleman and Walton, 32; and Ross, 12.
32. Letter, "Plough Project," General G.C. Marshall to Lieutenant-Colonel Robert T. Frederick, 16 June 1942, reproduced in Burhans, 11. See also Library and Archives Canada (hereafter cited as LAC), RG 24, File HQS 20-4-32, Mobilization and organization, (Vol. 1), Plough Project, (1 CSSBN), microfilm reel C-5436. The FSSF was activated on 5 July 1942. War Department, Secret letter AG 32c.2 (7-5-42) MR-M-GN, 5 July 1942. The Force was to be stationed at Fort William Henry Harrison, Helena, Montana. General Order No. 50, Major-General Joyce P.R. Davison, Headquarters 9th Corps Area, Fort Douglas, Utah, 9 July 1942.
33. Memorandum, Marshal to subordinate commanders, "Plough Project," 16 June 1942. LAC, RG 24, File HQS 20-4-32, Mobilization and organization, (Vol. 1), Plough Project, (1 SSBN), microfilm reel C-5436. See also Dziuban, 260; Burhans, 10–11; and Wood, 17.
34. Alan Muntz wings are detachable wings with detachable fairing to provide the flight characteristics needed to allow the machine to be towed as a glider.
35. Quoted in Burhans, 5–6. The Archimedean-screw propulsion system, championed by Pyke, was tested but proved to be inadequate, lacking the necessary power to propel the snow machine at an acceptable speed. Furthermore, it was unable to hold a grade, nor could it traverse non-snow terrain or free wheel down a hill.
36. Burhans, 7.
37. Interestingly, the only critic was Geoffrey Pyke who still pushed for a vehicle utilizing Archimedean-screw technology despite the contrary evidence. See Burhans, 8 and Lampe, 141–42.

38. Burhans, 8.
39. *Ibid.*, 17.
40. Lampe, 143–44; and Signals Report (Chief of Combined Operations), "Plough Scheme," 9 March 1943. PRO, DEFE 2/8, War Diary, Combined Operations Command.

CHAPTER 3

1. Don Mason, "'Air Commandos' Will Strike Hard at Axis." Newspaper clipping, unknown publication, 2nd Canadian Parachute Battalion War Diary. LAC, RG 24, Vol. 15301, August 1942.
2. Churchill felt that the Canadians would add value to the force and even suggested the force be named "The North American Force." See Adelman and Walton, 33.
3. Memorandum, PA to GOC First Canadian Army to senior officer Canadian Military Headquarters, 22 April 1942. LAC, RG 24, CMHQ, Vol. 12,305, File 3/Plough/1, Organization and operation of project plough; Memorandum, VCGS to DSD, 25 April 1942. LAC, RG 24, Series C-1, File HQS 20-1-32, "Formation FSSF Battalion," microfilm reel C-5481; Memorandum, DSD to D. Mech, HQS 5960, 27 April 1942, *Ibid.*; Memorandum, DSD to DMT, HQS 8960, 27 April 1942, *Ibid.*; Historical Section (GS) DND, "1st Canadian Special Service Battalion — Historical Report No. 5," DHH (hereafter cited as DHH, Historical Report No. 5), 22 February 1946; Major J.W. Ostiguy, "Historical Sketch of 1st Canadian Special Service Battalion," 14 March 1951. DHH, File 145.3003 (D1).
4. Letter, Parkin (NRC) to Chesley (DND), 30 April 1942. LAC, RG 24, Series C-1, File HQS 20-1-32, Vol. 2, "Formation FSSF Battalion," microfilm reel C-5481.
5. Message, Canmilitry [CMHQ] to Defensor [NDHQ], GS 1404, 23 April 1942. LAC, RG 24, CMHQ, Vol. 12,305, File 3/Plough/1 Organization and operations of proposed "Plough Project"; Note to file, HQS 8960, 2 May 1942; and Memorandum, DSD to D. Pers, 18 May 1942. Both LAC, RG 24, Series C-1, File HQS 20-1-32, "Formation FSSF Battalion," microfilm reel C-5481. See also Memorandum, CGS to VCGS, 13 June 1942. LAC, RG 24, Series C-1, File HQS 20-4-32, Mobilization and organization, (Vol. 1), Plough Project, (1 CSSBN), microfilm C-5436. The officers chosen were Captain T. Gilday (winter warfare specialist and later a regimental commanding officer of the FSSF) and Captain F.W. McEwen (technical officer).
6. See Letter, Crerar to Montgomery, 5 February 1942. LAC, RG 24, Vol. 10,765, File 2221C1(D126), "Raids — 2nd Canadian Division"; "Notes on Conference held on 6 March 1942." LAC, RG 24, Vol. 10750, File 220.C1.009 (D2), "Operations"; Memorandum, "Visit of LGen B.C.T. Paget GOC in C SE Comd," 6 September 1941. LAC, RG 24, Vol. 10,765, File 2221C1(D126), "Raids — 2nd Canadian Division"; Colonel C.P. Stacey, *The Canadian Army 1939-1945: An Official Historical Summary* (Ottawa: King's Printer, 1948), 44; and "The Message of Canada by the Rt. Hon. W.L. Mackenzie King, Prime Minister of Canada," *Hutchinsons Pictorial History of the War*, No. 1, Series 13, July-December 1941, 200.
7. Canada. Canada at War. A Summary of Canada's Part in the War, No. 17, August 1942, 11.

NOTES

8. "Memorandum of Conversation," S.D.1, 15 June 1942 and Memorandum, Murchie to the minister, 23 June 1942. LAC, RG 24, Series C-1, File HQS 20-4-32, Mobilization and organization, (Vol. 1), Plough Project, (1 CSSBN), microfilm reel C-5436.
9. Memorandum, CGS to VCGS, 13 June 1942. LAC, RG 24, Series C-1, File HQS 20-4-32, Mobilization and organization, (Vol. 1), Plough Project, (1 CSSBN), microfilm reel C-5436.
10. Naval Message, Admiralty 101, CCLO to CCO, 18 June 1942. LAC, RG 24, Series C-1, File HQS 20-4-32, Mobilization and organization, (Vol. 1), Plough Project, (1 CSSBN), microfilm reel C-5436; and Letter, Chesley (DND) to Mackenzie (NRC), 29 June 1942. LAC, RG 24, Series C-1, File HQS 20-4-32, Mobilization and organization, (Vol. 1), Plough Project, (1 CSSBN), microfilm reel C-5436. Pyke was eventually recalled to England and he retired.
11. DHH, Historical Report No. 5, 2. In reality, the decision was made days earlier. A Top Secret message stated, "Colonel Anderson representing Chief of Canadian General Staff has visited me and reported that under instruction from Ottawa he has today concluded an agreement with War Department for Canadian participation in PLOUGH project which will be under the direction and at the request of War Department." Naval Message, Admiralty 101, dated 18 June 1942. LAC, RG 24, Series C-1, File HQS 20-4-32, Mobilization and organization, Plough Project (1 SSBN), microfilm reel C-5436.
12. During the months of June and July 1942, the FSSF Table of Organization underwent several revisions. Memorandum from Lieutenant-Colonel W.A.B. Anderson, Staff Duties 1, (S.D.1) to the chief of the general staff, Lieutenant-General Kenneth Stuart, Ottawa, 20 June 1942. LAC, RG 24, Series C-1, File HQS 20-4-32, Mobilization and organization, (Vol. 1), Plough Project, (1 CSSBN), microfilm reel C-5436.
13. Memorandum, John Ralston, minister of national defence, 27 June 1942. LAC, RG 24, Series C-1, File HQS 20-4-32, Mobilization and organization, (Vol. 1), Plough Project, (1 CSSBN), microfilm reel C-5436; Memorandum, Murchie to MND, 10 July 1942. LAC, RG 24, Series C-1, File HQS 8974, Plough Project, microfilm reel C-5460; and Memorandum, CGS to MND, "Plough Project," 11 July 1942. LAC, RG 24, Series C-1, File HQS 20-4-32, Mobilization and organization, (Vol. 1), Plough Project, (1 CSSBN), microfilm reel C-5436.
14. Canada, *House of Common Debates* (hereafter cited as *Debates*), 10 May 1943, 2504; and Adrian Preston, "Canada and the Higher Direction of the Second World War 1939–1945," in *Canada's Defence: Perspectives on Policy in the Twentieth Century*, eds., B.D. Hunt and R.G. Haycock (Toronto: Copp Clark Pitman Ltd., 1993), 116.
15. *Debates*, 10 May 1943, 2504.
16. *Ibid.*, 2504.
17. See Pickersgill and Forster, The Mackenzie King Record, Vol. 1, 137–42; and Colonel Stanley W. Dziuban, *The U.S. Army in World War II. Special Studies: Military Relationships Between the United States and Canada 1939–1945* (Washington, D.C.: Department of the Army, 1959), 22–30. See also "Canada-U.S. Permanent Joint Board on Defence — Twenty-Fifth Anniversary," External Affairs, Vol. 17, No. 9, September 1965, 384–88; and H.L. Keenleyside, "The Canadian-U.S. Permanent Joint Board of Defence, 1940–1945," *Behind the Scenes*, Vol. 16, No. 1, Winter 1960–61, 51–75.

18. Letter from Lieutenant-Colonel C.M. Drury, military attaché, Canadian Legation, Washington to the Directorate of Military Operations and Intelligence, NDHQ, Washington, 7 July 1942. LAC, RG 24, Series C-1, File HQS 20-4-32, Mobilization and organization, (Vol. 1), Plough Project, (1 CSSBN), microfilm reel C-5436.
19. Memorandum, CGS to MND, "Plough Project," 11 July 1942. LAC, RG 24, Series C-1, File HQS 20-4-32, Mobilization and organization, (Vol. 1), Plough Project, (1 CSSBN), microfilm reel C-5436; "Minutes of a Meeting Held at NDHQ at 1730 hrs, 16 Jul 42, to discuss the organization of the 2nd Canadian Parachute Battalion," 27 July 1942. DHH, File 145.3009 (D5), Organization and administrative correspondence and instructions for the 1st Canadian Special Service Battalion, July 1942/December 1944; and DHH, Historical Report No. 5, 2.
20. Memorandum for file, "Canadian Parachute Battalion," 16 July 1942. LAC, RG 24, Series C-1, HQS 8846-1 (Vol. 4) Parachute Troops Organization and Training, microfilm reel C-5278; "Minutes of a Meeting Held at NDHQ at 1730 hrs, 16 Jul 42, to discuss the organization of the 2nd Canadian Parachute Battalion," 27 July 1942. Message, Canmilitry to Defensor, GSD 1430, 12 July 42. LAC, RG 24, CMHQ, Vol. 12305, File 3/Plough/1 Organization and operations of proposed "Plough Project"; DHH, File 145.3009 (D5), Organization and administrative correspondence and instructions for the 1st Canadian Special Service Battalion, July 1942/December 1944; and DHH, Historical Report No. 5, 2; and *Ibid*. The name was eventually redesignated in May 1943 to the 1st Canadian Special Service Battalion (see chapter 5). For the complete history of the 1st Canadian Parachute Battalion, see Bernd Horn and Michel Wyczynski, *Paras versus the Reich: Canada's Paratroopers at War, 1942-45* (Toronto: Dundurn Press, 2003).
21. Letter, Ralston to Howe, 10 July 1942. LAC, RG 24, Series C-1, File HQS 20-12-32, Ordnance Service — Plough Project, microfilm reel C-5460.
22. See Letter, Controller National Parks Bureau to Superintendent Banff National Park, 19 June 1942; Memorandum, VCGS to MND, 10 July 1942; "Extract," Colonel L.M. Chesley, DSD, 16 July 1942; Letter, ADM (Army) to DM Department of Munitions and Supply, 20 July 1942; Letter, ADM (Army) to ADM Department of Mines and Resources, 19 August 1942 — all LAC, RG 24, Series C-1, File HQS 20-12-32, Ordnance Service — Plough Project, microfilm reel C-5460.
23. LAC, RG 24, Series C-1, File HQS 20-12-32, Ordance Service — Plough Project, microfilm reel C-5460. See also Burhans, 37-38.
24. Transcript, "Talk Delivered Over Radio Station KFFA, Helena, Montana by Colonel Robert T. Frederick, U.S. Army, August 31 1942 As Guest of Montana Radio Forum (8:45 PM)" (hereafter, Frederick Radio Address). Hoover Institution Archives, Stanford University, Stanford, California (hereafter cited as HIA), Robert Tryon Frederick Papers, Box 5, File Speeches and writings, 1942-50.
25. *Ibid*.
26. Some of the Native tribe names considered were Pawnee; Iroquois and Blackfeet. R.T. Elson, "New Service Force may be called Braves," *The Herald*, 7 August 1942. War diary Appendix "A" entry, August 1942. LAC, RG 24, War Diaries, 2nd Canadian Parachute Battalion, Vol. 15,301. See also, Burhans, 16.

NOTES

27. R.T. Elson, "'Braves' May be Name of New Force Set-Up," *The Evening Citizen* (Ottawa), 7 August 1942. LAC, Newspaper section, microfilm reel N-17995, 3; and Burhans, 16.
28. See Burhans, 15–16.
29. The collar dogs (two crossed arrows) were the insignia formerly worn by the Indian scouts of the U.S. Army.
30. *Ibid.*, 16.
31. The Table of Organization of the FSSF changed frequently during the training period in the early months. See Monthly report of 2 Cdn Para Bn (AF) within the First Special Service Force. 1–31 August 1942. Item 1.Organization of the 1st Special Service Force. Report authored by Lieutenant-Colonel J.G. McQueen for the General Staff, NDHQ, Fort William Henry Harrison. LAC, RG 24, Series C-1, File HQS 20–16–32, (Vol. 1.) Monthly Reports, State of Project, 1 CSSBN, microfilm reel C-5468; and LAC, RG 24, Series C-1, File HQS 20–4–32, (Vol. 1) Mobilization and organization, Plough Project (1 SBN, microfilm reel C-5436).
32. See "Notes on interview with Col D.D. Williamson regarding historical sketch on force activities 1942/Dec1943," Italy: 1944. DHH, File 145.3011 (D1) 1 CSSBN, 2; Scott R. McMichael, *A Historical Perspective on Light Infantry* (Fort Leavenworth, Kansas: U.S. Army Command and General Staff College, 1987), 170–71; Ross, 14–16 & 48–49; Burhans, 15; DHH, Historical Report No. 5; Colonel Stanley W. Dziuban, *Military Relations Between the United States and Canada*, 262; and Stacey, *Six Years of War*, 105.
33. The organization of the FSSF did alter slightly over the course of its existence. For example, the section breakdown given reflects the organization that was actually used in fighting, rather than what was laid out in the original Plough Project framework (i.e., 12-man versus 9-man sections and the addition of a 2.36-inch anti-tank rocket launcher).
34. McMichael, 170–71; and Ross, 16.
35. General Order No. 50 regarding the activation of the 1st Special Service Force was issued by command of Major-General Joyce, Headquarters 9th Corps Area, Fort Douglas, Utah, 9 July 1942. www.execulink.comforKiska/FSSFHomepage.index.html, accessed 19 February 2009.
36. Press Release, Ottawa, 6 August 1942. LAC, RG 24, Series C-1, File HQS 20–4–32, Mobilization and organization (Vol. 1), Plough Project (1 CSSBN), microfilm reel C-5436.
37. A83 Bulletin, Washington, 6 August 1942. LAC, RG 24, Series C-1, File HQS 20–4–32, Mobilization and organization, (Vol. 1), Plough Project, (1 CSSBN), microfilm reel C-5436.
38. Telegram, Mawash Washington to Defensor Ottawa, MA 1461, 6 August 1942. LAC, RG 24, Series C-1, File HQS 20–4–32, Mobilization and organization, (Vol. 1), Plough Project, (1 CSSBN), microfilm reel C-5436.
39. For example see: "Create Unit of Canadian-U.S. Super-Fighters," *The Evening Citizen* (Ottawa), 6 August 1942, No. 41, 1, 12. LAC, Newspaper Section, microfilm reel N-17993; Ross Munro, "Albertan Second in Command of Allies' Super-Commandos," and "Calgarian is 2-i-c with Commandos," press clippings 6 August 1942. LAC, RG 24, Vol. 15301, 2 Cdn Para Bn War Diary, August 1942; "New Shock Troops to be Specialists on the Offensive," *Ottawa Journal*, 6 August 1942, Vol. 57, No. 201, 1, 12. LAC, Newspaper Section, microfilm reel N-29817; R.T. Elson, "Canadians Will Serve in Special U.S. Corps," *The Calgary Herald*, 6 August 1942, 10. LAC, Newspaper Section, microfilm reel C-252; "Army Forms 2 Air-Borne Divisions and

U.S. — Canadian Commandos," *The New York Times*, 7 August 1942, Vol. 91, No. 30,876, 1,18. LAC, Newspaper Section, microfilm N-2410; "2-Nation Commandos to be Fast, Furious Hard-Hitting Force," *The Evening Citizen*, Ottawa, 7 August 1942, No. 41, 13. LAC, Newspaper Section, microfilm reel N-17993; "Canada, U.S. Organize Hard-Hitting Joint Commando Unit," *The Globe and Mail*, 7 August 1942, Vol. 99, No. 28,906, 1. LAC, Newspaper Section, microfilm reel N-20035; and "First Special Service Force of U.S.A. Training in Helena," *The Helena Independent Daily*, 7 August 1942. Canadian Airborne Force Museum (hereafter cited as CAFM), Alastair Neely fonds, AB 2, 1 FSSF, Box 1, File No. 1, 1 July 1942–18 March 1943.

40. "Toronto Ski-Paratroopers," press clipping, August 1942. LAC, RG 24, Vol. 15301, 2 Cdn Para Bn War Diary, August 1942.
41. Memorandum, VCGS to minister, 3 August 1942. LAC, RG 24, Series C-1, File HQS 20–4-32, Mobilization and organization, (Vol. 1), Plough Project, (1 CSSBN), microfilm reel C-5436; P.C. 629, "At the Government House at Ottawa, Tuesday, the 26th day of January, 1943." DHH, File 145.3005 (D3) Instruction and direction for the 1st Canadian Special Service Battalion, January 1943/December 1944; PC 76/3711, Certified True Copy of a Minute of a Meeting of the Treasury Board, approved by His Excellency the Governor General in Council, on the 5th May, 1943; and Memorandum, MND to Governor General, 23 December 1943. LAC, RG 24, Series C-1, File HQS 8974, Vol. 2, Organization 4, microfilm reel C-5277.
42. Message, Defensor to Canmilitry, GSD 1350, 3 July 42. LAC, RG 24, CMHQ, Vol. 12305, File 3/Plough/1 Organization and operations of proposed "Plough Project"; and Canada, *Canada at War: A Summary of Canada's Part in the War*, No. 17, August 1942, 11.

CHAPTER 4

1. Ross Munro, "Albertan Second in Command Of Allies' Super-Commandos," Unidentified Canadian newspaper clipping, 6 August 1942. LAC, RG 24, Vol. 15301, August 1942.
2. "Lieutenant-Colonel W.A.B. Anderson spoke with Frederick on 25 June 1942 and confirmed that the MND had briefed the government regarding Canada's participation to the Plough Project. Anderson hopes to have an answer for Frederick within the next two days." Plough Project Diary, 25 June 1942, 55.
3. On the 26 June 1942, King told Ralston that he agreed that Canada share in this project by supplying an officer as second-in-command, training facilities for 500 other ranks, and the participation of the National Research Council in the project. Ralston, note to file, Ottawa, 27 June 1942. LAC, RG 24, File HQS 20–4-32, Mobilization and organization (Vol. 1), Plough Project (1 SSBN), microfilm reel C-5436.
4. Letter from Lieutenant-Colonel C.M. Drury, Assistant Military Attaché, Canadian Legation, Washington to the Directorate of Military Operations and Intelligence, National Defence Headquarters (hereafter cited as NDHQ), Washington, 7 July 1942. LAC, RG 24, Series C-1, File HQS 20–4-32, Mobilization, Organization, Plough Project (1 SSBN), microfilm C-5436.
5. The average age of the Forcemen between July 1942 and December 1943 was 26. This was considerably higher than that of other U.S. Army units. Lieutenant-Colonel Paul Adams, the

NOTES

Force's executive officer, later pointed out that this was a very important factor in the Force's cohesion and maturity. "The First Special Service Force," in Major Scott R. McMichael, *A Historical Perspective on Light Infantry* (Fort Leavenworth, KS: Combat Studies Institute, Research Survey No. 6, U.S. Army Command and General Staff College, 1987), 172.

6. Speech by Major-General Kenneth G. Wickham (U.S.A. Retired), First Special Service Force Association, 40th Annual Reunion, 14–16 August 1986, Colonial Motor Inn, Helena, Montana, Major-General Kenneth G. Wickham (U.S.A. Retired), 12.

7. Memorandum of a telephone conversation between Lieutenant-Colonel W.A.B. Anderson, Staff Duties, (S.D.1) and Lieutenant-Colonel Robert T. Frederick, Ottawa, 18 July 1942. LAC, RG 24, Series C-1, File HQS 20-4-32, Mobilization and organization, (Vol. 1), Plough Project, (1 CSSBN), microfilm reel C-5436.

8. Telegram from Lieutenant-Colonel C.M. Drury, Canadian Military Attaché, Washington to Lieutenant-Colonel W.A.B. Anderson, Defensor, Ottawa, 11 July 1942. The FSSF recruiting message was posted throughout U.S. Army camps in the Southwest and along the Pacific seaboard read, "Single men between ages 21 and 35 who had completed three years, or more grammar school within the occupational range of Lumberjacks, Forest Rangers, Hunters, Northwoodsmen, Game Wardens, Prospectors and Explorers." Burhans, 14. Several unit commanders saw Frederick's request for volunteers as an opportunity to empty their stockades. The detainees were presented with the option of volunteering for the Force, or continue serving their sentences. Many readily took up the offer. Messages were forwarded by certain commanders to the FSSF headquarters advising Frederick as to type of soldiers that they were sending to Fort William Henry Harrison. "All volunteers for your command have departed this date. Direct the officer in charge and armed guards to return to this station as soon as practicable." Another message read, "All personnel transferred to your command are en route except 42 men AWOL, 26 men sick not in line of duty and requiring further treatment, and 14 men in confinement awaiting final action on remission of sentences. These volunteers for your command will be transferred as soon as available." Adleman and Walton, 49. Conversely, Canadian recruiters screened out candidates who had bad disciplinary records. Many Canadian volunteers showed up to the interviews without their records. These were mailed out by their previous units and took time to arrive. This did not sit well with the interviewing officer. Vernon Doucette remembered, "The selection officer was a bit worried during the interview — For some reason, he was interested to see if I had a clear crime sheet." Sergeant Vernon J. Doucette (4th Coy, 3rd Regiment), interviewed by authors, 29 September 2003.

9. The message was often read out to troops on parade rather than posting the actual message.

10. Memorandum from Lieutenant-Colonel L.M. Chesley, to CGS, 10 July 1942. LAC, RG 24, Series C-1, File 20-4-32, Mobilization and organization, (Vol. 1), Plough Project, (1 CSSBN), microfilm reel C-5436.

11. Telegram G.S.D. 1430 CGS, to McNaughton, 12 July 1942. LAC, RG 24, Series C-1, File HQS 20-4-32, Mobilization and organization, (Vol. 1), Plough Project, (1 CSSBN), microfilm reel C-5436.

12. Memorandum from CGS to the AG, the quartermaster general (QMG) and the master general of the ordnance (MGO), Ottawa, 14 July 1942. Stuart's original proposal to organize,

raise, and equip the 1st Canadian Parachute Battalion was dated 10 July 1942. Mobilization of a Parachute Battalion, Ottawa, 10 July 1942. LAC, RG 24, Series C-1, File HQS 8846-1, Vol. 4, Parachute Troops, Organization and training, microfilm reel C-5277.

13. Memorandum from CGS to the AG, QMG and the MGO, Ottawa, 14 July 1942. LAC, RG 24, Series C-1, File HQS 8846-1, Vol. 4, Parachute Troops, Organization and training, microfilm reel C-5278.
14. Message from Canadian Military Attaché to Defensor, Washington, 16 July 1942. LAC, RG 24, Series C-1, File HQS 20-4-32, Mobilization and organization, (Vol. 1), Plough Project, (1 CSSBN), microfilm reel C-5436.
15. *Ibid.*, Note to file from Lieutenant-Colonel W.A.B. Anderson, General Staff, (GS), 14 July 1942.
16. *Ibid.*, Memorandum from CGS to the MND, 11 July 1942.
17. The physical standards listed in these documents were those that had been previously developed for the selection of 1 Cdn Para Bn personnel. As of 10 July 1942, the initial physical requirements for paratroops were:

    A. Alert, active, supple, with firm muscles and sound limbs: capable of development into aggressive individual fighter with great endurance.
    B. Age: officers — not over 32 years of age for captains and Lieutenants and not over 35 years for Majors; Other Ranks (ORs) 18–32 inclusive.
    C. Physically qualified as follows:

    1. Weight — maximum, not to exceed 185 pounds.
    2. Height — maximum, not to exceed 72 inches.
    3. Vision — Distant vision uncorrected must be 20/40 each eye.
    4. Feet — Greater than a non symptomatic 2nd degree pes planus to disqualify
    5. Genito-urinary system — recent venereal disease to disqualify.
    6. Nervous system — evidence of highly labile nervous system to disqualify.
    7. Bones, joints and muscles — Lack of normal mobility in every joint, poor or unequally developed musculature, poor coordination, asthemic habitus, or lack of at least average athletic ability to disqualify.
    8. Medical History — History of painful arches, recurrent knees or ankle injuries, recent fracture, old fractures with deformity, pain or limitation of motion, recurrent dislocation, recent severe illness, operation or chronic disease to disqualify.
    9. Other than listed above, the physical standards to be the same as Army Standard "A.1."

The Army definition of "A.1." category was: "The man shall be able to see to shoot or drive and can undergo severe strain without defects of locomotion and with only minor remediable disabilities. Age — between 22 and 32 years of age; Height — usual heights — minimum 5'2" max 6'; Weight — minimum 125 lbs, maximum 196 lbs; Visual Standards — 20/40 both

NOTES

eyes without glasses. Colour vision should be 'defective safe'; Hearing W.V. — 10ft. both ears, i.e. a man standing with his back to the examiner and using both ears, must be able to hear a forced whisper 10 feet away. Must have patent Eustachian Tubes; Dental — Men must not drop with false teeth, consequently there must be eight sound or reparable teeth (including two molars) in the upper jaw in good functional opposition to corresponding teeth in lower jaw; Injuries of limbs — it was agreed that men with old fractures of the lower limbs or spine, however well recovered, were not suitable. Flat-feet not acceptable. Must have full movements in all joints of lower limbs; Mental and intelligence standard: It was agreed that men with alert minds are required for these duties and that men with doubtful intelligence should be eliminated by an intelligence test." See: Letter, adjutant general to all district officers commanding, "Parachute Battalion, Serial No. 1351," 10 July 1942. DHH, File 171.009/D223; "Medical Standards for Paratroops," LAC, RG 24, Series C-1, File HQS 8846–1, Parachute Troops, Organization and training, microfilm C-5277, Vol. 15. "Appendix A — Physical Requirements for Officers; Appendix B — Physical Requirements for Other Ranks; Letter, Major-General H.F.G. Letson, Adjutant General to all district officers commanding; "Commandants of Petawawa Military Camp and RMC and G.O.C. in-C of Atlantic and Pacific Commands," LAC, RG 24, Series C-1, File HQS 8846–1, Vol. 4, Parachute Troops, Organization and training, microfilm reel C-5278. For additional information regarding the implementation of the selection criterion for Canadian parachute troops, see Chapter 3, "Canada's Hardy, Tanned Sons: Developing a Military Elite," in Lieutenant-Colonel Bernd Horn and Michel Wyczynski, *Paras Versus the Reich, 1942–1945* (Toronto: Dundurn Press, 2003), Chapter 3, 49–63.

18. Minutes of a meeting held At NDHQ at 1730 hours, 16 July 1942, to discuss the organization of the 2nd Canadian Parachute Battalion, Ottawa, 16 July 1942. DHH, File 112.3M3009 (D100), Training, 2 Cdn Para Bn, July 1942 to April 1943.

19. Memorandum of telephone conversation between Lieutenant-Colonel W.A.B. Anderson and Lieutenant-Colonel Frederick, Ottawa, 17 July 1942. LAC, RG 24, Series C-1, File HQS 20–4-32, Mobilization and organization, (Vol. 1), Plough Project, (1 CSSBN), microfilm reel C-5436.

20. Message from Major S.H. Muton, DAAG, Military District (MD) 10 to commandants of training centres, Winnipeg, 18 July 1942. DHH, File 168.009 (D43), Organization and administration of the 1 CSSBN, July 42 to May 1943.

21. Selection directive pertaining to 2nd Canadian Parachute Battalion from Colonel W. Line, director of personnel selection, to all army examiners, all assistant army examiners, and personnel selection staff, Ottawa, 16 July 1942. Directorate of Personnel Selection War Diary, 16 July 1942, Appendix 23. LAC, RG 24, Vol. 13302, July 1942. The Revised Examination "M" tests scores ranged from 0 to 211. The Canadian volunteers for the 2nd Canadian Parachute Battalion had to obtain a score in Group 3 over 140.

22. Selection directive pertaining to 2nd Canadian Parachute Battalion issued by Colonel W. Line, Director of Personnel Selection, to all army examiners, all assistant army examiners, and personnel selection staff, Ottawa, 16 July 1942. Directorate of Personnel Selection War Diary, 16 July 1942, Appendix 23. LAC, RG 24, Vol. 13302, July 1942.

23. Memorandum from Lieutenant-Colonel A.P. Sprange, Organization and planning (Org & P) to file, Ottawa, 26 July 1942. DHH, File 145.3009(D5), Organization and administration, correspondence and instructions for the 1 CSSBN, July 1942 to December 1944.
24. Telegram from CGS to McNaughton, 16 July 1942. LAC, RG 24, Series C-1, File HQS 20-5-32-2, Plough Command and Service Appointment, microfilm reel C-5439.
25. Message from Lieutenant-General K. Stuart, CGS to Lieutenant-General A.G.L. McNaughton, Ottawa, 3 July 1942. LAC, RG 24, CMHQ, Vol. 12305, File 3/Plough/1, Organization and operation of proposed "Plough Project."
26. Message from McNaughton to CGS, 27 July 1942. LAC, RG 24, Series C-1, File HQS 20-4-32, Mobilization and organization, (Vol. 1), Plough Project, (1 CSSBN), microfilm reel C-5436.
27. Telegram G.S. 331. Information on physical requirements being applied here for 1st Parachute Battalion, Ottawa, 5 August 1942. LAC, RG 24, Series C-1, File HQS 8846-1 (Vol. 11), Paratroops, Organization and training, microfilm reel C-5277.
28. "U.K. Men to Join Unit Here," *The Gazette* (Montreal), Vol. 171, No. 188, 7 August 1942, 10. LAC, Newspaper Section, microfilm reel N-32606.
29. "Returning to Canada to Join Paratroopers," *The Evening Citizen*, No. 41, 6 August 1942, 1. LAC, Newspaper Section, microfilm reel N-17993.
30. William Stewart, "Canadians as Parachutists in Britain Enjoy Thrills," 23 September 1942, unknown newspaper (clipping), 23 September 1942. 1st Canadian Parachute Battalion Association Archives.
31. Sergeant George Wright (1st Coy, 1st Regiment), interviewed by authors, 1 February 2001.
32. Peter Cottingham, *Once Upon A Wartime: A Canadian Who Survived the Devil's Brigade* (Brandon, Manitoba: Leech Printing, 1996), 30.
33. *Ibid.*
34. Note on parachute training from Brigadier M.H.S. Penhale, General Staff CMHQ to CMHQ Military Training (MT) (3), London, 27 August 1942. LAC, RG 24, CMHQ, Vol. 9830, File 2/Para Tps/1, document 40.
35. Sergeant George Wright (1st Coy, 1st Regiment), interviewed by authors, 1 February 2001.
36. Message CGS to McNaughton, 2 August 1942. LAC, RG 24, File HQS 20-4-32, Mobilization and organization, (Vol. 1), Plough Project, (1 CSSBN), microfilm reel C-5436.
37. Message from CGS to McNaughton, 5 August 1942. LAC, RG 24, CMHQ, Vol. 12305, File 3/Plough/, Organization and operations of proposed "Plough Project."
38. This group was the first group of Canadian soldiers to undergo British parachute training. LAC, RG 24, CMHQ, Vol. 9830, File 2/Para Tps/1, Report from Wing Commander M.A. Newnham, commander, Parachute Training School, R.A.F. Ringway to CMHQ, Military Training Branch, London, 15 September 1942. Of the 85 selected, 21 officers and 58 other ranks completed the course.
39. Letter from Major-General H.F.G. Letson to GOC-in-C Atlantic Command; GOC-in-C Pacific Command, all DO's C, commandant of Petawawa Camp and commandant RMC, Ottawa, 16 July 1942. LAC, RG 24, Series C-1, File HQS 8846-1, Vol. 3, Parachute Troops, Organization and training, microfilm reel C-5278.
40. Letter from CGS to the MND, 11 July 1942. LAC, RG 24, File HQS 20-4-32, Mobilization

NOTES

and organization, (Vol. 1), Plough Project, (1 CSSBN), microfilm reel C-5436. Minutes of a meeting held at NDHQ at 1730 hours, 16 July 1942, to discuss the organization of the 2nd Canadian Parachute Battalion. DHH, File 112.3M009 (D100), Training, 2 Cdn Para Bn, July 1942 to April 1943.

41. Message from Major S.H. Muton, DAAG, MD 10, to commandants of training centres, Winnipeg, 18 July 1942. DHH, File 168.009 (D43), Organization and administration of the 1 CSSBN, July 42 to May 1943.
42. *Ibid.*
43. J.D. Mitchell, "The War as I saw it from My Foxhole: My Days with the First Special Service Force," unpublished manuscript, 3–4.
44. Sergeant Lloyd D.M. Dunlop (6th Coy, 3rd Regiment), Communications Sergeant (2nd Battalion HQ), interviewed by authors, 1 October 2003.
45. Vernon Doucette (4th Coy, 3rd Regiment), interviewed by authors, 29 September 2003.
46. Donald Ballantyne (HQ detachment, 1st Battalion, 3rd Regiment), interviewed by authors, 12 September 2003.
47. Sergeant Lloyd D.M. Dunlop (6th Coy, 3rd Regiment), Communications Sergeant (2nd Battalion HQ), interviewed by authors, 1 October 2003.
48. Sergeant Eugene Forward (3rd Coy, 3rd Regiment), interviewed by authors, 9 October 2003.
49. Sergeant Sam Borditsky (HQ, 1st Regiment). Darryl Rehr, *Suicide Missions: The Black Devils*, The History Channel, A&E Television Network, Video Documentary, Digital Ranch, 2001.
50. 1 CSSBN War Diary, August 1942. Ross Munro, "Albertan Second in command of Allies' Super Commandoes," 6 August 1942. Unknown newspaper. LAC, RG 24, Vol. 15301.
51. Sam Barod (1st Regiment), interviewed by authors, 26 September 2003.
52. Sergeant Joe T. Jamieson (2nd Coy, 3rd Regiment), interviewed by authors, 1 October 2003.
53. Sergeant Eugene Forward (3rd Coy, 3rd Regiment), interviewed by authors, 1 October 2003.
54. Sergeant Vernon J. Doucette (4th Coy, 3rd Regiment), interviewed by authors, 29 September 2003.
55. Captain Ralph Wilson Becket, "The Stars and Jack," unpublished manuscript, 18–19. DHH, BIO-B fonds, Captain Ralph Wilson Becket.
56. *Ibid.* Message from Major S.H. Muton, DAAG, MD 10, to commandants of training centres, Winnipeg, 18 July 1942. DHH, File 168.009 (D43), Organization and administration of the 1 CSSBN, July 42 to May 1943.
57. Marion Webster, "This Photo will Hang," non-dated. Unknown newspaper. Authors' collection.
58. *Ibid.*
59. Selected American Forcemen were requested to fill out a form that listed "experience or knowledge of the following subjects: Surveying, mountain climbing, explosives, first aid, tractor driving, electrical machinery, electrical power transmission, water power installation, logging aircraft operation or maintenance, water supply systems, astronomy, meteorology, mining, navigation, radio operation, skiing, snow shoeing, winter expeditions, masonry constructions, steel constructions, telephone systems diesel engines, motor vehicle repair, railroad construction or operation, and highway or road building." Louis Conner Clelland's personnel file, 1943. CAFM, AB 2, FSSF, Vol. 1, File 13.

60. Sergeant Eugene Forward (3rd Coy, 3rd Regiment), interviewed by authors, 9 October 2003.
61. Private William "Sam" Magee (1st Regiment), interviewed by authors, 7 February 2002.
62. *Ibid.*
63. Sergeant Vernon J. Doucette (4th Coy, 3rd Regiment), interviewed by authors, 29 September 2003.
64. Sergeant William S.P. "Bill" Story (5th Coy, 2nd Regiment), interviewed by authors, 1 February 2000.
65. Donald Ballantyne (3rd Regiment), interviewed by authors, 26 September 2003.
66. Sergeant William Wiber (3rd Coy, 2nd Regiment). Rehr, *Suicide Missions*.
67. Sergeant Charlie Mann (4th Coy, 3rd Regiment), interviewed by authors, 15 October 2003.
68. Becket, 21.
69. Sergeant Joe Glass (1st Coy, 2nd Regiment). Greg Hancock and Wayne Abbott, *Daring to Die: The Story of the Black Devils*, Canada's History Television and National Geographic Channel, Video documentary, Northern Sky Entertainment, 2003.
70. J.D. Mitchell, 3–4.
71. Becket, 21.
72. McQueen was 29 years old. He studied and qualified at the Militia Staff College and the Canadian War Staff College. The future CO of 2nd Canadian Parachute Battalion was also an experienced company commander, staff captain at CMHQ, DAAG at 1st Canadian Division and 1st Canadian Corps, and second in command of The Calgary Highlanders (Overseas). Message from Lieutenant-General A.G.L. McNaughton to Lieutenant-General K. Stuart, CGS, London, 18 July 1942. LAC, RG 24, CMHQ, Vol. 12305, File 3/Plough/1, Organization and operation of proposed "Plough Project." Major-General J.C. Murchie to the minister of national defence, Ottawa, 19 July 1942. LAC, RG 24, Series, C-1, File HQS 20-5-32-2, Plough command and service appointment, microfilm reel C-5439.
73. Minutes of a meeting held at NDHQ at 1600 hours 28 July 1942 to discuss the organization and administration of the 2nd Canadian Parachute Battalion, Ottawa, 28 July 1942. LAC, RG 24, Series C-1, File HQS 20-1-11 (No. 3), Policy, composition and formation, unallotted battalions and unattached battalions, microfilm reel C-5472.
74. *Ibid.*
75. *Ibid.*
76. Sergeant Patrick Smith (4th Coy, 3rd Regiment), interviewed by authors, 7 October 2003.
77. Becket, 20–21.
78. Private Lorin Waling (1st Coy, 2nd Regiment), Hancock and Abbott, *Daring to Die*.
79. 1 CSSBN War Diary, 3, 5, 11, and 16 August 1942. LAC, RG 24, Vol. 15301, August 1942.
80. *Ibid.*, 24 August 1942.
81. 1 CSSBN War Diary, 1–31 August 1942. LAC, RG 24, Vol. 15301, August 1942.
82. *Ibid.*, 13 August 1942. McQueen's injury diagnosis: "1: Fracture, simple, complete, tibia right, distal end, posterior lip, fragment one centimetre in diameter, mild. 2: Fracture, simple, complete, comminuted fibula, right distal 1/3, mild. 3: Dislocation, ankle right, astragulus dislocated posterior, moderately severe." The injury was such that it required an extensive healing period. Interim Report, Training Casualties, Lieutenant-Colonel J.G. McQueen to

NOTES

General Staff, NDHQ, Fort William Henry Harrison, 15 August 1942, Appendix D. Report on Condition of Lieutenant-Colonel J.G. McQueen. LAC, RG 24, Series C-1, File HQS 20-16-32 (Vol. 1), Monthly Reports, State of Project, 1 CSSBN, microfilm reel C-5468.

83. Monthly report of the 2nd Canadian Parachute Battalion. Item 11. Recommendations. Report prepared by Lieutenant-Colonel D.D. Williamson to the secretary, NDHQ, Fort William Henry Harrison, 2nd Canadian Parachute Battalion (AF), 1 October 1942. DHH, File 145.3009 (D7), Monthly reports of 1 CSSBN.
84. *Ibid.*, Ottawa, 25 August 1942.
85. Canadian Army Routine Order 2423 — Volunteers For Special Units, Ottawa, 7 October 1942. LAC, RG 24, Vol. 1915, Canadian Army Routine Orders, Vol. 6.
86. The number of new candidates would eventually reach 150, 1 CSSBN War Diary, 30 August 1942, LAC, RG 24, Vol. 15301, August 1942.

CHAPTER 5

1. Monthly report on the organization and training of 2nd Canadian Parachute Battalion (AF) Within the 1st Special Service Force for the period 1 November 1944 to 9 January 1945. Item 5, Administration. Report authored by Lieutenant-Colonel J.F.R. Akehurst. DHH, File 145.3009 (D7), Monthly reports of 2 Cdn Para Bn/1 CSSBN, August 1942 to January 1945.
2. Previously, in 1916, the Canadian government and senior army commanders were dissatisfied with the administrative control structure regarding Canadian troops serving in the U.K. Furthermore, the fact that many Canadian formations and establishments were commanded by British officers did not help matters. To correct this situation the Canadian government appointed Sir George Perley as minister of Overseas Military Forces of Canada. Shortly after, in the fall of 1916, Perley named Major-General R.E. W. Turner, VC, to head the ministry's military staff. C.P. Stacey, *Arms, Men and Government: The War Policies of Canada* (Ottawa: Information Canada, 1974), 206–07.
3. As of 31 December 1939, CMHQ staff comprised of 23 officers, 28 other ranks, and 36 civilians. In 1940, staff increased to 124 officers, 518 other ranks, and 258 civilians, totalling 900. By the end of the war, CMHQ staff totalled 616 officers, 2712 other ranks, 745 civilians, totalling 4073. The paperwork processed by the staff soared from 165 pieces of incoming mail in 1940 to 1,500 units per day in 1944. See C.P. Stacey, *Six Years of War, The Army in Canada, Britain and the Pacific, Volume 1* (Ottawa: Queen's Printer and Controller of Stationery: 1957), 194–203; DHH, Canadian Military Headquarters Reports, 1940-48, C.P. Stacey, Report #5, *Canadian Military Headquarters*, 17 January 1941, 11 pages and C.P. Stacey, Report #6, *The Records Branch, CMHQ*, 20 January 1941, 5 pages.
4. Stacey, Arms, Men and Governments, 206–08.
5. The new appointments were C.G. Power as MND for Air; Angus L. Macdonald as MND for Naval Services; and Norman McLeod Rogers as MND for the Army. Stacey, *Six Years of War*, Vol. 1, 81.

6. The PJBD was a Canadian/American advisory board created following a meeting between President Franklin Roosevelt and Prime Minister Mackenzie King, in Ogdensburg, New York, 18 August 1940. Both heads of state discussed their mutual concerns regarding the defence of their countries. The membership comprised between four to five military members from each country. Colonel Stanley W. Dziuban, *United States Army in World War II, Special Studies, Military Relations Between The United and Canada, 1939–1945* (Washington, D.C.: Office of The Chief of Military History Department of Army, 1959), 31–34; and C.P. Stacey, *The Canadian-American Permanent Joint Board on Defence, 1940–1945*, Army Headquarter Report #7, 24 June 1945. DHH, Army Headquarter (AHQ) Reports.
7. Despite increasing military collaboration with the United States, the Canadian Military Mission continued to work closely with the British Military Mission in Washington.
8. Dziuban, 76. Also assisting the U.S. Joint Staff Planners was the Joint Intelligence Committee and the Army and Navy bureaus of public relations. Stacey, *Arms, Men and Governments*, 166.
9. Telegram from the Canadian minister in the United States to the secretary of state for external affairs, Canada, Washington, 3 July 1942. John Ralston fonds, LAC, MG 27, III, B 11, Military, 1939–1948, General, Subject files, Canadian Joint Staff, Secret file.
10. By the end of the month, following Combined Chiefs of Staff's meeting, on 30 July 1942, Pope drafted an extensive 16-point report detailing the Canadian Joint Staff's mandate and work with both the U.S. chiefs of staff and the British Joint Staff Mission. Maurice Pope fonds, LAC, MG 27, III, F4, Vol. 1, File Diary, 1942, page 60; Maurice A. Pope, *Soldiers and Politicians: The Memoirs of Lt.-General Maurice A. Pope* (Toronto: University of Toronto Press, 1962), 197.
11. Frederick also found it necessary to expedite and improve the exchange of Plough Project information between Washington and Ottawa. To improve this process, he requested that Lieutenant-Colonel Drury of the Canadian Legation in Washington and Lieutenant-Colonel W.A.B. Anderson in Ottawa select a lieutenant-colonel to act as an executive and operations officer for the Force. Plough Project Diary, 1942, 18 June 1942 entry, 36. HIA, Robert Tryon Frederick Papers, Box #1.
12. Telegram from Colonel L.N. Chesley, Director of Staff Duties to General Staff to the general officer–in–command, Pacific Command, Victoria, B.C., Ottawa, 27 June 1942. LAC, RG 24, Series C-1, File HQS 20-5-32-2, Plough command and service appointment, microfilm reel C-5439.
13. Telegram from McNaughton to Stuart, 18 July 1942. LAC, RG 24, CMHQ, Vol. 12,305, File 3/Plough/1 Organization and operation of proposal "Plough Project."
14. Memorandum from the adjutant general to the director adjutant general (B) and director of personnel, 24 July 1942. LAC, RG 24, Series C-1, File HQS 8846-1, Parachute Troops, Organization and training, microfilm reel C-5277; Letter from Lieutenant-Colonel D.D. Williamson to the director of staff duties, 15 July 1942, LAC, RG 24, Series C-1, File HQS 20-4-32, Mobilization or organization, (Vol. 1), Plough Project, (1 SSBN), microfilm reel C-5436.
15. It was the U.S. Army Personnel Branch of General Staff who suggested this proposed course of action. They argued that if Canadian personnel took this oath it would, in their view, greatly simplify the administrative process. Canadian and American personnel would be on

NOTES

equal footing regarding pay, records, and discipline. Furthermore, this would permit "mixture" of Canadian and U.S. personnel within small units. Telegram (MA 1234) from the Canadian Military Attaché to Director of Staff Duties, Washington, 12 July 1942. LAC, RG 24, Series C-1, File HQS 20-4-32 (Vol. 1), Mobilization and organization, Plough Project (1 SSBN), microfilm reel C-5436.

16. Plough Project Diary, 1942, 14 July 1942 entry, 101. HIA, Robert Tryon Frederick Papers, Box #1.
17. Kenneth G. Wickham, *An Adjutant General Remembers: Major General Kenneth Wickham; a Military Memoir* (Adjutant General's Corps Regimental Association, 1991), 10.
18. Memorandum from headquarters of the 1st Special Service Force to the director of staff duties, general staff, 15 July 1942. DHH, File 145.3009 (D5), Organization and administration, correspondence and instructions for 1 CSSBN, July 1942-December 1944.
19. Whereas this agreement required the approval of the Canadian government, the Americans forwarded it to General Moses and Colonel Nelson of General McNarney's office. They saw no problems with the document. Plough Project Diary, 1942, 16 July 1942 entry, 106. HIA, Robert Tryon Frederick Papers, Box #1.
20. Memorandum from headquarters of the 1st Special Service for the director of staff duties, general staff, 15 July 1942. DND DHH, File 145.3009 (D5), Organization and administration, correspondence and instructions for 1 CSSBN, July 1942 to December 1944.
21. Letter from Major D.D. Williamson to the Director of Staff Duties, 15 July 1942. LAC, RG 24, Series C-1, File HQS 20-4-32, Mobilization and organization (Vol. 1), Plough Project, 1 CSSBN, microfilm reel C-5436.
22. Letter from Major-General H.F.G. Letson to all district officers commanding, commandant of Petawawa Military Camp, commandant RMC and GOC-in-C, Atlantic and Pacific Commands, 16 July 1942. LAC, RG 24, Series C-1, File HQS 8846-1 Vol. 4, Parachute Troops, Organization and training, microfilm reel C-5278.
23. Minutes of a meeting held at NDHQ at 1730 hours, 16 July 1942, to discuss the organization of the 2nd Canadian Parachute Battalion, Ottawa, 16 July 1942. DHH, File 112,3M009 (D100), Training, 2nd Canadian Parachute Battalion, July 1942 to April 1943.
24. Minutes of a meeting held at NDHQ at 1730 hours, 16 July 1942, to discuss the organization of the 2nd Canadian Parachute Battalion, Ottawa, 16 July 1942. DHH, File 112.3M009 (D100), Training, 2nd Canadian Parachute Battalion, July 1942 to April 1943.
25. Minutes of a meeting held at NDHQ at 1600 hours 28 July 1942, to discuss the organization and administration of the 2nd Canadian Parachute Battalion, Ottawa, 28 July 1942. LAC, RG 24, Series C-1, File HQS 20-1011 (Vol. 3), Policy composition of formation, unallotted battalions and unattached, microfilm reel C-5472
26. Minutes of a meeting held at NDHQ at 1600 hours 28 July 1942, to discuss the organization and administration of the 2nd Canadian Parachute Battalion, Ottawa, 28 July 1942. LAC, RG 24, Series C-1, File HQS 20-1011 (Vol. 3), Policy composition of formation, unallotted battalions and unattached, microfilm reel C-5472.
27. Note to file from Lieutenant-Colonel W.A.B. Anderson regarding a meeting between Colonel Frederick, the chief of the general staff, the vice-chief of the general staff, the deputy chief

of the general staff (A) and Lieutenant-Colonel W.A.B. Anderson, (S.D. 1), 22 July 1942, Ottawa. LAC, RG 24, Series C-1, File HQS 20-4-32 (Vol. 1), Mobilization and organization, Plough Project (1 CSSBN), microfilm reel C-5436.

28. Memorandum from the CGS to MND, 3 August 1942. LAC, RG 24, Series C-1, File HQS 20-4-32, Mobilization and organization, Plough Project (1 CSSBN), microfilm reel C-5436.
29. *Ibid.*; and Instructions from the CGS to McQueen, 4 August 1942. LAC, RG 24, Series C-1, File HQS 20-4-32, Mobilization and organization, Plough Project (1 CSSBN), microfilm reel C-5436.
30. *Ibid.*
31. Preliminary instructions drafted by the CGS to McQueen, 4 August 1942. LAC, RG 24, Series C-1, File HQS 20-4-32, Mobilization and organization, Plough Project (1 CSSBN), microfilm reel C-5436. The OC of 2nd Canadian Parachute Battalion was instructed to keep a separate war diary relating to Canadian aspects of the Force. Minutes of a meeting held at NDHQ at 1730 hours, 16 July 1942, to discuss the organization of the 2nd Canadian Parachute Battalion, Ottawa, 16 July 1942. DHH, File 112,3M009 (D100), Training, 2nd Canadian Parachute Battalion, July 1942 to April 1943.
32. Letter from Anderson for the CGS to the adjutant general, the quartermaster general, and the master general of the ordnance, Ottawa, 5 August 1942. LAC, RG 24, Series C-1, File HQS 20-4-32, Mobilization and organization, Plough Project (1 CSSBN), microfilm reel C-5436.
33. As of 5 August 1942, Canadian personnel within the FSSF could hold the following positions and ranks: one colonel; four lieutenant-colonels; six majors, and 36 subalterns; total 47 officers, and 650 sergeants. Memorandum from Lieutenant-General Kenneth Stuart, CGS, signed off by Major-General J.C. Murchie to the adjutant general, 5 August 1942. LAC, RG 24, Series C-1, File HQS 20-1-11 (FD 15), Policy composition of formation unallotted battalions and unattached units, microfilm reel C-5481.
34. Memorandum from CGS, signed off by Major-General J.C. Murchie to the adjutant general, 5 August 1942. LAC, RG 24, Series C-1, File HQS 20-1-32-1,(Vol. 2), Policy, formation of FSSF, microfilm reel C-5481.
35. *Ibid.*
36. Lieutenant-Colonel J.G. McQueen, officer commanding, Monthly report on organization and training of 2 Cdn Para Bn (AF), within the 1st Special Service Force, August 1942. LAC, RG 24, Series C-1, File HQS 201-6-32 (Vol. 1), Monthly Reports, State of Project, 1 CSSBN, microfilm reel C-5468.
37. Frederick Radio Address.
38. Monthly report of 2 Cdn Para Bn/1 CSSBN (AF) within the 1st Special Service Force, Item 1, Allotment of Canadian Personnel, August 1942. LAC, RG 24, Series C-1, File HQS 201-6-32 (Vol. 1), Monthly Reports, State of Project, 1 CSSBN, microfilm reel C-5468.
39. Memorandum from Directorate of Organization to Directorate of Organization and Planning, Ottawa, 10 August 1942; Memorandum of the director personnel services to the Directorate of Organization and Planning, Ottawa, 27 August 1942. LAC, RG 24, Series C-1, File HQS 20-1-11 (Vol. 15), Policy composition of formation unallotted battalions and unattached units, microfilm reel C-5472.

NOTES

40. Memorandum from CGS to the adjutant general, 5 August 1942. LAC, RG 24, Series C-1, File HQS 20–1–32–1 (Vol. 2), Policy, Formation of FSSF, microfilm reel C-5481.
41. Memorandum from the Directorate of Organization and Planning to the Directorate of Organization and Administration, 10 August 1942. LAC, RG 24, Series C-1, File HQS 20–1–11 (No. 15), Policy composition of formation, unallotted battalions and unattached units, microfilm reel C-5472.
42. Directives issued by Major-General H.F.G. Letson to general officers commanding-in-chief and general officers commanding, 28 August 1942. DHH, File 112.3M3009 (D100), Training of the 2 Cdn Para Bn, July 1942-April 1943.
43. Letter from Frederick to Anderson, 17 August 1942. LAC, RG 24, Series C-1, File HQS 20–16–32 (Vol. 1), Monthly Reports, State of Project, 1 CSSBN, microfilm reel C-5468.
44. Note to file, [telephone conversations with McQueen and Frederick], Anderson, 17 August 1942. LAC, RG 24, Series C-1, HQS 20–1–11, Policy composition of formation, unallotted battalions and unattached units, microfilm reel C-5472.
45. Letter from Frederick to Anderson, 17 August 1942. LAC, RG 24, Series C-1, File HQS 20–16–32 (Vol. 1), Monthly Reports, State of Project, 1 CSSBN, microfilm reel C-5468.
46. Memorandum from Anderson to VCGS, 17 August 1942. LAC, RG 24, Series C-1, File HQS 20–1–11, Policy, composition of formation, unallotted battalions and unattached units.
47. Letter from VCGS to McQueen, 21 August 1942. DHH, File 145.3009 (D5), Organization and administrative correspondence, July 1942 to December 1944.
48. Major D.D. Williamson, Dufferin and Haldimand Rifles of Canada, was first commissioned in May 1929, and had been on active service since July 1940 during which time he served as a company commander and acted as 2IC of his regiment. He qualified for the rank of major at the company commanders' school at Royal Military College (RMC), October-November 1940. Letter from Lieutenant-Colonel J.G. McQueen to the secretary, NDHQ, 27 August 1942. DHH, File 145.3009 (D5), Organization and administrative correspondence and instructions for the 1 CSSBN, July 1942-December 1944.
49. Letter McQueen to the secretary, NDHQ, 27 August 1942. DHH, File 145.3009 (D5), Organization and administrative correspondence and instructions for the 1 CSSBN, July 1942-December 1944.
50. Instructions drafted by the CGS for McQueen, 9 September 1942. LAC, RG 24, Series C-1, File HQS 20–132, Policy, composition of formation of the 1 CSSBN, microfilm reel C-5481. Lieutenant-Colonel D.D. Williamson, Personnel file, LAC.
51. Memorandum from Anderson, Directorate of Staff Duties to Directorate of Personnel, 4 September 1942. LAC, RG 24, Series C-1, HQS File 20–5–32–2, Plough command and service appointment, microfilm reel C-5439.
52. Instructions drafted by the CGS for McQueen, 9 September 1942. LAC, RG 24, Series C-1, File HQS 20–1-32, Policy, composition of formation of the 1 CSSBN, microfilm reel C-5481.
53. Letter from the CGS to MND, 31 August 1942. LAC, RG 24, Series C-1, File HQS 20–5–32–2, Plough command and service appointment, microfilm reel C-5439.
54. Letter from the CGS to Pope, 9 September 1942. LAC, RG 24, Series C-1, File HQS 20–1–32 (Vol. 2), Policy, formation of the 1 CSSBN, microfilm reel C-5481.

55. Instructions issued by the CGS to Williamson, 9 September 1942. LAC, RG 24, Series C-1, File HQS 20-1-32 (Vol. 2), Policy, formation of the 1 CSSBN, microfilm reel C-5481.
56. Monthly report of 2 Cdn Para Bn/1 CSSBN (AF) within the 1st Special Service Force, 1–31 August 1942. Item 7: Pay. Letter from Frederick to Anderson, 17 August 1942. LAC, RG 24, Series C-1, File HQS 20–16–32 (Vol. 1), Monthly Reports, State of Project, 1 CSSBN, microfilm reel C-5468.
57. Monthly report of 2 Cdn Para Bn (AF) within the 1st Special Service Force, 1–31 August 1942. Item 7: Pay. LAC, RG 24, Series C-1, File HQS 20–16–32 (Vol. 1), Monthly Reports, State of Project, 1 CSSBN, microfilm reel C-5468.
58. Sergeant Charlie Mann (4th Coy, 3rd Regiment), interviewed by authors, 15 October 2003.
59. Monthly report of 2 Cdn Para Bn/1 CSSBN (AF) incorporated within the 1st Special Service Force, 1–31 September 1942. Item 13: Morale, 1 October 1942. DHH File 1453009 (D7). Monthly reports of 1 CSSBN.
60. Letter from Brigadier-General A.R. Mortimore, paymaster general (PMG) to Anderson, 29 August 1942. LAC, RG 24, Series C-1, File HQS 20-4-32 (Vol. 1), Mobilization and organization, Plough Project, (1 CSSBN), microfilm reel C-5436.
61. Letter Mortimore, P.M.G. to the adjutant general, 25 September 1942; Briefing note from DND Deputy-Minister Lieutenant-Colonel G.S. Currie to the minister, 26 September 1942. LAC, RG 24, Series C-1, File HQS 8846-1, Parachute troops, organization and training, microfilm reel C-5277.
62. Note to file from Anderson, reporting conversations with Lieutenant-Colonel Goforth, office of the PMG, and Lieutenant-Colonel McQueen, 26 August 1942. Letter from Anderson to the PMG, 27 August 1942. LAC, RG 24, Series C-1, File HQS 20-4-32 (Vol. 1), Mobilization and organization, Plough Project, (1 CSSBN), microfilm reel C-5436.
63. Letter Mortimore, PMG, to Anderson, 29 August 1942. LAC, RG 24, Series C-1, File HQS 20-4-32 (Vol. 1), Mobilization and organization, Plough Project, (1 CSSBN), microfilm reel C-5436.
64. Letter from the CGS to the MND, 8 September 1942. LAC, RG 24, Series C-1, File HQS 20-4-32 (Vol. 1), Mobilization and organization. Plough Project (1 CSSBN), microfilm reel C-5436.
65. Declaration to be signed by all officers and other ranks (in triplicate) posted to the 2nd Canadian Parachute Battalion, 27 August 1942. LAC, RG 24, Series C-1, File HQS 20-1-11 (FD 22), Policy composition of formation, unallotted battalions and unattached units, microfilm reel C-5472. War diary entry, 30 September 1942, 2 Cdn Para Bn/1 CSSBN War Diary, September 1942. LAC, RG 24, Vol. 15301.
66. War diary entry of 30 September 1942. 2 Cdn Para Bn/1 CSSBN War Diary, September 1942. LAC, RG 24, Vol. 15301. Monthly report of 2 Cdn Para Bn/1 CSSBN (AF) within the 1st Special Service Force, September 1942. Item 13, Moral. LAC, RG 24, Series C-1, File HQS 20-16-32 (Vol. 1), Monthly Reports, State of Project, 1 CSSBN, microfilm reel C-5468.
67. Monthly report of 2 Cdn Para Bn/1 CSSBN (AF) within the 1st Special Service Force, 1–30 September 1942. Item 13, Morale. LAC, RG 24, Series C-1, File HQS 20-16-32 (Vol. 1), Monthly Reports, State of Project 1 CSSBN, microfilm reel C-5468.

NOTES

68. War dairy entry, 30 September 1942. 2 Cdn Para Bn 1/1 CSSBN War Dairy, September 1942. LAC, RG 24, Vol. 15301.
69. Monthly report of 2nd Canadian Parachute Battalion 1 CSSBN (AF) within the 1st Special Service Force, 1–30 September 1942. Item 13, Morale. LAC, RG 24, Series C-1, File HQS 20-16-32 (Vol. 1), Monthly Reports, State of Project 1 CSSBN, microfilm reel C-5468.
70. Letter from CGS to the MND, 9 October 1942. DHH, File 112.352009 (D30), Paratroops.

CHAPTER 6

1. Donald Ballantyne, HQ detachment, 1st Battalion, 3rd Regiment, *The First Special Service Force — Canada's Unique Military Experiment* (Port Hope, ON: Unpublished manuscript, September 2003), 11.
2. Plough Project Diary, 3 July 1942 entry, 76. HIA, Robert Frederick Papers, Box 1. The fort was originally built in 1894 to accommodate a two battalion, or one regiment infantry post. A railway line and a road were built to connect the fort to the town of Helena. The base comprised a very large parade ground, a guardhouse, non-commission officers' quarters, officers' quarters, a bakery, quartermaster and commissary storehouses, administration and fuel buildings, stables, wagon sheds, shop buildings, and streetcar waiting room. "Fort Harrison," *The Helena Independent*, 11 November 1894.
3. Plough Project Diary, 4 July 1942 entry, 77. HIA, Robert Tryon Frederick Papers, Box 1.
4. Plough Project Diary, 7 July 1942 entry, 84. HIA, Robert Tryon Frederick Papers, Box 1.
5. Sergeant William "Bill" Story (5th Coy, 2nd Regiment), interviewed by authors, 7 February 2002.
6. Sergeant Charles Mann (4th Coy, 3rd Regiment), interviewed by authors, 15 October 2003; Rehr, *Suicide Missions*.
7. Mitchell, 6.
8. Ed Thomas, Auburn to Berlin: A World War II Memoir, 1936–1946: An Account of Preparation for Active Duty in World War II (Private Manuscript, 2005), 27–28.
9. Hicks, 72.
10. Springer, 18. Interview with Sergeant William "Bill" Story, 5th Coy, 2nd Regiment.
11. Sergeant William "Bill" Story (5th Coy, 2nd Regiment), interviewed by authors, 7 February 2002.
12. Sergeant Vernon J. Doucette (4th Coy, 3rd Regiment), interviewed by authors, 29 September 2003.
13. Plough Project Diary, 4 July 1942 entry, 79. HIA, Robert Tryon Frederick Papers, Box 1.
14. Sergeant William "Bill" Story (5th Coy, 2nd Regiment), interviewed by authors, 7 February 2002.
15. Becket, 22.
16. Springer, 20. Interview 1st Lieutenant Edwards Thomas, executive officer, 2nd Battalion, 2nd Regiment.
17. *Ibid.*, 17. Interview Second-Lieutenant Mark Radcliffe, commander 3rd Coy, 1st Battalion, 3rd Regiment.
18. *Ibid.*, 17. Interview Private Russell Wieneke, Parachute Platoon, Service Battalion.

19. Private William "Sam" Magee (1st Coy, 3rd Regiment; 6th Coy, 3rd Regiment), interviewed by authors, 7 February 2002.
20. *Ibid.*
21. *Ibid.*
22. Sergeant Peter Smith (4th Coy, 3rd Regiment), interviewed by authors. 7 October 2003.
23. Adleman and Walton, 63.
24. Sergeant Peter Smith (4th Coy, 3rd Regiment), interviewed by authors, 7 October 2003.
25. Sergeant Peter Kroll (4th Coy, 3rd Regiment), interviewed by authors, 10 October 2003.
26. Springer, 18. Interview Sergeant William 'Bill' Story, 5th Coy, 2nd Regiment.
27. Peppard, 41.
28. Private Eugene Forward (3rd Coy, 3rd Regiment), interviewed by authors, 9 October 2003.
29. Springer, 17. Interview Private John Dawson, 6th Coy, 2nd Battalion, 2nd Regiment.
30. Adleman and Walton, 65.
31. Private Eugene Forward (3rd Coy, 3rd Regiment), interviewed by authors, 9 October 2003.
32. Sergeant Charles Mann (4th Coy, 3rd Regiment), interviewed by authors, 15 October 2003.
33. Sergeant Joe Jamieson (6th Coy, 3rd Regiment), interviewed by authors, 1 October 2003.
34. Frederick Radio Address.
35. Burhans, 21.
36. Monthly report of 2 Cdn Para Bn/1 CSSBN. Item 5. Morale and Discipline. 2 Cdn Para Bn (AF), 31 August 1942. DHH, File 145.3009 (D7), Monthly report of 1 CSSBN.
37. Monthly report of 2 Cdn Para Bn/1 CSSBN (AF) with the 1st Special Service Force, Item 12. Discipline. 2 Cdn Para Bn (AF), 1 October 1942. DHH, File 145.3009 (D7), Monthly report of 1 CSSBN.
38. Monthly report of 2 Cdn Para Bn/1 CSSBN (AF). Item 6. Officers. 2 Cdn Para Bn (AF), 1 October 1942. DHH, File 145.3009 (D7), Monthly report of 1 CSSBN.
39. Adleman and Walton, 77.
40. William "Bill" Story, "The Early Days of The Force," www.thedropzone.org/training/story.html, 9, accessed 25 May 2011.
41. Lieutenant-Colonel J.B. Shinberger, FSSF Training Officer, *Drill Regulations*, Fort William Henry-Harrison, Helena, Montana, non-dated 10 pages. Gordon Sims fonds, CAFM.
42. Private Eugene Forward (3rd Coy, 3rd Regiment), interviewed by authors, 9 October 2003.
43. Story, "The Early Days of The Force," 9.
44. *Ibid.*
45. Letter from Gordon Sims to authors, Columbia, South Carolina, 16 September 2004. Story, *The Early Days of the Force*, 9.
46. Adleman and Walton, 77.
47. Sergeant Charles Mann (4th Coy, 3rd Regiment), interviewed by authors, 15 October 2003.
48. War diary entry, 22 October 1942. 2 Cdn Para Bn/1 CSSBN War Dairy, October 1942. LAC, RG 24, Vol. 15, 301.
49. Monthly report of 2 Cdn Para Bn. Item 14. Relationships. 2 Cdn Para Bn (AF), September 1942. LAC, RG 24, Series C-1, File HQS 20-16-32, Vol. 1, Monthly reports of 1 CSSBN, microfilm reel C-5468.

NOTES

50. Letter from Gordon Sims to authors, Columbia, South Carolina, 16 September 2004.
51. *Ibid.*
52. Colonel James Baldwin who served as the Force's S-4 officer wrote, "I doubt very much that you will find anything in regulations — Canadian or United States — that specified the insignia to be worn on the dress–up occasions." There were many things we did that were covered in headquarters (Force) that never got into official printing." Letter to Richard Ugino from Colonel (Retired), United States Army, Orval James Baldwin, Powell, Ohio, 17 September 1978. Canadian War Museum, George Metcalf Archival Collection, James Orval Baldwin, call number 58C 314.8
53. Minutes of a meeting held at NDHQ at 1600 hours, 28 July 1942, to discuss the organization of the 2 Cdn Par Bn, Item 16. LAC, RG 24, Series C-1, File HQS 20-1-11 (No. 3) Policy Composition of Formation unallotted Battalion and unattached, microfilm reel C-5472
54. Frederick Radio Address.
55. Plough Project Diary, 1942, 30 June 1942 entry, 66. HIA, Robert Tryon Frederick Papers, Box 1.
56. Letter from Major O.J. Baldwin, S-4, FSSF to Commanding General, Services of Supply, Washington, D.C., 3 September 1942.
57. *Ibid.*
58. *Ibid.*
59. Memorandum of Lieutenant-General Somervell, HQ Services of Supply, Military Personnel Division to Requirement Division Development Branch. Subject: Insignia for 1st Special Service Forces, 12 September 1942. Copy of document provided to authors by Gordon Sims.
60. Lieutenant-General Somervell, HQ Services of Supply, Military Personnel Division to Requirement Division Development Branch. 1st Endorsement, SPRMD 421.7 (9–3-42), 12 September 1942. Memorandum from Colonel W.A. Wood Jr., General Staff Corps, Director, Requirements Division, to Quartermaster General, Heraldic Section, 14 September 1942. Copy of document provided to authors by Gordon Sims.
61. Burhans, 15–16; and Adleman and Walton, 16.
62. Frederick Radio Address.
63. John R. Dawson and Don Kutemeire, First Special Service Force, 1942–1944, (Part 1), Military Illustrated Past and Present, June/July 1986, 7.
64. Bulletin from War Under-Secretary Robert Patterson regarding the creation of a new American-Canadian force of super-specialists in offensive warfare, Washington, 6 August 1942. LAC, RG 24, Series C-1, File HQS 20-4-32, Mobilization and organization of unallotted battalions and unattached units, microfilm reel C-5246.
65. R.T. Elson, Canadians will serve in Special U.S. Corps, *The Herald*, 6 August 1942. War Diary Appendix "A" entry, August 1942. LAC, RG 24, War Diaries, 2nd Canadian Parachute Battalion, Vol. 15, 301.
66. Russ Munro, Albertan Second in Command of Allies Super-Commando, *The Calgary Herald*, 6 August 1942, 1, 2. CAFM, AB 2, FSSF, Vol. 1, File 29.
67. R.T. Elson, Braves may be name of new Force set-Up, *The Evening Citizen*, 7 August 1942, 3. LAC, Newspaper Section, *The Evening Citizen*, No. 41, 7 August 1942, microfilm reel N-17993.

68. "Paratrooper training gave Red Snider real thrills," *The Evening Citizen*, 10 September 1942, No. 71, 1, 14. LAC, Newspaper Section, microfilm reel N-17994.
69. Hicks, 73–74.
70. Following photographic analysis, these ovals were only worn for a short time. Dawson and Kutemeire, *First Special Service Force, 1942–1944, (Part 1)*.
71. Becket, 73.
72. Report Dress Canadian Personnel 1st Special Service Force from Lieutenant-Colonel J.G. McQueen to Director of Staff Duties, Fort William Henry Harrison, Helena, Montana, non-dated. DHH, File 145.3009 (D5), Organization and administration, correspondence, July 1942 to December 1944.
73. Monthly report of the 2 Cdn Para Bn, 1–31 December 1942. LAC, RG 24, Series C-1, File HQS 20-16-32 (Vol. 1). Monthly Reports, State of Projects, 1 CSSBN, microfilm reel C-5468.
74. Letter from Frederick to Anderson, 17 August 1942. LAC, RG 24, Series C-1, File HQS 20-16-32, Vol. 1, Monthly Reports, State of Project, 1 CSSBN, microfilm reel C-5468.
75. War diary entry, 28 August 1942. 2 Cdn Para Bn/1 CSSBN, 28 August 1942. LAC, RG 24, War Diaries, 2 Cdn Para Bn/1 CSSBN, Vol. 15,301.
76. Letter from McQueen to Director of Staff Duties. DHH, File 145.3009 (D 5), Organization and administration correspondence, July 1942/December 1944.
77. Memorandum from Colonel H.A. Campbell, Directorate of Ordnance Service (A) to Anderson, Ottawa, 17 September 1942. LAC, RG 24, Series C-1, File HQS 20-1-11 (FD 22), Policy Composition of Formation Unallotted Battalion and unattached, microfilm reel C-5472.
78. Letter Williamson to McQueen, 5 December 1942. DHH, File 145.3009 (D5). Organization and administrative correspondence and instructions for the 1 CSSBN, July 1942 to December 1944.
79. Message from the Master-General of the Ordnance to McQueen, 14 September 1942. LAC, RG 24, Series C-1, File HQS 20-1-32 (Vol. 1), Policy, composition of formation of FSSF BN, microfilm reel C-5481.
80. Memorandum from the MND to CGS, 14 April 1943. LAC, RG 24, Series C-1, File HQS 20-1-32 (Vol. 1), Policy composition of formation of the FSSF battalion, microfilm reel C-5481.
81. Memorandum from the CGS to MND, 20 April 1943. LAC, RG 24, Series C-1, File HQS 20-1-32 (Vol. 2). Policy and composition, formation of the FSSF, microfilm reel C-5481.
82. Memorandum from CGS to MND regarding the Plough Project, 20 April 1943. Item 4. Uniforms and Badges. DHH File 112,21009 (D200) Correspondence DCGS (A+B with AG, January to September 1943.
83. Memorandum from CGS to MND, 28 May 1943. LAC, RG 24, Series C-1, File HQS 20-1-32, (Vol. 2), Policy and Composition and Formation of FSSF, microfilm reel C-5481.
84. *Ibid.*
85. *Ibid.*
86. Memorandum from CGS to MND, 28 May 1943. LAC, NA, RG 24, File HQS 20-1-32, (Vol. 2), Policy and Composition and Formation of FSSF, microfilm reel C-5481.

NOTES

87. Telegram from Colonel Frederick to Brigadier Weeks, 8 April 1943. Memorandum for Directorate of Staff Duties to the Pay-Master General, 3 May 1943. LAC, RG 24, Series C-1, File HQS 20-1-32, (Vol. 2) .Policy and composition and formation of FSSF, microfilm reel C-5481.
88. War diary entry, 8 April 1943. 2 Cdn Para Bn/1 CSSBN War Diary, April 1943. LAC, RG 24, War Diaries, Vol. 15, 301.
89. Story, "The Early Days of The Force," 7.
90. Speech given by Colonel Frederick to all FSSF officers, 22 October 1942, Fort William Henry Harrison (hereafter cited as Fredericks 22 October Speech). H IA. Robert Tryon Frederick Papers, Box 5, File Speeches and writing, 1942–1950. War diary entry, 22 October 1942. 2 Cdn Para Bn/1 CSSBN, October 1942. LAC, RG 24, War Diaries, 2 Cdn Para Bn/1 CSSBN, Vol. 15,301.
91. Staff Sergeant Gordon Sims (Force HQ), interviewed by authors, 14 September 2003.
92. Sergeant Vernon J. Doucette (4th Coy, 3rd Regiment), interviewed by authors, 29 September 2003.
93. Burhans, 48.
94. Peppard, 29.
95. *Ibid.*, 30, 32.
96. Sergeant Bill Story (5th Coy, 2nd Regiment.) interviewed by authors, 1 February 2002.

CHAPTER 7

1. Private Jack Callowhill (2nd Coy, 1st Regiment), interviewed by authors, 11 September 2003.
2. Monthly reports of 2 Cdn. Para Bn — August, September, November and December 1942. 2 Cdn. Parachute Bn (AF), 31 August 1942. DHH, File 145.3009 (D7), Monthly report of 1 CSSBN. Burhans, *The First Special Service Force*, 23.
3. *Ibid.*
4. Monthly report of 2 Cdn Para Bn Item 2. Training, Training General. 2 Cdn Para Bn (AF), 31 August 1942. DHH, File 145.3009 (D7), Monthly report of 1 CSSBN.
5. Personnel of the FSSF Base Echelon, Service Battalion totalled 25 officers and 521 enlisted men. FSSF Table of Organization, War Department, Washington 5 July 1942. LAC, RG 24 Series C-1, File HQS 20-4-32 (Vol. 1). Mobilization or organization, Plough Project (1 CSSBN), microfilm reel C-5436.
6. Sergeant Peter Smith (4th Coy, 3rd Regiment), interviewed by authors, 7 October 2003. Monthly report Of 2 Cdn Para Bn. 2 Cdn Para Bn (AF), 31 August 1942. DHH, File 145.3009 (D7), Monthly report of the 1 CSSBN.
7. Adleman and Walton, 77.
8. Monthly report of the 2 Cdn Para Bn. 2nd Cdn Parachute Bn. (AF), 1 October 1942. Item 6. Physical Training. DHH, File 145.3009 (D7). Monthly reports of 1 CSSBN.
9. Monthly report of the 2 Cdn Para Bn. 2 Cdn Para Bn. (AF), 1 October 1942. Item 6. Physical Training. DHH, File 145.3009 (D7). Monthly reports of 1 CSSBN.

10. Sergeant Joe T. Jamieson (6th Coy, 3rd Regiment), interviewed by authors, 1 October 2003.
11. Sergeant George Wright (1st Coy, 1st Regiment), interviewed by authors, 16 October 2003.
12. Sergeant Lloyd D.M. Dunlop (6th Coy, 3rd Regiment) interviewed by authors, 1 October 2003.
13. Sergeant Joe T. Jamieson (6th Coy, 3rd Regiment), interviewed by authors, 1 October 2003.
14. Sergeant Paul Schoeler (6th Coy, 3rd Regiment), interviewed by authors, 17 October 2003.
15. Despite Williamson's directives pertaining to discipline some Canadian personnel had been apprehended during the month of September, for car theft, breaking and entering, false registrations at hotels, and other infractions. The CO reported, however, that, "the local police have been most cooperative and friendly in their dealings with Canadian personnel, and have by their tact avoided what in a few cases could have been serious civilian charges ..." Monthly report Of the 2 Cdn Para Bn. 2 Cdn Para Bn (AF), 1 October 1942. Item 12. Discipline. DHH, File 145.3009 (D7). Monthly reports of 1 CSSBN.
16. Letter from Gordon Sims to authors, 16 September 2004.
17. Private Eugene Forward (3rd Coy, 3rd Regiment), interviewed by authors, 9 October 2003.
18. Sergeant Allen Lennox (4th Coy, 3rd Regiment), interviewed by authors, 2003.
19. Donald Ballantyne (HQ detachment, 1st Battalion, 3rd Regiment), interviewed by authors, 12 September 2003.
20. To expedite this training phase Troop Carrier Command loaned to the FSSF, six C-47s aircraft. Following this period, the FSSF was authorized to retain one aircraft to parachute qualify personnel who had been previously hospitalized, or later joined the unit as replacements. Burhans, 19.
21. Plough Project Diary, 18 July 1942, 111,112. HIA, Robert Tryon Frederick Papers, Box 1.
22. LAC, RG 24, Series C-1, File HQS 8846-1, Vol. 4. Parachute Troops, Organization and training, microfilm reel C-5278; and Interim report, training, casualties, 15 August 1942. LAC, RG 24, Series C-1, HQS 20-16-32 (Vol. 1), Monthly reports, State of Project, 1 CSSBN, microfilm reel C-5468.
23. Interim Report. Appendix B. Proportion of confirmed Casualties to Midnight 15 August., Canadian Troops. 2 Cdn Para Bn (AF), 15 August 1942. LAC, RG 24, Series C-1, File HQS 20-16-32, Vol. 1, Monthly Reports, State of Project, 1 CSSBN, microfilm reel C-5468.
24. In his first report, McQueen informed NDHQ that the minimum number of days to train U.S. candidates prior to jumping was two and the maximum six which averaged out to four days. The minimum number of days to train Canadian candidates prior to jumping was seven and the maximum nine which averaged out to eight days. Interim Report. Appendix B. Proportion of confirmed casualties to midnight 15 August 1942. 2 Cdn Para Bn (AF), 15 August 1942. LAC, RG 24, Series C-1, File HQS 20-16-32, Vol. 1. Monthly Reports, State of Project, 1 CSSBN, microfilm reel C-5468.
25. Private Eugene Forward (3rd Coy, 3rd Regiment), interviewed by authors. 9 October 2003.
26. Interim Report. 2 Cdn Para Bn (AF), 15 August 1942. LAC, RG 24, Series C-1, File HQS 20-16-32, Vol. 1. Monthly Reports, State of Project, 1 CSSBN, microfilm reel C-5468.
27. Gordon H. Baker, *First Special Service Force, August 1942-December 1944* (Dawson Creek, BC: Private Printing, 1998), 5.

NOTES

28. Sergeant Charlie Mann (4th Coy, 3rd Regiment), interviewed by authors, 15 October 2003.
29. Interim Report. Appendix A. Parachute Training. 2 Cdn Para Bn (AF), 15 August 1942. LAC, RG 24, Series C-1, File HQS 20–16–32, Vol. 1. Monthly Reports, State of Project, 1 CSSBN, microfilm reel C-5468.
30. Monthly report Of 2 Cdn Para Bn. Item 2. Training. 2 Cdn Para Bn (AF), 31 August 1942. DHH, File 145.3009 (D7), Monthly report of 1 CSSBN.
31. Adleman and Walton, 76–77.
32. As quoted in Hicks, 72.
33. Alan Blackwell, *70 Years Next to Paradise* (Bums Lake, BC: Power Line Productions of Burns Lake, 1999), 39.
34. Herb Peppard, *The Light Hearted Solider: A Canadian's exploit with the Black Devils* (Halifax, NS: Nimbus Publishing Ltd., 1994), 33, 35.
35. Sergeant Peter Smith (4th Coy, 3rd Regiment), interviewed by authors. 7 October 2003.
36. Interim Report. 2 Cdn Para Bn (AF), 15 August 1942, Appendix A, Parachute Training. LAC, RG 24, Series C-1, File HQS 20–16–32, Vol. 1. Monthly Reports, State of Project, 1 CSSBN, microfilm reel C-5468.
37. Sergeant Charlie Mann (4th Coy, 3rd Regiment), interviewed by authors, 15 October 2003.
38. Mitchell, 7.
39. Monthly report Of 2 Cdn Para Bn. Item 2: Training. 2 Cdn Para Bn (AF), 31 August 1942. DHH, File 145.3009 (D7), Monthly report of 1 CSSBN.
40. Sergeant Vernon J. Doucette (4th Coy, 3rd Regiment), interviewed by authors, 29 September 2003.
41. Hancock and Abbott, *Daring to Die*.
42. Monthly report of 2 Cdn Para Bn. Item 7. Casualties during Parachute Training. 2nd Cdn Para Bn (AF), 31 August 1942. DHH, File 145.3009 (D7), Monthly report of 1 CSSBN.
43. Sam Borod, (HQ detachment, 1st Regiment), interviewed by authors, 26 September 2003.
44. Quoted in Springer, 21.
45. Statistics showed American and Canadian injury rates were comparable: U.S. Troops: Officers, 12.5%; Enlisted Men 6.3%; Average 8.9%. Canadian Troops: Officers, 9%; ORs 3.5%; Average 4.3%. Policy of Special Service Force. Disposal of Unsuitable Personnel. Directive drafted by Lieutenant-Colonel J.G. McQueen, Fort William Henry Harrison, 15 August 1942. DHH, File 145.3009 (D5). Organization and administrative correspondence and instructions for 1 CSSBN, July 1942 to December 1944; and Briefing memorandum from Lieutenant-Colonel W.A.B. Anderson to MND, 26 August 1942. LAC, RG 24, Series C-1, File HQS 20–16–32, Vol. 1. Monthly Reports, States of Project, 1 CSSBN, microfilm reel C-5468.
46. Interim report prepared by McQueen for the General Staff, NDHQ, 15 August 1942. LAC, RG 24, File HQS 20–16–32, Vol. 1, Monthly Reports, State of Project, 1 CSSBN, microfilm reel C-5468.
47. Letter from Frederick to Anderson, 17 August 1942. LAC, RG 24 Series C-1, File HQS 20–16–32, Vol. 1, Monthly Reports, State of Project, 1 CSSBN, microfilm reel C-5468.
48. 31 August 1942 entry. 1 CSSBN War Diary, August 1942. LAC, RG 24, Vol. 15301.
49. 1 CSSBN War Diary, 31 August 1942. LAC, RG 24, Series C-1, Vol. 15301, August 1942.

50. *Ibid.*
51. As quoted in Hicks, 74.
52. Sergeant R.E. Blake (3rd Coy, 3rd Regiment), interviewed by authors, 7 October 2003.
53. Sergeant Lloyd D.M. Dunlop (6th Coy, 3rd Regiment), interviewed by authors, 1 October 2003.
54. Burhans, 21.
55. Sergeant Charlie Mann (4th Coy, 3rd Regiment), interviewed by authors, 15 October 2003.
56. Sergeant Jim Summersides (4th Coy, 3rd Regiment), interviewed by authors, 21 October 2003.
57. Sergeant Joe T. Jamieson (6th Coy, 3rd Regiment), interviewed by authors, 1 October 2003.
58. Sergeant Lloyd Dunlop (6th Coy, 3rd Regiment), interviewed by authors, 1 October 2003.
59. Private Eugene Forward (3rd Coy, 3rd Regiment), interviewed by authors, 9 October 2003.
60. Unknown author, *First Special Service Force, 9/42–12/44* (Unpublished manuscript), CAFM, FSSF Memories Collection.
61. Sergeant George Wright (1st Coy, 1st Regiment), interviewed by authors, 16 October 2003.
62. Sergeant Gordon Sims (Force Headquarters), interviewed by authors, 14 September 2003.
63. Private Morris Lazarus (5th Coy, 2nd Regiment), interviewed by authors, 3 October 2003.
64. Unknown author, First Special Service Force.
65. 2 Cdn Para Bn/1 CSSBN War diary, 11, 12, and 14 October 1942. LAC, RG 24, Vol. 15301.
66. Monthly report of the 2nd Canadian Parachute Battalion. 2 Cdn Para Bn, (AF), September 1942. Item 3, Small arms. DHH, File 145.3009 (D7). Monthly reports of 1 CSSBN.
67. Mitchell, 10.
68. Sergeant Joe Dauphinais, 1st Coy, 1st Battalion, 2nd Regiment. As quoted in Springer, 32.
69. The German weapons that were provided to the Forces as training aids were: MP 40 (Schmeisser) maschinen-pistole; MP 18 (Bergmann) 9-mm machine-pistol; MG 34, 7.92-mm multipurpose machine gun; Mauser rifle; as well as Panzerbüchse antitank rifles. Monthly report of the 2nd Canadian Parachute Battalion. 2 Cdn Para Bn. (AF), 1 September 1942. Item 3. Small arms. DHH, File 145.3009 (D7). Monthly reports of 2 Cdn Para Bn/1 CSSBN.
70. Private Eugene Forward (3rd Coy. 3rd Regiment), interviewed by authors, 9 October 2003.
71. O'Neill was born in Newmarket, County Cork, Ireland in 1905. In 1919, he took a job as a cabin boy on a tramp streamer headed for Asia. In 1925, O'Neil joined the Shanghai municipal police where he started as a policeman and eventually rose to the rank of sub-inspector. It was during that time that O'Neill studied judo, ju-jitsu, Chinese boxing, and foot fighting. In 1938, he left the Shanghai police force and moved to Tokyo where he became the security chief at the British embassy. During his stay in Japan, he obtained his 4th degree in judo. This distinction made him one of the highest non-Japanese judokas in the world. In 1941, as the Japanese forces invaded various parts of the Pacific, O'Neill fled to the Philippines and quickly relocated to Australia. Shortly after, he left for the United States and took a job as an instructor with the Office of Strategic Services. After a few months, he explored other opportunities. Eventually, he was hired on as a civilian instructor with the FSSF. At the end of the unarmed combat training course, O'Neil chose to remain with the Force and served as an intelligence officer and Frederick's bodyguard. Steven C. Brown, "Dermot M. O'Neill. One of

NOTES

the 20th Century's Most Overlooked Combative Pioneers," in *Journal of Asian Martial Arts*, Vol. 12, No 3, 2003, 19–33.

72. Plough Project Diary, 17 July 1942 entry, 108. HIA, Robert Tryon Frederick Papers, Box 1.
73. *Ibid.*
74. As quoted in Brown, 24.
75. Monthly report of the 2nd Canadian Parachute Battalion. 2 Cdn Para Bn (AF), 31 August 1942, Item 2, Training — Unarmed Combat. DHH, File 145.3009 (D7). Monthly reports of 1 CSSBN.
76. As quoted in Hicks, 75.
77. Burhans, 33.
78. Telephone interview conducted by Richard Ugino with Joe O'Brien, 3rd Coy, 2nd Regiment. Canadian War Museum, George Metcalf Archival Collection, James Orval Baldwin, Call number 58C 314.8
79. Mitchell, 9.
80. As quoted in Brown, 24.
81. Adleman and Walton, 70–71, 78–79.
82. Wright, 36–37.
83. On 23 June 1942, Fredrick asked Lieutenant-Colonel E.A.M. Wedderburn, a British commando officer, posted to the Plough Project if it was possible to obtain British demolition training manuals. Wedderburn stated that for security reasons his superiors preferred not to circulate such material. Instead, they offered the services of a qualified demolition expert. Frederick accepted this offer. HIA, Plough Project diary, 23, 27, 29 June, 17 July, 47, 48, 49, 60, 64, 110. Box #1, Robert Tryon Frederick Papers; and Burhans, 32.
84. Monthly report of the 2nd Canadian Parachute Battalion. 2 Cdn Para Bn, (AF), 5 November 1942. October 1942 training activities). Item 2: Training, D — Demolition. DHH, File 145.3009 (D7), Monthly reports of 1 CSSBN.
85. 2 Cdn Para Bn/1 CSSBN War Diary, October 1942. LAC, RG 24, Vol. 15301.
86. Monthly report of the 2nd Canadian Parachute Battalion. 2 Cdn Para Bn, (AF), 5 November 1942. Item 2: Training, D — Demolition. DHH, File 145.3009 (D7), Monthly reports of 1 CSSBN.
87. As quoted in Springer, 30–31.
88. Sergeant Peter Smith (4th Coy, 3rd Regiment), interviewed by authors, 7 October 2003.
89. Becket, 38.
90. Mitchell, 12.
91. Private Eugene Forward (3rd Coy, 3rd Regiment), interviewed by authors, 9 October 2003.
92. Sergeant Joe Dauphinais (1st Coy, 1st Battalion, 2nd Regiment). As quoted in Springer, 30.

CHAPTER 8

1. Speech delivered by Colonel Robert Frederick to the FSSF officers, Fort William Henry Harrison, 24 October 1942 (hereafter cited as Frederick 24 October Speech). HIA, Robert Tryon Frederick Papers, Box 5, Speeches and writings, 1942–1950.

2. When Churchill read the minutes of the 24 November 1942 Chiefs of Staff Committee meeting that revealed that the First Special Service Force "as now organized might be diverted to some task other than for which it was originally designated" he angrily sent a minutes to Mountbatten. "CCO," he wrote, "Not good enough. Draft for me to return to the charge." Minute by Churchill to CCO, on "Chiefs of Staff Committee: 326th (42) Meeting, 24 November 1942." PRO, DEFE 2/4, War Diary Combined Operations Command. On 25 November 1942, prime minister informed Field Marshal Sir John Dill that "I visualise Special Service Force [FSSF — 'plough scheme'] playing vital role in the ultimate re-conquest of Norway, and wish you, therefore, to press most strongly for their retention in this role." Draft telegram to Field Marshal Dill, "Chiefs of Staff Committee: 188th (42) Meeting (0) cdt, 25 November 1942." PRO DEFE 2/4, War Diary Combined Operations Command, Annex II.
3. Quoted in Burhans, 35. See also: Memorandum, McQueen to CGS, 8 October 1942. LAC, RG 24, Series C-1, HQS 20-4-32, Mobilization and organization (1st Special Service Battalion), microfilm reel C-5436; Message, Canmilitary to Defensor (Stuart to Murchie), GSD 2088, 8 October 1942. LAC, RG 24, Series C-2, CMHQ, Vol. 12,305, File 3/Plough/, Organization and operation of proposed Plough Project.
4. The SOE was a British secret service organization created in 1940 responsible for promoting subversive warfare in the occupied territories. See Wilkinson and Astley, *Gubbins & SOE:* and Dear, *Sabotage and Subversion.*
5. Memorandum, McQueen to CGS, 8 October 1942. LAC, RG 24, Series C-1, HQS 20-4-32, Mobilization Organization (1st Special Service Battalion), microfilm reel C-5436. See also Message, Canmilitary to Defensor (Stuart to Murchie), GSD 2088, 8 October 1942. LAC, RG 24, Series C-2, CMHQ, Vol. 12305, File 3/Plough/1. Organization and operation of Proposed Plough Project.
6. See Message, Military Attaché to DEFENSOR, Ottawa, MA 1286 16/7, 12 July 1942. LAC, RG 24, Series C-1, HQS 20-4-32, Mobilization Organization Plough Project (1 SSBN), microfilm reel C-5436; "Minutes of Meeting Held at C.O.H.Q. on 4.1.43 to discuss Long–and Short — Term Policy Regarding Norwegian Operations," para 4, "Cobblestone Operations." PRO, DEFE 2/6, COC War Diary; Cottingham, 49; and Burhans, 36. Letter from Major-General Wilhelm von Tangen Hansteen to Colonel Robert Frederick, London, 18 September 1942. HIA, Robert T. Frederick Papers, Box 8, Released records 1942–1948, August 2011.
7. Priority message from Frederick to Burhans, 26 September 1942. HIA, Robert T. Frederick Papers, Box 1, File Plough Project — Maps of Important Norway Hydro-electric station. Letter, Marshall to Pope, "Second Canadian Parachute Battalion," 17 October 1942. LAC, RG 24, Series C-1, HQS 20-2-32, Employment and Movement Operations, 1st Special Service Battalion, microfilm reel C-5489.
8. Telegram DEFENSOR to CANMILITRY, No. G.S.D. 2088, 8 October 1942. LAC, RG 24, Series C-1, HQS 20-2-32, Employment and Movement Operations, 1st Special Service Battalion, microfilm reel C-5489.
9. Telegram DEFENSOR to CANMILITRY, No. G.S.D. 2088, 8 October 1942. LAC, RG 24, Series C-1, HQS 20-2-32, Employment and Movement Operations, 1st Special Service Battalion, microfilm reel C-5489.

NOTES

10. Memorandum Major-General Thomas T. Handy to the Chief of Staff, 14 October 1942. HIA. Robert Tryon Frederick Papers, Box 1, File Plough Project — Maps of Important Norway Hydro-electric station.
11. Letter, Marshall to Pope, "Second Canadian Parachute Battalion," 17 October 1942. LAC, RG 24, Series C-1,HQS 20–2–32, Employment and Movement Operations, 1st Special Service Battalion, microfilm reel C-5489.
12. Letter from Marshall to Pope, 17 October 1942. HIA, Robert Tryon Frederick Papers, Box 1, File, Plough Project — Maps of important Norway hydroelectric stations.
13. Letter, Pope to CGS, "Second Canadian Parachute Battalion," 20 October 1942. LAC, RG 24, Series C-1, HQS 20–2-32, Employment an Movement Operations, 1st Special Service Battalion, microfilm reel C-5489. See also Telegram DEFENSOR to CANMILITRY, No. G.S.D. 2088, 8 October 1942. LAC, RG 24, Series C-1, HQS 20–2-32, Employment and Movement Operations, 1st Special Service Battalion.
14. *Minutes of the War Cabinet Committee*, 28 October 1942. LAC, RG 2, Series A-5-B, Cabinet War Committee, Minutes and documents of the Cabinet War Committee, Vol. 11, Meeting no. 201, 28 October, microfilm reel C-4874.
15. Telegram from Stuart to Pope, 29 October 1942. LAC, RG 24, Series C-1, File HQS 20–4–32, Vol. 1. Mobilization, organization, Plough Project (1 CSSBN), microfilm reel C-5436.
16. Minutes of the Cabinet War Committee meeting, 11 November 1942 Item, U.S. Canadian Special Service Force. LAC, RG 2, 7c, Vol. 11, Minutes and documents of the Cabinet War Committee meeting # 206, 11 November 1942.
17. Letter, Marshall to Pope, "Second Canadian parachute Battalion," 17 October 1942. LAC, RG 24, Series C-1, HQS 20–2-32, Employment and Movement Operations, 1st Special Service Battalion, microfilm reel C-5489.
18. Frederick studied the requirements of this possible deployment. On 23 October, he submitted a detailed report that recommended that the Force not be employed in the Caucasus. Memorandum from Frederick to the Deputy Chief of Staff, 28 October 1942. HIA, Robert Tryon Frederick Papers. Box 1, File Plough Project — maps of important Norway hydroelectric stations.
19. Letter, "Second Canadian Parachute Battalion," McNarney to Pope, 13 November 1942; Letter, McNarney to Pope, 20 November 1942. The Marshall Papers, Royal Military College (RMC), Kingston, microfilm reel 7:0317, University Publications of America, Bethesda, Maryland; and Burhans, 45–46.
20. The AGF HQ was responsible for overseeing and assessing FSSF training. Plough Project Diary, entries of 23- 27 June 1942, 1- 6 July 1942, 49- 81. HIA, Robert T. Fredrick Papers. Box 1, Plough Project Diary.
21. Memoranda from Lieutenant-Colonel Ridgely Gaither, GSC, to Chief of Staff Army Ground Forces ,Special Projects Branch, Training Division, G-3 Section, HQ, Army Ground Force, 24 September 1942. HIA, Robert Tryon Frederick Papers, Box 1, Memoranda, manuscripts, and maps, 1942.
22. *Ibid.*
23. *Ibid.*

24. *Ibid.*
25. *Ibid.*
26. Report from McNair to Frederick regarding the inspection of training activities for FSSF during the period 2–4 December 1942. HIA, Robert D. Burhans Papers, Box 1, File Training.
27. The new FSSF training standard, for all personnel, proposed by Burhans included: the ability to travel on skis for 45 miles with 20 pounds, in 12 hours, day or night; living in snow for 30 nights in improvised shelters; to send and receive messages on all Force radio sets and be able to start, drive, and stop locomotives. Memorandum, from Major Robert D. Burhan to Colonel Robert Frederick, Washington, 21 September 1942. HIA, Robert Tryon Frederick Papers, Box 1, File Miscellanea.
28. War diary entry of 23 November 1942. 2 Cdn Para Bn/1 CSSBN War Diary, November 1942. Training memoranda, 12 November 1942. LAC, RG 24, Vol. 15301.
29. Organization charts, FSSF, 28 February 1943. LAC, RG 24, Series, File HQS20-16-32, Vol. 1, Monthly reports, State of Project, 1 CSSBN, microfilm reel C-5468. See also Organization charts, FSSF, 13 October 1943. HIA, Robert Tryon Frederick Papers, Box 2, FSSF Correspondence, memoranda, order etc, 1942–1943 Speeches and writings, 1942–1950.
30. Burhans, 42–45.
31. These tests, explained Williamson to NDHQ, were similar to the Canadian Army's TOETs. Monthly report of the 2 Cdn Para Bn. 2 Cdn Para Bn. (AF), 5 November 1942. Item 2: Training, D -Demolition. DHH, File 145.3009 (D7). Monthly reports of 1 CSSBN.
32. War diary entry of 3 October 1942. 2 Cdn Para Bn/1 CSSBN War Diary, October 1942. LAC, RG 24, Vol. 15301.
33. Becket, 32.
34. *Ibid.*
35. Information and course curriculums can be found in the various FSSF training memoranda issued between October 1942 to June 1943.
36. Four week Training program. FSSF Training Officer, 20 October 1942, Annexe October 1942. LAC, RG 24, War Diary, 2 Cdn Para Bn/1 CSSBN, Vol. 15301.
37. Frederick 24 October Speech.
38. *Ibid.*
39. *Ibid.*
40. Training memoranda. FSSF Training Officer, October 1942, Annexe October 1942. LAC, RG 24, War Diary, 2 Cdn Para Bn/1 CSSBN, Vol. 15301.
41. Monthly reports of 2 Cdn. Para Bn. October 1942. Item 2. Training d) Demolition; November 1942. Item 5. Officers. 2 Cdn. Parachute Bn (AF), 31 October 1942. DHH, File 145.3009 (D7), Monthly report of 1 CSSBN.
42. Intelligence Training Bulletins # 2, 3, 4. Headquarters, FSSF, Fort William Henry Harrison, Helena, Montana. 4, 11, 18 November 1942. DHH, File 112.21009 (D200). Correspondence DCGS (A+B) with AG Jan/September 1943.
43. Sergeant George Wright (1st Coy, 3rd Regiment), interviewed by authors, 16 October 2003.
44. Quoted in Springer, 31.
45. *Ibid.*, 30.

NOTES

46. War diary entry of 7 October 1942. 2 Cdn Para Bn/1 CSSBN War Diary, October 1942. LAC, RG 24, Vol. 15301.
47. Quoted in Hicks, 75.
48. Monthly report of the 2 Cdn Para Bn. 2 Cdn Parachute Bn. (AF), October 1942. Item 2: Training, C) Small Arms. DHH, File 145.3009 (D7). Monthly reports of 1 CSSBN.
49. Cottingham, 44.
50. Peppard, 30.
51. The V-2 fighting knife was approved by Frederick on 7 September 1942. The FSSF commander was satisfied with the specifications and the sample sent by the Case Company. He requested that a sheath be manufactured so that the knife could hang low on the leg or suspended from either a trouser or a pistol belt. Plough Project Diary, 7 September 1942 entry. HIA, Robert Tryon Frederick Papers, Box 1, Plough Project Diary 1942.
52. Battle Drill Lectures and Precise, Coldstream Ranch, Vernon, British Columbia, 5th Edition, 27 January 1943. DHH, Canadian Battle Drill Training Centre, — Training Precise, January 1943, 245 pages.
53. War diary entry of 24 October 1942. 2 Cdn Para Bn/1 CSSBN War Diary, October 1942. LAC, RG 24, Vol. 15301.
54. Colonel Adna H. Underhill, *The Force, A Historical Novel Based On The Actual Training and Combat of the First Special Service Force in World War II* (Arizona Monographs: Tucson, Arizona, 1994), 46.
55. Lloyd D.M. Dunlop (6th Coy, 3rd Regiment), interviewed by authors, 1 October 2003.
56. George Wright (1st Coy, 1st Regiment), interviewed by authors, 16 October 2003.
57. Lloyd D.M. Dunlop (6th Coy, 3rd Regiment), interviewed by authors, 1 October 2003.
58. Cottingham, 48.
59. Eugene Forward (3rd Coy, 3rd Regiment), interviewed by authors, 9 October 2003.
60. Letter from Pope to Frederick containing a copy of PC 76/3711, Washington, 21 May 1943; Becket, 33–34.
61. Inspection report from McNair to Frederick, 29 December 1942. HIA, Robert D. Burhans Papers. Box 1, File Training.
62. Burhans believed, "His [inspector] clear purpose was to damn the whole Force enterprise, declaring the skiers not qualified, and the mountaineers not competent on the rocks. His eventual report was so caustic that it brought a reproof to Army Ground Forces for even bothering the Chief of Staff with its contents." Burhans, 50.
63. Peter Smith (4th Coy, 3rd Regiment), interviewed by authors, 16 October 2003.
64. Peter Smith (4th Coy, 3rd Regiment), interviewed by authors, 16 October 2003.
65. *Ibid.*
66. George Wright (1st Coy, 1st Regiment), interviewed by authors, 16 October 2003.
67. Peter Smith (4th Coy, 3rd Regiment), interviewed by authors, 16 October 2003.
68. Burhans, 49.
69. Frederick acknowledged the fact that Canadians were asked to accept and learn many U.S. training aspects as well as other issues that related to military life. He stated, "We tried to reach a common basis by giving a little from both sides, but due to the fact that we are using arms

and equipment and in the general all administrative services of the United States, it had been necessary to ask the Canadians to go much further that the Americans to reach this commons ground of training and living. I must at this time compliment all the Canadian officers and enlisted men of the Force for the splendid way in which they have accepted the changes in customs, training, and other phases of military life." Fredericks 22 October Speech.

70. War diary entry of 18 March 1943. 2 Cdn Para Bn/1 CSSBN War Diary, March 1943. LAC, RG 24, Vol. 15301.

71. Burhans, 56.

72. War diary entry of 24 April 1943. 2 Cdn Para Bn/1 CSSBN War Diary, April 1942. LAC, RG 24, Vol. 15301.

73. This latest training phase focused on the use of weapons to hone fire techniques and tactics; enhancing tactical training of all units beginning with the section and culminating with the Force; living under field conditions for an extended period of time; developing superior march techniques; operating as an assault force; planning and executing raiding operations; complete training on the following subject matter: communications, scouting and patrolling, intelligence and amphibious scouting; continue training and the development of replacements for all FSSF echelons and for continue all specialist training. All training sessions would include exercises that would focus on: assault problems; night raiding; night observations and subunit tactical field exercises. Training memorandum #71, issued by Colonel Paul D. Adams, Executive, FSSF, Fort Ethan Allen Vermont, 27 May 1943. LAC , RG 24, 2 Cdn Para Bn/1 CSSBN War Diary, Annexe E, Vol. 15301. Simultaneously, all replacements continued their indoctrination with the FSSF's Special Training Detachment No .1. Training memoranda #70 and 73, issued by Colonel Paul D. Adams, Executive, FSSF, Fort Ethan Allen Vermont, 27 May 1943. LAC, RG 24, 2 Cdn Para Bn/1 CSSBN War Diary, Annexe E, Vol. 15301. Regimental commanding officers were ordered to provide officers and NCOs to act as instructors during the various phases of the replacements training. The training involved: close-order drill; map reading; aerial photo reading; chemical defence; hand-to-hand combat; scouting and patrolling; parachute training; first aid; grenades; administration and inspection; and obstacle course training.

74. Prior to this meeting NDHQ staff and the MND had finalized three important outstanding issues. The first was inclusion of the 1st and 2nd Canadian Parachute Battalions in the Canadian Army's Order of Battle; the second was the issuance of Privy Council Order 629 authorizing Williamson and his officers in-theatre disciplinary powers and legal responsibilities over their Canadian personnel serving within the FSSF; and third, drafting and authorization of P.C. 76/371, which formalized administrative relationships and responsibilities of the Canadian component of the FSSF. General Order 290, 1943. LAC, RG 24, Series C-1, File HQS 8846-1, (Vol. 20), Parachute troops, organization and training, microfilm reel C-5278; Memorandum from the Letson to Ralston, 7 January 1943. LAC, RG 24, Series C-1, File 20-1-32 (Vol. 2), Policy, composition and formation of the FSSF, microfilm reel C-5481; and Letter from CGS to MND, Ottawa, 3 April 1943. LAC, RG 24, Series C-1, File HQS 20-1-32 (Vol. 1), Policy Composition of the formation of the FSSF battalion, microfilm reel C-5481; P.C. 76/3711. P.C. 76/3711, 5 May 1943. LAC, RG

NOTES

24, Series C-1, File HQS 20-4-32, Vol. 1. Mobilization, organization of Plough Project (1 CSSBN), microfilm reel C-5436.

75. War diary entry of 27 May 1943. 2 Cdn Para Bn/1 CSSBN War Diary, May 1943. LAC, RG 24, Vol. 15301.
76. As quoted in Burhans, 58.
77. War diary entry of 28 May. 2 Cdn Para Bn/1 CSSBN War Diary, May. LAC, RG 24, Vol. 15301.
78. Letter Pope to Williamson, 14 June 1943. DHH, File 145.3009(D5). Organization and administration, correspondence and instructions for 1 CSSBN, July 1942 and December 1944.
79. "The ships rolled like corks," recalled Charlie Mann, "A lot of us, including myself were sicker than dogs. It was a messy ride." Charlie Mann (4th Coy, 3rd Regiment), interviewed by authors, 16 October 2003.

CHAPTER 9

1. Peter Smith (4th Coy, 3rd Regiment), interviewed by authors, 7 October 2003.
2. War diary entry of 14 July 1943. 2 Cdn Para Bn/1 CSSBN War Diary. July 1943. LAC, RG 24, Vol. 15301.
3. Japanese offensive operations in the Aleutians began in June 1942. On 3–4 June 1942, Japanese bombers attacked Dutch Harbour. Then, the Japanese No. 3 Maizuru Special Landing Party composed of 500 marines led by Lieutenant- Commander Mukai Hifumi landed and occupied Kiska on 6 June 1942. The Japanese then proceeded to set up a series of anti-aircraft batteries while 20 vessels of the Imperial Japanese Navy dropped anchor in Kiska Harbour. G.W.L. Nicholson, *The Canadian Participation in the Kiska Operation*, 16 October 1944. DHH, Army Headquarter Report # 6, B) Japanese Occupation (2). See also, *The Enemy on Kiska*, intelligence summary complied by assistant chief of staff, G-2, Advanced Command Post, HQ Alaska Defence Command and Advance Intelligence Centre, North Pacific Area, 102 pages.
4. The Japanese naval forces deployed for the Battle of Midway, 3–7 June 1942, commanded by Admiral Isoroku Yamamoto, comprised of the largest battleship in the world, the 70,000-ton *Yamato*, eight aircraft carriers, 22 cruisers, 65 destroyers, and 21 submarines. Yamamoto also had at his disposal 600 aircraft. Comparatively, the American naval force comprised of three aircraft carriers, 75 various vessels and 230 planes. The battle ended on 7 June 1942. Losses were staggering; Japanese losses totalled: Ships sunk — 4 carriers and 1 cruiser. Total aircraft lost — 292. Casualties — 2,500 men. American losses totalled: Ships sunk- 1 carrier and 1 destroyer. Total aircraft lost — 145. Casualties — 307 men. John Ray, *The Illustrated History of WW II* (London, U.K.: Weidenfield & Nicolson, The Orion Publishing Group, 2003), 128–29. Losses in the Battle of Midway June 3–7, 1942. Http://International Midway Memorial Foundation, 2000, accessed 15 May 2012.
5. Advance Intelligence Centre, North Pacific Area. *Summary Picture: Japanese Development of Kiska Island, June 7, 1942–July 26, 1943*. Part I, Topographic Description of Kiska. 1–2.

6. The estimated total of naval Japanese personnel was 2540. The estimated grand total of the Japanese garrison, on Kiska, was somewhere between 6,176 to 7,714. Intelligence Memorandum No. 6. *A Study of Enemy Defensive Installations on Kiska Island as known 5 July 1943: Item 4) Personnel. 4.1) Army, 4.2) Navy. 19–20.* Report prepared by, G-2, Western Defense Command and Fourth Army. Headquarters Western Defense Command and Fourth Army, Presidio of San Francisco, California, 16. The RCR Archives, Historical Records fonds, Series 7: World War II, 1939–1945, Sub-series: 7–44, Operations: Kiska. Volume 11, File 43. Other reports estimated the Japanese garrison to be as high as 11,000 men.
7. The invasion force comprised four American and one Canadian task group. Each task group consisted of three battalion combat teams. Nicholson, *The Canadian Participation in the Kiska Operation*, 23.
8. Underhill, 101.
9. As Frederick watched his men train, he wondered if the clothing could adequately protect his men against the elements. "Clothing is suffering greatly due to the wet, mud and other hard conditions," observed the commander. "I am beginning to wonder if the clothing and equipment will hold up until the operation is started. We will be in a difficult position if not, and there are not sufficient replacements." Project Plough Diary — Section relating to the Kiska operations, 31 July 1942, 140. HIA, Robert Tryon Frederick Papers, Box 1.
10. Underhill, 101.
11. War diary entry of 24 July 1943. 2 Cdn Para Bn/1 CSSBN War Diary. July 1943. LAC, RG 24, Vol. 15301.
12. Project Plough Diary- Section relating to Kiska Operations, 30 July 1943, 128. HIA, Robert Tryon Frederick Papers, Box 1.
13. Quoted in John Prados, *Combined Fleet Decoded: The Secret History of American Intelligence and the Japanese Navy in World War II* (New York: Random House, Inc., 1995), 480. The Japanese losses were light: 15 dead, 13 wounded, and 12 buildings badly damaged. To escape the shelling and strafing, the Japanese garrison went below ground and lived in a series of elaborate caves. Johnson, 162.
14. American forces suffered 3,829 casualties: 549 killed; 1,148 wounded; 1,200 injuries due to the severe cold; 614 other casualties due to accidents, drowning, self-inflicted wounds, and psychiatric breakdowns. Japanese casualties were: 2,351 killed, many from disembowelment from their own. Only 28 Japanese soldiers were captured, no officers. Brain Garfield, *The Thousand-Mile War: World War II in Alaska and The Aleutians* (Garden City, New York: Doubleday & Company, Inc., 1969), 256.
15. A special training bulletin noted: "The Japanese soldier has been taught hatred by the Japanese Army War Lords. The soldier fears a violent end, thus he fights to the death, no matter how pointless his resistance may be. It is very important to capture Japanese personnel. They have been brainwashed with the Samurai traditions of an honourable fatal end, however they were never taught how to comport themselves when captured. For this reason a Japanese prisoner is extremely valuable; once captured and over the fear of immediate brutal murder, the Japanese [prisoner] vocalizes as though vaccinated with a phonograph needle, giving information of tremendous value." Special Memorandum #

NOTES

11 prepared by the Office of the Commanding General, ATF 9, 5 July 1943. CAFM, AB 2, FSSF, Vol. 1, File 18.

16. Peppard, 64.
17. Vernon J. Doucette (4th Coy, 3rd Regiment), interviewed by authors, 29 September 2003.
18. Underhill, 98.
19. Monthly report of the 2 Cdn Para Bn. 2 Cdn Para Bn (AF), July 1943. Item 3: Training. DHH, File 145.3009 (D7). Monthly reports of 1 CSSBN.
20. Jack, Martin, "Jack Martin's Life in the Force," unpublished recollections. 1 December 2004.
21. J. D. Mitchell, "The War as I saw it from my foxhole. My days with the First Special Service Force," unpublished manuscript, non-dated, 27.
22. War diary entry of 3 August 1943. 2 Cdn Para Bn/1 CSSBN War Diary. August 1943. LAC, RG 24, Vol. 15301. Project Plough Diary — Section relating to Kiska operations, 29 July 1943, 139. HIA, Robert Tryon Frederick Papers, Box 1
23. Peppard, 36
24. War diary entry of 1 August 1943. 2 Cdn Para Bn/1 CSSBN War Diary. August 1943. LAC, RG 24, Vol. 15301. This being the Force's first deployment, it took the cooks some time to learn how to cook dehydrated vegetables. "Our cook had no experience with them and did not do a very good job preparing them," explained Major Kenneth Wickham. Wickham, 36.
25. War diary entry of 5 August 1943. 2 Cdn Para Bn/1 CSSBN War Diary. August 1943. LAC, RG 24, Vol. 15301.
26. Colonel Paul D. Adams, FSSF executive officer, Island Force G-2 Periodic Report, FSSF Headquarters, 6 August 1943. Major S.E Shoemaker, S-2 Infantry, S-2 Periodic Report, 6 to 12 August 1943. No. 57. DHH, File 595.013 (D2) Kiska — 1 CSSBN Report. Report of activities of 1 CSSBN, period 1, August to 30 September 1943.
27. Memoranda, Aerial Photo Interpretation Report Kiska Island, July 15 to July 22, 1943, FSSF Headquarters, Seattle, Washington, 4 August 1943. DHH, File 595.013 (D2) Kiska — 1 CSSBN. Period 1, August to 30 September 1943. Kiska, 1 CSSBN Report. Report of activities of 1 CSSBN. Period 1, August to 30 September 1943. S-2 Periodic Report No. 56. Headquarters U.S. Troops, Office of the Intelligence Officer, 4–6 August 1943. DHH, File 595.013 (D2) Kiska — 1 CSSBN Report. Report of activities of 1 CSSBN, period 1 August to 30 September 1943.
28. During the last week in July, pilots reported a drop in Japanese activities. American journalist Keith Wheeler wrote: "No AA fire reported at Kiska since July 27 ... We flew six B-24's with 100-lb bombs today [August 11th] and made numerous individual bomb-runs at low altitude, 2,000 feet. No AA whatever, though our B-24's offer big and tempting targets. A 3-ship mission this afternoon also drew no AA. There has been none for fifteen days encountered by our squadron. This island appears desolate and unoccupied. We wonder if they have somehow withdrawn. The whole thing looks suspicious and baffling ... The Navy expects heavy casualties; I remember Colonel Eareckson's opinion expressed in June that Kiska has no strategic value and isn't worth a single life. We were told that five thousand or more may die in taking the sinister island, but we wonder. G-2 claims there are five to eight thousand Japanese on Kiska. The Navy has been in a cordon about the island. Yet, there was a lot of radar activity on July 22 — did the Japs evacuate by submarine?" Garfield, 284.

29. Burhans, 68–69.
30. This detachment of Alaskan Scouts totalled two officers and 62 other ranks. The detachment's moniker was "Kastners Cutthroats." "They were a tough bunch of Alaskan trappers and prospectors," commented the war diary chronicler, "who are familiar with this type of country and a few are attached to each company to assist in any way they can." War diary entry of 12 August 1943. 2 Cdn Para Bn/1 CSSBN War Diary. August 1943. LAC, RG 24, Vol. 15301.
31. Kiska, installations and trenches. Memoranda, Island Force G-2 Periodic Report, 6 August 1943. DHH, File 595.013 (D2) Kiska — 1 CSSBN. Period 1 August to 30 September 1943.
32. Burhans, 72.
33. War diary entry of 7 August 1943. 2 Cdn Para Bn/1 CSSBN War Diary. August 1943. LAC, RG 24, Vol. 15301.
34. Major Emil P. Eschenburg, Headquarters FSSF, Annex No. 5 to Field Order No. 5, 8 August 1943. LAC, RG 24, 2 Cdn Para Bn/1 CSSBN, Vol. 15301, Appendix D.
35. The boundary between the sectors were: Swallow Rocks (to Southern Sector) Louis Creek (to Southern Sector) Male Hill (to Northern Sector) and Mucker Hill (to Southern Sector). Colonel Robert T. Frederick, Field Order 5. Amchitka, Alaska, 8 August 1943. DHH, File 595.013(D2) Kiska, 1 CSSBN report. Report of activities of 1 CSSBN, period 1 August-30 September 1943.
36. For these two operations, 2nd Regiment was organized into three provisional battalions. Field Order, Headquarters, FSSF, Amchitka, Alaska, August 1943. HIA, Robert D. Burhans Papers, Box 2, File Little Kiska.
37. Vernon J. Doucette (4th Coy, 3rd Regiment), interviewed by authors, 29 September 2003.
38. Colonel Robert T. Frederick, Field Order 5. Item 3, 1st Regiment. Amchitka, Alaska, 8 August 1943. DHH, File 595.013(D2) Kiska, 1 CSSBN report. Report of activities of 1 CSSBN, period 1 August to 30 September 1943.
39. Quoted in Adleman and Walton , 97.
40. Donald Ballantyne (HQ detachment, 1st Battalion, 3rd Regiment), interviewed by authors, 15 September 2003.
41. Becket, 46.
42. The war diary chronicler of The Winnipeg Grenadiers (M.G.) described: "This mock landing took place today (15 August 1943) which is 'D' Day. Our ships were to participate while the American forces landed at Quisling Cove on the opposite side of the island. This mock landing included the use of assault boats which were filled with 'Dummies' ... The purpose of this mock landing was to draw reserves from other parts of the island especially in the vicinity of the U.S. troops who landed at Quisling Cove." War diary entry of 15 August 1943, The Winnipeg Grenadiers (M.G.) War Diary, August 1943. LAC, RG 24, Vol. 15292, August 1943.
43. Captain Becket devised a system to control the approach that consisted of a "loose line to pass down my line of rubber boats so that we could keep together and come into the beach perpendicularly instead of horizontally. I remembered that machine gun position and did not wish to present the Jap with a target of rubber boats all stretched out in front of him for a much easier target. I figured that we could drop the line and spread out just as we were landing — which is in fact what we did." Becket, 45.

NOTES

44. Sam Barod (3rd Coy, 1st Regiment) interviewed by authors, 26 September 2003.
45. Wright, 43.
46. Becket, 47.
47. *Ibid.*, 48.
48. Wright, 43.
49. On each of these beaches, designated personnel erected a vertical six-foot square panel bearing the color designating each beach. Additionally, signal lamps emitting the same color as the panel were placed beside each panel. Colonel Robert T. Frederick, Annex No. 3 to Field Order No. 5, Instructions for Marking Beaches. FSSF, 8 August 1943. DHH, File 595.013(D2) Kiska, 1 CSSBN report. Report of activities of 1 CSSBN, period 1 August to 30 September 1943.
50. George Wright (1st Coy, 1st Regiment), interviewed by authors, 16 October 2003.
51. Becket, 48.
52. General Staff Pacific Command; General Intelligence Notes No. 124. Land mines, grenades, and booby traps. 27 September 1943. RCR Archives, Historical Records fonds, Series 7: World War II, Sub-series: 7–44, 1939–1945, Operations: Kiska, Vol. 11, File 45.
53. Colonel Robert T. Frederick, Field Order 5, 8 August 1943. DHH, File 595.013(D2) Kiska, 1 CSSBN report. Report of activities of 1 CSSBN, period 1 August-30 September 1943. See also, Special Memorandum 12, Use of Panels in Air-Ground Support, 5 July 1943. Office of the Commanding General, ATF 9, Fort Ord, California. CAFM, AB 2, FSSF Vol. 1, File 18.
54. Becket, 49.
55. Colonel Robert T. Frederick, Field Order 5, 8 August 1943. DHH, File 595.013(D2) Kiska, 1 CSSBN report. Report of activities of 1 CSSBN, period 1 August-30 September 1943.
56. For information regarding the Japanese planning and evacuation of the Kiska garrison consult, Masataka Chihaya, "Mysterious Withdrawal from Kiska," in *United States Naval Institute Proceedings*, February 1954, Vol. 84, No. 2, 31–47.
57. A total of 5,200 Japanese soldiers were evacuated. Prados, 480. Because of the limited number of ships, Lieutenant-Commander Mukai, the Kiska garrison commander, ordered his soldiers to leave behind all unnecessary equipment including rifles and automatic weapons. These were disabled and dumped into the water. Furthermore, all heavy weapons throughout the island were disabled and all heavy equipment and material was destroyed. Garfield, 281.
58. Chihaya, 47.
59. War diary entry of 15 August 1943, 2 Cdn Para Bn/1 CSSBN War Diary, August 1943. LAC, RG 24, Vol. 15301, October 1943.
60. Mitchell, 31.
61. In the event that the rafts were perforated by enemy fire, each raft was equipped with a kit containing wooden plugs. "If a bullet struck our raft," explained Lloyd Dunlop, "we were to put a .30 caliber or .45 caliber wooden plug in it. It makes me laugh now. I don't think you'd have much of a chance of plugging these holes if they fired at you with machine guns." Lloyd D.M. Dunlop (6th Coy, 3rd Regiment), interviewed by authors, 10 October 2003.
62. Peter Smith (4th Coy, 3rd Regiment), interviewed by authors, 7 October 2003.
63. Peter Kroll (4th Coy, 3rd Regiment), interviewed by authors, 10 October 2003.

64. Annex No. 3 to Field Order No. 5, Instructions for Marking Beaches, FSSF, Amchitka, Alaska, 8 August 1943. 2 Cdn Para Bn/1 CSSBN War Diary, Appendix D. LAC, RG 24, Vol. 15301.
65. Lloyd D.M. Dunlop (6th Coy, 3rd Regiment), interviewed by authors 1 October 2003.
66. Baker, 14.
67. Major Thomas P. Gilday, CO, 1st Battalion, 3rd Regiment. Annex to No. 1 to Accompany Field Order No. 5. Headquarters, 1st Battalion, 3rd Regiment. 13 August 1943. CAFM, FSSF, AB 2, Vol. 1, File 23.
68. William "Sam" Magee (6th Coy, 3rd Regiment), interviewed by authors, 7 February 2002.
69. *Ibid.*
70. Nicholson, The Canadian Participation in the Kiska, 33.
71. During the advance, the war diary chronicler of Headquarters 13th Canadian Infantry Brigade logged the following entry regarding FSSF [3rd Regiment] alleged lack of fire discipline in the northern sector: "The Special Service boys, having seized their initial objectives (Ranger Hill), had pushed down towards the ridge of the Main Camp. Now, each man of the Special Force carried over 500 rounds of ammunition, and when they reached the ridge, rich in abandoned Japanese small arms weapons and smaller articles, they decided to lighten their original load. The result was that they conducted a field firing exercise in the valley west of Salmon Lagoon and in front of our troops. After a few brisk exchanges of fire between the 184 (Task Group) and the Canadian troops on one side and the SSF on the other, without casualties, the situation clarified itself. Throughout the night small bands of SSF withdrew through our lines." Quoted in Nicholson, *The Canadian Participation in the Kiska*, 23. Also, during the evening of 16 August at 2200 hours the following message was sent from Task Group 13 to HQ northern sector, "Please contact SSF and tell them to please stop firing mortar bombs as they are landing close to our lines." *Ibid.*, 28
72. Lloyd D.M. Dunlop (6th Coy, 3rd Regiment), interviewed by authors, 1 October 2003.
73. Charlie Mann (4th Coy, 3rd Regiment), interviewed by authors, 15 October 2003.
74. Eugene Forward (3rd Coy, 3rd Regiment), interviewed by authors, 9 October 2003.
75. Subsequent inspections uncovered an incredible maze of underground tunnels and facilities. Moreover, Corlett had in his possession a radiogram from the War Department stating that an American doctor who had visited Kiska in 1902 had allegedly seen mountain caves large enough to hide entire divisions. In order not to worry his troops before the invasion, Corlett opted not to share this information. Garfield, 289.
76. Chihaya, 47.
77. Charlie Mann (4th Coy, 3rd Regiment), interviewed by authors, 15 October 2003.
78. Vernon J. Doucette (4th Coy, 3rd Regiment), interviewed by authors, 29 September 2003.
79. Joe T. Jamieson (6th Coy, 3rd Regiment), interviewed by authors, 1 October 2003.
80. Eugene Forward (3rd Coy, 3rd Regiment), interviewed by authors, 9 October 2003.
81. Peter Smith (4th Coy, 3rd Regiment), interviewed by authors, 7 October 2003.
82. Japanese defences on Little Kiska consisted of three coastal defence guns. five medium anti-aircraft guns. and two light anti-aircraft guns. Intelligence Memorandum No. 6. *A Study of Enemy Defensive Installations on Kiska Island as known 5 July 1943*. Item F. Little Kiska Island. Report prepared by, G-2, Western Defense Command and Fourth Army.

NOTES

Headquarters Western Defense Command and Fourth Army, Presidio of San Francisco, California, 12. RCR Archives, Historical Records fonds, Series 7: World War II, Sub-series: 7-44, 1939–45, Operations: Kiska, Vol. 11, File 43.

83. Burhans, 80.
84. George Wright (1st Coy, 1st Regiment.), interviewed by authors, 16 October 2003.
85. Casualties included: 24 killed by own forces in the fog; four killed by booby-traps or mines; 50 wounded by booby-traps or friendly fire; and 130 sustained trench foot. Garfield, 288. Additionally, the Navy lost 70 dead and missing and 47 wounded when the destroyer *Amner Read* hit a mine on 18 August. *Aleutian Islands, The U.S. Army Campaigns of World War II*, www.army.mil/cmh/pg/brochures/aleut.htm, accessed 18 May 2012, 20.
86. Chihaya, 47.
87. The FSSF sustained two casualties: an American injured by friendly fire and a Canadian who sustained an injury while handling a hand grenade detonator. George Wright (1st Coy, 1st Regiment), interviewed by authors, 16 October 2003. Monthly report of the 1 CSSBN. Report prepared by Williamson to secretary of NDHQ, 1 CSSBN, (AF), Report covering the period of 1 August to 30 September 1943. Item 1: Strength. DHH, File 145.3009 (D7). Monthly reports of 1 CSSBN.
88. As cited in Garfield, 289.
89. *Ibid.*, 289.
90. Letter from Corlett to the Adjutant General War Department, 24 August 1943. LAC, RG 24, Series C-1, File HQS 20-1-32, Policy, composition of formation of FSSF BN, microfilm reel C-5481.
91. Letter from DeWitt, commanding, Western Defence Command to adjutant general, War Department, 24 August 1943, Commendation of First Special Service Force. LAC, RG 24, Series C-1, File HQS 20-1-32, Vol. 2. Policy and formation of FSSF battalion, microfilm reel C-5481.
92. Report prepared by Williamson to secretary of NDHQ, 1 CSSBN, (AF), Report covering the period of 1 August to 30 September 1943. Item 2: Operations in Kiska. DHH, File 145.3009 (D7). Monthly reports of 1 CSSBN.
93. George Wright (1st Coy, 1st Regiment), interviewed by authors, 16 October 2003.
94. Lloyd D.M. Dunlop (6th Coy, 3rd Regiment), interviewed by authors, 1 October 2003.
95. Vernon Doucette (4th Coy, 3rd Regiment), interviewed by authors, 29 September 2003.
96. Eugene Forward (3rd Coy, 3rd Regiment), interviewed by authors, 9 October 2003.
97. George Wright (1st Coy, 1st Regiment), interviewed by authors, 16 October 2003.
98. The evacuation of the Force from Kiska was very poorly executed. "The reports of abandoned clothing and equipment are very concerning," commented the war diary chronicler. "Clothing in perfectly good repair, rifles, carbines, pistols, rocket launchers were found trampled in the mud, quantities of 'C' rations had been opened and only partly consumed. Neglect and carelessness concerning clothing and equipment has always been noticed but this was an all-time high. This may be partly excused on the grounds of their leaving very hurriedly and earlier than expected." The following day, 22 August, the loading of the *John B. Floyd* was very poorly executed and managed. "The loading was strictly a mess, boxes were

dumped and jammed any old way," observed the war diary chronicler. "No attempt was made to keep each organization's boxes separate. A number were smashed wide open and some equipment will undoubtedly be damaged." Daily entries of 21 and 22 August 1943. 2 Cdn Para Bn/1 CSSBN War Diary. October 1943, Annexes A, B. LAC, RG 24, Vol. 15301.

99. Report on activities of 1 CSSBN from 1 August 1943 to 30 September 1943. DHH, File 595.013(D2) Kiska, 1 CSSBN report.
100. Other FSSF officer promotions were six battalion commanders promoted to the rank of lieutenant-colonel. Also, battalion second-in-command (2IC) were promoted to the rank of major. War diary entry of 16 September 1943. 2 Cdn Para Bn/1 CSSBN War Diary. September 1943. LAC, RG 24, Vol. 15301.

CHAPTER 10

1. Donald Ballantyne (HQ detachment, 1st Battalion, 3rd Regiment), interviewed by authors, 12 September 2003.
2. The Canadian War Committee of Cabinet approved the assignment of the 1st Canadian Special Service Battalion as part of the FSSF under General Eisenhower's command for special service in Italy or the Balkans on 14 October 1943. The following day the CGS sent a letter to Colonel Williamson notifying him of the decision. The CGS also clarified, "You are therefore permitted to commit the personnel of the First Canadian Special Service Battalion allocated as they maybe to sub-units within the First Special Service Force, to any operational employment deemed necessary and expedient on orders from Commander-in-Chief, Allied Forces in the Mediterranean Area, transmitted through the Officer Commanding, First Special Service Force." The CGS however reinforced, "You will continue to have a direct channel of communication to the Department of National Defense through the Canadian Army Staff at Washington." See Memorandum, MND to CGS, "Re: Employment of First Special Service Battalion," 14 October 1943; and Letter, CGS to Williamson, 15 October 1943. LAC, RG 24, Series C-1, File HQS-2-32, Employment and movement operation 1st Special Service Battalion, microfilm reel C-5489.
3. Letter, McNarney to Pope, 20 November 1942. LAC, RG 24, Series C-1, File HQS–2–32, Employment and movement operation 1st Special Service Battalion, microfilm reel C-5489.
4. Memorandum, CGS to MND, 3 June 1943. LAC, RG 24, Series C-1, File HQS–2–32, Employment and movement operation 1st Special Service Battalion, microfilm reel C-5489.
5. Briefing Note for Canadian War Committee of Cabinet, "Dispatch of First Canadian Special Service Battalion to United Kingdom, and its Employment in the European Theatre as an Integral Part of the First Special Service Force." LAC, RG 24, Series C-1, File HQS–2–32, Employment and movement operation 1st Special Service Battalion, microfilm reel C-5489. The CGS issued new administrative directives to Colonel Williamson on 19 October 1943. For the interim, the channel of communication between Williamson and NDHQ remained unchanged. Meanwhile, at CMHQ, the officer-in-charge of records was briefed on the 1 CSSBN and ordered to provide all required administrative support during the course of the

NOTES

battalion's upcoming deployment. As of the 27 October 1943, the 1 CSSBN totalled 38 officers and 571 other ranks. The unit was still under strength and needed an additional 10 officers and 131 ORs to reach its war establishment. Report prepared by Colonel D.D. Williamson to secretary of NDHQ, 1 CSSBN, (AF), Report covering the period of 1–27 October 1943. Item 1: Strength. DHH, File 145.3009 (D7). Monthly reports of 1 CSSBN.

6. Telegram, From Stuart to Pope, 7 October 1943. LAC, RG 24, Series C-1, File HQS–2–32, Employment and movement operation 1st Special Service Battalion, microfilm reel C-5489.
7. After the summit had been seized and resupply columns worked their way to the top, the cost of the previous assaults became evident. Private Forward recalled:

> The footing was quite bad. This trail was no more than 16 inches wide. Every time it rained, the soil washed away. This exposed little stones. They were loose and uneven. It was terrible to walk on these. At certain places, it was quite steep. At the beginning of the trail, there was an open area on both sides. As we got higher, maybe a little more than half way, we came upon the bodies of American soldiers from previous attacks. The Americans and British had made several attempts to capture the mountain. All had failed. A lot of the bodies had been stuffed into mattress covers. They had done this to drag the bodies down the mountain. But I guess those who were dragging these bodies were forced to abandon their dead comrades due to the continuous shelling. There were hundreds of bodies. As we made our way to the top there were more and more bodies ... It was terrible. It was then that reality of war had revealed itself to me. Private Eugene Forward (3rd Coy, 3rd Regiment, interviewed by authors, 9 October 2003.

8. Cited in Ray Routhier, *The Black Devils: A Pictorial History of the First Special Service Force* (Great Falls, MO: Advanced Litho Printing, 1982), 20.
9. Mitchell, 45–46. See also Underhill, 118.
10. Clark assigned the British 46th Division a diversionary role. They were to launch an assault against Hill 360 in an attempt to draw off German forces.
11. War diary entry, 24 November 1943, 2 Cdn Para Bn/1 CSSBN, November 1943. LAC, RG 24, Vol. 15301.
12. "Memories of the Battle of Mount La Difensa," By Donald Mackinnon, 1st Co. 2nd Regiment, FSSF. CAFM, FSSF First Hand Accounts and Memoirs (Sims fonds).
13. Private Eugene Forward (3rd Coy, 3rd Regiment), interviewed by authors, 16 October 2003.
14. Staff-Sergeant Gordon Sims (FHQ), interviewed by authors.
15. Underhill, 120.
16. Clark Lee, "American-Canadian Troops Are Crack Mountain Fighters," *The Independent Record*, 13 February 1944, 16. CAFM, Alastair Neely fonds, AB 22, 1 FSSF, Vol. 1, File 3, 9 December 1943 to 4 April 1944.
17. Mitchell, 45–46.
18. "Narrative History of Events, Period 1–9 December 1943," 2 Cdn Para Bn/1 CSSBN War Diary, HQ 2nd Regiment, FSSF, Appendix G. LAC, RG 24, Vol. 15301.

19. Ed Thomas, "First Special Service Force," personal memoir. CAFM, FSSF First Hand Accounts And Memoirs (Sims fonds).
20. *Ibid.*
21. Sergeant Bert Hopkins (2nd Coy, 2nd Regiment), interviewed by authors, 20 October 2003.
22. With regard to the use of ropes, one veteran explained, "It was on a slant, could always use your feet — had to have something to hang on to though." "Force History — notes, 2d Bn CP, Barnesville, 22 February 1945." HIA, R. D. Burhans fonds, Box 18, File: Narrative Notes Force History.
23. Underhill, 125.
24. See affidavits of Captain Eino O. Olson, Lieutenant W.S. Story, Technician Grade 4, C.F. Rigg, Lieutenant-Colonel Robert S. Moore, Major Walter S. Gray, Staff Sergeant K.R. S. Meiklejohn, all dated 29 December 1943. HIA, Robert D. Burhans Papers, Box 19, File British and Canadian Correspondence.
25. The actual time that the battle began is unclear. Various publications place it anywhere between 0400 hours to 0530 hours.
26. Sergeant Bert Hopkins (2nd Coy, 2nd Regiment), interviewed by authors, 20 October 2003.
27. "Memories of the Battle of Mount La Difensa, By Donald Mackinnon, 1st Co. 2nd Regt, FSSF," (hereafter cited as Mackinnon Memoir). CAFM, FSSF First Hand Accounts and Memoirs (Sims fonds).
28. "Interesting Tale of First Special Service Force Tells About Trip to Farmhouse Held by Krauts," *Helena News*, 8 April 1945, 1. CAFM, Neely fonds, AB 22, 26 June 1944 to 10 August 1947, Vol. 1, File 5.
29. Blackwell, 45. Peter Cottingham insisted, "It is impossible to describe the terror which the sound of even one incoming artillery shell can instill in a person." Cottingham, 103.
30. Underhill, 136.
31. Cited in Corporal Gordon Harold Baker, "First Special Service Force Aug. 1942–Dec. 1944" (hereafter cited as Baker Memoir), unpublished memoir, 20. CAFM, AB 28, Charlie Mann fonds.
32. Private Lorin Waling (1st Coy, 2nd Regiment). Hancock and Abbott, *Daring to Die*.
33. Cited in Baker Memoir, 20.
34. This story is widely told. For example see Baker Memoir, 21; Allen Cowperthewaite, "Maybe Difensa, Maggiore, Cassino, Are A Jumble Of Words To You, But They Represent Real Heroism," *The Independent Record*, 7 August 1955, Section 2, B-1; Routhier, 23; and Burhans, 106.
35. See John Nadler, *A Perfect Hell* (Toronto: Doubleday Canada, 2005), 118. Nadler's book is an excellent source of first person accounts of the battle. This incident is a great example of how "second hand" stories can take on a life of their own with serious consequences. Many German PWs were killed based on the justification that Rothlin was killed through treachery.
36. "Narrative History of Events, Period 1–9 December 1943," War Diary, HQ 2nd Regiment, FSSF, Appendix G. LAC, RG 24, Vol. 15301, 2 Cdn Para Bn/1 CSSBN War Diary. Some accounts would arguably place some of the weight of the decision not to attack on Colonel Williamson, the commander of 2nd Regiment, who showed extreme nervousness, fear, and lack of decisiveness.

NOTES

37. Quoted Hicks, 101.
38. Lieutenant-Commander Maxwell Hamilton, "The Greatest Fighting General of all Time," *The Retired Officer*, October 1981, 26.
39. Sergeant R.E. Blake (3rd Coy, 3rd Regiment), interviewed by authors.
40. Mitchell, 47.
41. *Ibid*. Mitchell noted that it took all night to reach the summit. They would drop the supplies and then bring down the wounded. He also stated, "We didn't carry weapons and that in itself gave us a naked feeling."
42. Sergeant George Wright (1st Coy, 1st Regiment), interviewed by authors, 16 October 2003. To avoid confusion, on 4 December Frederick ordered the 3rd Regiment to be solely responsible for resupplying the troops on the summit. In the Santa Maria barracks, a member of the 3rd Regiment had drawn a picture in charcoal on the wall of a Forceman with a large packboard laden with rations and ammunition that towered over the soldier. Above it, he wrote "Freddy's Freighters Difensa or Bust." The name stuck and the Force was often referred to by this nickname. Burhans, 98.
43. Major Gerald McFadden, Written account. CAFM, AB fonds 31, Eugene Forward.
44. Affidavit, Lieutenant-Colonel Robert S. Moore, 29 December 1943. HIA, Robert D. Burhans Papers, Box 19, File British and Canadian Correspondence.
45. *Ibid.*
46. He was reinforced with 1st Company, 3rd Regiment.
47. Cited in Burhans, 119.
48. Cited Hicks, 100.
49. Mackinnon Memoir.
50. "Notes on interview with Col. DD Williamson re historical sketch on force activities," 1942/December 1943. DHH, File 145.3011 (D1) 1 CSSBN.
51. The percentage is based on a combat echelon of approximately 1,800 men. DHH, Army Headquarters Report No. 5, 1st Canadian Special Service Battalion, 22 February 1946, 35. The evacuation of wounded was a very deliberate, difficult endeavour. It took six men to carry a litter with a seventh, holding a rope in the rear, acting as a brake. The trip from the summit to the bottom of the mountain took eight to 10 hours. Gord Baker recalled, "It was no easy chore packing a wounded suffering man down a rough mountain trail while the patient screamed at every jolt of the stretcher, especially at night when it was too dark for the bearer to see where he was walking half the time." Baker, 26.
52. DHH Army Headquarters Report No. 5, 1st Canadian Special Service Battalion, 22 February 1946, 36. Commendations became yet another administrative dilemma. Brigadier A.W. Beament from the Canadian Section at GHQ in Italy, sent a hasty memorandum to Canadian military headquarters on 6 December 1943, requesting direction on how to proceed with the award of American gallantry awards to Canadians in the FSSF as there was no protocol, and the Americans were pressing to award the medals quickly after an action as was their custom. NDHQ approved the receipt of American awards on 12 January 1944. Letter, Beament to senior officer, Canadian Military Headquarters, "Honours and Awards 1 Cdn Special Service Battalion," 6 December 1943. LAC, RG 24, Vol. 15301, 2 Cdn Para Bn/1 CSSBN War Diary, Appendix B.

53. DHH Army Headquarters Report No. 5 Historical Section (GS) Department of National Defence, 1st Canadian Special Service Battalion, 22 February 1946, 36.
54. Hamilton, 24.

CHAPTER 11

1. Baker, 25.
2. Cited in Nadler, 141.
3. Burhans, 138.
4. Letter, Frederick to commanding general, 5th Army, "Recommendation for Award," 18 December 1943. HIA, Robert D. Burhans Papers, Box 19, File British and Canadian Correspondence. The nomination itself is not hard to explain. After all, Colonel Williamson was the commander of 2nd Regiment who trained his personnel, planned the attack, and whose unit captured La Difensa, something larger formations had been unable to do. Almost by protocol alone, he would be expected to be rewarded by a substantive award. The stories of his behaviour apparently did not start to circulate until the regiment left the mountain. By the time Colonel Frederick would have had heard the full stories and conducted an investigation, the nomination would have already have been written. The actual affidavits by witnesses were not signed and dated until 29 December. Action was promptly taken once the scope of his behaviour was fully realized.
5. Memorandum, "Disposal (Adverse Report)." LAC, Personnel File, Williamson, D.D., 43–26748 MJ.
6. Memorandum, Colonel Donald Dobie Williamson, "Explanation of Adverse Report," 1 January 1944. LAC, Personnel File, Williamson, D.D., 43–26748 MJ.
7. Affidavit, Captain Eino O. Olson, 29 December 1943. HIA, Robert D. Burhans Papers, Box 19, File British and Canadian Correspondence. Eino remembered "while we were on Amchitka the same thing happened when the Colonel received our mission and came back to our CP."
8. *Ibid.*
9. Affidavit, Lieutenant W.S. Story, 29 December 1943. HIA, Robert D. Burhans Papers, Box 19, File British and Canadian Correspondence. Incredulously, Williamson would tell others, including Story, that he believed he had wounded the German "sniper." Years later Story publicly disagreed with an author who argued Frederick railroaded Williamson out of the FSSF. Story wrote, "I was so shattered by the Colonel's conduct during the attack on La Difensa ... I was the only one who knew exactly what happened as he made his way down past most of 2nd Battalion to seek out Col. Frederick at his forward HQ near Dr Evashwick's Aid Station. When Williamson got back up to the top, he commissioned me. I was struck by the thought he had done so to keep me quiet about his behaviour ... I resolved not to remain quiet, if asked by a senior officer in a formal hearing. In a session presided over by our Adjutant Lt. Col. Kenneth G. Wickham, I gave book, chapter and verse. I am sure now it was the most damning testimony, except for that of Col. Frederick, who preceded me and whom I met

NOTES

leaving as I was going into the tent. The typed letter for my signature I received later simply said I had lost confidence in Williamson's ability to lead. Wickham asked me to sign it, please, the way it was stated." Bill Story, "Snowplough and the Jupiter Deception — Book Review," *The Spearhead*, March-April 2006, 12.

10. Affidavit, Technician Grade 4, C.F. Rigg, 29 December 1943. HIA, Robert D. Burhans Papers, Box 19, File British and Canadian Correspondence.

11. *Ibid*. At one point on the descent, Williamson fell while holding his pistol and discharged a clip of ammunition. Rigg recalled, "the shots were coming too close to me for comfort, and I began to realize that the Colonel really didn't know what he was doing. I decided the best thing for me to do was for me to get back to my detachment." Rigg also revealed that the men in 2nd Regiment now referred to Colonel Williamson "as 'Fox Hole Willie' from observation that he was in his fox hole the biggest share of the time on la Difensa." *Ibid*.

12. See affidavits of Captain Eino O. Olson, Lieutenant W.S. Story, Technician Grade 4, C.F. Rigg, Lieutenant-Colonel Robert S. Moore, Major Walter S. Gray, Staff Sergeant K.R. S. Meiklejohn, all dated 29 December 1943. HIA, Robert D. Burhans Papers, Box 19, File British and Canadian Correspondence.

13. Sergeant Joe T. Jamieson (6th Coy, 3rd Regiment,), interviewed by authors, 1 October 2003.

14. Sergeant George Wright (1st Coy, 1st Regiment), interviewed by authors, 16 October 2003.

15. Donald Ballantyne (HQ Coy, 3rd Regiment), interviewed by authors, 12 September 2003.

16. Affidavit, Captain Eino O. Olson, 29 December 1943. HIA, Robert D. Burhans Papers, Box 19, File British and Canadian Correspondence.

17. Affidavit, Major Walter S. Gray, 29 December 1943. HIA, Robert D. Burhans Papers, Box 19, File British and Canadian Correspondence.

18. As of 3 January 1944, NDHQ, thru CMHQ, authorized 1 CSSBN to utilize Canadian Section HQ 2nd Echelon, Central Mediterranean Force, for administrative support. This saved the Canadian component of the FSSF resources and time since they could now deal directly with their Canadian headquarters in Italy instead of London, England.

19. Memorandum. to MGA, 5 January 1944. LAC, Personnel File, Williamson, D.D., 43–26748 MJ.

20. War diary entry, 1 January 1944, 2 Cdn Para Bn/1 CSSBN War Diary. LAC, RG 24, Vol. 15301.

21. Message, FLAMBO to CANMILITRY, ALA 1683, January 041815A/44. LAC, Personnel File, Williamson, D.D., 43–26748 MJ.

22. *Ibid*.

23. *Ibid*. Colonel Williamson, not surprisingly, protested his removal from command. According to an adjutant general's report, Williamson argued, "that he has been placed 'on the spot' by an unfair C.O. (Col Fredericks) and that he definitely has a case for reconsideration, having been the victim of differentiation." It goes on to state, "While he admits that he was 'jittery' on his first occasion under difficult conditions, his orders had been clear, and his unit had definitely done a good show and carried out superior orders." Memorandum, "Col. D.D. Williamson," To C.O.S. from Brigadier W.B. Wedd, 14 February 1944. LAC, Personnel File, Williamson, D.D., 43–26748 MJ.

24. Colonel Williamson's case is not without precedence. Anyone with operational experience can recount tales of individuals who in garrison and training were powerful forces but when faced with the reality of operations failed to live up to expectations. Conversely, others who merited little attention seemingly spring to life and rise to the challenge. In the Second World War, a similar Canadian case was that of Lieutenant-Colonel G.F.P. Bradbrooke, the CO of 1st Canadian Parachute Battalion who was also relieved following his combat debut during the invasion of Normandy for his inability to provide decisive leadership during that campaign. He also demonstrated nervousness and confined himself to his CP. Like Williamson, he too was a driving force behind the creation and training of his unit. However, although both were great organizers, administrators, and trainers, they were unable to face the rigors of combat. See Horn and Wycyznski, *Paras Versus the Reich*, 161–62; and Bernd Horn, "Bradbrooke, Nicklin and Eadie: A Tale of Command," in Bernd Horn, ed., *Intrepid Warriors: Perspectives on Canadian Military Leaders* (Toronto: Canadian Defence Academy Press/Dundurn, 2007), 223–60.
25. Memorandum, "On to Majo," Colonel Edwin A. Walker, 9 June 1944. HIA, Robert D. Burhans, Box 19, File Radicosa
26. Burhans, 149. Frederick, as commander Task Force "B" was also assigned the 36th Division artillery and "A" Coy, 109th Medical Battalion for casualty evacuation.
27. Memorandum, "Recommendation for Awards," 26 January 1944. HIA, Robert D. Burhans, Box 19, File Radicosa
28. "On to Majo," Walker.
29. *Ibid*.
30. Memorandum, "Honours and Awards," 18 January 1945. DHH, File 145.3009 (D2) Honours and Awards.
31. Sholto Watt, "Crack Mixed Force is Gradually Becoming American," *The Montreal Daily Star*, 8 April 1944, 13–28. LAC, *The Montreal Daily Star*, microfilm reel N-39719.
32. *Ibid*.
33. Letter, "Honours and Awards," 25 January 1945. DHH, File 145.3009 (D2), Honours and Awards.
34. "Headquarters Seventh Army, General Orders, Number 77," 15 September 1944. DHH, File 145.3009 (D2) Honours and Awards. Wright was ordered to withdraw because adjacent units were unable to press their attack. However, upon being informed one of his men was seriously wounded still on the battlefield, but could not be reached because of intense enemy fire, Wright "rushed twenty-five yards up the fire-swept slope, bodily lifted the man to his shoulders, and carried him one hundred and fifty yards to a litter team." He then directed his platoon in a successful withdrawal without further casualties. He was awarded the Distinguished Service Cross.
35. Watt, "Crack Mixed Force is Gradually Becoming American."
36. Memorandum, "Honours and Awards," 18 January 1945. DHH, File 145.3009 (D2) Honours and Awards.
37. Sergeant Lloyd D.M. Dunlop (6th Coy, 3rd Regiment), communications sergeant (2nd Battalion HQ), interviewed by authors.

NOTES

38. "On to Majo," Walker.
39. Sergeant George Wright (1st Coy, 1st Regiment), interviewed by authors.
40. "On to Majo," Walker.
41. The 3rd Battalion (133rd Infantry Regiment) remained on Hill 1109. It also acted as Task Force "B" reserve. Keyes had reinforced Task Force "B" with both the 1st and 2nd Battalions (133rd Infantry Regiment) to provide Frederick with the required strength to effect the pursuit.
42. The 2nd Battalion, 133rd Infantry Regiment was also known as the Japanese-American 100th Infantry Battalion.
43. From 8–10 January, approximately 50 percent of the 295 casualties suffered by the Force were a result of frostbite. DHH, Army Headquarters Report No. 5, 1st Canadian Special Service Battalion, 22 February 1946, 38.
44. Steve Goodwin, "One night you'd go for the kill, the next night you'd go for prisoners," *The Pictou Advocate*, 7 November 2003, 6–7.
45. Sergeant Paul Schoeler (6th Coy, 3rd Regiment), interviewed by authors, 17 October 2003.
46. Watt, "Crack Mixed Force is Gradually Becoming American."
47. Hamilton, 26.
48. One large problem facing the Canadians was tracing their wounded. The field hospitals were not reporting admissions, discharges, or diagnoses to the units or FSSF second echelon. As a result, the Canadians lost track of their soldiers as they entered the medical chain. Of 222 hospital cases in the aftermath of the latest combat, they could trace only about 50 individuals. Gilday suspected the others were evacuated through American channels to the United States. Letter, acting officer commanding 1st Canadian Special Service Battalion C.A. (A) to Cmd Cdn Army Staff, 31 January 1944. DHH, File 145.3009 (D7), Monthly reports of 1 Cdn Spec Svc Bn, August 1942 to January 1945; and Burhans, 162.
49. Report of activities of the 1st Canadian Special Service Battalion, C.A. (A) from 28 October to 15 December 1942. DHH, File 145.3009 (D7), Monthly reports of 1 CSSBN, August 1942-January 1945; Report of activities of the First Canadian Special Service Battalion, C.A. (A) from 16 December to 31 January 1942; Letter, acting officer commanding 1st Canadian Special Service Battalion C.A. (A) to Cmd Cdn Army Staff, 31 January 1944. DHH, File 145.3009 (D7) Monthly reports of 1 Cdn Spec Svc Bn, August 1942 to January 1945; and DHH Army Headquarters Report No. 5, 1st Canadian Special Service Battalion, 22 February 1946, 39. As always, there are slight differences in the actual numbers in different documents.
50. Letter from Gilday to OC Canadian Section, GHQ, 1st Echelon, Canadian Army, CMF, 15 January 1944. LAC, RG 24, Series C-2, CMHQ, Vol. 10404, File HQ Cdn 56/5/1 CSSBN/1, Correspondence, messages, policy procedures.
51. Report of activities of the 1st Canadian Special Service Battalion, C.A. (A) from 28th October to 15 December 1942. DHH, File 145.3009 (D7), Monthly reports of 1 CSSBN, August 1942-January 1945. Report of activities of the 1st Canadian Special Service Battalion, C.A. (A) from 16 December to 31 January 1942.
52. Letter from Gilday to OC Canadian Section, GHQ, 1st Echelon, Canadian Army, CMF, 15 January 1944. LAC, RG 24, Series C-2, CMHQ, Vol. 10404, File HQ Cdn 56/5/1 CSSBN/1, Correspondence, messages, policy procedures.

53. Report of the Activities of the 1st Canadian Special Service Battalion, C.A. (A) from 1 October 1943 to 27 October 1943. *Ibid.*
54. Letter from Gilday to OC Canadian Section, GHQ, 1st Echelon, Canadian Army, CMF, 15 January 1944. LAC, RG 24, Series C-2, CMHQ, Vol. 10404, File HQ Cdn 56/5/1 CSSBN/1, Correspondence, messages, policy procedures.
55. Letter from Weeks to major-general in charge of administration (through the deputy adjutant general), 17 January 1944. LAC, RG 24, Series C-2, CMHQ, Vol. 12540, File 6/1 Spec Serv Bn/1, Organization and administration.
56. Memorandum from CGS to the MND regarding the employment of the 1st Special Service Battalion, London, 2 February 1944. DHH, File 112.21009 (D195), Correspondence deputy chief of the general staff (A+B) with and from the minister to others. January-February 1944.
57. Letter from Gilday to OC Canadian Section, G.H.Q., 1st Echelon, Canadian Army, C.M.F., 15 January 1944. LAC, RG 24, Series C-2, CMHQ, Vol. 10404, File HQ Cdn 56/5/1 CSSBN/1, Correspondence, messages, policy procedures.

CHAPTER 12

1. Sergeant Peter Smith (4th Coy, 3rd Regiment), Interviewed by authors, 7 October 2003.
2. Cited in Raleigh Trevelyan, "Anzio-Blast & Counterblast," *History of the Second World War*, part 58, 1614.
3. For a detailed account of the Anzio campaign see: Lloyd Clark, *Anzio* (London: Headline Publishing Group, 2006); Raleigh Trevelyan, *Rome '44: The Battle For the Eternal City* (New York: Viking Press, 1981); Franz Kurowski, *Battleground Italy, 1943–1945* (Winnipeg: JJ Fedorowcz Publishing Inc, 2003); Roger Bender and George A. Petersen, *Herman Göring: From Regiment to Fallschirmpanzerkorps* (San Jose, CA: R. James Bender Publishing, 1975); and Franz Kurowski, *The History of Fallschirm Panzerkorps Herman Göring* (Winnipeg: J.J. Fedorowicz Publishing Inc., 1995). In actuality, within the first 22 hours, 6th Corps landed approximately 36,000 troops 3,069 vehicles, and 90 percent of their equipment.
4. The failure of Major-General Lucas to aggressively push forward became a controversy. By February, Churchill and General Alexander exerted considerable pressure on Clark to relieve Lucas of command, making him the scapegoat for the Allied failure to capitalize on the operational surprise they had achieved. Yet, Lucas followed his orders. The priority was to hold the beachhead and not to overextend. However, the caveat that can always plague a subordinate commander was Clark's last minute directive to push forward if possible, without accepting risk of being cut-off or endangering the bridgehead. As such, the commander on the ground is left open to criticism after the fact, once the situation is clearly evident as to enemy forces and capability.
5. Kurowski, 231.
6. Cited Trevelyan, 1614.
7. The Allies had approximately 61,000 troops in the beachhead at the beginning of February.

NOTES

Major Stanley C. Waters, "Anzio — The Role of the 1st Special Service Force," *Canadian Army Journal*, Vol. 2, Nos. 5 and 6, August-September 1948, 16–17.

8. Sixth Corps, "Intelligence Plan and G-2 Estimate of Enemy Situation," 062200 Mar 44. HIA, Robert D. Burhans Papers, Box 22, File Raid Reports — Anzio.
9. War diary entry, 1–2 February 1944, 2 Cdn Para Bn/1 CSSBN War Diary. LAC, RG 24, Vol. 15301, War Diary, 1–29 February 1944.
10. Underhill, 191.
11. "On to Majo," Walker.
12. War diary entry, 29 February 1944, 2 Cdn Para Bn War Diary. LAC, RG 24, Vol. 15301, War Diary, 1–29 February 1944. Gilday's number differ significantly from others. Most sources put the FSSF front line strength at approximately 1,200 men.
13. McFadden recollection in Hancock and Abbott, *Daring to Die*.
14. Donald J. Green, "Donald J. Green Memoir — Dear Alex" (hereafter cited as Green Memoir), unpublished manuscript, 1974. CAFM, Gordon Sims Papers, AB fonds 29.
15. Lieutenant Conrad Legault, "The Anzio Beachhead." HIA, Robert H. Adleman Papers, Box 12, File Conrad Legault.
16. Mitchell, 74.
17. Frederick was promoted to brigadier-general on 27 January 1944.
18. Thomas, "First Special Service Force, 9/42–12/44" (hereafter cited as Thomas Memoir), unpublished memoir, no date. CAFM, Gordon Sims Papers, AB fonds 29.
19. "Narrative Report, First Special Service Force 1 February to 29 February 1944." Summary of Operations, First Special Service Force Historical Records, War Department, The Adjutant General's Office Washington (hereafter cited as Narrative Report). CAFM, AB 2, 1 FSSF, Box 1.
20. War diary entry, 11 February 1944, 2 Cdn Para Bn/1 CSSBN War Diary. LAC, RG 24, Vol. 15301, War Diary, 1–29 February 1944.
21. Sergeant Jim Summersides (4th Coy, 3rd Regiment), interview with authors, 21 October 2003.
22. Susan Lentz, *Kenneth* (Bloomington, IN: Author House, 2007), 68.
23. Thomas Memoir. He also pointed out that they lived in these squalid conditions for 99 days.
24. *Ibid*.
25. Narrative Report.
26. Cited in Clark, 175.
27. War diary entry, 24 February 1944, 2 Cdn Para Bn/1 CSSBN War Diary. LAC, RG 24, Vol. 15301, War Diary, 1–29 February 1944.
28. War diary entry, 16 February 1944, 2 Cdn Para Bn/1 CSSBN War Diary. LAC, RG 24, Vol. 15301, War Diary, 1–29 February 1944.
29. S-2 Report #65, 17 February 1944. LAC, RG 24, Vol. 15301, 2 Cdn Para Bn/1 CSSBN War Diary, Appendix February.
30. War diary entry, 18 February 1944, 2 Cdn Para Bn/1 CSSBN War Diary. LAC, RG 24, Vol. 15301, War Diary, 1–29 February 1944.
31. Sergeant Jim Summersides (4th Coy, 3rd Regiment), interview with authors, 21 October 2003.
32. War diary entry, 29 February 1944, 2 Cdn Para Bn/1 CSSBN War Diary. LAC, RG 24, Vol. 15301, War Diary, 1–29 February 1944.

33. War diary entry, 29 February 1944, 2 Cdn Para Bn/1 CSSBN War Diary. LAC, RG 24, Vol. 15301, War Diary, 1–29 February 1944.
34. "Activities of the First Canadian Special Service Force Battalion, CA, (A) From 1st February 44 to 29th February 44." DHH, File 145.3009 (D7), Monthly reports of 1 Cdn SSF, August 1942/January 1945.
35. War diary entry, 29 February 1944, 2 Cdn Para Bn/1 CSSBN War Diary. LAC, RG 24, Vol. 15301, War Diary, 1–29 February 1944.
36. Letter from CGS to MND, 2 February 1942. DHH, File 112.21009 (D195), Correspondence DCGS (A+B) with and from the minister to others. January-February 1944; and Message from Beament to CGS, 11 February 1944. LAC, RG 24, Series C-2, CMHQ, Vol. 10404, File HQ Cdn 56/5/1 CSSBN/1, Correspondence, messages, policy procedures.
37. Telegram, Canadian Army Staff, Washington D.C. to NDHQ, 28 January 1944. LAC, RG 24, Series C-1, File HQ 20-2-32, employment and movement operations.
38. Letter from Gilday to OC Canadian Section, GHQ, 1st Echelon, Canadian Army, CMF, 15 January 1944. LAC, RG 24, Series C-2, CMHQ, Vol. 10404, File HQ Cdn 56/5/1 CSSBN/1, Correspondence, messages, policy procedures.
39. Message from Murchie to CGS, 19 February 1944. LAC, RG 24, Series C-2, CMHQ, Vol. 12540, File 6/1 Spec Serv Bn/1, Organization and administration.
40. Message Beament to CGS, 8 February 1944. *Ibid*.
41. Letter CGS to Brigadier-General Staff, 9 February 1944; Message from CGS to Murchie, 11 February 1944. *Ibid*.
42. Letter, Frederick to GOC 5th Army, "First Special Service Force," 19 February 1944. HIA, Robert T. Frederick Papers (hereafter cited as R.T.F.), Box 1, FSSF, memoranda, MSS, maps.
43. Letter, Frederick to GOC 5th Army, "First Special Service Force," 19 February 1944. HIA, R.T.F., Box 1, FSSF, memoranda, MSS, maps. Frederick noted, seemingly complained, that Canada supplied no support troops; that all administration and overhead, less Canadian pay and records are performed by U.S. troops; that there are substantive differences in policies, procedures and discipline; and that by necessity the U.S. Army provided all weapons, clothing, and equipment. Finally, Frederick also pointed out that due to the inclusion of Canadian personnel in the force "the British Government has had to be consulted and its agreement obtained for the force's employment."
44. *Ibid*. Frederick did concede, "When the force was activated, the Canadian Army furnished, in general, better qualified officers and enlisted men than did the United States Army, and this has resulted in a large number of the key positions being filled by Canadians."
45. Memorandum from Lieutenant-Colonel O.J. Baldwin to General Frederick, Subject: Matters Canadian, 20 February 1944. DHH, File 145.3009 (D5), Organization and administration, correspondence and instructions for 1 CSSBN, July 1942 to December 1944.
46. Memorandum from Lieutenant-Colonel C.H. Walker, assistant adjutant general, to Brigadier E.G. Weeks, officer in command, Canadian Section, Sec. GHQ, 1st Echelon, London, 6 March 1944. LAC, RG 24, Series C-2, CMHQ, Vol. 10404, File HQ Cdn 56/6/1 CSSBN/1, 200A5.009 (D53). Correspondence, message, policy procedures.
47. The Americans also requested a program be put in place to automatically cover activity wastage

NOTES

rates and battle casualty replacements to ensure the provisions of additional monthly reinforcements that would be sent from Canada. LAC, RG 24, Series C-2, CMHQ, Vol. 10404, File HQ Cdn 56/6/1 CSSBN/1, 200A5.009 (D53). Correspondence, message, policy procedures.

48. The new revised form was titled "Special Declaration." The original form prepared in August 1942 was titled, "Declaration To Be Signed by All Officers And Other Ranks to 2nd Canadian Parachute Battalion." The wording in the new form had been revised to reflect the unit's current designation and possible future work with an airborne unit of the Canadian Army. Letter Weeks to HQ 1 CBRGp, 25 March 1944. LAC, RG 24, Series C-2, CMHQ, Vol. 10404, File HQ Cdn 56/6/1 CSSBN/1, 20A5.009 (D53), Correspondence, messages, policy and procedures.
49. Message from Murchie to CGS, 19 February 1944. LAC, RG 24, CMHQ, Vol. 12540, File 6/1 Spec Serv Bn/1, Organization and administration; and Letter from Weeks to HQ 1 CBRGp, 10 March 1944. LAC, RG 24, Series C-2, CMHQ, Vol. 10404, File HQ Cdn 56/6/1 CSSBN/1, 20A5.009 (D53), Correspondence, messages, policy and procedures.
50. Sergeant John Rowe (4th Coy, 1st Regiment), interviewed by authors, 22 October 2003.
51. Letter Haldeny to Cdn Sec GHQ, 1 Ech. LAC, RG 24, Series C-2, CMHQ, Vol. 10404, File HQ Cdn 56/6/1CSSBB/1 200A5.009 (D53). Correspondence, messages, policy procedures.
52. Memorandum, Weeks to MND, 3 October 1944. LAC, RG 24, Series C-2, CMHQ, Vol. 12540, File 6/1 Spec Serv Bn/1/2, Organization and administration.
53. Sergeant George Wright (1st Coy, 1st Regiment), interviewed by authors, 16 October 2003.
54. Activities of the 1st Canadian Special Service Battalion. CA (A), from 1–30 April 1944. DHH, File 145.3009 (D7). Monthly reports of 1 CSSBN, August 1942 to January 1945.
55. Letter from Staff Duty 1(A) to Staff Duty 1, 1 June 1944. LAC, RG 24, Series C-1, File HQS 20-1-32, (Vol. 2), Policy, function of FSSF Battalion, microfilm reel C-5481.
56. Letter Akehurst to adjutant general, 3 May 1944. DHH, File 145.3009 (D3), Instruction and directives for the 1 CSSBN, June 1943 to December 1944. Weeks clarified that the present authorized official War Establishment for the 1 CSSBN was 47 officers and 583 men. Letters from Weeks to Akehurst, 24 May and 30 June 1944. LAC, RG 24, Series C-2, CMHQ, File HQ Cdn 56/6/1 CSSBN/1, 200A5.009 (D53), Correspondence, messages, policy, procedures; and Letter Weeks to Officer IC, Cdn Sec GHQ 2 ECH AAI, 24 May 1944. LAC, RG 24, Series C-2, CMHQ, File HQ Cdn 56/6/1 CSSBN/1, 200A5.009 (D53), Correspondence, messages, policy, and procedures.
57. "Activities of the First Canadian Special Service Force Battalion, CA, (A) From 1st April to 30th April 44." DHH, File 145.3009 (D7), Monthly reports of 1 Cdn SSF, August 1942/ January 1945.
58. Legault, "The Anzio Beachhead."
59. Sergeant Paul Schoeler (6th Coy, 3rd Regiment), Interview by authors, 17 October 2003.
60. *Ibid.*
61. Corporal Gordon Harold Baker, "First Special Service Force Aug. 1942-Dec. 1944" (hereafter cited as Baker Memoir), unpublished manuscript, no date . CAFM, Charlie Mann fonds.
62. Sergeant George Wright (1st Coy, 1st Regiment), interview by authors, 16 October 2003.
63. Green Memoir.
64. Lentz, 70.

65. "IPW [interrogation Prisoner of War] Report," 18 February 1944. LAC, RG 24, Vol. 15301, 2 Cdn Para Bn/1 CSSBN War Diary, Appendix February.
66. James O'Neill, "Devils in Baggy Pants," *YANK: The Army Weekly*, 29 December 1944. CAFM, AB 2, FSSF, File 1, Box 2.
67. Cited in Hicks, 122.
68. "SSF Respected by Jerry," *Powder River Gazette* (Unofficial newsletter), Vol. 1, No. 3, February 29 [1944]. CAFM, Gordon Sims Papers, AB fonds 29.
69. Tom Gilday, "Tom Gilday," in Blake Heathcote, ed., *Testaments of Honour: Personal Histories of Canada's War Veterans* (Toronto: Doubleday Canada, 2002), 233.
70. Waters, "Anzio — The Role of the 1st Special Service Force," 19.
71. Clark sacked Major-General Lucas for his sluggish performance and inability to breakout of the Anzio beachhead.
72. Memorandum, "Conservation of Supplies," Truscott to subordinate commanders, 6 March 1944. LAC, RG 24, 2 Cdn Para Bn/1 CSSBN War Diary, Vol. 15,301, Appendix 5.
73. War diary entry, 28 May 1944. LAC, RG 24, 2 Cdn Para Bn/1 CSSBN War Diary, Vol. 15,302.
74. Letter, Frederick to GOC Sixth Army Group, "Recommendation for the Award of Unit Citation to First Special Service Force," 20 November 1944, 3. HIA, Robert T. Frederick Papers, Box 1, File memoranda, mss, map 1942. One FSSF officer captured the accomplishments of the Force at Anzio: "We held damn near a third of the Beachhead perimeter, initially with a little more than a 1,000 men and never with more than 2,500. By aggressive patrolling and night attacks in up to battalion strength, we were able to keep Jerry off balance, push is line back from one to two miles, take more than 500 prisoners, and kill well over 1,000 of Hitler's heroes." Underhill, 235.
75. Lieutenant-Colonel Ralph Becket, Transcript of 1999 DHH, taped interviews (hereafter cited as Becket Transcript), 138. LAC, IDCCISM 306330–306340. The Anzio bridgehead had proved costly. In the approximate four months of occupation, the Allies suffered 7,000 killed, 36,000 wounded, and 44,000 non-battle casualties that required hospitalization. Clark, 321.
76. William Sheldon, "Battle -1944 — Anzio to Rome" (hereafter cited as Sheldon Memoir), unpublished memoir, 2. CAFM, Gordon Sims Papers, AB fonds 29.
77. "Summary of our Operations, 1–31 May 1944." Summary of Operations, First Special Service Force Historical Records, War Department The Adjutant General's Office Washington. CAFM, AB 2, FSSF, Box 1.
78. Becket Transcript.
79. *Ibid.*
80. Baker Memoir.
81. "Summary of Enemy Operations, 1–31 May 1944." "B" indicated local time.
82. "Activities of the First Canadian Special Service Bn, CA (A) From 1 May to 10 June 44." DHH, File 145.3 (D2) 1 Cdn SSF, Operations in Italy 1 May to 3 July 1944.
83. Sheldon Memoir. As always, the variance in numbers become difficult to nail down. Fear, memory, exaggeration, multiple sighting of the same vehicle, vantage point, hearsay, etc all play into the recollection of numbers.

NOTES

84. Thomas Memoir.
85. Wickham, 45.
86. Wright, 54.
87. Mitchell Memoir.
88. Sergeant John Rowe (4th Coy, 1st Regiment), interview by authors.
89. Sheldon Memoir.
90. Green Memoir.
91. "Summary of our Operations, 1–31 May 1944."
92. Green Memoir.
93. *Ibid.*
94. Becket Transcript.
95. *Ibid.*
96. *Ibid.*
97. "S-3 Report No. 122, Summary of Allied Situation," 1 June 1944. LAC, RG 24, 2 Cdn Para Bn/1 CSSBN War Diary, Vol. 15,302, Appendix June.
98. "Field Order No. 26," 3 June 1944. LAC, RG 24, War Diary, 1 CSSBN, Vol. 15,302, Appendix June.
99. "Activities of the First Canadian Special Service Bn, CA (A) From 1 May to 10 June 44." DHH, File 145.3 (D2) 1 Cdn SSF, Operations in Italy 1 May-3 July 1944; and "S-3 Report No. 124, Summary of Allied Situation," LAC, RG 24, 2 Cdn Para Bn/1 CSSBN War Diary, Vol. 15,302. The Howze Armoured Task Force consisted of the 81st Reconnaissance Battalion and the 13th Armoured Infantry.
100. War diary entry, 3 June 1944. LAC, RG 24, 2 Cdn Para Bn/1 CSSBN War Diary, Vol. 15,302.
101. "Activities of the First Canadian Special Service Bn, CA (A) From 1 May to 10 June 1944."
102. Colonel Walker, as the commander of the FSSF, would later write a letter to Lieutenant-General Clark, commander, 5th Army, substantiating the Force's claim of first Allied troops into Rome. He wrote, "The foremost elements of this command in the approach on Rome on 4 June 1944, were the 2d and 4th companies of the First Regiment. These companies formed the infantry component of an infantry-tank column approaching the city along Highway 6. The tanks of this column were provided by the 13th Armored Regiment. The column arrived at what is presumed to be the city boundary at 0630 hours. At this point there was a large sign on Highway 6, stating in one word, Roma." Letter, Walker to GOC 5th Army, "Entry of First Special Service Force into City of Rome," 10 July 1944. Summary of Operations, First Special Service Force Historical Records, War Department The Adjutant General's Office Washington. CAFM, AB 2, FSSF, Box 1.
103. "Statement of Captain Gus M. Heilman concerning entry of First Special Service Force troops into the City of Rome on 4 June 1944." Summary of Operations, First Special Service Force Historical Records, War Department The Adjutant General's Office Washington. CAFM, AB 2, 1 FSSF, Box 1.
104. Sheldon Memoir.
105. *Ibid.*
106. *Ibid.*

107. Seymour Korman, "Brig. Gen. Robert T. Frederick Tells How Special Service Troops Were First Allies to Enter Rome," Unknown newspaper clipping, 14 June 1944. CAFM, AB 22, Alastair Neely fonds, Vol. 1, File 4.
108. "Activities of the First Canadian Special Service Bn, CA (A) From 1 May to 10 June 44." DHH, File 145.3 (D2) 1 Cdn SSF, Operations in Italy 1 May to 3 July 1944; and "S-3 Report No. 125, Summary of Allied Situation," 5 June 1944. LAC, RG 24, 2 Cdn Para Bn/1 CSSBN War Diary, Vol. 15,302, Appendix January.
109. William G. Shelton, "William G. Shelton, 1st Lieutenant, Platoon Commander/Company Commander," in Ed Thomas, "Rome Stories. Accounts by Members of the U.S.-Canadian 1st Special Service Force Of the Entry into Rome on June 4, 1944," unpublished manuscript. CAFM, Gordon Sims Papers, AB fonds 29.
110. Underhill, 270.
111. Green Memoir.
112. *Ibid.*
113. War diary entry, 6 June 1944. LAC, RG 24, 2 Cdn Para Bn/1 CSSBN War Diary, Vol. 15,302.
114. "Summary of Enemy Operations, 1–30 June 1944." Summary of Operations, First Special Service Force Historical Records, War Department The Adjutant General's Office Washington. CAFM, AB 2, 1 FSSF, Box 1.
115. *Ibid.*
116. "S-3 Report No. 125, Summary of Allied Situation," 5 June 1944. LAC, RG 24, 2 Cdn Para Bn/1 CSSBN War Diary, Vol. 15, 302, Appendix January.
117. War diary entry, 6 June 1944. LAC, RG 24, 2 Cdn Para Bn/1 CSSBN War Diary, Vol. 15, 302.
118. "Activities of the First Canadian Special Service Battalion From 11 June to 3 July 44." DHH, File 145.3 (D2) 1 Cdn SSF Ops in Italy, 1 May to 3 July 1944. The strength of the American contingent in the combat echelon was 71 officers and 1,131 other ranks. The service battalion, which was all American, was 52 and 644, respectively. *Ibid.*
119. This is based on the entire makeup of the FSSF (i.e., combat and support echelons) using the data provided in the Canadian report: "Activities of the First Canadian Special Service Battalion From 11 June to 3 July 44." DHH, File 145.3 (D2) 1 Cdn SSF Ops in Italy, 1 May to 3 July 1944.
120. Frederick was promoted to major-general in August and in December 1944, was appointed commanding general, 45th Infantry Division, which he held until December 1945. Post war, he held a series of command and staff appointments culminating in division command of the 4th Infantry Division in Fort Ord California, a position he held from December 1948-February 1949. He finished his career in a series of staff appointments. He retired from the military as a major-general on 31 March 1952 due to physical disability. Among his many awards was the Distinguished Service Cross (DSC) with one Bronze Oak Leaf Cluster; one Distinguished Service Medal with Bronze Oak Leaf Cluster; Silver Star; Legion of Merit with one Bronze Oak Leaf Cluster; bronze Star Medal with one Bronze Oak Leaf Cluster; Air Medal; Purple Heart with one Silver and Two Bronze Oak Leaf Clusters; American Defence Service Medal; American Campaign Medal; Asiatic-Pacific Campaign Medal with one Silver Service Star; Army of Occupation Medal with Germany Clasp; World War II Victory Medal; Combat

NOTES

Infantryman Badge; Croix de Guerre with Palm (French); Legion D'Honneur (Officer) with Croix de Guerre with Palm (second award); Order of St. Charles (Grand Officer) (Monaco), Commander, Order of the Crown (Italy); Silver Medal with Valor (Italy); Liberation Cross of Haakon VII (Norway); and Grand Commander of the Order of George the First (Greece). Department of Army, "Statement of Military Service of Robert Tyron Frederick 017 196," CAFM, Gordon Sims Papers, AB fonds 29. See also Hicks, *The Last Fighting General*.

121. Donald Ballantyne (3rd Regiment), interview by authors, 15 September 2003.
122. Private William "Sam" Magee (1st Regiment), interview by authors, 7 February 2002.
123. Private Waling in Hancock and Abbott, *Daring to Die*.
124. Frederick was not the only departure. On 28 June 1944, the 1 CSSBN war diary recorded, "Lt. Colonel Gilday's request for transfer back to the Canadian Army was approved to-day. He had reached the end of his tether at swallowing American Army methods. He had done an excellent job as battalion commander and was offered command of a regiment recently but wants no further part of the Force. He goes with the best wishes of those who served with him and no few Canadian officers will be envious of his getting back into his own army." Interesting to note, at first Colonel Walker had offered command of the 3rd Regiment to Gilday. When he learned that Gilday had requested a return to the Canadian Army, he wrote a deficiency report to accompany Gilday's departure. War diary entry, 28 June 1944. LAC, RG 24, 2 Cdn Para Bn/1 CSSBN War Diary, Vol. 15,302.

CHAPTER 13

1. Becket, 203.
2. As of 1 May 1944, 1 CSSBN strength totalled 53 officers and 676 other ranks. Of this total, three officers and 86 ORs were in hospital. On 10 June 1944, the battalion strength on paper was 48 officers and 588 ORs. The effective strength, however, was 32 officers and 396 other ranks. The 1 CSSBN was short 16 officers and 192 ORs. The strength of the American Forcemen, in the combat echelon, totalled 60 officers and 1,030 ORs. In addition, there were 13 officers and 552 ORs in hospital. The FSSF Service Battalion totalled 57 officers and 775 ORs including those in hospital. Report prepared by Akehurt to NDHQ. Report covering the period of 1 May to 10 June 1943. Item 2: Strength. DHH, File 145.3009 (D7). Monthly reports of 1 CSSBN. August 1942-January 1945.
3. Report covering the period of 1 May to 10 June 1944. Item 7: Reinforcements. DHH, File 145.3009 (D7). Monthly reports of 1 CSSBN. August 1942-January 1945.
4. With these new reinforcements, the battalion's strength was now listed at 650 all ranks. Report covering the period of 11 June to 3 July 1944. Item 7: Reinforcements. DHH, File 145.3009 (D7). Monthly reports of 1 CSSBN. August 1942-January 1945. War diary entry, 23 June 1944, 2 Cdn Para Bn/1 CSSBN War Diary. LAC, RG 24, Vol. 15302.
5. Brigadier E.G. Weeks, Officer IC, Cdn Sec GHQ1 Ech AAI, Memo to file, 28 June 1944. LAC, RG 24, File HQCDn 56/5/1 CSSBN/1 200A5.009 (D53) Correspondence, messages, policies and procedures.

OF COURAGE AND DETERMINATION

6. Once subunit training was completed, the reinforcements underwent two operational readiness tests. The first consisted of a series of company level fire and movements exercises. The second consisted of a physical fitness test consisting of: a route march with full field equipment; a 182-metre swim; rubber boat races, and rope climbing with full equipment. Lieutenant-Colonel K.G. Wickham, Executive Officer, Field Exercise #1, Company in the attack exercise, 28 June 1944. LAC, RG 24, 2 Cdn Para Bn/1 CSSBN War Diary, Vol. 15302, Appendix June; and Lieutenant-Colonel K.G. Wickham, executive officer, physical fitness test, 28 June 1944. LAC, RG 24, 2 Cdn Para Bn/1 CSSBN War Diary, Vol. 15302, Appendix June.
7. The gap between the American and Canadian effective strength continually increased. In his August 1944 monthly report, Akehurst provided the following numbers: Canadian effective strength 55 officers and 641 ORs. American effective strength, combat echelon, 53 officers and 1,064 ORs; service battalion 47 officers and 626 ORs. Report covering the period of 1–31 August 1943. Item 2: Strength. DHH, File 145.3009 (D7). Monthly reports of 1 CSSBN. August 1942-January 1945.
8. CAFM, Gordon Sims fonds; and Burhans, 250.
9. War diary entry, 8 July 1944, 2 Cdn Para Bn/1 CSSBN War diary. LAC, RG 24, Vol. 15302.
10. The APD acronym stands for AP = transport, D = destroyer.
11. Estimate of the enemy situation, Annex 2 to Field Order 1 DR, FSSF HQ, 25 July 1944; Annex 4 Composition of Forward Supply Echelon, 28 July 1944. Annex 4 to Adm 01 to Field Order 1 DR FSSF HQ, 28 July 1944; Adm Order No. 1 to Accompany Field Order 1 DR, FSSF HQ, 28 July 1944. LAC, RG 24, Series C-1, File HQS 20–16–32, Vol. 3, Monthly Reports and State of Project, microfilm reel C-5469.
12. Originally, this operation was called Operation Anvil. It was to be launched simultaneously with Operation Overlord in order to force the enemy to leave a greater percentage of its forces in southern France. However, resources were an issue. Following the successful landing in Normandy, naval elements could be now transferred to the Mediterranean and provide Lieutenant-General Patch with the required naval support to transport and land his troops.
13. The German forces in Southern France were rated as second and third grade troops. They were largely composed of older personnel, wounded soldiers, and *Volksdeutsche* from Poland and Czechoslovakia. Most of the front line divisions had been previously reallocated to other operational theatres. As of spring 1944, only 11 divisions remained. Four of these divisions were described as static divisions, meaning that they had no vehicles. The equipment and weaponry consisted of captured outdated weapons from various countries. As for armour, only the 11th Panzer Division was available. However, two of its tank battalions had been taken and sent to another theatre. Steven J. Zaloga, *Operation Dragoon 1944: France's other D-Day* (London, England: Osprey Publishing Ltd., 2009), 16–19.
14. The units that were part of the 1 ABTF were: British units — 2nd Independent Parachute Brigade Group and 2nd Chemical Battalion. American units — 517th Parachute Regimental Combat Team; 509th Parachute Infantry Combat Team; 550th Glider Infantry Battalion with one platoon of 887th Engineer Company attached; 551st Parachute Infantry Battalion and attached platoon of the 887th Engineer Company; and the 602nd Pack Howitzer Field

NOTES

Artillery Battalion. Michel de Trez, *First Airborne Task Force, Pictorial History of the Allied Paratrooper in the Invasion of Southern France* (Belgium: D-Day Publishing, 1998), 7.

15. The Iles d'Hyeres are a grouping of five Mediterranean islands that are part of the Var Department of southeast France. These consisted of the Geins Peninsula, Iles de Porquerolles, Port-Cros, Iles du Bagaud, and Ile de Levant.
16. "The Attack of Ile de Port Cros," unknown author, non-dated . CAFM, FSSF Memoirs Collection.
17. The Forcemen were supposed to be towed to about 900 metres from the beaches. However many veterans recalled that they were left on their own at a much further distance. Moreover, the Forcemen complained of the noise of the LCA crews and accompanying PT boats. Many thought that the advance toward the landing sites had been compromised. Memorandum, "Lessons learned from the French Campaign, since 15 August 1944," C. Comments concerning naval activities, 2 November 1944, FSSF. DHH, File 145.3009 (D5), Organization and administration correspondence and instruction for 1 CSSBN, July 1944 to December 1944.
18. John Rowe (4th Coy, 1st Regiment), interviewed by authors, 22 October 2003.
19. Intelligence reports estimated the German forces on Port-Cros to total 200 men. These were suspected to be part of a Radar detachment and a security detachment. Estimate of the enemy situation. 1) Enemy dispositions, 1b) Ile de Port-Cros. Appendix 1 to Annex 2 of FO 29, FSSF HQ, In the Field, 3 August 1944. LAC, RG 24, Series C-1, File HQS 20–16–32, Vol. 3, Monthly reports and State of Projects, microfilm reel C-5469.
20. "The Attack of Ile de Port Cros."
21. The island's dimensions were 3.21 kilometres long by 1.60 kilometres wide. Terrain Study — Iles d'Hyeres. Item 3, Port Cros. Appendix 2 to Annex 2 of FO 29, FSSF HQ, In the Field, 3 August 1944. LAC, RG 24, Series C-1, File HQS 20–16–32, Vol. 3, Monthly reports and State of Projects, microfilm reel C-5469.
22. The interrogated prisoners revealed that they were part of 1st Battalion, 917th Grenadier Regiment part of 242nd Regiment stationed on both Port-Cros and Ile Levant. Burhans, 262. Appendix 4 to Annex 2 to FO 29, Battle Order [of the German Army] in Southern France, item 2) 242 Infantry Division, HQ, FSSF, In the Field, 3 August 1944. Colonel Edwin A. Walker, Field Order (FO) 29, FSSF, In the Field, Italy, 4 August 1944. LAC, RG 24, 2 Cdn Para Bn/1 CSSBN, War Diary, Vol. 15302, August 1944, Annex. Following the capture of the "artillery battery" on Ile De Levant, information gathered from prisoners revealed that the island was defended by 120 men of 3rd Coy, 917th Grenadier Regiment. Section 2 — Intelligence, Summary of Enemy Operations, 1–31 August 1944. LAC, RG 24, Vol. 10993, File 284SF1.013 (D1) Operations.
23. Fort l'Eminence was built during the Napoleonic era. It was part of Toulon's outer fortification system. "The central fort was concrete and rock amalgam structure, the sides and top 12 feet thick. On top of the roof was an additional 20 feet of earth and gravel. Three sides of outer wall were sheer drops of 40 to 80 feet and the fourth was on ground level on which the only road into the fort was constructed. A deep wide moat separated the inner and outer walls. All around fields of fire were affected by clearing all trees and bush to ground level." "The Attack of Ile de Port Cros." UP correspondent Clinton B. Conger provided additional

details regarding the Fort de l'Eminence formidable defences, "Fort de l'Eminence had a moat between 30 to 40 feet deep, with the approaches covered by four rows of trenches with strong stone machine-gun nests in four rows and a double apron of barbed wire. The walls were 30 feet high at the lowest point, consisting of two stone walls three feet thick sandwiching 10 to 15 feet of earth between them." Clinton B. Conger, Canuck-Yank Unit Wins Epic Victory, *The Montreal Star*, Tuesday, 18 August 1944, Vol. 76, No. 193, 1, 14, microfilm reel N-39722.

24. Record of 1st Regiment FSSF during mission occupation of Isle De Port-Cros — D-1/D-Day. LAC, RG 24, 2 Cdn Para Bn/1 CSSBN War diary, Vol. 15302, Appendix 9.
25. *Ibid.*
26. Jim Summersides (4th Coy, 1st Regiment), interviewed by authors 21 October 2003.
27. John Rowe (4th Coy, 1st Regiment), interviewed by authors, 22 October 2003.
28. Burhans, 267. Record of 1st Regiment FSSF during mission occupation of Isle De Port-Cros — D-1/D-Day. LAC, RG 24, 2 Cdn Para Bn/1 CSSBN War diary, Vol. 15302, Appendix 9. "The Attack of Ile de Port Cros."
29. Section 2 — Intelligence. Summary of our Operations, 1–31 August 1944. LAC, RG 24, Vol. 10993, File 284SSF1.013 (D1), Reports on Operations. 1 SSF, Italy, January- October 1944.
30. Section 2 — Intelligence. Summary of our Operations, 1–31 August 1944. LAC, RG 24, Vol. 10993, File 284SSF1.013 (D1), Reports on Operations. 1 SSF, Italy, January to October 1944.
31. Record of 1st Regiment FSSF during mission occupation of Isle De Port-Cros — D-1/D-Day. LAC, RG 24, 2 Cdn Para Bn/1 CSSBN War Diary, Vol. 15302, Appendix 9.
32. The island was eight kilometres long by 1.6 kilometres wide with its highest elevation being 130 meters. The estimated strength of Ile de Levant enemy forces was thought to be: two infantry companies; one battery coast defence, and service personnel totalling 400 men. Terrain Study — Iles d'Hyeres. Item 2. Ile de Levant. Appendix 2 to Annex 2 of FO 29, FSSF HQ, In the Field, 3 August 1944. LAC, RG 24, Series C-1, File HQS 20–16–32, Vol. 3, Monthly reports and State of Projects, microfilm reel C-5469. Estimate of the enemy situation. 1) Enemy dispositions, 1a) Ile de Levant. Appendix 1 to Annex 2 of FO 29, FSSF HQ, In the Field, 3 August 1944. LAC, RG 24, Series C-1, File HQS 20–16–32, Vol. 3, Monthly reports and State of Projects, microfilm reel C-5469.
33. Walker, Field Order (FO) 29, FSSF, In the Field, Italy, 4 August 1944. LAC, RG 24, 2 Cdn Para Bn/1 CSSBN, War Diary, Vol. 15302, August 1944, Annex.
34. Earlier reconnaissance reported that there were 20 possible landing sites on Ile de Levant's south coast. Of these 15 could be considered for landings but presented various challenges. 2nd Regiment landed on beaches identified by reconnaissance teams as sectors 11 and 13. Sector 11 was described as a "small inlet suitable for infantry landing up stream valley in dead ground to road. Tracks exist is valley. Bushes and small trees afford cover. Road at this point about 70 feet high." Sector 13 was described as, "suitable for rubber boats to land infantry. Fairly steep slopes leading to shrubs and small trees, with ground sloping gently towards the old Penitentiary ruins distant about 1100 yards, through vineyards and grown trees." Terrain Study — Iles d'Hyeres. Item 2: Ile de Levant, b) South coast scrambles. Appendix 2 to Annex 2 of FO 29, FSSF HQ, In the Field, 3 August 1944. LAC, RG 24, Series C-1, File HQS 20–16–32,

NOTES

Vol. 3, Monthly reports and State of Projects, microfilm reel C-5469. Exact topographical descriptions of the 3rd Regiment's landing sites could not be confirmed. Only information available was coordinates Z376899 and Z377902. Operations–Section 1. Summary of our operations, 1–31 July 1944. CAFM, AB fonds 2, FSSF, Vol. 2, War Department, The Adjutant General's Office, Washington. W.D. Records Branch, AGO, Historical Records Section, Field Order 4, HQ, 2nd Regiment, FSSF, 9 August 1944. CAFM, Charlie Mann fonds.

35. Underhill, 281.
36. Peter Smith (4th Coy, 3rd Regiment), interviewed by authors, 7 October 2003.
37. Becket, 192.
38. *Ibid.*, 192.
39. Underhill, 283.
40. Peter Kroll (4th Coy, 3rd Regiment), interviewed by authors, 10 October 2003.
41. Sergeant Howard Rutsey, staff writer, *The Maple Leaf*, with the First Special Service Force, non-dated (September 1944). CAFM, Charles Mann fonds.
42. Underhill, 283.
43. Section 2 — Intelligence. Summary of our Operations, 1–31 August 1944. LAC, RG 24, Vol. 10993, File 284SSF1.013 (D1), Reports on Operations. 1SSF, Italy, January– October 1944
44. Lloyd D.M. Dunlop (6th Coy, 3rd Regiment), interviewed by authors, 1 October 2003. 1 CSSBN losses were 13 killed and 38 wounded. Casualties 1 Cdn Spec Service Bn for Significant Periods of Operations, (HQ54-27-22-3 (DR4), 11 January 1946 as listed in Appendix "B" of 1st Canadian Special Service Battalion, Army Headquarters Report No. 5 Historical Section (G.S.), 26 February 1946. DHH.
45. Underhill, 283.
46. Conger, 1 and 14.
47. As quoted in Adleman and Walton, 230.
48. War diary entries of 12–30 August 1944. LAC, RG 24, 2 Cdn Para Bn/1 CSSBN War diary, Vol. 15302.
49. Letter, Colonel C.L. Laurin, director of records, to director of administration, NDHQ, 11 March 1944. LAC, RG 24, File HQS 20-16-32. Vol. 2DD. Monthly reports. State of Projects, 1 CSSBN, microfilm reel C-5468.
50. Airborne operations commenced on 15 August 1944 before dawn and continued throughout the day. The 1 ABTF was parachuted into three drop zones in the Le Muy area. A total of 9,112 airborne personnel, 400,000 pounds of equipment and supplies, 213 artillery pieces and anti-tank guns, and 221 vehicles were transported by air over the Mediterranean and dropped behind enemy lines. De Trez, 8.
51. Walker, Field Order 30, FSSF, 20 August 1944. LAC, RG 24, 2 Cdn Para Bn/1 CSSBN War Diary, Vol. 15302.
52. *Ibid.*
53. The German 19th Army, 62nd Corps, under Lieutenant-General Ferdinand Neuling, occupied and defended the French coastline from Toulon to the French Italian border. Major-General Otto Fretter-Pico's 148th Division was deployed in the areas through which the FSSF had to advance. Chapter 4, "German Plans and Organization," Jeffrey J. Clarke, *U.S.*

Army in WW II. European Theatre of Ops. Riviera to the Rhine, www.ibibilo.org/hyperwar/USA/USA-E-Riviera/index.html, accessed 21 May 2012

54. II. Estimate of the enemy situation. 6) Units in contact. 7) Reserves. Annex 2 to Field Order 30, Intelligence Annex, HQ, FSSF, Frejus, France, 20 August 1944. LAC, RG 24, 2 Cdn Para Bn/1 CSSBN War Diary, Vol. 15302.
55. Operations–Section 1. Summary of our operations, 1–31 August 1944. CAFM, AB fonds 2, FSSF, Vol. 2, War Department, The Adjutant General's Office, Washington. W.D. Records Branch, AGO, Historical Records Section.
56. Memorandum: Lessons learned from the French Campaign, since 15 August 1944, Phase 2 — Rapid Pursuit of an enemy in orderly retreat. FSSF, 2 November 1944. LAC, RG 24, 2 Cdn Para Bn/1 CSSBN War Diary, Vol. 15302.
57. The FSSF Cannon Company was formed from absorbed elements of the Ranger Cannon Company which fought with the Force in Anzio. A Ranger Cannon Company consisted of four halftracks. Each vehicle was identified using the playing card club, diamond, heart, and spade designations. The armament consisted of a French 75-mm cannon, .50-calibre and .30-calibre machine guns, and for mountain operations one 81-mm mortar. Memorandum: Lessons learned from the French Campaign, since 15 August 1944, Phase 2 — Rapid pursuit of an enemy in orderly retreat. The Cannon Company. FSSF, 2 November 1944. LAC, RG 24, 2 Cdn Para Bn/1 CSSBN War Diary, Vol. 15302.
58. Entry of 24 August 1944. 2) Chronology. Section 2 — Intelligence Summary of Enemy Operations, 1–31 August 1944. LAC, RG 24, Vol. 10993, File 284SF1.013 (D1), Operations.
59. Joe T. Jamieson (6th Coy, 3rd Regiment), interviewed by authors, 1 October 2003.
60. Green Memoir, 67.
61. Captain Finn W. Roll, Intelligence prisoner of war report. HQ, FSSF. 22 August 1944. LAC, RG 24, 2 Cdn Para Bn/1 CSSBN War diary, Vol. 15302. Of the 32 prisoners captured on the 22 August, 20 were Poles. Entry of 22 August 1944. 2) Chronology. Section 2 — Intelligence Summary of Enemy Operations, 1–31 August 1944. LAC, RG 24, Vol. 10993, File 284SSF1.013 (D1). Reports on Operations, 1SSF, Italy, January to October 1944.
62. The training of new Forcemen continued back in Santa Maria Capua Vetere, Italy. Moreover, returning FSSF wounded arrived daily at the FSSF training facilities. On 30 August, 60 Canadians and 191 American reinforcements arrived at the FSSF Command Post at St-Roman, France. A second replacement-training group of 225 Americans, recruited from 7th Army replacements centres, were sent to the FSSF training school. Operations–Section 1. Summary of our operations, 1–31 August 1944. CAFM, AB fonds 2, FSSF, Vol. 2, War Department, The Adjutant General's Office, Washington. W.D. Records Branch, AGO, Historical Records Section.
63. Becket, 204.
64. Memorandum: Lessons learned from the French Campaign, since 15 August 1944.
65. Private E. Scharf, Interrogation of Prisoners of War, HQ, FSSF, In the field, 29 August 1944. LAC, RG 24, 2 Cdn Para Bn/1 CSSBN War Diary, Vol. 15302.
66. Captain Finn W. Roll, Intelligence prisoner of war report. HQ, FSSF 22 August 1944. LAC, RG 24, 2 Cdn Para Bn/1 CSSBN War Diary, Vol. 15302.

NOTES

67. Unidentified (officer of 2nd Regiment, could be Major Murray D. Kirkwood, commanding officer of 1st Battalion, 2nd Regiment) "Memoires," Unpublished, non-dated , 35. CAFM, FSSF Memories Collection.
68. S-3 Periodic Report No 134. Our Operations for Period, 25–26 August 1944. HQ, FSSF, 26 August 1944. Operations–Section 1. LAC, RG 24, 2 Cdn Para Bn/1 CSSBN War diary, Vol. 15302. Summary of our operations, 1–31 August 1944. DND, CFB Petawawa, AB fonds 2, FSSF, Vol. 2. War Department, The Adjutant General's Office, Washington. W.D. Records Branch, AGO, Historical Records Section.
69. Summary of our operations, 1–31 August 1944. CAFM, AB fonds 2, FSSF, Vol. 2. War Department, The Adjutant General's Office, Washington. W.D. Records Branch, AGO, Historical Records Section. German POW's are listed in August daily entries. 2) Chronology. Section 2 — Intelligence Summary of Enemy Operations, 1 -31 August 1944. LAC, RG 24, Vol. 10993, File 284SSF1.013 (D1) Reports on Operations. 1SSF, Italy, January- October 1944.
70. Section V — Medical. Information consolidated by FSSF HQ from daily blotter form submitted to surgeon, Seventh Army covering month of August 1944, pertaining to FSSF personnel only. LAC, RG 24, Vol. 10993, File 284SSF1.013 (D1). Reports on Operations 1 SS Force, Italy, January-October 1944; and Report prepared by Lieutenant-Colonel J.F.R Akehurst to secretary of NDHQ, A.P.O 4994, c/o U.S. Army, Italy, 1 CSSBN, (AF), Report covering the period of 1–31 August 1944, Item 2: Strengths, DHH, File 145.3009 (D7), Monthly reports of 1 CSSBN, August 1942 to January 1945. Casualties 1 Cdn Spec Service Bn for Significant Periods of Operations, (HQ54–27–22–3 (DR4), 11 January 1946 as listed in Appendix "B" of 1st Canadian Special Service Battalion, Army Headquarters Report No. 5, Historical Section (G.S.), 26 February 1946.
71. S-3 Periodic report No. 146. Our operations for period, 6–7 September 1944. HQ, FSSF, 7 September 1944. LAC, RG 24, 2 Cdn Para Bn/1 CSSBN War diary, Vol. 15302.
72. Memorandum: Lessons learned from the French Campaign, since 15 August 1944.
73. Green Memoir.
74. Becket, 208–09.
75. War diary entry of 16 September 1944. LAC, RG 24, 2 Cdn Para Bn/1 CSSBN War diary, Vol. 15302.
76. War diary entry of 30 September 1944. LAC, RG 24, 2 Cdn Para Bn/1 CSSBN War diary, Vol. 15302.
77. Report prepared by Akehurt to secretary of NDHQ, Report covering the period of 1–30 September 1944. Item 6: Discipline and Morale. DHH, File 145.3009 (D7). Monthly reports of 1 CSSBN. August 1942-January 1945.
78. Operations–Section 1. Summary of our operations, 1–30 September 1944. CAFM, AB fonds 2, FSSF, Vol. 2. War Department, The Adjutant General's Office, Washington. W.D. Records Branch, AGO, Historical Records Section.
79. Report prepared by Akehurt to secretary of NDHQ. Report covering the period of 1 -31 October 1944. Item 5: Administration. DHH, File 145.3009 (D7). Monthly reports of 1 CSSBN. August 1942-January 1945.

80. Operations–Section 1. Summary of our operations, 1–31 October 1944. LAC, RG 24, Vol. 10993, Reports on Ops. File 284SSF1.013 (D1) Reports on Operations. 1SSF, Italy, January-October 1944.
81. Section 2 — Intelligence. Summary of enemy operations, 1–31 October 1944. LAC, RG 24, Vol. 10993, File 284SSF1.013 (D1), Reports on Operations. 1SSF, Italy. January to October 1944.
82. Unidentified (officer of 2nd Regiment, could be Major Murray D. Kirkwood, commanding officer of 1st Battalion, 2nd Regiment), "Memoires," unpublished, non-dated, 41. CAFM, FSSF Memories Collection.
83. Operations–Section 1. Summary of our operations, 1–31 October 1944. LAC, RG 24, Vol. 10993, Reports on Ops, File 284SSF1.013 (D1), Reports on Operations, 1 SSF, Italy, January-October 1944.
84. War diary entries 1–30 September and 1–31 October 1944. LAC, RG 24, 2 Cdn Para Bn/1 CSSBN War diary, Vol. 15302.
85. War diary entry of 12 October 1944. LAC, RG 24, 2 Cdn Para Bn/1 CSSBN War diary, Vol. 15302.
86. The continued requests to provide reinforcements to the 1 CSSBN was now starting to frustrate Brigadier Weeks. He wrote to the minister explaining that as of the 30 September 1944, a total of 24 officers and 494 ORs had been sent to the battalion. During September, another request had been received from Akehurst for an additional five officers and 90 ORs. The GOC, 1st Canadian Corps, refused this request and instructed Weeks that "no further reinforcements would be sent to 1 Cdn Spec Serv Bn." Memorandum Weeks, to MND, 3 October 1944. LAC, RG 24, Series C-2, CMHQ, Vol. 12540, File 6/1 Spec Serv Bn/1/2, Org and Adm.
87. War diary entry of 10 October 1944. LAC, RG 24, 2 Cdn Para Bn/1 CSSBN War diary, Vol. 15302.
88. War diary entry of 8 October 1944. LAC, RG 24, 2 Cdn Para Bn/1 CSSBN War diary, Vol. 15302. Lieutenant-Colonel Becket took over command of the battalion. This unforeseen turn of events surprised 1 CSSBN personnel. The war diary chronicler related that Lieutenant-Colonel Akehurst, "will be missed both in and Battalion and the Force, he is a most capable officer and highly regarded by all ranks…" On 8 October, Akehurst returned to FSSF Base Echelon awaiting directives from 1st Echelon as to his next course of action. Even though Becket assumed command for a very short time, he was unclear as to the reason why Akehurst left. Becket, 260. On 11 October, Akehurst briefed Becket on all the ongoing battalion administrative files. On the 22 October, Akehurst left to go to 1st Echelon, in Rome and was expected to return in about one week. Akehurst returned on 2 November following a visit with General E.L.M. Burns. During their conversation, Burns advised Akehurst to travel to London and discuss with Lieutenant-General Stuart the future of the 1 CSSBN. Meanwhile, Akehurst reassumed the command of the 1 CSSBN. On 16 November, Akehurst accepted a temporary position working for Major-General Frederick until he received instructions from the commander of 1st Canadian Corps to go to England. On 21 November, Akehurst received a telegram from Sixth Army Group regarding future of the Force's Canadian element. Akehurst left the next day for London to protest the Sixth Army Group's proposed

NOTES

plans regarding the 1 CSSBN. The following day Akehurst left for London to meet with senior CMHQ officers to discuss issues regarding the battalion. Akehurst returned from London on the 30 November and rejoined the battalion. War diary entries of 11, 22 October, 2, 16, 21, 22, 30 November 1944. LAC, RG 24, 2 Cdn Para Bn/1 CSSBN War diary, Vol. 15302.

89. Memorandum, Weeks to the MND, 3 October 1944. LAC, RG 24, Series C-2, CMHQ, Vol. 12540, File 6/1 Spec Serv Bn/1/2, Org and Adm.
90. Memorandum, Stuart to MND, 7 October 1944. LAC, RG 24, Series C-2, CMHQ, Vol. 12540, File 6/1 Spec Serv Bn/1/2, Org and Adm.
91. Memorandum from the office of the deputy chief of the general staff to the chief of the general staff, 13 October 1944. LAC, RG 24, Series C-1, File HQs 20-1-32, Vol. 2. Policy Formation of FSSF Bn, microfilm reel C-5481.
92. Underhill, 302.
93. Eugene Forward, (3rd Coy, 3rd Regiment), interviewed by authors, 1 October 2003.
94. Underhill, 302.
95. Memorandum: Lessons learned from the French Campaign, since 15 August 1944.
96. Casualties 1 Cdn Spec Service Bn for Significant Periods of Operations, (HQ54-27-22-3 (DR4), 11 January 1946 as listed in Appendix "B" of 1st Canadian Special Service Battalion, Army Headquarters Report No. 5, Historical Section (G.S.), 26 February 1946.
97. Memorandum: Lessons learned from the French Campaign, since 15 August 1944.
98. Message from General Jacob Loucks Devers, commander, Sixth Army Group to 1st Airborne Task Force HQ, 10 November 1944. DHH, File 145.3009 (D3). Instruction and directives for 1 CSSBN, January 1943-December 1944. The message was quickly forwarded to Akehurst. Angered by this unexpected news, the CO drafted a document arguing for his battalion's retention and future service within the Canadian Army and travelled to London to plead his case. Memorandum, Akehurst, "Return of Canadian personnel, namely 1 Cdn Sp Sv Bn to reinforcement channels of Canadian Army," 21 November 1944. LAC, RG 24 Series C-2, CMHQ, Vol. 12540, File 6/1 Spec Serv Bn/1/2, Organization and administration, The 1 CSSBN war diary entry of 21 November 1944 confirmed that Akehurst had received Devers's message, "and plans to leave for London tomorrow (22 November 1944) to protest the proposed plans." War diary entry of 21 November 1944. LAC, RG 24, 2 Cdn Para Bn/1 CSSBN War diary, Vol. 15302.
99. Memorandum, Akehurst, "Return of Canadian personnel, namely 1 Cdn Sp Sv Bn to reinforcement channels of Canadian Army," 21 November 1944. LAC, RG 24 Series C-2, CMHQ, Vol. 12540, File 6/1 Spec Serv Bn/1/2, Organization and administration.
100. Message from Allied Army Italy, to 1st Canadian Corps, 27 November 1944, LAC, RG 24, Vol. 10404, File HQS 56/6/1 CSSBN/1/2 200A5.009 (D53). Correspondence, message, policy procedures.
101. NDHQ sent messages to all echelons involved in the disbandment of the 1 CSSBN instructing that, "no publicity be given to disbandment but if at later date it should be decided to make public announcement we would expect to be consulted in advance with regards to wording of release and to arrange for simultaneous announcement here." NDHQ gave no reason for its request for secrecy. Message from Defensor, Ottawa to Canmilitry, 7 November

1944. LAC, RG 24, Series C-2, CMHQ, Vol. 12540, File 6/1 Spe Ser Bn/1/2, Organization and administration. This message was then relayed by CMHQ to 1st Canadian Army. CMHQ instructed that the message be forwarded to SHAEF. Message from Canmilitry to 1st Canadian Army, 10 November 1944. LAC, RG 24, Series C-2, CMHQ, Vol. 12540, File 6/1 Spe Ser Bn/1/2, Organization and administration.

CHAPTER 14

1. Private Morris Lazarus (5th Coy, 2nd Regiment), interviewed by authors, 3 October 2003.
2. Underhill, 303. American historian, Colonel Dziuban explained, "the very nature and status of the Force required frequent attention of the Combined Chiefs of Staff for proposals for employment of this group of less than 2,000 men, as well as diplomatic exchanges to obtain Canadian acceptance of proposals — all in all an inordinate amount of high-level consideration in relation to the size of the Force. But, from the point of view of Canadian-U.S. relations, the unique experiment was a remarkable success." Dziuban, *Military Relations Between The United States and Canada*, 268–69.
3. During this visit, Akehurst was in London, from 22–30 November 1944, attending various meetings with CMHQ staff regarding the disbandment of the 1 CSSBN. War diary entry, 28 November 1944, 2 Cdn Para Bn/1 CSSBN War Diary. LAC, RG 24, Vol. 15302.
4. Dunn's report, Item 16. Report (1 CSSBN, Disbandment) from Dunn to chief of staff, CMHQ, 9 December 1944. LAC, RG 24, Vol. 13599, War Diary, 2nd Ech AAI, December 1944, Appendix 95.
5. Brigadier W.N. Bostock discussed with the DAA and QMG Canadian Liaison Section, 6th Airborne Division, of the possibility of sending 1 CSSBN parachute-trained personnel to 1st Canadian Parachute Battalion. The liaison officer stated that he would gladly take all the officers immediately and absorb some of the NCOs. Memorandum from Bostock to deputy adjutant general, 25 November 1944. LAC, RG 24, Series C-2, CMHQ, Vol. 12540, File 6/1 CSSBN/1/2, Organization and administration. Message from CANDEX, Allied Army Italy, to 1st Canadian Corps, CDN 02E, November 1944. LAC, RG 24, Series C-1, NDHQ, Vol. 10404, File HQ 56/6/1 CSSBN/1/2, 200A5.009 (D53). Correspondence, messages, policy procedures.
6. Message to Foulkes, 27 November 1944. LAC, RG 24, Series C-2, CMHQ, Vol. 12540. File 6/1 Spec Serv Bn/1/2, Organization and administration.
7. Message from CANDEX Allied Army Italy, to 1 CBR GP CDH, 02E AAI PMCT, AAI, 11 November 1944. LAC, RG 24, Series C-2,CMHQ, Vol. 10404, File HQ 56/6/1 CSSBN/1/2, 200A5.009 (D53). Correspondence, message policy procedures.
8. Memorandum of recommendation by Akehurst, 24 November 1944. LAC, RG 24, Series C-2, CMHQ, Vol. 12540, File 6/1 CSSBN/1/2, Organization and administration.
9. *Ibid*.
10. Letter, from Montague, 28 November 1944. LAC, RG 24, Vol. 10624, File 215C1.009 (D243), Reinforcements.

NOTES

11. Memorandum regarding special formation from Major Edward H. Clay, Adjutant, HQ FSSF, 4 December 1944. CAFM, Gordon Sims fonds.
12. *Ibid.*
13. War diary entry, 5 December 1944, 2 Cdn Para Bn/1 CSSBN War diary. LAC, RG 24, Vol. 15302.
14. Peter Kroll (4th Coy, 3rd Regiment), interviewed by authors, 10 October 2003.
15. War diary entry, 5 December 1944, 2 Cdn Para Bn/1 CSSBN War diary. LAC, RG 24, Vol. 15302.
16. "Many of Famous First Special Service Force serving in Norway. Disbanding of Braves was a sad day Corp[oral] Otis C. Crabbe Jr. writes to wife residing here," *The Independent Record*, 11 June 1945, 5. CAFM, AB 22, Alastair Neely fonds, Vol. 1, File 5.
17. Peter Smith (4th Coy, 3rd Regiment), interviewed by authors, 7 October 2003.
18. Vernon J. Doucette (4th Coy, 3rd Regiment), interviewed by authors, 29 September 2003.
19. Charlie Mann, quoted in Rehr, *Suicide Missions.*
20. Bert Hopkins (2nd Coy, 2nd Regiment), interviewed by authors, 20 October 2003.
21. Green Memoir.
22. Item 6) Discipline and morale. Monthly report of the activities of the 1 CSSBN from 1 November 1944 to 9 January 1945. DHH, File 145.3009 (D7). Monthly reports of 1 CSSBN, August 1942 to January 1945.
23. Sergeant John Rowe (4th Coy, 1st Regiment), interviewed by authors 22 October 2003.
24. Peppard, 174–75.
25. Unidentified author, *First Special Service Force* (Unpublished manuscript, non-dated). CAFM, FSSF, Memories Collection.
26. War diary entries 8, 9 December 1944. LAC, RG 24, Vol. 13579, Canadian Section, GHQ, 1st Echelon, Allied Armies Italy.
27. War diary entry, 18 December 1944, 2 Cdn Para Bn/1 CSSBN War diary. LAC, RG 24, Vol. 15302.
28. Item 5) Administration. Monthly report of the activities of the 1 CSSBN from 1 November 1944 to 9 January 1945. DHH, File 145.3009 (D7). Monthly reports of 1 CSSBN, August 1942 to January 1945.
29. Brigadier Thomas Graeme Gibson, GOC, 1 CBRG stated that 1 CSSBN personnel remaining Italy had to undergo NCO and Canadian weapons refresher courses before they could considered as reinforcements. Memo to 1st Canadian Base Reinforcement Group war diary. 9 December 1944. LAC, RG 24, Series C-1, NDHQ, Vol. 10404, File HQS 56/6/1 CSSBN/1/2 2000A.5009 (D53). Correspondence, messages, and policy procedures.
30. War diary entry of 16 December 1944. LAC, RG 24, Vol. 16711, HQ, 1 Canadian Base Reinforcement Group.
31. War diary entry of 17 December 1944, 2 Cdn Para Bn/1 CSSBN War diary. LAC, RG 24, Vol. 15302. The reorganization of 1 CSSBN into two groups was completed on 17 December 1944. War diary entry of 17 December 1944. LAC, RG 24, Vol. 16711, HQ, 1 Canadian Base Reinforcement Group.
32. Item 6) Discipline and morale. Monthly report of the activities of the 1st Canadian Special

Service Battalion from 1 November 1944 to 9 January 1945. DHH, File 145.3009 (D7). Monthly reports of 1 CSSBN, August 1942 to January 1945.

33. Message from Foulkes to Montague, 11 December 1944. LAC, RG 24 Series C-2, CMHQ, Vol. 12540, Files 6/1 Spec Serv Bn/1/2, Organization and administration.

34. Letter from Foulkes, to general officers commanding, 1 Canadian Infantry Division and 5 Canadian Armoured Division, 11 December 1944. LAC, RG 24, 2 Cdn ParaBn/1 CSSBN, War Diary, Vol. 15302.

35. Memorandum from Christie Command to officer commanding 1st, 2nd, and 3rd Battalions, 20 December 1944. A copy of this memo was forwarded to Major J.V.J. Biscoe who was overseeing the transfer of 1 CSSBN personnel to the CIC. DHH, File 145.3009 (D3). Instruction and directives for 1 CSSBN, January 1943 to December 1944.

36. Major A.T. Brown, GSO2 of HQ, 1st Canadian Base Reinforcement Group, Canadian Army, CMF issued Operational Instruction No. 4, 16 December 1944 providing directives to the 2 Canadian Non-Effective Transit Depot (NETD) personnel regarding upcoming training requirements for the parachute qualified 1st Canadian Special Service Battalion sent to their location. DHH, File 145.3009 (D3). Instructions and directions for the 1 CSSBN, January 1943 to December 1944. War diary entry of 17 December 1944. LAC, RG 24, Vol. 16711, HQ, 1 Canadian Base Reinforcement Group.

37. Item 6) Discipline and morale. Monthly report of the activities of the 1st Canadian Special Service Battalion from 1 November 1944 to 9 January 1945. DHH, File 145.3009 (D7). Monthly reports of 1 CSSBN, August 1942 to January 1945.

38. War diary entry, 27 December 1944, 2 Cdn Para Bn/1 CSSBN War diary. LAC, RG 24, Vol. 15302.

39. Memorandum from Weeks to ADAG (A), 9 January 1945. LAC, RG 24, Series C-2, CMHQ, Vol. 12540, File 6/1 Spec Serv Bn/1/2, Organization and administration.

40. Item 7) General. Monthly report of the activities of the 1st Canadian Special Service Battalion from 1 November 1944 to 9 January 1945. DHH, File 145.3009 (D7). Monthly reports of 1 CSSBN, August 1942 to January 1945.

41. War diary entry, 9 January 1945, 2 Cdn Para Bn/1 CSSBN War diary. LAC, RG 24, Vol. 15302. Brigadier W.H.S. Macklin DCGS, CMHQ, issued CMHQ Directive No. 120 regarding NDHQ's instruction regarding the disbandment of the FSSF and 1 CSSBN. "Please note that NDHQ instructed that no publicity whatever is to be given concerning the recent disbandment of the Special Service Force. In this connection the U.K. censorship has a permanent stop on this as well as other disbandments, and the personnel of the unit have already been briefed regarding loose talk and including the information in letters." CMHQ, Office Instruction No. 120. LAC, RG 24, Series C-2, CMHQ, Vol. 12540, File 6/1 Spec Serve Bn/1/2, Organization and administration. On 12 January, a letter was sent from the CGS to the Director of Censorship explaining that the Supreme Commander, Allied Expeditionary Forces request that for reasons of military security no publicity whatsoever be given regarding the disbandment of the FSSF and 1 CSSBN. Thus, nothing regarding this event was to be published in Canada. Furthermore, the chief postal and telegraph censors was informed to, "take all necessary steps to ensure that there is no leakage by means of communications over

NOTES

which they exercise authority." Letter from CGS to Mr. F. Charpentier, director of censorship, 12 January 1945. LAC, RG 24, Series C-1, NDHQ, File HQS 20-1-32, Vol. 2, Policy, formation of FSSF BN, microfilm reel C-5481.

42. After Order No. 1, 18 December 1945 issued by Directorate of Records supplement to daily Order No. 1, dated 9 January 1945. LAC, Part 2 Orders, 2 Cdn Para Bn/1 CSSBN.

43. The General Order number confirming the disbandment was G.O. 203/45. The authority number confirming the transfer of ex 1 CSSBN personnel to the #5 CITR was Auth 406/ Spec Serv Bn/1 (AAG)/12 January 1945. After that Order No. 1, 18 December 1945 issued by Directorate of Records supplement to daily Order No. 1, dated 9 January 1945. LAC, Part 2: Orders, 2 Cdn Para Bn/1 CSSBN. The disbandment was confirmed on 31 January 1945, in the CMHQ's Administrative Order, No. 14. CMHQ Administrative Order, No. 14, Part "A" U.K. stated that "No. 1 Canadian Special Services Battalion, a) Approval is granted for the disbandment of Series 1354/1 — 1 Cdn SS Bn wef 10 January 1945 (Authority CSG 139). B) Serial 1354/1 will disband under instrs of HQ CRU." LAC, RG 24, Series C-2, CMHQ, Vol. 1 2540, File 6/1 Spec Serv Bn/1/2. Organization and administration.

44. Letter from Akehurst (CO, 7 Cdn Inf Trg Bn) to Commander 13 Cdn Inf Trg Bde, 3 April 1945. LAC, Lieutenant-Colonel J.F.R Akehurst personnel file.

45. George Wright (1st Coy, 1st Regiment), interviewed by authors, 16 October 2003.

46. Minutes of meeting (Personnel of PAR Corps Training On American Weapons to Canada). NDHQ, Ottawa, 6 June 1945. List of Para Corps trained on American weapons included., London, England, 3 June 1945. LAC, RG 24 Series C-1, NDHQ, File HQS 20-1-32. Policy, Composition of Formation of FSSF Bn, microfilm reel, C-5481.

47. Wright, 61.

48. Peter Smith (4th Coy, 3rd Regiment), interviewed by authors, 7 October 2003.

49. Joe Jamieson (6th Coy, 3rd Regiment), interviewed by authors, 1 October 2003.

50. Letter from Murchie to MND, 23 April 1945. LAC, RG 24, Series C-1, NDHQ, File HQS 20-1-32. Policy composition of formation of FSSBn, microfilm reel C-5481.

51. The document was logged as P.C. 71/3341, and signed off by Treasury Board on 7 May 1945. LAC, RG 2, Orders in Council, Vol. 4462, 23 April 1945. The document was identified as a secret document with a non-publication order. Order-in-Council, P.C.71/3341, 7 May 1945. LAC, RG 24, Series C-1, NDHQ, File HQS 20-1-32, Vol. 2, Policy Formation of the FSSF Bn, microfilm reel C-5481. CMHQ was informed of this Order-in- Council on 4 June 1945. Note from Adjutant-General, Major-General A.E. Walford, NDHQ to CMHQ, 4 June 1945. LAC, RG 24, Series C-1, NDHQ, File HQS 20-4-32 Vol. 1. Mobilization and organization. Plough Project (1 SSBN), microfilm reel C-5436.

52. Memorandum from DCGS (A) to CGS, Ottawa, 6 January 1945. LAC, RG 24, Series C-1, NDHQ, File HQS 20-1-32, Vol. 2. Policy Formation of the FSSF Bn, microfilm reel C-5481. It seems that the publication of this event did not cause concern with the War Department staff. This disbandment of 1 CSSBN was published in General Order G.O. 203, 1945, Disbandment — Active units.

53. Burhans, 316-20.

54. "Many of Famous First Special Service Force serving in Norway. Disbanding of Braves was a

sad day Corp[oral] Otis C. Crabbe Jr writes to wife residing here," *The Independent Record*, 11 June 1945, 5. CAFM, AB 22, Alastair Neely fonds, Vol. 1, File 5.
55. Burhans, 316–20.
56. *Ibid.*, 298.
57. List of fatal casualties in 1st Canadian Special Service Battalion and 1st Canadian Parachute Battalion, 1939/45, 27 December 1948 by War Service Records. DHH, File 145.3065 (D1). Casualties.
58. The British awards and honours were: Distinguished Service Order — 2; Member of the Order of The British Empire — 1; Military Medal — 2; Distinguished Conduct Medal — 1; Mention in Despatches — 11. American Awards: Distinguished Service Cross — 6; Silver Star Medal — 39; Oak Leaf Cluster Bronze Star Medal — 1; Bronze Star Medal — 24. Appendix "C," List of British and American decorations awarded to personnel in 1st Canadian Special Service Battalion, HQS 54-27-94-14 (Records 3), 16 January 1946. Major G.W.L. Nicholson, Report No. 5, Historical Section (G.S.) Department of National Defence, The 1st Canadian Special Service Battalion, 22 February 1946, 56, 60–61.
59. The total numbers of awards and decorations awarded to FSSF personnel were: Distinguished Service Cross — 20; Legion of Merit — 5; Silver Star Medal — 121; Bronze Star Medal — 140; Air Medal — 1; Soldier's Medal — 1; Purple Heart — 1406; Good Conduct Medal — 1049; Combat Infantryman's Badge — 2416. Cited in "Campaigns, Battle Honors, and Decorations and Awards of the First Special Service Force," Special Feature #9, in Ross. *The Supercommandoes*, 279.

EPILOGUE

1. Sergeant Charlie Mann (4th Coy, 3rd Regiment), interviewed by authors, 15 October 2003.
2. Staff-Sergeant Gordon Sims (FHQ), interview by authors.
3. Sergeant Bert Hopkins (2nd Coy, 2nd Regiment), interviewed by authors, 20 October 2003.
4. Private Lorin Waling (1st Coy, 2nd Regiment). Hancock and Abbott, *Daring to Die*.
5. Staff-Sergeant Gordon Sims (FHQ), interview with authors.
6. Sergeant Vernon J. Doucette (4th Coy, 3rd Regiment), interviewed by authors, 29 September 2003.
7. Sergeant Joe Glass (1st Coy, 2nd Regiment). John Nadler, "Neighbours In Arms: At Anzio, Canucks and Yanks — in the same uniform — paved the way to victory," *Maclean's*, Vol. 117, No. 20, 17 May 2004, 44.
8. Staff Sergeant Bill Story (HQ detachment, 2nd Regiment). Hancock and Abbott, *Daring to Die*.
9. Sergeant Joe T. Jamieson (6th Coy, 3rd Regiment), interviewed by authors, 1 October 2003.
10. Sergeant George Wright (1st Coy, 1st Regiment), interviewed by authors, 16 October 2003.
11. "Sturdy, Hard-Hitting Canadian-American Army Unit Writing New Military History," *The Montreal Daily Star*, 6 April 1944, 12. There are many other examples given throughout this book.

NOTES

12. "Helena Largely Is Responsible for Instilling Driving Power in Force, Leader Says" *The Independent Record*, 19 September 1945, 5. CAFM, AB 22. Alastair Neely fonds, 26 June 1944 to 10 August 1947, File 5.
13. In the Second World War, SOF was arguably defined as special men, special training, special missions.
14. The JAS/CJATC mission included:

    a. Research in Airportability of Army personnel and equipment;
    b. User Trials of equipment, especially under cold weather conditions;
    c. Limited Development and Assessment of Airborne equipment; and
    d. Training of Paratroop volunteers; training in Airportability of personnel and equipment; training in maintenance of air; advanced training of Glider pilots in exercises with troops; training in some of the uses of light aircraft.

    See "The Organization of an Army Air Centre In Canada," 29 November and 27 December 1945. DHH, 168.009 (D45).
15. For a detailed history of the Canadian Special Air Service Company, see Bernd Horn, "A Military Enigma: The Canadian Special Air Service Company, 1948–49," *Canadian Military History*, Vol. 10, No. 1, Winter 2001, 21–30.
16. "SAS Company — JAS (Army), 13 June 1947." LAC, RG 24, File HQS 88–60–2, reel C-8255.
17. "SAS Company," 30 October 1947, 4 and "Requested Amendment to Interim Plan — SAR," 11 September 1947. LAC, RG 24, File HQS 88–60–2, reel C-8255.
18. "SAS Company — JAS (Army), 13 June 1947, Appendix A." LAC, RG 24, File HQS 88–60–2, reel C-8255.
19. "Special Air Service Company — Implementation Policy," 12 September 1947. LAC, RG 24, File HQS 88–60–2, reel C-8255.
20. "SAS Company," 30 October 1947 (Air S94), LAC, RG 24, File HQS 88–60–2, reel C-8255.
21. "SAS Terms of Reference," 16 April 1948; "Duties of the SAS Coy," 29 January 1948; SAS Coy — Air Training Directive," December 1948. LAC, RG 24, File HQS 88–60–2, reel C-8255.
22. "SAS Company," 27 October 1948. LAC, RG 24, File HQS 88–60–2, reel C-8255.
23. Interviews of former serving members by authors.
24. See Horn, Bastard Sons; George Kitching, *Mud and Green Fields: The Memoirs of Major-General George Kitching* (St. Catharines, ON: Vanwell Publishing Ltd., 1986), 248; and "Command, Mobile Striking Force," 21 October 1948. DHH, 112.3M2 (D369).
25. The 1 CSSBN battle honours awarded by the Canadian government include: Monte Camino, Monte La Difensa, Monte la Remetanea, Monte Majo, Height 720 (Monte Samucro), Radicosa, Monte Vischiataro, Anzio, Rome, Advance to the Tiber, Monte Arrestino, Rocca Massima, Colle Ferro, Italy 1943–1944, Iles d'Hyeres, Grasse, Villeneuve-Loubert, Vence, Drap, L'Escarene, La Turbie, Menton, Southern France, Franco-Italian Border.
26. Concurrently, the lineage and honours of "B" Coy, 1st Ranger Battalion (from the Second World War) and the 5th Ranger Coy (from the Korean War) were also assigned to the 1st Special Forces Group. The 1st Special Forces Group was actually created on 1 April 1956,

with the activation of the 14th Special Forces Operational Detachment (SFOD) at Fort Bragg, North Carolina. It was established by hand-selecting individuals from the 77th Special Forces Group (Airborne). These individuals, as well as individuals from the 12th, 13th, and 16th SFODs, were specifically selected and trained with the objective of establishing a special operations capability in the Asian-Pacific theatre. On 24 June 1957, the 1st Special Force Group (Airborne) was officially activated at Camp Drake Japan. The actual group activation ceremonies were conducted 14 July 1957 at Fort Buckner, Okinawa. Between 1957–60, the 1st Special Forces Group sent mobile training teams to conduct missions in Thailand, Taiwan, the Philippines, Indonesia, and South Vietnam. During this time, 1st Special Forces Group strength increased from 55 personnel in July 1957, to 364 personnel by October 1960. See Memorandum, "Change in Status of Units," from HQ, Department of the Army, 19 April 1960. CAFM, Gordon Sims Papers, AB fonds 29.
27. *Debates*, 12 May 1966, 19, 7 December 1966, 10823 and 30 January 1967, 12417. See also Paul Hellyer, MND, *Address on the Canadian Forces Reorganization Act*, 7 December 1966, 19.
28. Special Committee on Defence: Minutes of Proceedings and Evidence, 21 June 1966, 298–99.
29. Colonel D.H. Rochester, "The Birth of a Regiment," *The Maroon Beret*, 20th Anniversary Issue, 1988, 34.
30. For a definitive history of the Canadian Airborne Regiment, see Horn, *Bastard Sons*.
31. "Formation of the Canadian Airborne Regiment — Activation and Terms of Reference," 15 May 1967, 3.
32. *Ibid.*, 3. Interestingly, Lieutenant-General Anderson was a staff officer working on the Plough Project in the Second World War.
33. *Ibid.*, 2.
34. "Canadian Airborne Regiment — Operational Concept, Annex C" (written by the Canadian Airborne Regiment planning staff) and "Role, Capabilities and Employment," *CFP 310 (1) — Airborne, Volume 1: The Canadian Airborne Regiment*, 1968, Chapter 1, Section 2.
35. *CANFORGEN 02*, dated 041846Z Feb 08. This status is afforded to combatant units whose functional purpose is to close with and conquer, neutralize, or destroy the enemy as an effective fighting force. Only combatant military units are entitled to be publicly recognized for active participation in battle against a former and armed enemy through the award of battle honours and honorary distinctions. *CANFORGEN 03*, dated 041846Z Feb 08. The Canadian Airborne Regiment also perpetuated the lineage and battle honours of the 1st Canadian Parachute Battalion.
36. The FLQ Crisis, also known as the "October Crisis," was the culmination of a series of terrorist events staged by members of the *Front de libération du Québec* (FLQ). Beginning in 1963, the FLQ carried out a series of terrorist acts including bombings, bank robbery, and theft of explosives and weapons. On 5 and 8 October 1970, FLQ cells kidnapped British Trade Commissioner James Cross and Quebec's minister of labour, Pierre Laporte. The kidnappings prompted Quebec Premier, Robert Bourassa, with the support of Montreal Mayor Jean Drapeau, to ask that the federal government invoke the War Measures Act. With the influx of military troops, the widespread condemnation of the FLQ after they murdered Pierre

NOTES

Laporte, and the roll-up of the majority of active FLQ cells, the crisis was over by the end of December. The last military forces were withdrawn by early January of 1971.

37. The move and reorganization, however, became a defining moment for the Canadian Airborne Regiment. It signalled nothing short of the organization's eventual demise. Of prime importance, and instrumental to the regiment's subsequent decline, was the loss of independent formation status. It was now simply an integral part of the newly created SSF. The Canadian Airborne Regiment became nothing more than just another infantry unit, albeit an airborne one. See Horn, *Bastard Sons*, 143–84.

38. The SSF was formerly 2nd Canadian Mechanized Brigade Group (CMBG). It reverted back to 2nd CMBG in 1995.

39. Incidents included: the mistreatment of prisoners on several occasions; the alleged unjustified shooting and resultant death of an intruder; and the torture death of an apprehended thief. These occurrences ultimately defined the Canadian Airborne Regiment's achievements in the public consciousness. See Horn, *Bastard Sons*, 185–248.

40. See Horn, *Bastard Sons*, 185–209.

41. *Ibid.*, 217–48.

42. See Peter Harclerode, *Secret Soldiers: Special Forces in the War Against Terrorism* (London: Cassell & Co, 2000); Paul de B. Taillon, *The Evolution of Special Forces in Counter-Terrorism* (Westport: Praeger, 2001); Benjamin Netanyahu, *Fighting Terrorism* (New York: Noonday Press, 1995); Christopher Dobson and Ronald Payne, *The Terrorists* (New York: Facts on File, 1995); and Brian MacDonald, ed., *Terror* (Toronto: The Canadian Institute of Strategic Studies, 1986).

43. Brigadier-General Ray Romses, the first JTF 2 CO, stated that part of the rationale for the transfer was the government's emphasis on "economizing how it did business." As such, with the Cold War over and DND looking for new roles, the deputy ministers of the various departments rationalized that the 75 RCMP officers at SERT, who only trained, would be more beneficial doing actual police work, while DND, which was effective at training and looking for a new role, could do HR/CT.

44. The original recommendation for the unit name by Lieutenant-Colonel Romses was the Canadian SAS. However, Colonel Michael O'Brien, the DCDS J3 operations officer, who was Romses's immediate boss "wanted a unique name." During a visit to the U.S. with the deputy minister, Bob Fowler, they had visited a U.S. unit with the title JTF 4. Both were enamoured with the name and on return O'Brien insisted on JTF 2. Interview with Colonel Bernd Horn, 21 June 2008.

45. Direct actions, or DAs, are short duration strikes and other precise small-scale offensive actions conducted by special operation forces to seize, destroy, capture, exploit, recover or damage designated targets. Direct action differs from conventional offensive action in the level of physical and political risk, operational techniques, and the degree of discriminate and precise use of force to achieve specific objectives. Special reconnaissance, or SR, missions are conducted to collect or verify information of strategic or operational significance. These actions complement and refine other collection methods but are normally directed upon extremely significant areas of interest. Sensitive site exploitation (SSE) is a

type of direct action operation involving the gathering of intelligence and/or evidence from a specific area or location. SSEs may be conducted in friendly, hostile, denied, or politically sensitive territory. SSEs may include the destruction of weapons, munitions, or equipment if the aforementioned items cannot be recovered. If there is no reasonable expectation of encountering enemy or hostile forces, SOF would not be required.

46. All non-attributed quotes are based on interviews with Colonel Bernd Horn.
47. David Pugliese, "Releasing Information on Canadians who fought with the famed Devil's Brigade during Second World War could harm national security, brass claims," *Ottawa Citizen*, 4 October 2006, A1.
48. Tarina White and Theresa Tayler, "Devil's Brigade Survivors Honoured," *Calgary Herald*, 15 August 2005, A11. The Combat Infantryman Badge (CIB) is awarded to infantry or Special Forces personnel who "must be personally present and under hostile fire while serving in an assigned infantry or Special Forces primary duty, in a unit actively engaged in ground combat with the enemy." The CIB was approved by the U.S. secretary of war on 7 October 1943. On 8 February 1952, the chief of staff, U.S. Army, approved a proposal to add stars to the CIB to indicate award of the badge in separate wars. Letter, "Permanent Orders 098–41," Award: Combat Infantry Badge, Department of the Army, 8 April 2005. On 18 August 2006, The U.S. Army authorized the award of the Bronze Star Medal for Service to the living former members of the FSSF for their service to the U.S. Army during the Second World War. The Bronze Star was established by the U.S. president on 4 February 1944, "for heroic or meritorious achievement of service, not involving aerial flight, in connection with operations against an opposing armed force."
49. See Bernd Horn, "The Canadian SOF Legacy," in Dr. Emily Spencer, ed., *Special Operations Forces: A National Capability* (Kingston: CDA Press, 2011); and Bernd Horn, *We Will Find a Way: Understanding Canadian Special Operations Forces* (Tampa, FL: Joint Special Operations University, March 2012).
50. One negative side effect was CANSOFCOM's initial flirtation with the concept of secrecy without due thought, which created an absurd situation. CANSOFCOM/DND censors quickly moved to classify records and information on the FSSF, such as the name and where it fought as secret because officials stated release would be "injurious to the conduct of international affairs, the defence of Canada or any state allied or associated with Canada or the detection, prevention or suppression of subversive or hostile activities." This was later dropped. David Pugliese, "Releasing Information on Canadians who fought with the famed Devil's Brigade during Second World War could harm national security, brass claims," *Ottawa Citizen*, 4 October 2006, A1.
51. This status is afforded to combatant units whose functional purpose is to close with and conquer, neutralize, or destroy the enemy as an effective fighting force. Only combatant military units are entitled to be publicly recognized for active participation in battle against a former and armed enemy through the award of battle honours and honorary distinctions. CANFORGEN 03, dated 041846Z Feb 08.
52. CANFORGEN 02, dated 041846Z Feb 08. "Perpetuation is a uniquely Canadian system that provides a means of preserving military operational honours for successive generations. The

NOTES

system was developed by the Army and used extensively to safeguard the record of service of Canadian expeditionary force units during the First World War. The system has changed little over the years. Only combatant units that have gained an honour and/or distinction in the field may be perpetuated and only serving combatant units with a proven link to the previous one can claim and be awarded the honour of perpetuation." *Ibid.*

53. David Poe, "Duty, Honor and Valor values espoused during Menton Week," IMCOM, 19 December 2011.
54. *Ibid.*
55. Mark Iype, "Black Devils honoured with own tartan," *National Post*, 30 March 2011, A2.
56. The MND's award for Operational Excellence recognizes members of the Defence Team who have demonstrated excellence, while deployed overseas in the achievement of outstanding results for DND. The award is open to individuals, units, and organizations at all levels. CANSOFCOM was the first to receive the new award in 2011 for its contribution and impact to the fight in Afghanistan.

ANNEX B

1. The vast majority of historians writing on the FSSF make no reference to Operation Jupiter, the Plough Project, and the FSSF as there is no link. However, two of the more recent publications on the FSSF do. One in passing, the other bases its thesis and title on it and makes the claim to uncover new information and to correct the historical record. However, the text itself fails to provide any documentation or sources that actually substantiate the claim that Plough and the FSSF were involved in the "Jupiter Deception." Conversely, after an exhausting search of the historical record, this annex provides the necessary evidence to discount the claim.
2. "Extract from Winston Churchill, *The Hinge of Fate*." LAC, RG 25, D-1, Department of External Affairs, Vol. 829, File 2, Under-Secretary's Office Papers, Operation Jupiter.
3. "Operation Jupiter, Prime Minister to General Ismay, for COS Committee, 1 May 1942," excerpt from Winston Churchill, *The Hinge of Fate*. LAC, RG 25, D-1, Department of External Affairs, Vol. 829, File 2, Under-Secretary's Office Papers, Operation Jupiter. On 2 June 1942, Churchill wrote a memorandum to his War Cabinet Chiefs of Staff Committee. "About 70 German bombers and 100 fighters established north of Norway in only two airfields, protected by about ten or twelve thousand effective fighting men, are denying us all entry into Norway and taking a heavy toll of our convoys. If we could gain possession of these airfields and establish an equal force there, not only would the Northern sea route to Russia be kept open, but we should have set up a second front on a small scale from which it would be most difficult to eject us." Memorandum, Winston Churchill to War Cabinet Committee, "Operation Jupiter," 2 June 1942. LAC, MG 30, E133, A.G.L. McNaughton fonds, Series 3, Canadian Army Overseas 1921, 1939–1949, Vol. 135, File P.A. 1-7-1 Jupiter Original.
4. "War Cabinet Joint Planning Staff. Operation Jupiter Draft Report by Joint Planning Staff," 24 June 1942, 1. DHH, File 693.023 (D1).

5. Memo, "Re — Operation Jupiter," CGS, Lieutenant-General G.G. Simonds, to Historical Section (GS) Army HQ, 9 August 1955. DHH, File 112.011 (D1). Simonds noted that Churchill accepted the appreciation of the special training staff in August and the subject was buried.
6. "Extract from Winston Churchill, *The Hinge of Fate*." LAC, RG 25, D-1, Department of External Affairs, Vol. 829, File 2, Under-Secretary's Office Papers, Operation Jupiter. Although Churchill spoke these words, he continued to lobby for Operation Jupiter. Lieutenant-General McNaughton revealed that even though the chiefs of staff said no, "Churchill refused to take no for an answer." McNaughton's assessment was that "Churchill would not accept defeat." He stated, "Churchill insisted plans be written up for the contingency of Jupiter in case opportunity arose." McNaughton himself didn't believe in the plan. He assessed, "It was in fact an Arctic Gallipoli designed to satisfy to some extent the unfortunate demands of the Russians and the clamour of public opinion in America and Britain for a second front." "Interview with General Andrew G.L. McNaughton in regards to Operation Jupiter (ca. 1950)," Canadian War Museum Collection, audio tape, track 1: 0355; 0500; 0900; and 1015.
7. Winston Churchill, himself an accomplished adventurer, journalist, and soldier, held a heroic and romantic image of war. His concept of conflict was irretrievably moulded during the South African War of 1899–1902. To Churchill, the offensive was all that mattered. He believed that audacity and willpower constituted the only sound approach to the conduct of war. General Archibald Wavell wrote, "He [Churchill] always accused commanders of organizing 'all tail and no teeth.'" Similarly, General Alan Brooke recalled, "He [Churchill] is like a child that has set its mind on some forbidden toy. It is no good explaining that it will cut his fingers or burn him. The more you explain, the more fixed he becomes in his idea." See Eliot A. Cohen, *Commandos and Politicians* (Cambridge: Center for International Affairs, Harvard University, 1978), 37–40; Maxwell Schoenfeld, *The War Ministry of Winston Churchill* (Ames: The Iowa State University Press, 1972), 124; Patrick Cosgrove, *Churchill at War Alone 1939–1940* (London: William Collins Sons & Co. Ltd., 1974), 95; and David Jablonsky, *Churchill: The Making of a Grand Strategist* (Carlisle Barracks: Strategic Studies Institute, U.S. Army War College, 1990), 92 and 125.
8. McNaughton, Personal memorandum PA 1-7-1 (capturing meeting at War Office, on 17 September 1942), 20 September 1942. LAC, MG 30, E133, A.G.L. McNaughton fonds, Series 3, Canadian Army Overseas 1921, 1939–1949, Vol. 135, File P.A. 1-7-1 Jupiter Original.
9. See "Operation Jupiter, Prime Minister to General Ismay, for COS Committee, 1 May 1942," excerpt from Winston Churchill, *The Hinge of Fate*; and Telegram, for Stuart to McNaughton, 24 September 1942. Both LAC, RG 25, D-1, Department of External Affairs, Vol. 829, File 2, Under-Secretary's Office Papers, Operation Jupiter. At one point a total of six divisions were contemplated.
10. See "'Operation Jupiter,' Prime Minister to General Ismay For COS committee, 16 September 1942," excerpt from Winston Churchill, *The Hinge of Fate*. LAC, RG 25, D-1, Department of External Affairs, Vol. 829, File 2, Under-Secretary's Office Papers, Operation Jupiter.
11. Extract from Winston Churchill, *The Hinge of Fate*. LAC RG 25, D-1, Department of External Affairs, Vol. 829, File 2, Under-Secretary's Office Papers, Operation Jupiter. Canadian Prime

NOTES

Minister Mackenzie King's real concern was what he perceived as Churchill's neglect to include the Americans in the plan. "In our view," wrote King to Churchill in a cable, "the operation envisaged is of a scale and significance which bring it within the realm of major strategy decisions in respect of which should be shared by the United States." He warned, "You are aware of the extent to which US and Canadian Forces are cooperating on this continent as well as in Europe. Were the President not to be advised and his approval obtained in advance of the proposed mission its personnel and its object the almost certainly would feel that he should have been given an opportunity to express his views." Telegram, Defensor to Canmilitry, 24 September 1942. LAC, MG 30, E133, A.G.L. McNaughton fonds, Series 3, Canadian Army Overseas 1921, 1939–49, Vol. 135, File P.A. 1–7-1 Jupiter Original.

12. "Operation Jupiter, Prime Minister to General Ismay, for COS Committee, 1 May 1942," excerpt from Winston Churchill, *The Hinge of Fate*. LAC, RG 25, D-1, Department of External Affairs, Vol. 829, File 2, Under-Secretary's Office Papers, Operation Jupiter.

13. Even after the demise of Operation Plough, the British were eager to gain access to the Weasel for operational purposes.

14. An exhaustive search of the FSSF files at the Canadian national archives and the Directorate of History and Heritage at DND as well as a search of the Frederick, Burhan, and Adelman papers at the Hoover Institute at Stanford University, as well as an analysis of secondary sources has turned up only the six-page staff check done by Frederick's staff officer. Even the book *Snow Plough and the Jupiter Deception* provides no clear documentary evidence that the FSSF was ever drawn into the operation.

15. HIA, Memorandum, "Memorandum on an Invasion of Northern Norway," Lieutenant-Colonel A.D. Dahl to Colonel Frederick, 12 September 1942. Robert Tyron Frederick Papers, Box 1, File Memorandum, mss, maps, 1942. Not surprisingly, Dahl concluded that the FSSF could be used "to advantage" in some form or another in an invasion scenario. Its skeletal and basic composition compared to the detailed planning evident in the voluminous appreciations done on Operation Jupiter indicate this was a very cursory exercise that was not at all connected to the Jupiter planning staffs. Its date also indicates this was done well past the submission of the Operation Jupiter proposed plan.

16. HIA, Colonel Robert T. Frederick handwritten notes/diary of the visit, 17 September 1942. Robert Tyron Frederick Papers, Box 1, File Telephone conversations. Interestingly, Lord Mountbatten also stated that "General M[arshall] had given the impression that there would be ample US aircraft in the British Isles for the project." Frederick further noted that "Lord M[ountbatten] believes it is up to the US to provide the aircraft and that an adequate number of C-54 for the project should be produced." *Ibid*.

17. HIA, Frederick handwritten notes/diary of the visit, 18 September 1942.

18. McNaughton was actually against visiting Stalin to sell him on Operation Jupiter. McNaughton stated in an interview, "it was not my task trying to sell a bunch of stale muffins to Stalin." He went on to say, "the last thing the Russians wanted was to start a second front up there. This is not an operation our Allies want. I didn't believe in it." "Interview with General Andrew G.L. McNaughton in regards to Operation Jupiter (ca. 1950)," Canadian War Museum Collection, audio tape, track 3, 04:45; 0526; 0544; and 0643.

19. Extract from Winston Churchill, *The Hinge of Fate*. LAC, RG 25, D-1, Department of External Affairs, Vol. 829, File 2, Under-Secretary's Office Papers, Operation Jupiter.
20. Letter, Churchill to Mackenzie King, 25 September 1942. LAC, RG 25, D-1, Department of External Affairs, Vol. 829, File 2, Under-Secretary's Office Papers, Operation Jupiter.
21. Memorandum, Lieutenant-Colonel McQueen to CGS, 6 October 1942. LAC, RG 24, Series C1, File HQS 20-4-32, Mobilization and organization of unallocated battalions. microfilm reel C-5246. Lieutenant-Colonel McQueen confirmed, "It was understood at the time [creation of FSSF] that the United States Army would take the task [Plough Project] over completely." In addition, as early as 12 August 1942, Lord Mountbatten wrote Colonel Frederick and stated, "if, at this stage, you would prefer to cut adrift from Combined Operations Headquarters and carry on making an entirely independent plan without further reference to us, I should quite understand your point of view …" HIA, Letter, Mountbatten to Frederick, 12 August 1942. Robert Tyron Frederick Papers, Box 8, File Declassified Papers.
22. Colonel C.P. Stacey wrote, "From July through September 1942 much of General McNaughton's attention and the energies of some of his best staff officers, were devoted to a project which he undertook to study at the request of the British authorities; the possibility of a large-scale military operation directed against the airfields in Northern Norway from which German aircraft were striking at our convoys to Russia. The scheme was a hazardous one, but it was finally abandoned only after long discussion and study." Excerpt from C.P. Stacey, *The Canadian Army*. LAC, RG 25, D-1, Department of External Affairs, Vol. 829, File 2, Under-Secretary's Office Papers, Operation Jupiter.
23. See "War Cabinet Joint Planning Staff. Operation Jupiter Draft Report by Joint Planning Staff," 24 June 1942, 5,7 and 9. DHH, File 693.023 (D1); "War Cabinet. Chiefs of Staff Committee. Operation "Jubilee," 7 August 1942, Appendices M and N. DHH, 693.023 (D24); and "Minutes of First Meeting of Special Planning Staff held on 13th July, 1942, War Diary of Cardwell Committee Operation Jupiter, 9 July 42 — 8 Aug 1942, Vol 1." DHH, File 803N1 (D1) Diaries, war, Cardwell Committee.
24. War Cabinet Joint Planning Staff," Operation Jupiter — Report by the Joint Planning Staff, 23 September 1942. LAC, MG 30, E133, A.G.L. McNaughton fonds, Series 3, Canadian Army Overseas 1921, 1939-1949, Vol. 135, File P.A. 1-7-1 Jupiter Original.
25. Undoubtedly, as the commander of Canadian forces overseas, McNaughton was aware of Operation Plough and the FSSF. Nonetheless, the Operation Jupiter estimate makes not a single mention of Operation Plough or the FSSF. In fact, its stated concern with the lack of information dealing with Norway, troops prepared or preparing for Arctic operations, or equipment suitable for such operations leads the reader to the conclusion that while McNaughton may have been aware the planning staff had no idea that Operation Plough or the FSSF even existed. The only reference made by McNaughton on Operation Plough and the FSSF occurs in his war diary on 1 September 1942, when he notes he received a courtesy call from Colonel Frederick and Brigadier Lushington, the chief-of-staff of Combined Operations Command headquarters, to discuss the "Plow scheme and other matters related to the unit," and in his personal memorandum on 22 September 1942 in which he captures his visit with Prime Minister Churchill (19 September 1942). In the meeting which covered a wide

NOTES

spectrum of activities and topics, McNaughton and Churchill discussed "Plow." The focus was the actual vehicle manufactured by Studebaker and "the value of these vehicles for recce and sabotage in winter." See War diary for Lieutenant-General A.G.L. McNaughton, 6 August 1942 and 1 Sep 1942. LAC, MG 30, E133, A.G.L. McNaughton fonds, Series 3, Canadian Army Overseas 1921, 1939–49, Vol. 135, File P.A. 1–7–1 Jupiter Original; and Lieutenant-General A.G.L. McNaughton, Personal Memorandum, 22 September 1942. LAC, MG 30, E133, Series 3, Canadian Army Overseas 1921, 1939–49, Vol. 135, File P.A. 1–7–1 Jupiter Original.

26. Letter, Marshall to Pope, "Second Canadian Parachute Battalion," 17 October 1942. A study of the possible employment of the FSSF in the Caucasus was investigated by Frederick's staff. Their conclusion was not to employ the Force in the region because of the difficulty of operating the vehicles in the steep and rugged mountains, as well as the likelihood that the Germans would have already advanced through the area. HIA, Memorandum, Frederick to the deputy chief of staff of the Army, "Proposed Caucasus Operations by 1st Special Service Force," 28 October 1941. Robert T. Frederick Papers, Box 1, File Miscellany.

27. Memorandum, MND to CGS, "Re: Employment of First Special Service Battalion," 14 October 1943.; and Letter, CGS to Williamson, 15 October 1943. LAC, C-5489, File HQS-2–32, Employment and movement operation 1st Special Service Battalion. See also briefing note for Canadian War Committee of Cabinet, "Despatch of First Canadian Special Service Battalion to United Kingdom, and its Employment in the European Theatre as an Integral Part of the First Special Service Force." LAC, RG 24, Series C-1, File HQS–2–32, Employment and movement operation 1st Special Service Battalion, microfilm reel C-5489.

28. A report written by Canadian military headquarters dated 23 September 1942, "showed conclusively that no basis exists for a modification of Plan Jupiter review, which under existing circumstances would bring our participation into the realm of a practical operation of war." Telegram, from Stuart to McNaughton, 24 September 1942. LAC, RG 25, D-1, Department of External Affairs, Vol. 829, File 2, Under-Secretary's Office Papers, Operation Jupiter. Stuart went on to say that as a result "there is no background for realistic military discussions with the Russian General Staff." The plan was scrubbed before it actually was even realistically begun.

29. Lieutenant-General Simonds affirmed, "'Torch' had been decided upon in the meantime and 'Jupiter' was eventually used as a 'cover plan' for that operation." Memo, "Re — Operation Jupiter," CGS, Lieutenant-General G.G. Simonds, to Historical Section (GS) Army HQ, 9 August 1955. DHH, File 112.011 (D1).

30. "War Cabinet Joint Planning Staff. Operation Jupiter Draft Report by Joint Planning Staff," 24 June 1942, 2. DHH, File 693.023 (D1). In fact, the appreciation stated that "the plan was dependent" on the Americans providing the ships and aircraft.

GLOSSARY

AAA	Anti-Aircraft Artillery
AAI	Allied Armies in Italy
AB	Airborne
ACGS	Assistant Chief of the General Staff
ADAG	Assistant Deputy Adjutant General
AFG	Army Ground Force
AFG HQ	Army Ground Force Headquarters
AG	Adjutant General
AGO	Adjutant General's Office
APD	Destroyer Escort Transport
Appx	Appendix
ATF 9	Amphibious Training Force, No. 9
ATO	Afghan Theatre of Operations
AWOL	Absent Without Official Leave
BAR	Browning Automatic Rifle
Bn	Battalion
BSP	Basic Security Plan
CA	Canadian Army
CAFM	Canadian Airborne Forces Museum
CANSOFCOM	Canadian Special Operations Command
Cdn	Canadian

Cdn AB Regt	Canadian Airborne Regiment
Cdn SAS Coy	Canadian Special Air Service Company
Cdo	Commando
CCO	Chief of Combined Operations
CDS	Chief of the Defence Staff
CFB	Canadian Forces Base
CFOO	Canadian Forces Organizational Order
CGS	Chief of the General Staff
CIGS	Chief of the Imperial General Staff
CJATC	Canadian Joint Air Training Centre
CJSM	Canadian Joint Staff Mission
CMBG	Canadian Mechanized Brigade Group
CMF	Central Mediterranean Force
CMHQ	Canadian Military Headquarters
CMM	Canadian Military Mission
CO	Commanding Officer
COC	Combined Operations Command
Coy	Company
CP	Command Post
CPP	Close Personal Protection
CPAT	Contingency Planning Assistance Team
CRU	Canadian Reinforcement Unit
CSOR	Canadian Special Operations Regiment
CSSBN	Canadian Special Service Battalion
CT	Counter Terrorism
CTS	Canadian Training School
DA	Direct Action
DAAG	Deputy Assistant Adjutant-General
D.C.	District of Columbia
DCGS	Deputy Chief of the Defence Staff
DDMA	Defence Diplomacy Military Assistance
Det	Detachment
DHH	Directorate of History and Heritage
DND	Department of National Defence
DSD	Director Staff Duties
DZ	Drop Zone
Ech	Echelon
ETO	European Theatre of Operation
FA	Field Artillery
FFI	French Forces of the Interior
FMC	Force Mobile Command
FSSF	First Special Service Force

GLOSSARY

GD	General Duty
GHQ	General Headquarters
GOC	General Officer Commanding
GS	General Staff
HALO	High Altitude Low Opening
HIA	Hoover Institute Archives
HQ	Headquarters
HQS	Headquarters Secret
HRH	His/Her Royal Highness
HMS	His Majesty's Ship
HR	hostage rescue
IC	Internal Combustion or In Charge (depending on context)
Inf	Infantry
IQ	Intelligence Quotient
JAS	Joint Air School
JTF2	Joint Task Force Two
Km	Kilometres
LAC	Library and Archives Canada
LCA	Landing Craft, Assault
LCI	Landing Craft, Infantry
LMG	Light Machine Gun
LST	Landing Ship, Tank
M.A.	Military Attaché
MD	Military Districts
MG	Machine Gun
MGO	Master General of the Ordnance
MND	Minister of National Defence
MP	Military Police
Mt	Mount
NDHQ	National Defence Headquarters
NCO	Non-Commissioned Officer
NEO	Non-Combatant Evacuation Operations
NOB	Navy Operations Base
NRC	National Research Council
OCTU	Officer Cadet Training Unit
OEF	Operation Enduring Freedom
OIC	Officer-in-charge
OTC	Officers' Training Centre
OR	Other Rank
Org & P	Organization and Planning
OSS	Office of Strategic Services
OSRD	Office of Scientific Research and Development

PC	Privy Council
PJBD	Permanent Joint Board of Defence
PMG	Pay-Master General
PPCLI	Princess Patricia's Canadian Light Infantry
Pte	Private
PW	Prisoner of War
QMG	Quarter Master General
R22R	Royal 22nd Regiment
RAF	Royal Air Force
RCAF	Royal Canadian Air Force
RCR	Royal Canadian Regiment
Recce	Reconnaissance
Regt	Regiment
Ret'd	Retired
RMC	Royal Military College
RR	Railroad
RTU	Return to Unit
RUSI	Royal United Service Institute
SAS	Special Air Service
SC	Staff Captain
SERT	Special Emergency Response Team
SFG	Special Forces Group
SHAEF	Supreme Headquarters Allied Expeditionary Force
SNAFU	Situation Normal All Fucked Up
SOE	Special Operations Executive
SOTF	Special Operations Task Force
SP	Self-Propelled
SS	Special Service (U.K.) or Schutzstaffeln (German)
SSF	Special Service Force
SSE	Sensitive Site Exploitation
SR	Strategic Reconnaissance
TD	Tank Destroyer
TOS	Taken on strength
U.K.	United Kingdom
UP	United Press
U.S.A.	United States of America
VCGS	Vice-Chief of the Defence Staff
WE	War Establishment
1 ABTF	1st Airborne Task Force
1 Cdn Para Bn	1st Canadian Parachute Battalion
1 Cdn Para Trg Coy	1st Canadian Parachute Training Company
1 Cdn Para Trg Bn	1st Canadian Parachute Training Battalion

GLOSSARY

1 CBRG	1st Canadian Base Reinforcement Group
1 CSSBN	1st Canadian Special Service Battalion
1 SFG	1st Special Forces Group
2 Cdn NETD	2nd Canadian Non-Effective Transit Depot
2 Cdn Para Bn	2nd Canadian Parachute Battalion
5 CITR	No 5 Canadian Infantry Training Regiment
7 Cdn Inf Trg Bn	7th Canadian Infantry Training Battalion
7 CITB	7th Canadian Infantry Training Brigade

ACKNOWLEDGEMENTS

A project of this magnitude owes its finalization to many hands. As such, we wish to thank all those who directly, or indirectly, assisted us with our endeavour to capture the uniqueness and outstanding contribution of the First Special Service Force and its role in North American military history. Therefore, there is nowhere better to start than by thanking Charlie Mann for agreeing to do the Foreword and all the veterans of the Force who gave freely of their time, recollections, documents, and photographs so that we could compile this volume. For both their service and their assistance, we are eternally grateful.

We would be remiss if we did not thank Warren Sinclair and Valerie Casbourn of the DND Directorate of History and Heritage, who provided great assistance in allowing us to access key documentation. In this vein, we would also like to pass on our appreciation to Roxanne Merritt, the curator of the JFK Special Warfare Museum; the Still Picture Reference Team, National Archives and Records Administration (NARA), College Park, Maryland, U.S.A.; Nicholas Siekierski, assistant archivist for exhibits and outreach, Hoover Institution Archives, Stanford University, California; Joe Drouin Enterprises and Mrs. Anne Frederick-Hicks, all of whom provided advice and/or access to photographs, as well as clarification on key issues.

Key to the publication of the book was the assistance of some talented individuals who provided artwork, maps, and graphic support. We owe a great debt to Katherine Taylor who painted the incredible cover art, Ted Zuber for his artwork within the book, and Roger Chabot who also allowed us to use his impressive Anzio painting. As well, we must acknowledge Amy Pierrson, Shannon Myra, and the late William Constable for their assistance with maps and graphics.

In addition, there were a number of people behind the scene who assisted with research and those who provided helping hands to get the large number of small things done. As such, we wish to thank Dr. Emily Spencer and Cathy Shepherd for their invaluable assistance with research. As well, we are greatly appreciative of the help that Karen Bassie, Wilson Becket, Leading Seaman Christopher Hibbs (CAFM), Holly Picard, and Captain Dennis Power extended to us.

Furthermore, we must thank Nigel Heseltine and Cheryl Hawley, as well as the entire Dundurn design and editing team for turning our manuscript into the polished work before you.

Finally, but certainly not least, we need to thank our wives, Kim and Sue, for their patience, forbearance, and immense tolerance in allowing us to pursue our endless historical endeavours and projects.

ABOUT THE AUTHORS

Courtesy Bernd Horn.

COLONEL BERND HORN, OMM, MSM, CD, Ph.D., is an experienced Canadian Forces infantry officer and military educator. He has held numerous key command and staff appointments, which include deputy commander, Canadian Special Operations Command; commanding officer, 1st Battalion, The Royal Canadian Regiment; and officer commanding 3 Commando, The Canadian Airborne Regiment. Dr. Horn is also an adjunct professor of history at the Royal Military College of Canada and Norwich University. He has authored, co-authored, edited, and co-edited over 35 books and over 100 chapters and articles on military history and military affairs.

Courtesy Michel Wyczynski.

MICHEL WYCZYNSKI has worked for Library and Archives Canada for the past 33 years, primarily in political and military archives. He has also served, for the past 35 years as an NCO with Le Regiment de Hull, Royal Canadian Armoured Corps, reserve unit. He has co-authored books and authored chapters and articles on various aspects of Canadian Airborne history and material history, as well as New France colonial military history. In addition, he served as an archival consultant for various militia and regular force units and he is the honorary archivist for the Canadian Airborne Forces Museum, the 1st Canadian Parachute Battalion Association, and the Airborne Regiment Association of Canada.

INDEX

Numbers in italics refer to images and their captions.

Achnacarry, Scotland, 19
Adak, 143, 144, 145
Adams, Colonel Paul D., 138
Afghan Theatre of Operations (ATO), 91
Afghanistan, 290–91, 292, 294
Air Force, 19, 24–25, 57, 58, 68, 126, 146, 279
Air-Ground Liaison Team, 150, 151
Aircraft, 21, 38–39, 41, 107, 108, 109–10, 121, 122–23, 158, 171, 244, 283, 288
    American, 144, 148
        C-54 Transport, 34–35, 304
    British
        Lancaster Bomber, 26, 34–35, 121
    German
        Stuka, 13, 26
Akehurst, Lieutenant-Colonel Jack F. R., 60, 67, 160, 188, 191, 210–11, 220, 223, 239, 243, 245, 250, 257–61, 264–69, 271–73, *274*
Alan Brooke, General, 15, 300–01
Alaska, 68, 85–86, 141, 142, 144, 148–49, 151, 153, 156

Alaskan Scouts, 148–49, 150–51, 153, 156
Alban Hills, 207, 208
Aleutians, 7, 68, 141–42, 143, 144, 148, 205
Alexander, General H.R., 224, 241
Algeria, 165, *167*
Allard, General Jean Victor, 282, 283
Amchitka, 144, *145*, 146, *147*, 148, 150, 154
Anderson, Lieutenant-Colonel W.A.B., 44, 69, *70*, 77, 80, 284
Anzio, 11, 47, 207, *208*, 209, 210, 213, 214, *215*, 216, *220*, 221, 223–24, 229, 230, 231, 237, 239, 257, 270
Appleyard, Major Geoffrey, 19
Archimedean screw-driven vehicles, 37, 38
Army Ground Force Headquarters, United States (AFG HQ), 36, 126, 127–28, 135
Artena, 229, 230, 231, 232
Artillery Forward Observer Party, 601st Field Artillery, 151, 214
Arundel Castle, 272
Athabasca Glacier, 46

Attu, 143, 144, 146
Avellino, 191, 219, 268

Baker, Corporal Gordon Harold, 108, 156, 177, 187, 226
Baldwin, Major O.J., 93–94
Ballantyne, Donald, 59, 61, 85, 106, 152, 165, 191, 237
Banak, 300
Banff National Park, 46
Basic Security Plan (BSP), 282
Battle Honours, 282, 285, 292
Beach 10, Kiska, 153, 154
Beacon, Sergeant O.C., 267
Beament, Brigadier-General A. Warwick, 191, 192, 217
Becket, Lieutenant-Colonel Ralph Wilson, 59–60, 61, 62, 88, 96, 120, 129, 135, 152, 153–54, 182, 225, 230, 231, 239, 246, 247, 248, 252, 254, 257, 263, 264
Belgium, 32
Black Devils, 7, 11–12, 222, 223
Blackwell, Alan, 109, 177
Blossburg, Montana, 136
Bodo, 300
Bohr, Niels, 32

Bombardier snowmobiles/snow machines, *46*
Borditsky, Sam, 59
Boulogne, France, 15, 23
Bourne, Lieutenant-Colonel J.G., 16, 248
Bourne, Lieutenant-General Sir Alan, 64
Braves, 47
Braves Bulletin, 47
British Air Force
    No.1 Parachute Training School, RAF Station, Ringway, 58
British Army
    1 Mountain Division, 303
    2nd Parachute Brigade, 250–51
    49th Division, 303
    52 Division, 303
    56 Division, 169
British Military Mission, Washington, D.C., 68
British Navy
    Ships
        HMS *Campbeltown*, 26
        HMS *Ramillies*, 245
British War Office, 67
Brooke, General Sir Alan, 15, 30, 300–01
Bruneval, France, 26
Burhans, Lieutenant-Colonel Robert D., 100, 117, 118, 123, 128, 138, 139, 303–04
Burma, 143

Cabinet War Committee (Canadian), 125
Callowhill, Jack, 103
Camp Borden, Ontario, 64
Camp Bradford, Navy Operations Base (NOB), Norfolk, Virginia, *73*, 138
Camp Debert, Nova Scotia, 64–65
Camp Grafton, Ramsey, North Dakota, 85
Camp McDowell, San Francisco, 142
Camp Patrick Henry, 165
Camp Petawawa, Ontario, 286, 291–92
Camp Sarcee, Alberta, 61, 62
Camp Stoneman, Pittsburg, California, 162
Camp Valcartier, Quebec, 64
Campbell, Colonel H.A., 97
Canadian Airborne Regiment (Cdn AB Regt), *283*, *284*, 285, *286*, *287*, 288

Canadian Army
    1st Canadian Base Reinforcement Group, 219
    1st Canadian Brigade, 264
    1st Canadian Corps, 219, 264, 269
    1st Canadian General Reinforcement Unit, 192
    1st Canadian Infantry Division, 270
    1st Canadian Parachute Battalion (1 Cdn Para Bn), 45, 53, 56, 58, 124, 135, 264, 274, 279
    1st Canadian Special Service Battalion (1 CSSBN), 67, 203–04, 275, 292, 296, 297
    1st Echelon, 15th Army Group, 217
    2nd Canadian Non-Effective Transit Depot (2 Cdn NETD), 271
    2nd Canadian Parachute Battalion (2 Cdn Para Bn), 45, 54, 58, 60, 62, 64, 70–71, 72, 73, 74, 75, 76, 78, 79, 80, 81, 82, 92, 97, 99, 115–16, 124, 135, 139, 140, 295
    3 Wing, Canadian training School, 271
    No. 5 Canadian Infantry Training Regiment (5 CITR), 273
    13th Brigade, 156
    Officer Cadet Training Unit (OCTU), 271
    Training Brigade, Vernon, British Columbia, 273–74
    Victoria Rifles, 91
Canadian Army Pacific Command, 69
Canadian Army Parachute Pay, 80
Canadian Battle Drill School, Vernon, British Columbia, 134
Canadian Chiefs of Staff, 68, 69
Canadian Dependent's Allowances, 80
Canadian Forces (CF), 279, 283–86, 288, 289, 290–92
Canadian Joint Air Training Centre (CJATC), 279, 280, 281
Canadian Joint Staff, Canadian Legation, Washington, *69*, 79, 124
Canadian Joint Staff Mission, 68–69

Canadian Military Headquarters (CMHQ), 51, 67, 192, 204, 223, 258, 259, 260–61, 263, 264, 269, 271, *272*
Canadian Military Mission (CMM), 68
Canadian Special Air Service Company (Cdn SAS Coy), 279
Canadian Special Operations Forces Command (CANSOFCOM), *289*, 291–92
Canadian Training School (CTS), 271
Cannes, France, 250
Caparo Hill, 202
Cargo Carrier, Light, T-15, 38, *see also* Weasel
Carpathians, 30
Casablanca, 165, *167*
Castellar, France, 257, 258
Castillon, France, 257, 258
Cavalaire Bay, France, 250
Cavaliere, France, 241
Central Mediterranean Force (CMF), 218
Ceppagna, 188
Cherbourg, France, 275, 299
Chesley, Colonel L.M., 53, 82
Chief of Combined Operations, 24–25, 29, 30, 34, 42, 121, 122
Chief of the Defence Staff (CDS), 283, 289, 291, 292
Chief of the General Staff (CGS), 43–44, 44, 53–54, 56, 67, 69, 70, 74, 75, 76, 78–79, 8, 83, 93, 97–99, 124, 125, 140, 205, 259, 274–75, 282
Chief of the Imperial General Staff (CIGS), 15, 22–23
Chiefs of Staff Committee, 24–25, 29
Christie, Colonel J.H., 270
Churchill, Winston, 10, 13, 14, 15–17, 22–25, 29, 31, *33*, 34–37, 41, *45*, 50, 121, 185, 207, 209, 224, 299–302, 304
Cisterna, 224, 227
Clark, Lieutenant-General Mark, 11, 167, 168, 184–85, 187, 283, 208, 209, 224, *225*, 231, 240, 273
Clarke, Colonel Dudley W., 15–16, 23
Cole, Ray E., 38
Colle Ferro, 230, 231
Combined Operations Command (COC), 23–24
Comer, Lieutenant-Colonel, 94

400

INDEX

Commando Depot, 19
Commando Holding Unit, 19
Conger, Clinton, 249
Corlett, General Charles, 144–45, 149, 161, 162
Cottingham, Peter, 57, 133, 135
Crabbe Jr., Corporal Otis C., 265, 275
Crerar, Lieutenant-General Harry, 192
Cyclotron, 32

D'Artois, Captain Guy, 281
D'Hyeres Islands, France, 242
Dahl, Lieutenant-Colonel A.D., 301, 303–04
Dauphinais, Joe, 116, 119, 120
De Lattre de Tassigny, 241
Department of Mines and Resources (Canadian), 46
Department of Munitions and Supply (Canadian), 46
deuterium oxide, 32, *see also* heavy water
Devers, Lieutenant-General Jacob L., 240, 241, 260
Devil's Brigade, 7, 290
DeWitt, Lieutenant-General J.L., 161, 162
Dill, General Sir John, 15–16
Director of combined operations command, 24
Directorate of Staff Duties (DSD), 53, 69
Doucette, Vern, 59, 61, 88, 100, 110, 147, 150, 159, 162, 266, 278
Duncan, Brigadier Nigel, 37
Dunlop, Lloyd D.M., 59, 106, 112, 113, 135, 156, 158, 162, 198, 248
Dunn, Colonel Michael A., 263, 264
Durance River, France, 250
Durnford-Slater, Brigadier John, 18–19, 23, 25
Dutch Harbour, Aleutains, 143

Earl, Ross, 114
Eden, Anthony, 23
Eisenhower, Major-General Dwight "Ike," 35, *36*, *43*, 165, 167, 217–18
Eliasson toboggan, 38
Elson, R.T., 95
Empress of Scotland, 165
England 14, 16, 20, 25, 27, 34, 42–43, 44, 51, 59–60, 89, 114, 120, 121, 260–61, 271, 274, 301, 302

English Channel, 57
Enigma, 25
Europe, 12, 15, 16, 25, 26, 29, 32, 33–34, 35, 275, 288, 294, 299, 300
European Theatre of Operation (ETO), 275

Farrar-Hockley, Brigadier Anthony, 21
Fenton, Sergeant Tom, 171, 173
Ferguson, Lieutenant-Colonel G.A., 74
Fifth Army, US, 203, 231, 232
Firestone Tire Corporation, 38
First Special Forces, 282
First Special Service Force (FSSF)
   1st Regiment, 113, 149, 150–56, 160, 171, *178*, 181, 182, 188, 193, 195, 199, 200–01, 202, 210, 224, 225, 226, 229, 227, 229, 230, 231, 232, 235, 236, 242, 243, 244, 245, 249
   2nd Regiment, 145, *147*, 150, 154, 155–56, 169–70, 171, 172–73, 174, 176, 177, 178, 179, 181–82, 191, 192, *193*, 194–95, 210, 224, 229, 231, *235*, 236, 246, 248, 251, 255, 256, 258, 260
   3rd Regiment, 145, 149, 150, 155–56, 158, 160, 171, 181, 192, 193–96, 199–201, 202, 210, 225, 229, 230, 231, 232, 235, 237, 237, 239, 242, 245–46, 247, 248, 251, 252, 264–65
   Cannon Company, 253
   Regimental Headquarters, 194
   Service Battalion, 194
First World War, 13, 44, 67, 285
Force Mobile Command (FMC), 282
Forino, Italy, 271
Fort Arbousier, Ile de Levant, 248
Fort Benning, Georgia, 87, 107, 108, 111, 135
Fort Bragg, North Carolina, 107, 282, *286*, 288
Fort de l'Eminence, Port-Cros Island, 243, 245
Fort de Lestissac, Port-Cros Island, 244
Fort Ethan Allen, Arlington, Vermont, 139–40, 142, 162, 165
Fort Lewis, Washington, 38, 288, *293*

Fort William Henry Harrison, Montana, 63, *71*, 78, 79, 82, 85, 87, 88, *93*, 95, 100, 104–05, 106, 107, 109, 117, 126
Fortin de la Vigie, Port-Cros Island, 243
Forward, Eugene, 59, 60, 89–90, 91, 106, 108, 113, 116, 135, 150–51, 158, 159, 162, 171, 256, 260
Foster, Major-General H.W., 270
France, 7, 13, 14, 24, 26, *43*, 44, *264*, 270
France, Southern, 12, 237, 239, 241, 250, 258
Frederick, (Lieutenant-Colonel to Major-General) Robert T., 10, 34, 35, 36–37, 39, 41, 43, 47, 51, 52, 54, 59, 67, *71*, 72, 74, 76–78, 80, 85, 86, 87, 88, 90, 91, 92, 93–94, 96, 97, 98, 99, 101, 105, 107–09, 111, *112*, *115*, 116–17, 119, 120, 121–22, 123, 125–26, 127–28, 129, 130, 131–32, 133, 135, 136, 139, 141, 144, 145, 146, 147, 148, 149, 154, 155, 159, 160, 161–63, 168, 171, 173, 175, 176, 177, 178, 179, 181, 182, 183, 184, 185, 189, 190–91, 192, 195, 200, 202–03, 211, 213, 218, 223, *225*, 231, 232, 234, 235, 237, 239, 241, 250–51, 252, 256, 258, 278, 301–02
French
   Army
      2nd Corps, 167, 187, 188, 192, 202, 241
   Commandos, 241
   French Forces of the Interior (FFI), 256, 257
Free Norwegian Forces, 25–26

Gaither, Colonel Ridgely, 126, 127
Gallagher, Captain Dan, 198
German Army
   7th *Luftwaffe Jaeger* Battalion, 222
   10th Army, 224, 230, 231
   14th Army, 208
   19th Army, 242, 250
   148th Infantry Division (148th Inf Div), 254
   Army Group G, 241
Gertrude Cove, Kiska, 152, 154
Gilbert Islands, 143

Gilday, Lieutenant-Colonel Thomas P., 156–57, 196, 198, 203–04, 205, 215, 216, 217, 218, 222
Glass, Joe, 61, 178, 278
Gold Bar, The, 119
Goodfellow, Colonel Preston, 117
Goodrich Tire Corporation, 38
Gouroch, Scotland, 271
Grasse, France, 252
Gray, Major Walter, 179, 182, 183, 191
Green, Sergeant Donald J., 211, 222, 230, 236, 246, 254, 267
Greenock, Scotland, 271
Grenoble, France, 250
Gubbins, Lieutenant-Colonel/Brigadier Colin, 16, 301
Guernsey, Island of, 23
Gustav Line, 167, 202, 207, 208

Hahn, Otto, 31
Hansteen, Major-General Wilhelm von Tangen, 122
Harvey, Royal Engineers, British Army, Major, 119
Harvey, Staff Sergeant Frank, 196–97
heavy water, 9, 32
Heilman, Captain Gus, 232
Helena, Montana, *63*, 72, 85, 87, 88, *93*, 96, 107, 108, 119, 133, 138, 278, 294
Herald, The, 95
Hill 720, 187–88
Hill 750, 194
Hill 907, 177, 179, 181–82, 183, 184–85, *see also* Remetanea
Hill 960, 173, *see also* La Difensa
Hill 1109, 188, 192, 195, 199, 200, 201, 202, *see also* Mount Vischiatro
Hill 1270, 200–01, 202
Hillier, General Rick, 291, 292
Hitler, Adolf, 26, 31–32, 59, 185, 230, 231, 300
Hitler's Commando Order, 26
Hoffmeister, Major-General B.M., 270
Home Defence, 16, 22–23, 55, 68
Home Forces, 22
Hopkins, Harry, 34
Hopkins, Sergeant Bert, 174, 266, 277
Howe, C.D., 46
Hubbard, Second-Lieutenant Fred, 88

Ile de Levant, France, 245, 246
  FSSF landing points
    Blue Scramble Beachhead, 151, 153, 246
    Green Scramble Beachhead, 246
    Purple Scramble Beachhead, 246
    Red Scramble Beachhead, 156, 246
Imperial Japanese Army, 142
independent companies, 16, 19
Ismay, General Hastings, 14, 22
Italy, 7, 9, 11, 31, 39, 126, 135, 165, 167, 168, 185, 187, 205, 208, 209, 217, 219, 224, *235*, 250, 255, 260, 263, 264, 268, 269, 270

Jamieson, Sergeant Joe T., 59, 90, 106, 159, 190, 254, 274, 278
Japan, 147, 274
Japanese Navy
  Imperial Destroyer Squadron One, 155
  Squadrons, 155
Jasper National Park (Canada), 46
Johnson, Lieutenant-Colonel H.R., 36
Joint Air School (JAS), 279, 282
Joint Chiefs of Staff, 68

Kamchatka Peninsula, 142
Keene, Major Robert A., 62
Kesselring, Field Marshal Albert, 208, 209
Keyes, Major-General Geoffrey, 167, 168
Keyes, Admiral of the Fleet Sir Roger, 24
Kiil, Captain, 138
Kimura, Rear Admiral Masatomi, 155
Kincaid, Admiral Thomas C., 144, 161
King, William Lyon Mackenzie, 44, 45, 140, 302
Kirk, Rear-Admiral Alan G., 139
Kirkenes, 300
Kirkwood, Major Murray D., 258
Kiska, Aleutians, 7, 11, 126, 142, 143, 144, 145, 146, 148, 149, 150, 152, 156–57, 158, 160, 161, 162, 165
Kiska Harbour, 154–55, 158, 160

Knaben Mine, Norway, 31
Kroll, Peter, 89, 156, 248, 265
Kuluk Bay, 145

La-Hay-du-Puits, Normandy, France, 275
Laghet, France, 256
Lago Albano, 237, 239
Lame Hill Ridge, Kiska, 154
Landing Force Reserve, Kiska, 152
Langly, Dave, 260
Lansdowne Park, Ottawa, 62
Lard Hills, Kiska, 151
Larry Hill, Kiska, 151, 154
Lasso Hill, Kiska, 153
Lazarus, Morris, 114, 263
L'Escarene, France, 256
Le Lavandeau, France, 242
Le Muy, France, 241, 250
Lee, Clark, 203
Legault, Lieutenant Conrad, 211
Lend Ridge, Kiska, 153
Lennox, Allen, 106
Leopards, 23
Letson, Major-General H.F.G., 58, 64, 70, 76
Lewis, Walter, 133
Libby, Montana, 133
Lief Cove, Kiska, 154
Liggett, Chaplain, Captain O.E., 265
Lilac Hill, Kiska, 153
Lilly Beach, Kiska, 151
Lily Creek, Kiska, 153
Lime, Colonel, E., 55
lineage, 288, 292
Link Hill, Kiska, 151, 154
Liri Valley, 11, 167, 187, 188, 231
Little Kiska, 144, 150, 152, 154, 160
Littoria, 212, 227
Lofoten Islands, 25
Long Range Desert Group, 9, 27
Loup River flats, *264*, 265
Low Countries, 13
Lucas, Major-General John P., 208
Lulu Hill, Kiska, 150–51

Mackinnon, Donald, 171, 175
Macklin, Brigadier W.H.S., 271
MacWilliam, Lieutenant-Colonel Tom, 169–70, 176, 178
Magee, William "Sam," 61, 88, 158
Maggiore, Monte, 167, 175, 179, 183, 184, *184*
Mair, Major W. Winston, 249

INDEX

Manual for Courts-Martial, U.S. Army, 72
Mann, Staff-Sergeant Charlie, 8, 61, 79, 86, 90, 108, 109, 253, 266, 277
Maritime Alps, France, 250, *251*, 252, 255, 263
Marseille, 249, 250, 257, 268
Marshall, Lieutenant-Colonel Alfred C., 150
Marshall, General George C., 34, *35*, 124
Martin, Captain I.H., 134
Martin, Jack, 147
Mason, Don, 41
Mason-Dixon Line, 89
McDougall, Ken, 213, 222
McFadden, Major Gerald, 181, 210–11
McNarney, Lieutenant-General J.T., 44, 49
McNaughton, Lieutenant-General A.G.L., 41, *42*, 53, 56, 58, 62, 124, 275, 302, 303
McQueen, Major J.G., 62, 63, 70, 75, 76, 77–80, 83, 90, 93, 97, 108, 110, 111, 117, 119, 124
Mediterranean theatre, 165
Menton, France, 12, 256, 258, 263
Menton Days, 286, 292, *293*
Merritt, Captain William, 245, 395
Midway, 143, 144
Mignano Gap, 167, 187, 188–89
military attaché, Washington, 54, 70, 75
military police (MPs), 119
Million dollar mountain, 173
minister of national defence (MND), 43, 68
Minto, Robert, 133
Minutes of the War Cabinet Committee, The, 125
Mitchell, Lieutenant J. D., 61, 86, 109–10, 116, 118, 120, 147, 156, 173, 179, 180–81, 196, 211, 229
molybdenum, 31
Monaco, France, 256
Montana, 49, *63*, 72, 85, 87, *93*, 124, 127, 133, 136, 138, 278, 294
Moore, Lieutenant-Colonel Robert S., 182, 189, 191, 245–46, 248, 255
Mortimore, Brigadier A.R., 80, 81
Moses, Brigadier-General Raymond G., 37–38

Mount Arrestino, 224, 229
Mount Camino, 167, 168–69, 173, 179, 182, 183–84
Mount La Difensa, 11, 135, 167–68, *169*, *170*, *172*, 173, 174, 175, *176*, 179, *180*, 183, 184–85, 187, 189, 191, 207, 209, see also Hill 960
Mount Majo, 187–88, 192, 194–95, 196, 199, *200*, 201, 202
Mount Rainier, 38
Mount Remetanea, 177, 178, 179, 182, 183, see also Hill 907
Mount Sammucro, 167–68, 187, 188, *197*
Mount Steffano, 194, 195
Mount Vischiatro, 188, see also Hill 1109
Mountbatten, Vice-Admiral Lord Louis, 10, 14, 24–25, 29, 30, 31, *33*, 34, 35, 36, 39, 41, 42, 43, 122, 301
Munro, Ross, 51, 95
Muntz, Alan, 37
Murchie, Major-General, Lieutenant-General John C., 42, 43, 58, 77–78, 124, 274–75
Mussolini Canal, *209*, 210, 211–12, 212, 224, 225

Naples, Italy, 165, 209–10, 223, 237, 239, 268, 271
Narvik, 300
National Defence Headquarters (NDHQ), 45, 51, 52, 54, 55, 60, 62, 63, 64, 67, 69, 70–71, 72, 73, 74, 75, 76, 77, 78, 79–80, 81, 82, 93, 96–97, 98, 111, 135, 140, 162, 217, 257, 258, 259, 263, 264, 274, 279, 281, 287, 289, 292, 298
National Research Council (NRC), 41, 45
Navy, 19, 68, 138
Nazis, 27, 49
Nimitz, Admiral Chester W., 161
Nola, Italy, 268
Norsk-Hydro Plant, Vemork (Rjukan) Norway, 32
North American Force, 50
North Borneo, 143
Norway, 9, 13, 16, 24, 25, 26, 30–31, 32, 39, 41, 122, 222–23, 275, 299, 300, 301–04

Office of Scientific Research and Development (OSRD), 37–38
officers' training centre (OTC)
   Brockville, Ontario, 58, 64
   Gordon Head, British Columbia, 58, 64
Ogdensburg Agreement, 10, 44
Olson, Captain Eino, 189
O'Neill, Dermont M. "Pat," 117–18, 134, 147, 179
Operation Buffalo, 224
Operation Bruno, 240
Operation Cottage, 149
Operation Dragoon, 12, 241
Operation Enduring Freedom (OEF), 290–91
Operation *Fischfang*, 214
Operation Grasshopper, 224
Operation Jupiter, 299, 301–04
Operation Raincoat, 168
Operation Shingle, 207
Operation Sledgehammer, 299
Operation Torch, 300, 302
Operation Turtle, 224
Operations Division of the General Staff (U.S.), 34, 125–26
Oran, Algeria, 165, *167*
Ottawa, Ontario, 41, 44, 51, 60, 62, 63, 78, 83, 98, 140, 162, 174, 288, 289, 290, 294

Palestine, 15
parachute school, Fort Benning, Georgia, 107
Parachute Training School, Royal Air Force Station, Ringway, Manchester, 58
Parliament, 44
Patch, Lieutenant-General Alexander M., 241–42, 250
Patterson, American War Under-Secretary Robert P., 49, 94
Pearl Harbour, Hawaii, 68, 143
Peillon, France, 256
Penhale, Brigadier M.H.S., 257
Peppard, Sergent Herb, 100–01, 109, 133, 146, 148
Permanent Joint Board of Defence (PJBD), 44
perpetuation, 279, 285–86, 292
Perry, Tony, 89, 196, 199
Petsamo, 300
Phare du Titan, Ile de Levant, 247
Philippines, 143

Pier 41, San Francisco, 142
Ploesti, Rumania, 9, 31
Plough Force, 39, 44, 47, 48, 122
Plough Project, 31, *33*, 34, 35, *36*, 37, 39, 41, *42*, 43, 45, 46–47, 50, 51, 53, 56, 63, 65, 69, *71*, 73, 77, 78, 79, 85, 122, 165, 205, 299, 301–04
Po River, Italy, 31
Poland, 13
Pollack Force, 227, 229
Pope, Major-General Maurice, 69, 78–79, 93, 124, 125, 141, 217
Porchak, Walter "Wally," 274
Port Croix, France, 245
Port de l'Avis, Ile de Levant, 248
Portal, Air Chief Marshal Charles, 121
Presenzano, 171
Princess Patricia's Canadian Light Infantry (PPCLI), 281
Project Plough, *see* Plough Project
Propriano, Corsica, 241
Putnam, Palmer C., 38
Pyke, Sir Geoffrey Nathaniel, 9, 29–30, 31, 34, 35, 36, 37, 39, 41, 43–44

Quisling, 25–26
Quisling Cove, Kiska, 150–51, 153

Radcliffe, Second-Lieutenant Mark, 88
Radicosa, 192, *193*, *194*, *195*, 201, 202
Ralston, James Layton, *43*, 44, 46, *68*, 81, 97, 125
Ranger Hill, Kiska, 158
Rapido plain, 202
Ready, Brigadier-General Joseph L., 149–50, 159
Rich, Sergeant John, 195
Rigg, Technician Fourth Class C.F., 190
Riot Hills, Kiska, 158
Rivers, Manitoba, 279
Robber Hill, Kiska, 149, 160
Robin Creek, Kiska, 158
Rocca d'Evandro, 183
Rocca Massima, 229
Rochester, Colonel Don H., 283
Roll, Captain Finn W., 254, 265
Roosevelt, Franklin D., 15, 34, 35, 44, *45*, 89, 302, 304
Rose Hill, Kiska, 158
Rothlin, Captain Bill, 171, 177–78

Rowe, Sergeant John, 219, 229, 243, 244, 267
Royal 22nd Regiment (R22R), 281
Royal Air Force (RAF), 58, 121
Royal Canadian Air Force (RCAF), 279–80, 281
Royal Canadian Regiment (RCR), 281
Royal Engineers, 119, 303
Royal Marines (RM), 16
Rumania, 31, 39
Russia, 31
Russians, 31, 299
Ryan, Lieutenant Dan, 119–20, 153
Ryan's Special, 120

San Francisco, 141, 142, 161, 162
Sangro River, 167
Santa Maria Capua Vetere, 165, *168*, 171, 184, 187, 188, 203, 209, 250
Santa Maria di Castellabate, 240, 249
Saskatchewan Glacier, Banff National Park, 46
Schoeler, Sergeant Paul, 106, 203, 221
Scotland, 19, 271, 302
Scramble Emerald Beach, Port-Cros Island, 243
Scramble Scarlet Beach, Port-Cros Island, 243
Second World War, 7, 8, 9, 292, 294
Section MO9, 16
Segula Island, Aleutians, 160
Shanghai Police Force, 117
Sheldon, Lieutenant William, 224, 227, 229, 232, 234, 235
Shilo, Manitoba, 218, 279
Shinberger, Major John, 86, 126, 129–30
Shu-mines, 254
Siagne River, France, 251, 252
Siam, 143
Simonds, Lieutenant-General G.G., 304
Sims, Gordon, 92, 100, 106, 114, 277, 278
Smith, Peter, 62, 88, 89, 105, 109, 111, 112, 119, 137, 143, 156, 207, 246, 266, 274
Snider, Sergeant George "Red," 95
Solomon's Island (Chesapeake Bay, Maryland), 139
Somalia, 287
Somerville, Lieutenant-General, 94
Sör Vaagso, Norway, 25

Sospel, France, 258
Spearhead, 94
Special Air Service (SAS), 9, 22, 279, *280*, 281, 282, 283, 284, 285, 289, 290
Special Forces (SF) 282, 284, 286, 288, *289*, 292, 294
Special Operations Executive (SOE), 27, 121–23, 301, 304,
special operations forces (SOF), 9, 29, 279, 282, 284, 289, 290–91
Special Service Force (SSF), 286
special service units, 64
Special Services Branch, 47
St. Nazaire, France, 26
St. Raphael, France, 241, 250
St. Tropez, France, 250
Stirling, Lieutenant David, 22
Storm Troops, 23
Story, Lieutenant Bill, 61, 89, 91, 101, 190, 278
Stuart, Lieutenant-General Kenneth, 42–43, *53*, 54, 56, 58, 69, 74, 75–76, 79, 81, 82, 93, 98, 99, 124, 205, 217–18, 259
Studebaker Corporation, 47
Summersides, Sergeant Jim, 113, 213, 216, 244
Sun Life Assurance Company of Canada building, London, U.K., 67
support echelon/service battalion, 48, 67
Supreme Headquarters Allied Expeditionary Force (SHAEF), 43
Surles, General, 93
Sutherland, Colonel Edwin M., 149, 154
Svolvaer, Norway, 25
Sweden, 25
Swisher, Sergeant Ralph, 195
Sylvabelle, France, 250

Takahashi, Private, 146
Task Force "A," 275
Task Force "B," 195, 200, 202
Task Force Howze, 232, 235, 236
Telecommunications Research Establishment, UK, 26
Thomas, Major Edward H., 86, 88, 139, 171, 174, 178, 182, 211, 212, 213, 228, 248
Thompson, Major-General Julian, 22

INDEX

Thompson sub-machine gun, 103, 116, 130, 197, 198
Tiber River, 232, 235, 236
Tiger tank, 228, 229
Tirpitz, 26
Tor Sapienza, 232, 235
Toulon, France, 242, 250
Tragino Aqueduct, Italy, 25
Tromso, 300
Truscott, Major-General Lucian King, 223, 241

Underhill, Lieutenant Adna U., 134, 145, 146, 172, 177, 209–10, 236, 246, 248, 249, 260, 263
Union Minière, Belgium, 32
United States Army chief of finance, 72
United States Army director requirements division, 94
United States Army HQ, 72
United States Army Parachutist Badge, 111, 272
United States Army Quartermaster General Heraldic Section, 94
United States Army's Oath of Service and Obedience, 71
United States Engineering Board, 119
United States Joint Chiefs of Staff, 68
United States Joint Staff Planners Committee, 69
United States of America
    Army
        1st Special Forces Group (1 SFG), 282, 288, 292, *293*
        2nd Chemical Battalion, 258
        3rd Division, 227, 230, 231, 237
        13th Armoured Regiment, 232
        17th Infantry Regiment, 154
        36th Division, 167, 179, 181, 184, 187
        44th Anti-Aircraft Artillery (AAA) Brigade, 260
        45th Division, 200, 216, 241
        81st Reconnaissance Battalion, 232
        82nd Airborne Division, 275
        87th Mountain Regiment, 154
        99th Infantry Battalion, 275
        100th Infantry Battalion, 261
        101st Airborne Division, 275
        133rd Infantry Regiment, 195, 200–02
        141st Infantry Regiment, 188
        142nd Infantry Regiment, 175, 179, 184, 189
        168th Infantry Regiment, 202
        184th Infantry Regiment, 156
        442nd Regimental Combat Team, 261
        463rd Parachute Field Artillery Battalion, 258
        474th Infantry Regiment, 275
        509th Parachute Infantry Combat Team, 251, 256
        601st Field Artillery Battalion, 252
        602nd Field Artillery Battalion, 258
        887th Airborne Engineer Company, 252
    Navy
        USS *Augusta*, 245
        Dominican Victory, 275
        SS *John B. Floyd*, 142, 145
        USS *Kane*, 151, 155–56
        SS *Nathaniel Wyeth*, 142, 145
        USS *Thomas Jefferson*, 139

Vaagso, Norway, *see* Sör Vaagso
Valbonne, France, 150–51
Valmontone, 224, 230, 231, 234
Van Ausdale, Sergeant Howard, 171, 173–74
Van Nostrand, Dr. (Colonel) Fred, 192
Vega Bay, Kiska, 152
Vemork (Rjukan), Norway, 32
Via Casilina, 234–35
Ville D'Oran, 268
Villeneuve-Loubet, France, 255, 261, 263
Volturno River, 167

Waling, Lorin, 62, 177, 237, 277–78
Walker, Lieutenant-Colonel Edwin A., *159*, 160, 167, 168, 192, 193–94, 196, 199, 210, 229, 237, 240, 244, 248, 250–51, 254, 256, 257, 259, 260, 261, 262, 265, 267, 275
War Cabinet Secretariat, UK, 14
War Department, US, 36–37, 38, 44, 50, 93, 161, 259
War Department planning staff, US, 78
War Measures Act, 74
War Office, UK, 16, 21, 22, 24, 30, 34, 67, 122
War Production Board, 37
Washington D.C., 34, 35, 37–38, 39, 44, 51, 54, 68, 69, 93, 122, 124, 217, 294
Waters, Major Stanley, 223
Watt, Sholto, 203
Wavell, General Sir Archibald, 15
Weasel, 38, *39*, 46, 47, 48, 103, 104–05, *120*, 126, 128, 130, 138, 301, *see also* Cargo Carrier, Light, T-15
Wedderburn, Major E.A.M, 37, 38, 121
Weeks, Brigadier E.G., 218, 219, 259, 259, *272*, 273, 273, *274*
Weiss, General Friedrich, 242
West Kiska Lake, Kiska, 149, 156–58
Whittle, D.G., 74
Wiber, William, 61
Wickham, Lieutenant-Colonel Ken G., 52, 71, 72, 228
Wickham-Williamson Agreement, 72
Wieneke, Russell, 88
Williamson, Colonel D.D., 64, 69–70, 71, 72, 77, 78–80, 81–82, 83, 90, 92, 93, 97, 98–99, 105–06, 129, 133, 138, 140, 141–42, 155, 162–63, 169, 170–71, 175, 179, 182, 184, 189–90, 191, 192
Winter Line, 167, 187
Witchcraft Point, Kiska, 149, 156
Wright, Staff Sergeant A.L., 198
Wright, Sergeant George, 57–58, 106, 113, 133, 137, 152, 153, 160, 162, 219, 228–29, 278
Wright, Sergeant Joe, 190–91
Würzburg radar, 26

Yamamoto, Admiral Isoroku, 143

BY THE SAME AUTHORS

Tip of the Spear
An Intimate Account of 1 Canadian Parachute Battalion, 1942–1945
Colonel Bernd Horn and Michel Wyczynski
978-1-550023886
$39.99

In the midst of the Second World War, the Germans introduced a new kind of warfare that had never been seen before, featuring a new kind of soldier: the paratrooper. The public and military alike were astonished by the feats of daring and martial prowess displayed by the intrepid troops, who soon became the epitome of the modern combat soldier.

The Allies countered by setting up their own airborne forces. In Canada, 1 Canadian Parachute Battalion was established to serve as the "tip of the spear" of Allied attacks. In fact, it was this battalion that was first into Normandy for the D-Day invasion.

Tip of the Spear tells in stunning black-and-white pictures the story of the Battalion from its inception in 1942 to its disbandment in 1945. Without question, the Battalion — or more accurately, its members — laid the foundation and established the airborne legacy that other Canadian airborne establishments could proudly follow and build on.

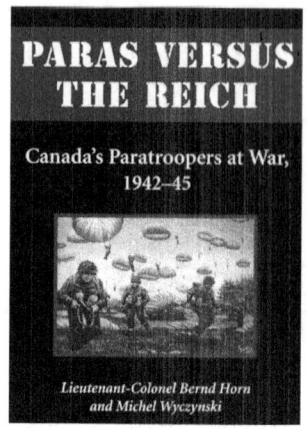

Paras Versus the Reich
Canada's Paratroopers at War, 1942–1945
Colonel Bernd Horn and Michel Wyczynski
978-1-550024708
$29.99

This meticulously researched book traces the development of airborne forces from their earliest mythology to their earth-shattering debut in the Second World War. More importantly, it reveals in exacting detail the story of Canada's paratroopers — from the early resistance to their establishment, the rigorous selection process and gruelling training, to their unrivalled combat record. It tells the story of the 1st Canadian Parachute Battalion, which never failed to achieve its assigned missions, nor did it ever lose an objective once captured. Through the pages of this book the reader will experience the exceptional courage, endurance, fighting skills, and tenacity of Canada's paratroopers in the Second World War.

Visit us at
Dundurn.com
Definingcanada.ca
@dundurnpress
Facebook.com/dundurnpress

www.ingramcontent.com/pod-product-compliance
Lightning Source LLC
Chambersburg PA
CBHW060308240426
43661CB00059B/2698